The **Princeton Review**®

SAT Subject Test™

MATH 2

PREP

3rd Edition

The Staff of The Princeton Review

PrincetonReview.com

Penguin
Random
House

The Princeton Review
110 East 42nd St, 7th Floor
New York, NY 10017
Email: editorialsupport@review.com

Published in the United States by Penguin Random House LLC,
New York, and in Canada by Random House of Canada, a division
of Penguin Random House Ltd., Toronto.

Some of the content in The Princeton Review SAT Subject
Test™ Math 2 Prep has previously appeared in Cracking the
SAT Subject Test™ in Math 2, 2nd Edition, published as a trade
paperback by Random House, an imprint and division of Penguin
Random House LLC, in 2017.

ISBN: 978-0-525-56899-5
ISSN: 2687-8488

SAT Subject Tests™ is a trademark owned by the College Board,
which is not affiliated with The Princeton Review.

The Princeton Review is not affiliated with Princeton University.

Editor: Chris Chimera
Production Artists: Jennifer Chapman
Production Editors: Lee Elder and Liz Dacey
Content Contributor: Christina Becker

Printed in the United States of America.

10 9 8 7 6 5 4 3 2 1

3rd Edition

Editorial

Rob Franek, Editor-in-Chief
David Soto, Director of Content Development
Stephen Koch, Student Survey Manager
Deborah Weber, Director of Production
Gabriel Berlin, Production Design Manager
Selena Coppock, Managing Editor
Aaron Riccio, Senior Editor
Meave Shelton, Senior Editor
Chris Chimera, Editor
Eleanor Green, Editor
Orion McBean, Editor
Brian Saladino, Editor

Penguin Random House Publishing Team

Tom Russell, VP, Publisher
Alison Stoltzfus, Publishing Director
Amanda Yee, Associate Managing Editor
Ellen Reed, Production Manager
Suzanne Lee, Designer

Acknowledgments

Special thanks to Christina Becker and Chris Knuth for their tremendous effort to develop the new content in this edition. Thanks also to Aaron Lindh, High School Content Director, for his contributions to this title, and to those who have worked on this book in the past. Our gratitude as well to the stellar production team of Jennifer Chapman, Lee Elder, and Liz Dacey: they literally make this book look good.

Special thanks to Adam Robinson, who conceived of and perfected the Joe Bloggs approach to standardized tests, and many other techniques in the book.

Contents

(Free) Content
at PrincetonReview.com/prep

As easy as 1·2·3

1 Go to PrincetonReview.com/prep and enter the following ISBN for your book:
9780525568995

2 Answer a few simple questions to set up an exclusive Princeton Review account. *(If you already have one, you can just log in.)*

3 Enjoy access to your **FREE** content!

Once you've registered, you can...

- Access a third Math 2 practice test

- Take a full-length practice SAT and/or ACT

- Get valuable advice about the college application process, including tips for writing a great essay and where to apply for financial aid

- If you're still choosing between colleges, use our searchable rankings of *The Best 385 Colleges* to find out more information about your dream school

- Access comprehensive study guides and a variety of printable resources, including additional bubble sheets, score conversion tables, and chapter summary pages

- Check to see if there have been any corrections or updates to this edition

- Get our take on any recent or pending updates to the SAT Subject Test Math 2

Need to report a potential **content** issue?

Contact **EditorialSupport@review.com** and include:

- full title of the book
- ISBN
- page number

Need to report a **technical** issue?

Contact **TPRStudentTech@review.com** and provide:

- your full name
- email address used to register the book
- full book title and ISBN
- Operating system (Mac/PC) and browser (Firefox, Safari, etc.)

Look For These Icons Throughout The Book

 ONLINE ARTICLES

 ONLINE PRACTICE TESTS

 PROVEN TECHNIQUES

 APPLIED STRATEGIES

Part I
Orientation

Chapter 1
Introduction

Welcome to the SAT Subject Test Math 2! This chapter will help you get familiar with this book and learn how to use it most effectively. We'll also talk about when to take the test and how to determine which level to take. (If you're flipping through this book in the bookstore, this chapter's for you!)

WHAT IS THE SAT SUBJECT TEST MATH 2?

The SAT Subject Test Math 2 is a standardized test in mathematics. Colleges use this test to assist in admissions decisions and to place incoming students in classes at the right level. This test is written by the College Board, a company that also writes several other tests. The College Board makes money by charging students to take the SAT and SAT Subject Tests, and then to send the scores to colleges.

The SAT Subject Test Math 2 has 50 multiple-choice questions and is one hour long. The test is scored from 200 to 800 points. The SAT Subject Test Math 2 covers a range of mathematical topics, from basic algebra to trigonometry and statistics.

Many colleges require some SAT Subject Tests (frequently two, but occasionally one or three). The subjects available are varied: two in mathematics, three in science, two in history, one in English, and twelve in foreign languages. Different schools have different preferences and requirements for which tests to take. For example, an engineering program may want to see one math and one science. Check each school's website to determine how many tests you must take and which ones (if any) are preferred.

What's on the Test?

The content of the SAT Subject Test Math 2 is approximately as follows:

Topic	Math Level 2
Functions	12 questions
Trigonometry	10 questions
Algebra	9 questions
Coordinate Geometry	6 questions
Solid Geometry	3 questions
Statistics	4 questions
Miscellaneous	6 questions
TOTAL	50 questions

As you can see, the SAT Subject Test Math 2 focuses on material you learned in your Geometry, Algebra II, and Precalculus classes. When it asks questions about basic concepts, it does so by including the concepts in a more complicated problem. For example, there are no direct questions about plane geometry. However, you will need to be able to apply the concepts of plane geometry to questions about coordinate geometry or spatial geometry.

You may be overwhelmed by the number of different topics which appear on the SAT Subject Test Math 2. Fear not! The test is written with the expectation that most students have not covered all the material on the test. Furthermore, you can do well on this test even if you haven't covered *everything* that may show up on the test.

Math Level 1 or 2?

We'd love to say that this decision boils down completely to your comfort level with the material in each course, but the truth is that not every school accepts the Math 1 results. You should therefore base your decision primarily on the admission requirements of the schools that interest you.

Math 2 is appropriate for high school students who have had a year of Trigonometry or Precalculus and have done well in the class. You should also be comfortable using a scientific or graphing calculator. If you hate math, do poorly on math tests, or have not yet studied Trigonometry or Precalculus, the SAT Subject Test Math 2 is probably not for you. It's worth noting, however, that while this test is difficult, the test is scored on a comparatively generous curve. If you find yourself making random (or "silly") mistakes more than anything else, the Math 2 scoring grid may work in your favor.

Colleges also receive your percentile (comparing you to other test takers), as well as your scaled (200–800) score. For the most part, they pay attention to the scaled score and ignore the percentile. However, to the small extent that percentiles matter, Math 1 has considerably more forgiving percentiles. People who take Math 2 are generally really good at math; about 13% of them get a perfect score! Less than 1% of Math 1 test-takers get a perfect score, though. As a result, a 790 on Math 2 is only in the 85th percentile (about 13% get an 800 and 2% get a 790), while a 790 on Math 1 is still in the 99th percentile. The disparity between the percentiles continues down the entire score range.

If you are very unsure about which test to take, even after working practice questions and taking practice tests, you can take both tests.

WHEN SHOULD I TAKE THE SAT SUBJECT TEST MATH 2?

The right time to take the SAT Subject Test Math 2 varies from person to person. Many students take the test at the end of a Precalculus class in school. (Precalculus also goes by many other names, such as Trigonometry, Advanced Functions, or other less recognizable names.) Some students take Math 2 during or at the end of an AP Calculus course.

The SAT Subject Tests are offered six times per year, and no test date is easier or harder than any other test date. The most popular test dates are in May and June, because these are at the end of a school year when the material is freshest in the student's mind. Whenever you choose to take the test, make sure you have time to do some practice beforehand, so that you can do your best (and not have to take the thing again!).

THE CALCULATOR

The SAT Subject Test Math 2 is designed to be taken with the aid of a calculator. Students taking this test should have a scientific or graphing calculator and know how to use it. A "scientific" calculator is one that has keys for the following functions:

- the values of π and e
- square roots
- raising to an exponent
- sine, cosine, and tangent
- logarithms

Calculators without these functions will not be as useful. Graphing calculators are allowed. The graphing features on a graphing calculator are helpful on a fairly small number of questions per test, and they are necessary for about 0–1 questions per test. If you're going to take a graphing calculator to the test, make sure you know how to use it. Fumbling over your calculator trying to figure something out during the test is just not a productive use of your time!

This book is going to focus on the TI-84. If you have another family member of the TI-80 series, know that these comments still apply to you with minor adjustments. Check with your manual for specific key stroke changes. If you have a scientific calculator, we'll be showing you your key stroke changes in the sidebars throughout the manual.

> **The College Board Predictor**
> The College Board says that for the SAT Subject Test Math 2, a calculator may be useful or necessary for about 55–65 percent of the questions.

Certain kinds of calculators are not allowed. For example, a calculator with a QWERTY keyboard (like a computer keyboard) is not allowed. Your calculator must not require a wall outlet for power and must not make noise or produce paper printouts. There will be no replacements at the test center for malfunctioning or forgotten calculators, though you're welcome to take a spare, as well as spare batteries. Laptops, tablets, and cell phones are also not allowed as calculators.

Bottom line: You need a calculator for this test. Certain things will be easier with a graphing calculator, but it is most important that you are comfortable using your calculator.

HOW TO USE THIS BOOK

It's best to work through the chapters of this book in sequence, since the later chapters build on the techniques introduced in earlier chapters. If you want an overall review of the material on the SAT Subject Test Math 2, just start at the beginning and cruise through to the end. This book will give you all the techniques and knowledge you need to do well on the test. If you feel a little shaky in certain areas of math and want to review specific topics, the chapter headings and subheadings will also allow you to zero in on your own problem topics. As with any subject, pay particular attention to the math topics you don't like—otherwise, those are the ones that will burn you on the real test.

If you really want to get your money's worth out of this book, you'll follow this study plan.

- Take the diagnostic full-length practice test that appears in Part II.
- Score your test and review it to see where your strengths and weaknesses lie.
- Focus on the chapters associated with the questions that you got wrong or didn't understand.
- Read through each section of a chapter carefully until you feel that you understand it.
- Try the practice questions at the end of that section.
- Check your answers, and review any questions you got wrong until you understand your mistakes.
- Once you finish all the sections in a chapter, try the Comprehensive Drill at the end of that chapter.
- Check your answers, and review any questions you got wrong until you understand your mistakes.
- Go back and review the chapters which cover material you're still struggling with.
- Take the final in-book full-length practice test. Then score and review it.

If you put in the work and study what's in this book, you'll be prepared for anything that the College Board may throw at you on the day of the real test.

Study Guide
In your free online student tools, you'll find a printable copy of two different study guides that you can use to plot out your progress through this book.

Need More?
You can also visit CollegeBoard.org for more information and test questions. Also, don't forget to register your book online for access to a third full-length practice test!

Chapter 2
Strategy

It's easy to get the impression that the only way to excel on the SAT Subject Test Math 2 is to become an expert on myriad mathematical matters. However, there are many effective strategies that you can use. From Pacing to Process of Elimination to using your calculator, this chapter takes you through the most important general strategies so you can start practicing them right way.

CRACKING THE SAT SUBJECT TEST MATH 2

It's true that you have to know some math to do well, but there's a great deal you can do to improve your score without staring into math books until you go blind.

Several important strategies will help you increase your scoring power.

- The questions on the SAT Subject Test Math 2 are arranged in order of difficulty. You can think of a test as being divided roughly into thirds, containing easy, medium, and difficult questions, in that order.
- The SAT Subject Test Math 2 is a multiple-choice test. That means that every time you look at a question on the test, the correct answer is on the paper right in front of you.
- The College Board writes incorrect answers on the SAT Subject Test Math 2 by studying errors commonly made by students. These are common errors that you can learn to recognize.

The next few pages will introduce you to test-taking techniques that use these features of the SAT Subject Test Math 2 to your advantage, which will increase your score. These strategies come in two basic types: section strategies (which help you determine which questions to do and how much time to spend on them) and question strategies (which help you solve an individual question once you've chosen to do it).

SECTION STRATEGY

The following represents a sample scoring grid from the SAT Subject Test Math 2. Note that scoring scales will vary from test to test, so this is just a general guide.

Raw Score	Scaled Score	Percentile	Raw Score	Scaled Score	Percentile
43–50	800	87	17	570	22
42	790	85	15–16	560	20
41	780	82	—	550	18
40	770	79	14	540	15
39	760	77	13	530	14
38	750	73	12	520	12
37	740	71	—	510	10
36	730	68	11	500	8
35	720	66	10	490	7
34	710	62	—	480	6
33	700	61	9	470	4
31–32	690	58	8	460	3
30	680	56	—	450	3
29	670	53	7	440	2
28	660	50	6	430	2
27	650	47	—	420	1
26	640	44	—	410	1
24–25	630	40	4–5	400	1
23	620	37	—	390	1-
22	610	33	3	380	1-
21	600	31	2	370	1-
19–20	590	28	1	360	1-
18	580	25			

A few things are notable:

- While it's theoretically possible to score less than a 350, to do so would require you to score a negative number of raw points (i.e., do worse than simply randomly guessing). Practically speaking, the scoring range on the SAT Subject Test Math 2 is from 350–800.
- On some test dates, some scores are not possible, such as 420 in the test shown above.
- The scoring grid for the SAT Subject Test Math 2 is very forgiving, especially at the top end. Anything from 43 to 50 raw points gets you a "perfect" 800, and 33 raw points out of a possible 50 is still a 700. However, the percentiles are brutal: a 700 is only the 61st percentile!

Pacing

The first step to improving your performance on the SAT Subject Test Math 2 is *slowing down*. That's right: you'll score better if you do fewer questions. It may sound strange, but it works. That's because the test-taking habits you've developed in high school are poorly suited to the SAT Subject Test Math 2. It's a different kind of test.

One Point Over Another?
A hard question on the SAT Subject Test Math 2 isn't worth more points than an easy question. It just takes longer to do, and it's harder to get right. It makes no sense to rush through a test if all that's waiting for you are tougher and tougher questions—especially if rushing worsens your performance on the easy questions.

Think about a free-response math test. If you work a question and get the wrong answer, but you do most of the question right, show your work, and make a mistake that lots of other students in the class make (so the grader can easily recognize it), you'll probably get partial credit. If you do the same thing on the SAT Subject Test Math 2, you get one of the four wrong answers. But you don't get partial credit for choosing one of the listed wrong answers; you lose a quarter-point. That's the *opposite* of partial credit! Because the SAT Subject Test Math 2 gives the opposite of partial credit, there is a huge premium on accuracy in this test.

Your Last Test
For your "last test," use your last SAT Subject Test Math 2 (real or practice), if you've taken one. If you've taken the SAT, use your Math score. You can also use a PSAT score. If you've taken the ACT instead, multiply your math score by 20 (so a 25 in Math becomes a 500 for the purpose of pacing on the SAT Subject Test Math 2). If you haven't taken any of these tests, make an educated guess!

How Many Questions Should I Do?

Use the following chart to determine how many questions you should attempt the next time you take an SAT Subject Test Math 2:

On your last test, you scored:	On your next test, attempt:	If you get this many raw points...	You'll get a score near:
200–550	30	23	600
560–600	35	28	650
610–650	40	33	700
660–700	45	38	750
710–800	50	44	800

As you improve, your pacing goals will also get more aggressive. Once you take your next practice test and score it, come back to this chart and adjust your pacing accordingly. For example, if you initially scored a 550, but on your second test you scored a 610, then use the 610–650 line for your third test, and you may score a 700 (or even higher!).

Personal Order of Difficulty (POOD)

You probably noticed that the previous chart doesn't tell you *which* questions to do on the SAT Subject Test Math 2, only how many. That's because students aren't all the same. Even if a certain question is easy for most students, if you don't know how to do it, it's hard for you. Conversely, if a question is hard for most students but you see exactly how to do it, it's easy for you. Most of the time, you'll find lower-numbered questions easy for you and higher-numbered questions harder for you, but not always, and you should always listen to your Personal Order of Difficulty (POOD).

Develop a Pacing Plan

The following is an example of an aggressive pacing plan. You should begin by trying this plan, and then you should adapt it to your own needs.

First, do questions 1–20 in 20 minutes. They are mostly easy, and you should be able to do each one in about a minute. (As noted above, though, you must not go so quickly that you sacrifice accuracy.) If there is a question that looks more time-consuming, but you know how to do it, mark it so that you can come back to it later, but move on.

Second, pick and choose among questions 21–50. Do only questions that you are sure you can get right quickly. Mark questions that are more time-consuming (but you still know how to do them!) so that you can come back to them later. Cross out questions that you do not know how to do; you shouldn't waste any more time on them.

Third, once you've seen every question on the test at least once and gotten all the quick points that you can get, go back to the more time-consuming questions. Make good choices about which questions to do; at this point, you will be low on time and need to make realistic decisions about which questions you will be able to finish and which questions you should give up for lost.

This pacing plan takes advantage of the test's built-in order of difficulty and your POOD. You should move at a brisk but not breakneck pace through the easy questions so that you have enough time to get them right but not waste time. You should make sure that you get to the end of the test and evaluate every question, because you never know if you happen to know how to do question 50; it may be harder for most students than question 30, but it just may test a math topic that you remember very well from class (or this book). Delaying more time-consuming questions until after you've gotten the quick and easy points maximizes your score and gives you a better sense of how long you have to complete those longer questions, and, after some practice, it will take only a few seconds to recognize a time-consuming question.

A Note About Question Numbers

As you cruise through this book, you'll run into practice questions that seem to be numbered out of order. That's because the numbers of the practice questions tell you what position those questions would occupy on a 50-question SAT Subject Test Math 2. The question number gives you an idea of how difficult the College Board considers a given question to be.

QUESTION STRATEGY

It's true that the math on the SAT Subject Test in Math 2 gets difficult. But what exactly does that mean? Well, it *doesn't* mean that you'll be doing 20-step calculations, or huge, crazy exponential expansions that your calculator can't handle. Difficult questions on this test require you to understand some slippery mathematical *concepts,* and sometimes to recognize familiar math rules in strange situations.

This means that if you find yourself doing a 20-step calculation, stop. There's a shortcut, and it probably involves using one of our techniques. Find it.

Know Your Job (RTFQ)

Have you ever started reading a fairly lengthy word problem in math, get to the end, and only find yourself having to go back to the beginning for a second run-through just to recall the info you've already found? In a test that only lasts 60 minutes, *every single second matters.*

When time is involved in a test, careless mistakes seem to happen without fail. On a test that is designed with traps for you to fall for, it's almost guaranteeing a couple (or more) incorrect answers even though you know exactly *how* to do the required math. Help secure arriving at the correct answer by starting each question with four key letters in mind: $R - T - F - Q$. This stands for **R**ead **T**he **F**inal **Q**uestion.

The most important part of getting the question right is ensuring that you actually answer what the question is asking for you. Next time you encounter a lengthy math question, go to the end, RTFQ, and underline it. This will make your job for the question pop off the page, so you always have the finish line in mind. By understanding and knowing your requirement for the question, you'll be more open to identifying relevant details during your read through of the question the first time.

Process of Elimination (POE)

It's helpful that the SAT Subject Test Math 2 contains only multiple-choice questions. After all, this means that eliminating four answers that cannot possibly be right is just as good as knowing what the right answer is, and it's often easier. Eliminating four answers and choosing the fifth is called the Process of Elimination (POE).

POE can also be helpful even when you can't get down to a single answer. Because of the way the test is scored (plus one raw point for a correct answer and minus a quarter-point for an incorrect answer), if you can eliminate at least one answer, it is to your advantage to guess.

So, the bottom line.

To increase your score on the SAT Subject Test Math 2, eliminate wrong answer choices whenever possible, and guess aggressively whenever you can eliminate anything.

There is a major elimination technique you should rely on as you move through the test: Ballparking.

Ballparking

Sometimes, you can approximate an answer:

> You can eliminate answer choices by Ballparking whenever you have a general idea of the correct answer. Answer choices that aren't even in the right ballpark can be crossed out.

Take a look at the following three questions. In each question, at least one answer choice can be eliminated by Ballparking. See whether you can make eliminations yourself. For now, don't worry about how to do these questions—just concentrate on eliminating answer choices.

6. If $x^{\frac{3}{5}} = 1.84$, then $x^2 =$

(A) −10.40
(B) −3.74
(C)   7.63
(D)   10.40
(E)   21.15

Here's How to Crack It

You may not have been sure how to work with that ugly fractional exponent. But if you realized that x^2 can't be negative, no matter what x is, then you could eliminate (A) and (B)—the negative answers—and then guess from the remaining answer choices.

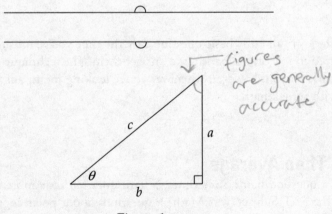

figures are generally accurate

Figure 1

13. In Figure 1, if $c = 7$ and $\theta = 42°$, what is the value of a ?

(A) 0.3
(B) 1.2
(C) 4.7
(D) 5.2
(E) 6.0

Here's How to Crack It

Unless you're told otherwise, the figures that the SAT Subject Test Math 2 gives you are drawn accurately, and you can use them to ballpark. In this example, even if you weren't sure how to apply trigonometric functions to the triangle, you could still approximate based on the diagram provided. If *c* is 7, then *a* looks like, say, 5. That's not specific enough to let you decide between (C), (D), and (E), but you can eliminate (A) and (B). They're not even close to 5. At the very least, that gets you down to a 1-in-3 guess—much better odds.

---

22. The average (arithmetic mean) cost of Simon's math textbooks was $55.00, and the average cost of his history textbooks was $65.00. If Simon bought 3 math textbooks and 2 history textbooks, what was the average cost of the 5 textbooks?

    (A) $57.00
    (B) $59.00
    (C) $60.00
    (D) $63.50
    (E) $67.00

Here's How to Crack It

Here, once again, you might not be sure how to relate all those averages. However, you could realize that the average value of a group can't be bigger than the value of the biggest member of the group, so you could eliminate (E). You might also realize that, since there are more $55 books than $65 books, the average must be closer to $55.00 than to $65.00, so you could eliminate (C) and (D). That gets you down to only two answer choices, a 50/50 chance. Those are excellent odds.

These are all fairly basic questions. By the time you've finished this book, you won't need to rely on Ballparking to answer them. The technique of Ballparking will still work for you, however, whenever you're looking for an answer you can't figure out with actual math.

Can I Trust The Figure?

In order to intentionally mislead you, sometimes the College Board inserts figures that are deliberately inaccurate. When the figure is wrong, the College Board will print underneath, "Note: Figure not drawn to scale." When you see this note, trust the text of the problem, but don't believe the figure, because the figure is just there to trick you.

"Better" Than Average

What makes a question hard? Sometimes, a hard question tests more advanced material. For example, on the SAT Subject Test Math 2, questions about polar coordinates are rare before question 20. Sometimes a hard question requires more steps, four or five rather than one or two. But more often, a hard question has trickier wording and better trap answers than an easy question.

The College Board designs its test around certain trends and traps, looking to catch the average student with the sort of tricks and problems that have tripped test-takers up in the past. While this does mean that you'll have to be alert, it also means that many of these questions have predictable wrong answers, and you can use this knowledge to "beat" the curve. When the College Board writes a question that mentions "a number," it counts on students to think of numbers like 2 or 3, not numbers like −44.76 or 4π. The College Board counts on students to think of the most obvious thing, like 2 or 3 instead of −44.76 or 4π. Don't be led astray by the urge to choose these; instead, use it to your advantage.

There is nothing on the SAT Subject Test Math 2 that hasn't been taught to students, which means that in order to trip students up, the test-writers need to make students pick a wrong answer. It does that by offering answers that are too good to be true: tempting oversimplifications, obvious answers to subtle questions, and all sorts of other answers that seem comforting and familiar. Take a step back. Try eliminating choices like these and then pick and check another one instead.

28. Ramona cycles from her house to school at 15 miles per hour. Upon arriving, she realizes that it is Saturday and immediately cycles home at 25 miles per hour. If the entire round-trip takes her 32 minutes, then what is her average speed, in miles per hour, for the entire round-trip?

(A)   17.0
(B)   18.75
(C)   ~~20.0~~
(D)   21.25
(E)   22.0

Here's How to Crack It

This is a tricky problem, and you may not be sure how to solve it. You can, however, see that there's a very tempting answer among the answer choices. If someone goes somewhere at 15 mph and returns at 25 mph, then it seems reasonable that the average speed for the trip should be 20 mph. For question 28, however, that's far too obvious to be right. Eliminate (C).

> **Stop and Think**
>
> Anytime you find an answer choice immediately appealing on a hard question, stop and think again. The College Board collects data from thousands of students in trial tests before making a question a scored part of their tests. If it looks that good to you, it probably looked good to many of the students taking the trial tests. That attractive answer choice is almost certainly a trap. The right answer won't be the answer most people would pick. On hard questions, obvious answers are wrong. Eliminate them.

34. If θ represents an angle such that $\sin 2\theta = \tan \theta - \cos 2\theta$, then $\tan^2 \theta =$

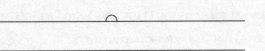

(A) $-\sqrt{2}$
(B)   0
(C)   1
(D) $2\sqrt{2}$
(E) It cannot be determined from the information given.

Here's How to Crack It

On a question like this one, you might have no idea how to go about finding the answer. That "It cannot be determined" answer choice may look awfully tempting. You can be sure, however, that (E) will look tempting to *many* students. It's too tempting to be right on a question this hard. You can eliminate (E).

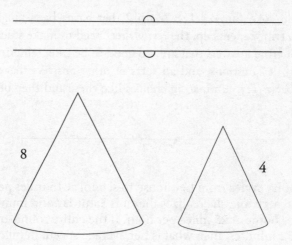

48. If the above cones are similar, and the volume of the larger cone is 64, then what is the volume of the smaller cone?

    (A)   2
    (B)   4
    (C)   8
    (D) 16
    (E) 32

Here's How to Crack It

This one may seem simple: the smaller cone is half as tall as the larger cone, so its volume must be $\frac{64}{2} = 32$. But wait! This is question number 48. That means that most test-takers will miss it. We'll cover how to tackle this question easily in the Plane and Solid Geometry chapter, but before you turn the page, be sure to cross out 32, as it's a trap answer!

SO DO I HAVE TO KNOW MATH AT ALL?

The techniques in this book will go a long way toward increasing your score, but there's a certain minimum amount of mathematical knowledge you'll need in order to do well on the SAT Subject Test Math 2. We've collected the most important rules and formulas into lists. As you move through the book, you'll find these lists at the end of each chapter.

The strategies in this chapter, and the techniques in the rest of this book, are powerful tools. They will make you a better test taker and improve your performance. Nevertheless, memorizing the formulas on our lists is as important as learning techniques. Memorize those rules and formulas, and make sure you understand them.

Using That Calculator

Behold the First Rule of Intelligent Calculator Use:

> Your calculator is only as smart as you are.

It's worth remembering. Some test-takers have a dangerous tendency to rely too much on their calculators. They try to use them on every question and start punching numbers in even before they've finished reading a question. That's a good way to make a question take twice as long as it has to.

The most important part of problem solving is done in your head. You need to read a question, decide which techniques will be helpful in answering it, and set up the question. Using a calculator before you really need to do so will keep you from seeing the shortcut solution to a problem.

When you do use your calculator, follow these simple procedures to avoid the most common calculator errors.

- Check your calculator's operating manual to make sure that you know how to use *all* of your calculator's scientific functions (such as the exponent and trigonometric functions).
- Clear the calculator at the beginning of each problem to make sure it's not still holding information from a previous calculation.
- Whenever possible, do long calculations one step at a time. It makes errors easier to catch.
- Write out your work! Label everything, and write down the steps in your solution after each calculation. That way, if you get stuck, you won't need to do the entire problem over again. Writing things down will also prevent you from making careless errors.
- Keep an eye on the answer choices to see if the College Board has included a partial answer designed to tempt you away from the final answer. Eliminate it!

> **Scientific or Graphing?**
> The College Board says that the SAT Subject Test Math 2 is designed with the assumption that most test-takers have graphing calculators. The College Board also says that a graphing calculator may give you an advantage on a handful of questions. If you have access to a graphing calculator and know how to use it, you may want to choose it instead of a scientific calculator.

Above all, remember that your brain is your main problem-solving tool. Your calculator is useful only when you've figured out exactly what you need to do to solve a problem.

Bubbling in Chunks

Since the goal of the subject test is to maximize time efficiency for that hour, treat each set of two pages as a set of answers to bubble. What that means is that when you're working through the test on your first pass, for each two pages that you're working on, when you've completed working the questions you plan to on the first pass, hop over to the scantron and bubble the answers you've gotten all at once.

The benefit to this is to minimize the hectic "back-and-forth" multi-tasking and keep you focused on one thing at a time. When you commit to an answer for a question, circle it in the book and jot the letter to the left of the question number for ease of identification when you are bubbling. The other additional benefit is that, for just a couple of seconds, the only thing you have to technically "worry" about is that you just color inside the lines on your scantron. This is also a great way to kind of rest and regroup for the next two pages.

When it is getting close to time expiring, about 5 minutes left, then bubble in whatever answers you haven't yet, and continue to bubble as you go from then until the end of the test. When time is about to expire, you don't want to have a handful of answers to bubble in with only mere seconds remaining!

Part II
Diagnostic
Practice Test

Chapter 3
Practice Test 1

MATHEMATICS LEVEL 2

For each of the following problems, decide which is the BEST of the choices given. If the exact numerical value is not one of the choices, select the choice that best approximates this value. Then fill in the corresponding oval on the answer sheet.

Notes: (1) A scientific or graphing calculator will be necessary for answering some (but not all) of the questions on this test. For each question, you will have to decide whether or not you should use a calculator.

(2) The only angle measure used on this test is degree measure. Make sure that your calculator is in degree mode.

(3) Figures that accompany problems on this test are intended to provide information useful in solving the problems. They are drawn as accurately as possible EXCEPT when it is stated in a specific problem that its figure is not drawn to scale. All figures lie in a plane unless otherwise indicated.

(4) Unless otherwise specified, the domain of any function f is assumed to be the set of all real numbers x for which $f(x)$ is a real number. The range of f is assumed to be the set of all real numbers $f(x)$, where x is in the domain of f.

(5) Reference information that may be useful in answering the questions on this test can be found below.

THE FOLLOWING INFORMATION IS FOR YOUR REFERENCE IN ANSWERING SOME OF THE QUESTIONS ON THIS TEST.

Volume of a right circular cone with radius r and height h:
$$V = \frac{1}{3}\pi r^2 h$$

Lateral area of a right circular cone with circumference of the base c and slant height ℓ: $S = \frac{1}{2}c\ell$

Volume of a sphere with radius r: $V = \frac{4}{3}\pi r^3$

Surface area of a sphere with radius r: $S = 4\pi r^2$

Volume of a pyramid with base area B and height h:
$$V = \frac{1}{3}Bh$$

USE THIS SPACE FOR SCRATCHWORK.

1. If $2y + 6 = \dfrac{c}{9}(y + 3)$ for all y, then $c =$

(A) $\dfrac{1}{9}$

(B) 2

(C) 9

(D) 15

(E) 18

GO ON TO THE NEXT PAGE

MATHEMATICS LEVEL 2—*Continued*

2. The relationship between a temperature F in degrees Fahrenheit and a temperature C in degrees Celsius is defined by the equation $F = \frac{9}{5}C + 32$, and the relationship between a temperature in degrees Fahrenheit and a temperature R in degrees Rankine is defined by the equation $R = F + 460$. Which of the following expresses the relationship between temperatures in degree Rankine and degrees Celsius?

(A) $R = \frac{9}{5}C - 32 + 460$

(B) $R = \frac{9}{5}C + 32 + 460$

(C) $R = \frac{9}{5}C + 32 - 460$

(D) $R = \frac{9}{5}C + 860$

(E) $R = \frac{9}{5}C - 828$

3. What is the slope of a line containing the points $(1, 13)$ and $(-3, 6)$?

(A) 0.14
(B) 0.57
(C) 1.75
(D) 1.83
(E) 6

4. If $a + b + c = 12$, $a + b = 4$, and $a + c = 7$, what is the value of a ?

(A) −2

(B) −1

(C) $\frac{3}{23}$

(D) 2

(E) $\frac{23}{3}$

GO ON TO THE NEXT PAGE

5. If $g(x) = 2e^x - 2$ and $h(x) = \ln(x)$, then $g(h(7)) =$

(A) 7.69
(B) 12
(C) 14
(D) 26.43
(E) 31.98

USE THIS SPACE FOR SCRATCHWORK.

6. The intersection of a cylinder and a plane could be which of the following?

    I.   A circle
    II.   A triangle
    III. A rectangle

(A) I only
(B) II only
(C) I and III only
(D) II and III only
(E) I, II, and III

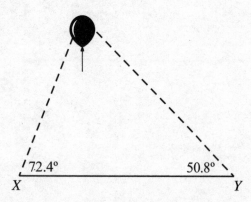

7. The figure above shows a helium balloon rising vertically. When the balloon reaches a height of 54 inches, the angles of elevation from points X and Y on the ground are 72.4° and 50.8°, respectively. What is the distance, in inches, between points X and Y?

(A) 61.17
(B) 72.29
(C) 84.15
(D) 124.72
(E) 236.44

GO ON TO THE NEXT PAGE

USE THIS SPACE FOR SCRATCHWORK.

8. What is the value of y^2 if $y = \sqrt{34^2 - 30^2}$?

 (A) 256^2
 (B) 256
 (C) 16
 (D) 4
 (E) 2

9. The points in the xy-plane are transformed so that each point $A\ (x, y)$ is transformed to $A'\ (3x, 3y)$. If the distance between point A and the origin is c, then the distance between the point A' and the origin is

 (A) $\dfrac{1}{c}$
 (B) $\dfrac{c}{3}$
 (C) c
 (D) $c\sqrt{3}$
 (E) $3c$

10. If $p(q(x)) = \dfrac{3\sqrt{x^2 - 2} + 2}{\sqrt{x^2 - 2} - 2}$ and $p(x) = \dfrac{3x + 2}{x - 2}$, then $q(x) =$

 (A) $x^2 - 2$
 (B) x^2
 (C) x
 (D) $\sqrt{x^2 - 2}$
 (E) $\sqrt{x}$

GO ON TO THE NEXT PAGE

11. If x is the degree measure of an angle such that $0° < x < 90°$ and $\cos x = 0.6$, then $\sin(90° − x) =$

    (A) 0.4
    (B) 0.5
    (C) 0.6
    (D) 0.7
    (E) 0.8

USE THIS SPACE FOR SCRATCHWORK.

12. The set of points defined by the equation $x^2 + y^2 + z^2 = 4$ is

    (A) a point
    (B) a line
    (C) a circle
    (D) a plane
    (E) a sphere

13. The graph of the function g, where

$$g(x) = \frac{7}{x^2 − 6x + 9}$$, has a vertical asymptote

at $x =$

    (A) 0 only
    (B) 3 only
    (C) 7 only
    (D) 0 and 3 only
    (E) 0, 3, and 7

GO ON TO THE NEXT PAGE ⟶

USE THIS SPACE FOR SCRATCHWORK.

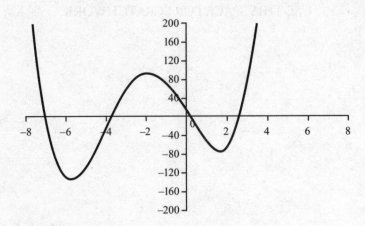

14. The graph of $y = x^4 + 8x^3 - 4x^2 - 64x + k$ is shown above. Which of the following could be the value of k ?

(A) 1,240
(B) 520
(C) 14
(D) −14
(E) −1,240

15. If $\sin x = 0.6743$, then $\csc x =$

(A) 0.6481
(B) 0.8374
(C) 1.2953
(D) 1.4830
(E) 1.9637

GO ON TO THE NEXT PAGE

16. Sarah is planning a vacation at a hotel that costs $80 per night. Sarah must also pay the $170 airfare to get there and will also pay for an equally priced hotel room for a friend who will be visiting her on three of the nights. Which of the following correctly expresses the average cost, in dollars, for each night as a function of n, the number of nights of the vacation?

USE THIS SPACE FOR SCRATCHWORK.

(A) $f(n) = \dfrac{80n + 410}{n - 3}$

(B) $f(n) = \dfrac{80n + 170}{n - 3}$

(C) $f(n) = \dfrac{80n + 410}{n + 3}$

(D) $f(n) = \dfrac{80n + 410}{n}$

(E) $f(n) = \dfrac{80n + 170}{n}$

17. Which of the following is an equation whose graph is a set of points equidistant from the points $(0, 0)$ and $(6, 0)$?

(A) $x = 3$
(B) $y = 3$
(C) $x = 3y$
(D) $y = 3x$
(E) $y = 3x + 3$

GO ON TO THE NEXT PAGE

18. What is the sum of the infinite geometric series

$$\frac{1}{9} + \frac{1}{27} + \frac{1}{81} + \frac{1}{243} + \dots \ ?$$

(A) $\frac{5}{36}$

(B) $\frac{1}{6}$

(C) $\frac{1}{3}$

(D) 1

(E) $\frac{4}{3}$

USE THIS SPACE FOR SCRATCHWORK.

19. Which of the following is equivalent to $a - b \geq a + b$?

(A) $a \leq b$
(B) $a \leq 0$
(C) $b \leq a$
(D) $b \leq 0$
(E) $b \geq 0$

20. If m and n are in the domain of a function g and $g(m) > g(n)$, which of the following must be true?

(A) $mn \neq 0$
(B) $m > n$
(C) $m < n$
(D) $m = n$
(E) $m \neq n$

GO ON TO THE NEXT PAGE ⟹

21. In a certain office, the human resources department reports that 60% of the employees in the office commute over an hour on average each day, and that 25% of those employees who commute over an hour on average each day commute by train. If an employee at the office is selected at random, what is the probability that the employee commutes over an hour on average by train?

    (A) 0.10
    (B) 0.15
    (C) 0.20
    (D) 0.25
    (E) 0.30

USE THIS SPACE FOR SCRATCHWORK.

22. To the nearest degree, what is the measure of the second smallest angle in a right triangle with sides 5, 12, and 13 ?

    (A) 23°
    (B) 45°
    (C) 47°
    (D) 60°
    (E) 67°

23. Which of the following is an equation of a line perpendicular to $y = 3x - 5$?

    (A) $y = 5x - 3$

    (B) $y = -3x + 5$

    (C) $y = -\dfrac{1}{3}x + 5$

    (D) $y = -\dfrac{1}{3}x + 4$

    (E) $y = \dfrac{1}{-3x + 5}$

GO ON TO THE NEXT PAGE ⇒

24. What is the range of the function $g(x) = -2 + 5\cos(3x + 7\pi)$?

    (A) $-1 \le g(x) \le 1$
    (B) $-5 \le g(x) \le -1$
    (C) $-5 \le g(x) \le 5$
    (D) $-7 \le g(x) \le 3$
    (E) $-7 \le g(x) \le 5$

USE THIS SPACE FOR SCRATCHWORK.

25. Of the following list of numbers, which has the greatest standard deviation?

    (A) 1, 2, 3
    (B) 2, 2, 2
    (C) 2, 4, 6
    (D) 4, 7, 10
    (E) 6, 8, 10

26. The formula $F = Ie^{0.06y}$ gives the final amount F that a bank account will contain if an initial investment I is compounded continuously at an annual interest of 6% for y years. Using this formula, after how many years will an initial investment of $100 be worth approximately $600 ?

    (A) 5.2
    (B) 6.0
    (C) 13.0
    (D) 22.4
    (E) 29.7

GO ON TO THE NEXT PAGE

USE THIS SPACE FOR SCRATCHWORK.

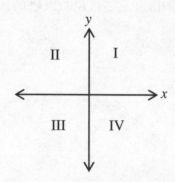

27. If $\cos \theta < 0$ and $\dfrac{\sin \theta}{\cos \theta} > 0$, then θ must be in
which quadrant in the figure above?

(A) I
(B) II
(C) III
(D) IV
(E) There is no quadrant in which both conditions are true.

28. If $g(-x) = -g(x)$ for all real numbers x and if $(4, 9)$ is a point on the graph of g, which of the following points must also be on the graph of g ?

(A) $(-9, -4)$
(B) $(-4, -9)$
(C) $(-4, 9)$
(D) $(4, -9)$
(E) $(9, 4)$

If a is a multiple of 10, then a is a multiple of 5.

29. If a is an integer, which of the following CANNOT be inferred from the statement above?

(A) If a is a multiple of 5, then a is a multiple of 10.
(B) If a is not a multiple of 5, then a is not a multiple of 10.
(C) a is a multiple of 10 implies that a is a multiple of 5.
(D) A necessary condition for a to be a multiple of 10 is that a is a multiple of 5.
(E) In order for a to be a multiple of 5, it is sufficient that a be a multiple of 10.

GO ON TO THE NEXT PAGE

30. In how many different orders can 8 different colors of flowers be arranged in a straight line?

    (A)   8
    (B)   64
    (C)   40,320
    (D)   80,640
    (E) 16,777,216

USE THIS SPACE FOR SCRATCHWORK.

31. What value does $\dfrac{2x}{\ln(x+1)}$ approach as x approaches 0 ?

    (A) 0
    (B) 0.5
    (C) 1
    (D) 2
    (E) It does not approach a unique value.

32. If $f(x) = |7 - 5x|$, then $f(1) =$

    (A) $f(-1)$

    (B) $f(0)$

    (C) $f\left(\dfrac{3}{5}\right)$

    (D) $f(2)$

    (E) $f\left(\dfrac{9}{5}\right)$

33. What is the period of the graph of
    $y = 3\tan(2\pi x + 9)$?

    (A) $\dfrac{\pi}{2}$

    (B) $\dfrac{1}{2}$

    (C) 3

    (D) $\dfrac{3}{2}$

    (E) $\dfrac{3\pi}{2}$

GO ON TO THE NEXT PAGE

MATHEMATICS LEVEL 2—*Continued*

USE THIS SPACE FOR SCRATCHWORK.

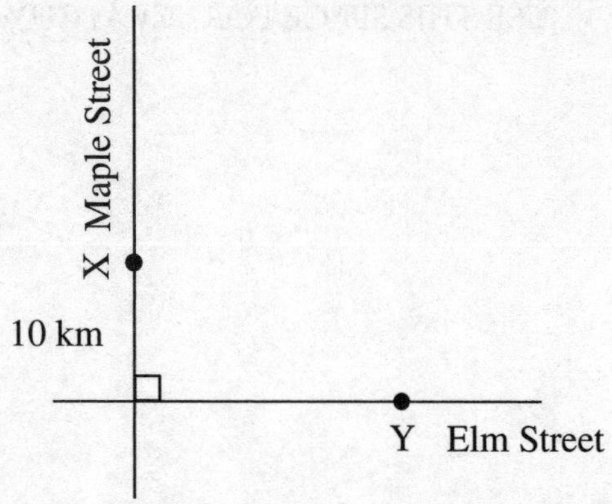

34. The figure above shows a map of Maple Street and Elm Street. Katherine is biking from Point X to Point Y. The straight-line distance from Point X to Point Y is 40 kilometers. If Katherine bikes at an average speed of 15 km per hour along Maple Street and Elm Street, how long will it take Katherine to get to Point Y ?

(A) 40 minutes
(B) 2 hours and 35 minutes
(C) 2 hours and 40 minutes
(D) 3 hours and 15 minutes
(E) 3 hours and 35 minutes

x	$g(x)$
−2	0
−1	−3
0	2
1	0
2	0

35. If g is a polynomial of degree 4, five of whose values are shown in the table above, then $g(x)$ could equal

(A) $g(x) = \left(x + \frac{1}{2}\right)(x + 1)(x + 2)^2$

(B) $g(x) = (x - 2)(x - 1)(x + 2)(x + 3)$

(C) $g(x) = (x - 2)\left(x + \frac{1}{2}\right)(x + 1)(x + 2)$

(D) $g(x) = (x - 3)(x - 2)(x - 1)(x + 2)$

(E) $g(x) = (x - 2)(x - 1)\left(x + \frac{1}{2}\right)(x + 2)$

GO ON TO THE NEXT PAGE

36. The only distinct prime factors of an integer m are 2, 3, 5, and 13. Which of the following could NOT be a factor of m?

    (A) 6
    (B) 9
    (C) 12
    (D) 26
    (E) 35

USE THIS SPACE FOR SCRATCHWORK.

37. If $0 \le x \le \dfrac{\pi}{2}$ and $\cos x = 4\sin x$, what is the value of x?

    (A) 0.245
    (B) 0.250
    (C) 0.328
    (D) 1.217
    (E) 1.326

38. If $g(x) = 3\sqrt{5x}$, what is the value of $g^{-1}(15)$?

    (A) 0.04
    (B) 1.73
    (C) 3.17
    (D) 5.00
    (E) 25.98

39. The Triangular Number Sequence T_n can be defined recursively as

    $$T_1 = 1$$
    $$T_n = T_{n-1} + n \text{ for } n > 1$$

    What is the 11th term of the sequence?

    (A) 45
    (B) 55
    (C) 66
    (D) 78
    (E) 91

GO ON TO THE NEXT PAGE

40. If $f(x) = x^3 + x^2 - 16x + 12$, which of the following statements are true?

    I. The equation $f(x) = 0$ has three real solutions.
    II. $f(x) \geq -8$ for all $x \geq 0$
    III. The function is increasing for $x > 2$.

    (A) I only
    (B) III only
    (C) I and III only
    (D) II and III only
    (E) I, II, and III only

USE THIS SPACE FOR SCRATCHWORK.

GO ON TO THE NEXT PAGE

USE THIS SPACE FOR SCRATCHWORK.

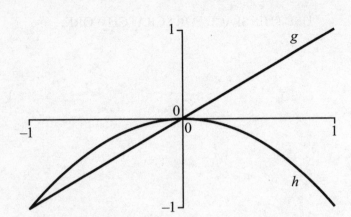

41. Portions of the graphs of g and h are shown above. Which of the following could be a portion of the graph of gh?

(A)

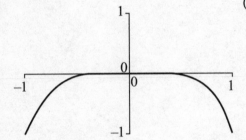

(B)

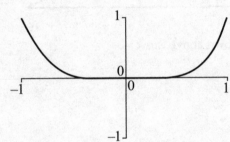

(C)

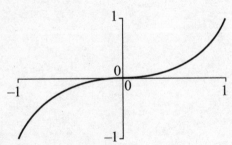

(D)

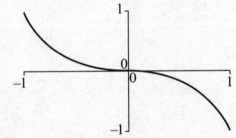

(E)

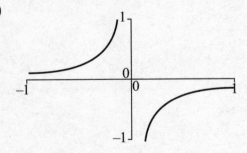

GO ON TO THE NEXT PAGE

USE THIS SPACE FOR SCRATCHWORK.

42. The set of all real numbers y such that $y = \sqrt{y^2}$ is

    (A) all real numbers
    (B) no real numbers
    (C) negative real numbers only
    (D) nonnegative real numbers only
    (E) zero only

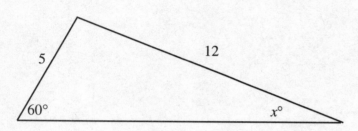

43. In the triangle shown above, sin x =

    (A) $\dfrac{5}{13}$

    (B) $\dfrac{5}{12}$

    (C) $\dfrac{5\sqrt{3}}{12}$

    (D) $\dfrac{5\sqrt{3}}{24}$

    (E) $\dfrac{12}{13}$

44. The length, width, and height of a rectangular solid are 6, 3, and 2. What is the length of the longest segment that can be drawn between two vertices of the solid?

    (A) 6

    (B) $3\sqrt{5}$

    (C) 7

    (D) 12

    (E) 18

GO ON TO THE NEXT PAGE

MATHEMATICS LEVEL 2—*Continued*

USE THIS SPACE FOR SCRATCHWORK.

45. If $\log_n 2 = a$ and $\log_n 5 = b$, then $\log_n 50 =$

(A) $a + b$
(B) $a + b^2$
(C) ab^2
(D) $a + 2b$
(E) $a + 5b$

46. If $\cos x = a$, then, for all x, in the interval $0 < x < \frac{\pi}{2}$, $\tan x =$

(A) $a^2 + 1$

(B) $\frac{1}{1 - a^2}$

(C) $\frac{a}{1 - a^2}$

(D) $\frac{1}{\sqrt{1 - a^2}}$

(E) $\frac{\sqrt{1 - a^2}}{a}$

47. Which of the following shifts in the graph of $y = x^2$ would result in the graph of $y = x^2 + 4x + c$, where c is a constant greater than 5 ?

(A) Left 2 units and up $c - 4$ units
(B) Right 2 units and down $c - 4$ units
(C) Right 2 units and down $c + 4$ units
(D) Left 2 units and up $c + 4$ units
(E) Right 4 units and up c units

GO ON TO THE NEXT PAGE

48. If the height of a right square pyramid is increased by 12%, by what percent must the side of the base be increased, so that the volume of the pyramid is increased by 28% ?

    (A) 3%
    (B) 7%
    (C) 10%
    (D) 36%
    (E) 56%

USE THIS SPACE FOR SCRATCHWORK.

49. If Matrix X has dimensions $a \times b$ and Matrix Y has dimensions $b \times c$, where a, b, and c are distinct positive integers, which of the following must be true?

    I. The product XY exists and has dimensions $a \times c$.
    II. The product XY exists and has dimensions $b \times b$.
    III. The product YX does not exist.

    (A) I only
    (B) II only
    (C) III only
    (D) I and III only
    (E) II and III only

GO ON TO THE NEXT PAGE

USE THIS SPACE FOR SCRATCHWORK.

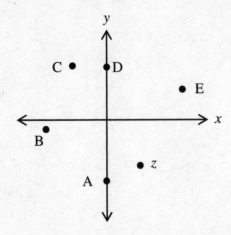

50. If z is the complex number shown in the figure above, which of the following could be iz ?

(A) A
(B) B
(C) C
(D) D
(E) E

STOP

IF YOU FINISH BEFORE TIME IS CALLED, YOU MAY CHECK YOUR WORK ON THIS TEST ONLY. DO NOT WORK ON ANY OTHER TEST IN THIS BOOK.

Chapter 4
Practice Test 1:
Answers and
Explanations

PRACTICE TEST 1 ANSWER KEY

The following answer key has been specifically formatted for diagnostic purposes. Please use the "Correct" column to check off the questions you not only answered correctly, but feel you fully understood. Use a squiggle to mark questions you used POE to guess on, or weren't sure about. Once you've marked up this table use either just the wrong answers OR the wrong and the unsure answers to tally up a percentage for each chapter.

If you are pressed for time, begin your review (in sequential order) with the chapters in which you scored the lowest percentage.

Question Number	Question Answer	Correct?	See Chapter(s) #
1	E		5
2	B		5
3	C		8
4	B		5
5	B		10
6	C		7
7	A		9
8	B		6
9	E		8
10	D		10
11	C		9
12	E		8
13	B		10
14	C		8
15	D		9
16	D		10
17	A		8
18	B		12
19	D		5
20	E		10
21	B		6
22	E		9
23	D		8
24	D		10
25	D		11

Question Number	Question Answer	Correct?	See Chapter(s) #
26	E		12
27	C		9
28	B		10
29	A		12
30	C		11
31	D		12
32	E		10
33	B		9
34	D		7
35	E		10
36	E		6
37	A		9
38	D		10
39	C		12
40	E		10
41	D		10
42	D		6
43	D		9
44	C		7
45	D		12
46	E		9
47	A		10
48	B		7
49	D		12
50	E		12

CHAPTER 5 TEST SCORE SELF-EVALUATION

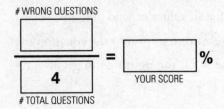

WRONG QUESTIONS

4

TOTAL QUESTIONS

= %

YOUR SCORE

CHAPTER 6 TEST SCORE SELF-EVALUATION

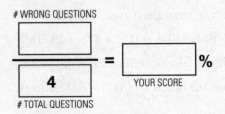

WRONG QUESTIONS

4

TOTAL QUESTIONS

= %

YOUR SCORE

CHAPTER 7 TEST SCORE SELF-EVALUATION

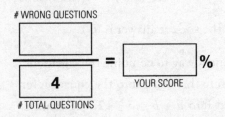

WRONG QUESTIONS

4

TOTAL QUESTIONS

= %

YOUR SCORE

CHAPTER 8 TEST SCORE SELF-EVALUATION

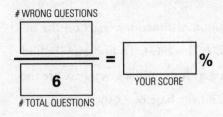

WRONG QUESTIONS

6

TOTAL QUESTIONS

= %

YOUR SCORE

CHAPTER 9 TEST SCORE SELF-EVALUATION

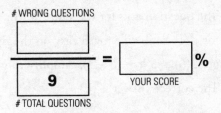

WRONG QUESTIONS

9

TOTAL QUESTIONS

= %

YOUR SCORE

CHAPTER 10 TEST SCORE SELF-EVALUATION

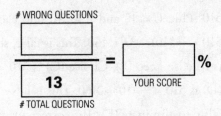

WRONG QUESTIONS

13

TOTAL QUESTIONS

= %

YOUR SCORE

CHAPTER 11 TEST SCORE SELF-EVALUATION

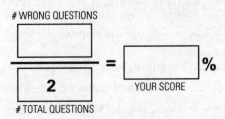

WRONG QUESTIONS

2

TOTAL QUESTIONS

= %

YOUR SCORE

CHAPTER 12 TEST SCORE SELF-EVALUATION

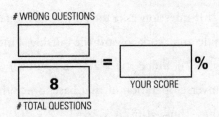

WRONG QUESTIONS

8

TOTAL QUESTIONS

= %

YOUR SCORE

PRACTICE TEST 1 EXPLANATIONS

1. **E** The question asks for the value of c in an equation that is true for all values of y, so plug in a value for y. To make the math easy on the right side, plug in $y = 6$. Substitute $y = 6$ into the equation to get $2(6) + 6 = \dfrac{c}{9}(6 + 3)$. Simplify to get $18 = \dfrac{c}{9}(9)$. Cancel the 9s on the right side to get $18 = c$. The correct answer is (E).

2. **B** The question asks for the relationship between R and C. Since there are variables in the choices, plug in. Let $C = 10$. If $C = 10$, then $F = \dfrac{9}{5}(10) + 32 = 50$. If $F = 50$, then $R = 50 + 460 = 510$. Plug $C = 10$ and $R = 510$ into each choice and eliminate any that aren't true. Choice (A) is $510 = \dfrac{9}{5}(10) - 32 + 460$. This is false, so eliminate (A). Choice (B) is $510 = \dfrac{9}{5}(10) + 32 + 460$. This is true, so keep (B). Choice (C) is $510 = \dfrac{9}{5}(10) + 32 - 460$. This is false, so eliminate (C). Choice (D) is $510 = \dfrac{9}{5}(10) + 860$. This is false, so eliminate (D). Choice (E) is $510 = \dfrac{9}{5}(10) - 828$. This is false, so eliminate (E). The correct answer is (B).

3. **C** To find the slope of a line, use the slope formula: $slope = \dfrac{y_2 - y_1}{x_2 - x_1}$. Let $(x_1, y_1) = (1, 13)$ and $(x_2, y_2) = (-3, 6)$. The slope of the line is $\dfrac{6 - 13}{-3 - 1} = \dfrac{-7}{-4} = 1.75$. The correct answer is (C).

4. **B** The question includes three equations and three variables, so find a way to combine the equations. Because the second equation provides a value for $a + b$, substitute this value into the equation for $a + b + c$ to get the value of c. When $a + b = 4$ is substituted into $a + b + c = 12$, the result is $4 + c = 12$. Subtract 4 from both sides to get $c = 8$. Now, substitute $c = 8$ into $a + c = 7$ to get $a + 8 = 7$. Subtract 8 from both sides to get $a = -1$. The correct answer is (B).

5. **B** This question asks for $g(h(7))$. On questions involving composition of functions, start on the inside and work toward the outside. Find $h(7)$. Since $h(x) = \ln(x)$, $h(7) = \ln(7)$. To find $g(h(7))$, find $g(\ln(7))$. Since $g(x) = 2e^x - 2$, $g(\ln(7)) = 2e^{\ln(7)} - 2$. Recall that logarithms with a given base are the inverse operation of that base. Since the base of ln is e, the ln and the base of e cancel each other out. Thus, $g(\ln(7)) = 2e^{\ln(7)} - 2 = 2(7) - 2 = 12$. As an alternative, use your calculator to find that $\ln(7) \approx 1.94591015$, and thus $2e^{\ln(7)} - 2 = 2e^{1.94591015} - 2 = 12$. The correct answer is (B).

6. **C** The question asks for which of the three listed figures could be the intersection of a plane and a cylinder. Go through one at a time. For (I), since the bases of a cylinder are circles, the plane could intersect the cylinder in a way that the plane contains one of the bases and forms a circle.

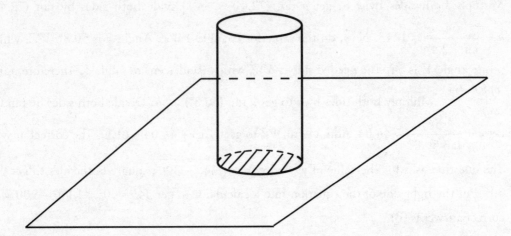

Since the intersection could form a circle, (I) must be included. Eliminate (B) and (D), which don't include (I). Try (II). There doesn't seem to be an obvious way to form a triangle. However, don't eliminate (II) right away in case there is a way that isn't obvious. Try (III). Determine whether a rectangle can be formed. If the plane passes through the diameters of each base, then a rectangle is formed.

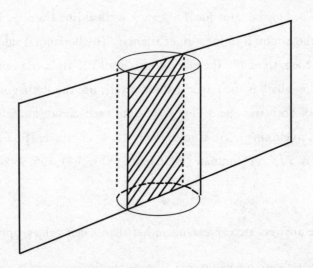

Therefore, (III) must be included, so eliminate (A). Now, come back to (II). If the plane is parallel to the bases, a circle is formed rather than a triangle. If the plane is perpendicular to the bases, a rectangle is formed. If the plane is at any other angle, a curved path is formed, so the result cannot be a triangle. Therefore, eliminate (E), which includes (II). The correct answer is (C).

7. **A** The question asks for the distance between X and Y. Use the vertical height to form two right triangles. Find the base of each triangle. The sum of the two bases will be the distance between X and Y. For reference, call the balloon point Z and the point on the ground directly below the balloon point W. Look at triangle XWZ. Angle X is 72.4°. WZ, which is opposite the angle X, is 54. The needed side is XW, which is adjacent to the angle X. Therefore, $\tan 72.4° = \dfrac{opp}{adj} = \dfrac{54}{a}$.

Multiply both sides by a to get $a \tan (72.4°) = 54$. Divide both sides by $\tan (72.4°)$ to get $a = \dfrac{54}{\tan 72.4°} \approx 17.13$. Now, do the same for triangle YWZ. Angle Y is $50.8°$. WZ, which is opposite angle Y, is 54. The needed side is YW, which is adjacent to angle Y. Therefore, $\tan 50.8° = \dfrac{opp}{adj} = \dfrac{54}{a}$. Multiply both sides by a to get $a \tan (50.8°) = 54$. Divide both sides by $\tan (50.8°)$ to get $a = \dfrac{54}{\tan 50.8°} \approx 44.04$. Add XW to WZ to get $17.13 + 44.04 = 61.17$. The correct answer is (A).

8. **B** The question asks for the value of y^2. Since $y = \sqrt{34^2 - 30^2}$, square both sides to get $y^2 = 34^2 - 30^2$. Put the right side of the equation into a calculator to get $34^2 - 30^2 = 1{,}156 - 900 = 256$. The correct answer is (B).

9. **E** Because there are variables in the choices, plug in. Pick coordinates for point A. Because the question involves distance, choose a point that can be used to make a Pythagorean triple. Let A be $(x, y) = (3, 4)$. Point A' is $(3x, 3y) = (9, 12)$. The distance between A and the origin is c. Draw a segment vertically from A to the x-axis and a line from $(3, 4)$ to the origin, forming a right triangle. The distance to the x-axis is 4, and the distance along the x-axis is 3. Therefore, this is a 3:4:5 right triangle, and $c = 5$. Do the same for A'. Draw a vertical line from $(9, 12)$ to the x-axis and a line from $(9, 12)$ to the origin, forming a right triangle. The horizontal side has a length of 9, and the vertical side has a length of 12. Therefore, this is a 9:12:15 right triangle, and the distance from A' to the origin is 15, which is the target. (Alternatively, use the Pythagorean Theorem to determine the hypotenuse of both triangles.) Plug $c = 5$ into each choice and eliminate any that aren't 15. Choice (A) is $\dfrac{1}{5}$, so eliminate (A). Choice (B) is $\dfrac{5}{3}$, so eliminate (B). Choice (C) is 5, so eliminate (C). Choice (D) is $5\sqrt{3}$, so eliminate (D). Choice (E) is $3(5) = 15$, so keep (E). The correct answer is (E).

10. **D** Even though the answers are expressions rather than exact values, apply PITA here by substituting in each answer choice for x into $p(x)$. The composite function $p(q(x))$ is going to contain radical expressions, so eliminate (A), (B), and (C) immediately since neither those choices nor $p(x)$ contain radicals. Plugging (D) in for x in $p(x)$ gives $\dfrac{3\sqrt{x^2 - 2} + 2}{\sqrt{x^2 - 2} - 2}$, which is identical to $p(q(x))$, so keep (D). Plugging (E) in gives $\dfrac{3\sqrt{x} + 2}{\sqrt{x} - 2}$, which is missing the -2's under the root symbols that are present in $p(q(x))$, so eliminate (E). As an alternative, plug in a value for x to get a decimal value for $p(q(x))$. Plugging in 3 for x gives $p\big(q(3)\big) = \dfrac{3\sqrt{3^2 - 2} + 2}{\sqrt{3^2 - 2} - 2} \approx 15.389$, which will be the target number. Plugging in 3 to each answer choice will give a value for $q(x)$, which can

then be plugged back in to $p(x)$ to match the target. For (D), if $q(3) = \sqrt{3^2 - 2} = \sqrt{7}$, then

$$p(q(3)) = p(\sqrt{7}) = \frac{3\sqrt{7} + 2}{\sqrt{7} - 2} \approx 15.389,$$ which matches the target answer. Plugging 3 into the other

choices doesn't lead to the target, so eliminate them. The correct answer is (D).

11. **C** The question asks for sin $(90° - x)$. There are two possible approaches to this problem. One is to find the value of x by using the inverse cosine function. If cos $x = 0.6$, then take the inverse cosine of both sides to get $x = \cos^{-1}(0.6) \approx 53.13$. Therefore, sin $(90° - x) \approx$ sin $(90° - 53.13°) \approx 0.6$. Alternatively, use the identity cos $x =$ sin $(90° - x)$. Therefore, if cos $x = 0.6$, then sin $(90° - x) = 0.6$ Using either method, the correct answer is (C).

12. **E** In xyz-coordinates, a graph with the equation $x^2 + y^2 + z^2 = r^2$ is a sphere with center at the origin. This equation may seem familiar as it is closely related to the standard form of the equation for a circle centered at the origin $(x^2 + y^2 = r^2)$ but extended to three dimensions. This may provide a clue to the answer if you don't know the equation of a sphere. However, if this equation is not familiar, the question can still be answered using POE. Find points that satisfy this equation. Start with points (2, 0, 0), (0, 2, 0), and (0, 0, 2). Because there is more than one point, eliminate (A). These three points do not form a line, so eliminate (B). These points could make a circle, plane, or sphere, so plug in more points. Try (–2, 0, 0), (0, –2, 0), and (0, 0, –2). These six points are not on the same plane, so eliminate (D). Since all points in any circle must be on the same plane, eliminate (C), as well. Only one choice remains. The correct answer is (E).

13. **B** The question asks for the x-values at which g has vertical asymptotes. A function has a vertical asymptote for x-values at which the denominator is 0 and the factor that makes the denominator equal to 0 cannot be canceled out with the numerator. Since the numerator of g cannot be factored, only worry about where the denominator is 0. Set $x^2 - 6x + 9 = 0$. Factor the left side, finding two factors of 9 with a sum of –6. These are –3 and –3. Therefore, the factored form of the equation is $(x - 3)(x - 3) = 0$. Set both factors to equal to 0 and solve. In both cases, the equation is $x - 3 = 0$, so add 3 to both sides to get $x = 3$. The correct answer is (B).

14. **C** The question asks for the value of k, which is the constant term in the polynomial. The constant term represents the y-intercept. According to the graph, the curve crosses the y-axis between 0 and 40. Only one choice is between these. The correct answer is (C).

15. **D** The question asks for csc x, which is equivalent to $\frac{1}{\sin x}$. Substitute the value of sin x given by the question to get csc $x = \frac{1}{\sin x} = \frac{1}{0.6743} \approx 1.4830$. The correct answer is (D).

16. **D** The question asks for the average cost for each night, which is $\frac{total\ cost}{\#\ of\ nights}$. There are variables in the choices, so plug in. Let $n = 4$. Since n represents the number of nights, let this be the

denominator. Determine the total cost. Her stay at the hotel costs $80 per night for four nights for a total of 4 × $80 = $320. Furthermore, the three-night hotel stay for her friend costs 3 × $80 = $240. She must also pay airfare, which is $170. Therefore, the total cost is $320 + $240 + $170 = $730, and the average cost is $\frac{\$730}{4}$ = $182.5. This is the target number. Plug $n = 4$ into each of the choices, and eliminate any that aren't 182.5. Choice (A) is $\frac{80(4) + 410}{4 - 3}$ = 730. Eliminate (A). Choice (B) is $\frac{80(4) + 170}{4 - 3}$ = 490. Eliminate (B). Choice (C) is $\frac{80(4) + 410}{4 + 3}$ ≈ 104.29. Eliminate (C). Choice (D) is $\frac{80(4) + 410}{4}$ = 182.5. Keep (D). Choice (E) is $\frac{80(4) + 170}{4}$ = 122.5. Eliminate (E). The correct answer is (D).

17. **A** The set of points equidistant between two points is the perpendicular bisector of the segment whose endpoints are the two points. The segment with endpoints (0, 0) and (6, 0) lies on the line $y = 0$ and has midpoint (3, 0). Since a line in the form $y = c$, where c is a constant, is a horizontal line, the perpendicular line must be a perpendicular line the form $x = k$, where k is a constant. To be a bisector, the line must go through the midpoint, which is (3, 0), so the line is $x = 3$.

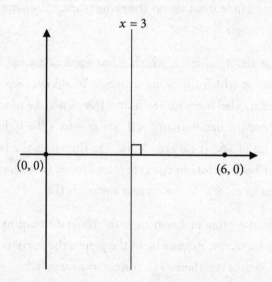

Alternatively, sketch the two points and sketch each of the choices. Choices (B), (C), (D), and (E) all have points that are clearly closer to (0, 0) to (6, 0) and vice versa, so they can be eliminated. The correct answer is (A).

18. **B** A geometric series is one with nth term ar^{n-1}, where a represents the first term, and r represents the common ratio, i.e., the number by which each term must be multiplied to get the next term. If

$0 < r < 1$, then the sum of an infinite series can be found using the formula $\dfrac{a}{1-r}$. The first term is $\dfrac{1}{9}$,

fill in this for a. To find the common ratio, set up the equation $\dfrac{1}{27} = r\left(\dfrac{1}{9}\right)$. Multiply both sides by

9 to get $r = \dfrac{9}{27} = \dfrac{1}{3}$. Therefore, the sum is $\dfrac{\frac{1}{9}}{1-\frac{1}{3}} = \dfrac{\frac{1}{9}}{\frac{2}{3}} = \dfrac{1}{9} \times \dfrac{3}{2} = \dfrac{3}{18} = \dfrac{1}{6}$. Alternatively, ballpark by

finding the sum of the known terms on a calculator $\dfrac{1}{9} + \dfrac{1}{27} + \dfrac{1}{81} + \dfrac{1}{243} \approx 0.1646$. This is close to

$\dfrac{1}{6} = 0.1\overline{6}$. Using either method, the correct answer is (B).

19. **D** Simplify the inequality by combining like terms. Subtract a from both sides to get $-b \geq b$. Add b to both sides to get $0 \geq 2b$. Divide both sides by 2 to get $0 \geq b$. This can be rewritten as $b \leq 0$. The correct answer is (D).

20. **E** Recall that in a function, each input can yield only one output. In stating that $g(m) > g(n)$, the question has told us that the outputs for m and n are different. Thus, they can't be the same input, and so $m \neq n$. As an alternative, since the question says *must be true*, eliminate any choice that can be false. It is unknown whether g is increasing, decreasing, or neither, so attempt as many cases as is needed to eliminate four choices. Let g be an increasing function. Try $g(x) = x$. In this case, if $g(m) > g(n)$, then $m > n$. Eliminate (C) and (D). Furthermore, it could be that $m = 2$ and $n = 0$. In this case, $mn = 0$, so eliminate (A) as well. Now try $g(x) = -x$. In this case, if $g(m) > g(n)$, $-m > -n$. Divide both sides by -1 to get $m < n$. Eliminate (B). The correct answer is (E).

21. **B** The question involves percents, so plug in 100 as the total number of employees in the office. 60% of the employees commute over an hour each day on average. Since 60% of 100 is 60, exactly 60 employees commute over an hour each day on average. 25% of those 60 employees commute by train. Since 25% of 60 is $\dfrac{25}{100} \times 60 = \dfrac{1}{4} \times \dfrac{60}{1} = \dfrac{60}{4} = 15$, there are 15 employees who commute over an hour by train. The question asks for the probability that a randomly selected employee commutes over an hour on average by train. There are 15 employees who do this out of 100 total employees, so the probability is $\dfrac{15}{100} = 0.15$. The correct answer is (B).

22. **E** The second smallest angle is the one opposite the second shortest side. The second shortest side is the 12. Mark the angle opposite the 12 as $x°$. The hypotenuse is 13. Therefore, $\sin x = \dfrac{opp}{hyp} = \dfrac{12}{13}$. Since $\sin x = \dfrac{12}{13}$, take $\sin^{-1}$ of both sides to get $x \approx 67.38$. The question asks for the nearest degree, so the correct answer is (E).

23. **D** The question asks for the equation of the line perpendicular to $y = 3x - 5$. In the xy-plane, perpendicular lines have slopes that are negative reciprocals. Find the slope of $y = 3x - 5$. For a line in the form $y = mx + b$, the slope is represented by m. Therefore, the slope of $y = 3x - 5$ must be 3. Find a choice that represents the equation of a line with a slope of $-\frac{1}{3}$. Choice (E) is not the equation of a line, so eliminate (E). The remaining choices are in $y = mx + b$ form, so select the choice with $m = -\frac{1}{3}$. The correct answer is (D).

24. **D** The question asks for the range of $g(x)$, which is a cosine function. The range of $\cos(x)$ is $-1 \le \cos(x) \le 1$. Anything that's inside the parentheses does not affect the range. The coefficient 3 only affects the period and not the range. Similarly, 7π only shifts the graph to the left and does not affect the range. Therefore, the range of $\cos(3x + 7\pi)$ is $-1 \le \cos(3x + 7\pi) \le 1$. The coefficient 5 changes the amplitude, which is defined as half the distance from the maximum and minimum values of the cosine graph. Therefore, the range of $5\cos(3x + 7\pi)$ is $-5 \le 5\cos(3x + 7\pi) \le 5$. The constant -2 represents a downward shift, so subtract 2 from both the maximum and the minimum. Therefore, the range of $g(x)$ is $-7 \le g(x) \le 3$. The correct answer is (D).

25. **D** The question asks for the list with the greatest standard deviation. Standard deviation refers to how spread out the numbers are in a set of data, so the list with the greatest standard deviation is the list in which the numbers are farthest apart. The numbers in (D) have the greatest separation. The correct answer is (D).

26. **E** First, plug in the known values into the equation. The initial investment is $100, so plug in $I = 100$. The account needs to be worth $600, so plug in $F = 600$ to get $600 = 100e^{0.06y}$. Solve for y. Divide both sides by 100 to get $6 = e^{0.06y}$. Take the natural log of both sides, which will cancel the base e to get $\ln(6) = 0.06y$ and $1.791759 = 0.06y$. Divide both sides by 0.06 to get $29.86 = y$, which is closest to 29.7. The correct answer is (E).

27. **C** The question asks for the location of θ on the xy-plane. Use the unit circle. In the unit circle, $\cos\theta$ is equivalent to the x-coordinate, and $\sin\theta$ is equivalent to the y coordinate. If $\cos\theta < 0$, then $x < 0$. The x-coordinate is negative in Quadrants II and III. Eliminate (A) and (D). The question also states that $\dfrac{\sin\theta}{\cos\theta} > 0$. If a fraction is positive, then the numerator and denominator must be of the same sign. Since $\cos\theta$ is negative, so is $\sin\theta$. Thus, the y-coordinate must be negative. The x- and y-coordinate are both negative in Quadrant III, so the correct answer is (C).

28. **B** The question asks for what point must be on the graph of g. Since the question has provided both a point $(4, 9)$ and an equation $g(-x) = -g(x)$, plug the point into the equation. The given point $(4, 9)$ tells you that $x = 4$ and $g(4) = 9$. Plugging 4 in for x gives $g(-4) = -g(4)$, and plugging 9 in for $g(4)$ gives $g(-4) = -9$. Since $g(-4) = -9$, the point $(-4, -9)$ must also be on the graph of g. As an alternative, notice that $g(-x) = -g(x)$ is the definition of an odd function, which tells you that points in the first quadrant will also appear in the third quadrant but with the appropriate signs. Since

both x and y are negative in the third quadrant, the first quadrant point $(4, 9)$ will become $(-4, -9)$. The correct answer is (B).

29. **A** The question asks for what statement CANNOT be inferred from the given statement. Because the question says CANNOT, ignore the CANNOT and mark each choice as Y or N depending on whether it can be inferred. The given statement is a conditional statement in the form *if p then q*. In the original statement, *a is a multiple of 10* and *b is a multiple of 5*. A conditional statement is logically equivalent to its contrapositive, which is in the form *if not q, then not p*. Therefore, the contrapositive of the given statement *If a is a multiple of 10, then a is a multiple of 5* is *If a is not a multiple of 5, then a is not a multiple of 10*. Go through each choice one at a time. Choice (A) is in the form *if q then p*. A reversal of the order of the original condition statement cannot be assumed to be equivalent to the original. (For example, consider $a = 15$.) Mark this choice as N. Choice (B) is the contrapositive. The contrapositive is logically equivalent, so mark this choice with Y. Choice (C) rephrases an *if p then q* statements as an *p implies q*. This is logically equivalent, so mark this choice with Y. Choice (D) discusses a necessary condition. For a statement in the form *if p then q*, p is referred to as the sufficient condition and q is referred to as the necessary condition. Since (D) refers to q as the necessary condition, mark (D) with Y. Similarly, (E) refers to p as the sufficient condition, so mark (E) with Y. Four choices are marked as Y and one choice is marked with N, so select the choice marked with N. The correct answer is (A).

30. **C** The question asks for how many different arrangements of 8 flowers in a line. Draw 8 spaces in a line for the 8 flowers. Consider the number of possibilities for each space. For the first space, any of the 8 flowers can be chosen, so put an 8 in the first space. Once that flower is chosen, there are 7 possible flowers remaining for the second space, so put a 7 in the second space. Similarly, there are 6 flowers remaining for the 3rd space, 5 for the 4th space, 4 for the 5th space, 3 for the 6th space, 2 for the 7th space, and 1 for the 8th space. Because the question asks for *different orders*, the order matters, so multiply the numbers in the spaces without doing any division to get $\underline{8} \times \underline{7} \times \underline{6} \times \underline{5} \times \underline{4} \times \underline{3} \times \underline{2} \times \underline{1} = 40{,}320$. The correct answer is (C).

31. **D** The question asks for what value an expression approaches as x approaches 0. Plug in a value close to 0. Let $x = 0.1$. In a calculator, compute $\dfrac{2(0.1)}{\ln(0.1 + 1)}$ to get 2.098. Eliminate (A), (B), and (C) because they are not close to 2.098. To determine whether the answer could be (E), plug in a value for x that is slightly less than 0. Let $x = -0.1$. In a calculator, compute $\dfrac{2(-0.1)}{\ln(-0.1 + 1)}$ to get 1.898. This is still close to 2, so the function does approach 2 as x approaches 0. As an alternative, graph $\dfrac{2x}{\ln(x + 1)}$ on a graphing calculator. The graph is a mostly smooth graph with a hole at $(0, 2)$. Using either method, the correct answer is (D).

32. **E** The question asks for something equal to $f(1)$. Replace x with 1 in $f(x)$ to get $f(1) = |7 - 5(1)| = 2$. Go through the choices and find the one equal to 2. In (A), $f(-1) = |7 - 5(-1)| = 12$. Eliminate (A). In (B), $f(0) = |7 - 5(0)| = 7$. Eliminate (B). In (C), $f\left(\dfrac{3}{5}\right) = \left|7 - 5\left(\dfrac{3}{5}\right)\right| = 4$. Eliminate (C). In (D), $f(2) = |7 - 5(2)| = 3$. Eliminate (D). In (E), $f\left(\dfrac{9}{5}\right) = \left|7 - 5\left(\dfrac{9}{5}\right)\right| = 2$. Keep (E). The correct answer is (E).

33. **B** The question asks for the period of a tangent graph. For a tangent equation in the form of $y = A\tan(Bx + C)$, the period is only affected by the value of B, which is a horizontal stretch transformation, and is equal to the expression $\dfrac{\pi}{|B|}$. In this equation $B = 2\pi$, so the period is $\dfrac{\pi}{|2\pi|} = \dfrac{\pi}{2\pi} = \dfrac{1}{2}$. Alternatively, graph the equation, and note that there is only one zero per period. Therefore, the distance between the zeros is equal to the period. The correct answer is (B).

34. **D** The question asks for how long it would take Katherine to get from Point X to Point Y along Maple Street and Elm Street. Because this is a rate question, use the formula $d = rt$, with d representing distance, r representing rate, and t representing time. According to the question, the rate is 15 kilometers per hour, so substitute $r = 15$ to get $d = 15t$. To get the time, find the distance. According to the question, the straight-line distance from Point X to Point Y is 40 kilometers. However, the question also says that she bikes along Maple Street and Elm Street, so don't use the straight-line distance for d. Instead use the sum of the distances from Point X to the intersection and from the intersection to Point Y for d. The distance from the Point X to the intersection is 10. To find the distance from intersection to Point Y, use the Pythagorean Theorem: $a^2 + b^2 = c^2$. Draw the straight-line distance from Point X to Point Y and label it 40. Since 40 is the hypotenuse, plug in $a = 10$ and $c = 40$ to get $10^2 + b^2 = 40^2$. Simplify to get $100 + b^2 = 1600$. Subtract 100 from both sides to get $b^2 = 1500$. Take the square root of both sides to get $b \approx 38.7298$. To get the total distance, add this to the distance from Point X to the intersection to get $d = 10 + 38.7298 = 48.7298$. Plug this into the equation to get $48.7298 = 15t$. Divide both sides by 15 to get $t \approx 3.2487$. This is the time in hours. Because it is between 3 and 4 hours, eliminate (A), (B), and (C). The remaining two choices only differ by the remainder in minutes. To get the remainder in minutes, set up the proportion $\dfrac{0.2487 \text{ hr}}{x \text{ min}} = \dfrac{1 \text{ hr}}{60 \text{ min}}$. Cross-multiply to get $x \approx 15$ minutes. Therefore, the total time is 3 hours and 15 minutes. The correct answer is (D).

35. **E** The question asks for what could equal $g(x)$. The choices are in factored form. In the factored form of a polynomial, each factor is in the form $(x - r)$ where r is one of the roots, so find the roots. The roots of an equation are the values of x at which the value of the function is 0. According to the table $g(x) = 0$, when $x = -2$, 1, and 2. Therefore, the factors $(x + 2)$, $(x - 1)$, and $(x - 2)$ must be included in the equation of the function. Eliminate (A) and (C). Plug the remaining points into the answer choices. Begin with $f(0) = 2$. In (B), $f(0) = (0 - 2)(0 - 1)(0 + 2)(0 + 3) = 12$, so eliminate (B). In (D), $f(0) = (0 - 3)(0 - 2)(0 - 1)(0 + 2) = -12$, so eliminate (D). In (E), $f(0) = (0 - 2)(0 - 1)$ $\left(0 + \dfrac{1}{2}\right)(0 + 2) = 2$, so keep (E). The correct answer is (E).

36. **E** The question asks for what could NOT be a factor of m, an integer whose only distinct prime factors are 2, 3, 5, and 13. A factor of m must, by definition, divide m evenly with no remainder. Since these are the only prime numbers used to make up m, any factors of m can only be made up of these four primes as well. Therefore, if a number has any prime factor other than 2, 3, 5, or 13, the number cannot be a factor of m. Find the prime factors of each choice. Because the question says NOT, ignore the NOT. Instead mark a choice with Y if it could be a factor and N if it could not be. The prime factors of 6 are 2 and 3. Since 2 and 3 are prime factors of m, this could be a factor, so mark (A) with Y. The prime factors of 9 are 3 and 3. Since 3 is a prime factor of m, this could be a factor, so mark (B) with Y. The prime factors of 12 are 2, 2, and 3. Since 2 and 3 are prime factors of m, this could be a factor, so mark (C) with Y. The prime factors of 26 are 2 and 13. Since 2 and 13 are prime factors of m, this could be a factor, so mark (D) with Y. The prime factors of 35 are 5 and 7. Since 7 is not a prime factor of m, this cannot be a factor, so mark (E) with N. Four choices are marked with Y and one choice is marked with N, so select the choice marked with N. The correct answer is (E).

37. **A** The question asks for the value of x. There are values in the choices, so PITA. Start with (C). If $x = 0.328$, then $\cos x \approx 0.947$ and $4\sin x \approx 1.289$. These are not equal, so eliminate (C). If it's not clear to you which direction to go in from (C), don't spend time debating—pick one and go. Try (B). If $x = 0.250$, then $\cos x \approx 0.969$ and $4\sin x \approx 0.990$. These are not equal, so eliminate (B). Try (A). If $x = 0.245$, the $\cos x \approx 0.970$ and $4\sin x \approx 0.970$. Although a calculator indicates that the values are not exactly equal, the answer choices on the test are rounded, so if they are extremely close, they can be taken to be equal. Since this choice works, the correct answer is (A).

38. **D** The question asks for the value of $g^{-1}(15)$. The function g^{-1} is defined as the inverse of g. For inverse functions, if $g(x) = y$, then $g^{-1}(y) = x$. Therefore, $y = 15$ and the question asks for the value of x. Since the question asks for the value of x and there are numbers in the choices, PITA. Plug the choices in for x and eliminate any for which $f(x)$ is not 15. Start with (C). If $x = 3.17$, then

$g(x) = g(3.17) \approx 11.944$. This is not 15, so eliminate (C). The answer must be greater, so eliminate (A) and (B), as well. Try (D). If $x = 5$, then $g(x) = g(5) = 15$. This matches the target, so the correct answer is (D).

39. **C** The question asks for the 11th term of the Triangular Number Sequence. To find a term in a recursive sequence, start at the beginning. The definition states that $T_1 = 1$ and that $T_n = T_{n-1} + n$ for $n > 1$. Therefore, $T_2 = T_1 + 2 = 1 + 2 = 3$. Continue to T_{11}.

$T_3 = T_2 + 3 = 3 + 3 = 6$.
$T_4 = T_3 + 4 = 6 + 4 = 10$.
$T_5 = T_4 + 5 = 10 + 5 = 15$.
$T_6 = T_5 + 6 = 15 + 6 = 21$.
$T_7 = T_6 + 7 = 21 + 7 = 28$.
$T_8 = T_7 + 8 = 28 + 8 = 36$.
$T_9 = T_7 + 9 = 36 + 9 = 45$.
$T_{10} = T_9 + 10 = 45 + 10 = 55$.
$T_{11} = T_{10} + 11 = 55 + 11 = 66$.

While the above series of equations might look intimidating at first, as you work through the first few you may start to notice a pattern that will help you move through the problem faster. In this case, the solution is really just adding up the integers from 1 to 11. The correct answer is (C).

40. **E** The question asks which statements are true about the function $f(x) = x^3 + x^2 - 16x + 12$ are true. If a graphing calculator is available, graph the function. The graph crosses the x-axis three times, so (I) is true. Also, the graph has a relative minimum at $(2, -8)$, is increasing at all points to the right of $(2, -8)$, and has no points for which $y < -8$ on the positive side of the x-axis. Therefore, (II) and (III) are true as well. If no graphing calculator is available, then factor to determine the number of solutions. One method is to test factors of 12 for a solution. The factors of 12 are 1, 2, 3, 4, 6, and 12. Try $x = 1$. Since $f(1) = 1^3 + 1^2 - 16(1) + 12 = -2$, $x = 1$ is not a solution. Try $x = 2$. Since $f(2) = 2^3 + 2^2 - 16(2) + 12 = -8$, $x = 2$ is not a solution. Since $f(3) = 3^3 + 3^2 - 16(3) + 12 = 0$, $x = 3$ is a solution and $(x - 3)$ is one factor. Rewrite $x^3 + x^2 - 16x + 12$ in a way that makes it easy to factor $(x - 3)$. First, rewrite it as $x^3 - 3x^2 + 3x^2 + x^2 - 16x + 12$, and factor the first two terms to get $x^2(x - 3) + 4x^2 - 16x + 12$. Now, rewrite it as $x^2(x - 3) + 4x^2 - 12x + 12x - 16x + 12$, and factor $4x^2 - 12x$ to get $x^2(x - 3) + 4x(x - 3) - 4x + 12$. Now factor $-4x + 12$ to get $x^2(x - 3) + 4x(x - 3) - 4(x - 3)$. Factor $(x - 3)$ to get $(x - 3)(x^2 + 4x - 4)$. Now determine the number of factors of $x^2 - 4x + 4$. To determine the number of factors of a quadratic in the form $ax^2 + bx + c$, use the discriminant: $b^2 - 4ac$. If the discriminant is positive, there are two real solutions. If the discriminant is 0, there is one real solution. If the discriminant is negative, there are no real solutions. In the quadratic $x^2 + 4x - 4$, $a = 1$, $b = 4$, and $c = -4$, so $b^2 - 4ac = 4^2 - 4(1)(-4) = 32 > 0$. Since the discriminant is positive, $x^2 + 4x - 4$ has two solutions and $(x - 3)(x^2 + 4x - 4)$ has three solutions. Thus, (I) is true. Eliminate (B) and (D). Test (II), which says that $f(x) \geq -8$, for all $x \geq 0$. Set up $x^3 + x^2 - 16x + 12 \geq -8$. Get one side equal to 0. Add 8 to both sides to get

$x^3 + x^2 - 16x + 20 \geq 0$. Similarly, factor the polynomial on the right by testing the factors of 20: 1, 2, 4, 5, 10 and 20. Since $1^3 + 1^2 - 16(1) + 20 = 6$, $x = 1$ is not a solution. Since $2^3 + 2^2 - 16(2) + 20 = 0$, $x = 2$ is a solution, so $(x - 2)$ is a factor. Rewrite $x^3 + x^2 - 16x + 20$ as $x^3 - 2x^2 + 2x^2 + x^2 - 16x + 20 = x^2(x - 2) + 3x^2 - 16x + 20 = x^2(x - 2) + 3x^2 - 6x + 6x - 16x + 20 = x^2(x - 2) + 3x(x - 2) - 10x + 20 = x^2(x - 2) + 3x(x - 2) - 10(x - 2) = (x - 2)(x^2 + 3x - 10)$. Factor to get $(x - 2)(x - 2)(x + 5) = (x - 2)^2(x + 5)$. Therefore, the expression $x^3 + x^2 - 16x + 20 = 0$ when $x = 2$ and $x = -5$. The statement only refers to what happens when $x \geq 0$, so ignore $x = -5$. Since $x^3 + x^2 - 16x + 20 = 0$, when $x = 2$, $x^3 + x^2 - 16x + 12 = f(x) = -8$, when $x = 2$. Determine what happens to the left and right of $x = 2$. If $x = 1$, then $f(1) = 1^3 + 1^2 - 16(1) + 12 = -2 \geq -8$. If $x = 3$, then $f(3) = 3^3 + 3^2 - 16(3) + 12 = 0 \geq -8$. Therefore $f(x) \geq -8$, whenever $x \geq 0$, so (II) is true. Eliminate (A) and (C). Only one choice remains. The correct answer is (E).

41. **D** The question asks which of the following could be a portion of the graph of gh, the product of the graphs of g and h. Look at the graphs in pieces. When x is negative, the graphs of g and h are both negative. Therefore, the product must be positive. Eliminate (A) and (C), which are negative when x is negative. If x is positive, g is positive but h is negative, so the product must be negative. Eliminate (B), which is positive when x is positive. If $x = 0$, the f and g are both 0, so the product is 0, and the graph of the product must go through the origin. Eliminate (E), which does not go through the origin. The correct answer is (D).

42. **D** The question asks what set of real numbers makes the equation true. Plug in values of y. Try $y = 0$. If $y = 0$, then the equation $0 = \sqrt{0^2}$ is true. Eliminate (B) and (C), which indicate that 0 should not be included. Plug in a positive number. Try $y = 2$. If $y = 2$, then the equation $2 = \sqrt{2^2}$ is true. Eliminate (E), which says that 2 should not be included. Now, try a negative. Try $y = -2$. If $y = -2$, then the equation $-2 = \sqrt{(-2)^2}$ is false. Eliminate (A), which says that -2 should be included. Only one choice remains. As an alternative, recall that the square root symbol refers to the principal square root, and will only yield positive numbers or zero unless it is preceded by $\pm$. Since y is equal to the principal root of something, y cannot be negative. Eliminate (A) and (C). Also, within the domain $y \geq 0$, the principal square root can be canceled with the second power, which gives you the equation $y = y$, and thus is true for all $y \geq 0$. Using either method, the correct answer is (D).

43. **D** The question asks for sin x. The triangle is not necessarily a right triangle. In non-right triangles, use the law of sines: $\dfrac{\sin a}{A} = \dfrac{\sin b}{B}$. The side opposite the 60° angle is 12 and the side opposite the $x°$ angle is 5. Plug these into the formula to get $\dfrac{\sin 60}{12} = \dfrac{\sin x}{5}$. Cross-multiply to get 5sin (60) = 12sin (x). Use the 30-60-90 right triangle to get $\sin(60) = \dfrac{\sqrt{3}}{2}$. Therefore, $\dfrac{5\sqrt{3}}{2} = 12\sin(x)$. Divide both sides by 12 to get $\dfrac{5\sqrt{3}}{24} = \sin(x)$. The correct answer is (D).

44. **C** The question asks for the longest segment that can be drawn between two vertices of the rectangular solid. The longest segments are always the diagonals that go through the center of the rectangular solid.

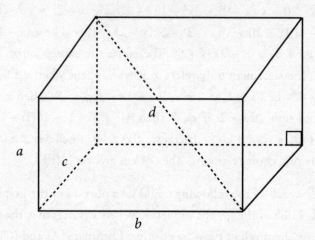

To find the length of one of them, use the three-dimensional version of the Pythagorean Theorem: $a^2 + b^2 + c^2 = d^2$, where a, b, and c represent the dimensions of the rectangular solid and d represents the diagonal. Plug in the dimensions to get $6^2 + 3^2 + 2^2 = d^2$. Simplify the left side to get $49 = d^2$. Take the square root of both sides to get $7 = d$. The correct answer is (C).

45. **D** The question asks for $\log_n 50$. The question also uses variables to represent $\log_n 2$ and $\log_n 5$, so put $\log_n 50$ into those terms. Notice that 2 and 5 are the prime factors of 50. Since $50 = 2 \times 5^2$, $\log_n 50 = \log_n (2 \times 5^2)$. A product within a log is equal to the sum of the logs. Therefore, $\log_n (2 \times 5^2) = \log_n (2) + \log_n (5^2)$. An exponent within a log can be moved in front of the log as a coefficient. Therefore, $\log_n (2) + \log_n (5^2) = \log_n (2) + 2\log_n (5)$. Since $\log_n 2 = a$, and $\log_n 5 = b$, $\log_n (2) + 2\log_n (5) = a + 2b$. Alternatively, plug in $n = 10$ and use a calculator to get $\log 2 \approx 0.301$, $\log 5 \approx 0.699$, and $\log 50 = 1.699$. Therefore, $a = 0.301$, $b = 0.699$, and the target is 1.699. Go through the choices and eliminate any that aren't 1.699. Choice (A) is $0.301 + 0.699 = 1$, so eliminate (A). Choice (B) is $0.301 + 0.699^2 = 0.790$, so eliminate (B). Choice (C) is $(0.301)(0.699)^2 = 0.147$, so eliminate (C). Choice (D) is $0.301 + 2(0.699) = 1.699$, so keep (D). Choice (E) is $0.301 + 5(0.699) = 3.796$, so eliminate (E). The correct answer is (D).

46. **E** The question asks for $\tan x$. There are variables in the choices, so plug in. Since $\cos x = a$, plug in for x and find a. To make sure the numbers are easy, plug in $x = \dfrac{\pi}{3}$ radians, which is equivalent to 60°. If $x = \dfrac{\pi}{3}$, then $a = \cos\left(\dfrac{\pi}{3}\right) = \dfrac{1}{2}$. The question asks for $\tan x$. Since $x = \dfrac{\pi}{3}$,

$\tan x = \tan \dfrac{\pi}{3} = \tan 60° = \sqrt{3} \approx 1.73$. This is the target. Go through the choices and eliminate any that aren't close to 1.73. Choice (A) is $\left(\dfrac{1}{2}\right)^2 + 1 = 1.25$. This is not close to 1.73, so eliminate

(A). Choice (B) is $\dfrac{1}{1 - \left(\dfrac{1}{2}\right)^2} = \dfrac{1}{1 - 0.25} = \dfrac{1}{0.75} = 1.333$. This is not close to 1.73, so eliminate (B).

Choice (C) is $\dfrac{\dfrac{1}{2}}{1 - \left(\dfrac{1}{2}\right)^2} = \dfrac{\dfrac{1}{2}}{1 - 0.25} = \dfrac{\dfrac{1}{2}}{0.75} = 0.667$. This is not close to 1.73, so eliminate (C).

Choice (D) is $\dfrac{1}{\sqrt{1 - \left(\dfrac{1}{2}\right)^2}} = \dfrac{1}{\sqrt{1 - 0.25}} = \dfrac{1}{\sqrt{0.75}} = 1.15$. This is not close to 1.73, so eliminate (D).

Choice (E) is $\dfrac{\sqrt{1 - \left(\dfrac{1}{2}\right)^2}}{\dfrac{1}{2}} = \dfrac{\sqrt{1 - 0.25}}{\dfrac{1}{2}} = \dfrac{\sqrt{0.75}}{\dfrac{1}{2}} = 1.732$. This is close to 1.73, so keep (E). The

correct answer is (E).

47. **A** The question asks for the shift in the graph. There are variables in the choices, so plug in. Since c is a constant greater than 5, plug in $c = 6$. Then, the equation is $y = x^2 + 4x + 6$. To determine the shift, find the vertex by getting the equation in vertex form. Complete the square. Set $y = 0$ to get $0 = x^2 + 4x + 6$. Subtract 6 to move the constant to the other side to get $-6 = x^2 + 4x$. Add the square of half the coefficient on x to both sides. The coefficient is 4, half of 4 is 2, and the square of 2 is 4. Add 4 to both sides to get $-2 = x^2 + 4x + 4$. Factor the right side to get $-2 = (x + 2)^2$. Add 2 to both sides to get $0 = (x + 2)^2 + 2$. Replace 0 with y to get $y = (x + 2)^2 + 2$. Now, the equation is in the form $y = (x - h)^2 + k$, where (h, k) represents the vertex of the parabola. Therefore, the vertex is $(-2, 2)$. Since the vertex of $y = x^2$ is $(0, 0)$, the graph shifts to the left 2 units. Eliminate (B), (C), and (E). The graph also shifts up 2 units. Since $c = 6$, (A) says that the graph shifts up $6 - 4 = 2$ units, while (D) says that the graph shifts $6 + 4 = 10$ units. Eliminate (D). The correct answer is (A).

48. **B** The question is asking for the percent that the side of the base must be increased. Since the question is asking for a percent change in some unknown value, the hidden plug in approach is the best to use here. The volume formula for a rectangular pyramid is $V = \dfrac{1}{3} lwh$, where l and w represent the length and width, respectively, of the base, and h represents the height of the pyramid. First,

plug in numbers just to calculate a starting volume. Since the base of the pyramid is a square, the length and width will be the same. Let $l = 2$, $w = 2$, and $h = 3$. Plugging into the formula yields $V = \frac{1}{3}(2)(2)(3) = 4$. Next, calculate the increased volume of the pyramid: 28% of 4 = 0.28 × 4 = 1.12. The volume that is 28% greater is 4 + 1.12 = 5.12. The question states that the height is increased by 12%, so calculate the new height: 12% of 3 = 0.12 × 3 = 0.36. The height that is 12% greater is 3 + 0.36 = 3.36. Finally, plug the new values calculated for volume and height into the formula to figure out the new values for length and width, which will both just equal x since the values are equal: $(5.12) = \frac{1}{3}(x)(x)(3.36)$. Simplifying results in $5.12 = 1.12x^2$. Divide both sides by 1.12 to get $4.571428571 = x^2$, and $x = 2.138089935$. The original side length was 2, and the question is asking for the percent the side length needs to be increased. Use the percent change formula of $\frac{difference}{original} \times 100$ to find the percent change: $\frac{2.138089935 - 2}{2} \times 100 = 6.904496765$, which is closest to 7%. The correct answer is (B).

49. **D** The question asks which statements must be true, and the statements involve the dimensions and existence of matrix products. To see whether a matrix product exists, write out the dimensions in the product side by side. If the inside values are the same, the product exists. For the product XY, we would write $a \times b$, $b \times c$. Since the values on the inside are the same (b, b), the product exists. To determine the dimensions of the product when it does exist, cancel the inside dimensions. Thus for $a \times b$, $b \times c$, the b's cancel, and the product becomes an $a \times c$ matrix. Therefore, (I) is true and (II) is false, so eliminate (B), (C), and (E). Do the same for the product YX by writing $b \times c$, $a \times b$. In this case, the values on the inside (c, a) are different since a and c are distinct integers, and thus the product does not exist. Therefore, (III) is true, so eliminate (A). The correct answer is (D).

50. **E** The question asks what could be iz. Plug in for z, which is a complex number in Quadrant IV. A complex number in Quadrant IV is in the form $a + bi$, where $a > 0$ and $b < 0$. Let $z = 2 - 3i$. Multiply both sides by i to get $iz = 2i - 3i^2$. Since $i^2 = -1$, $iz = 2i - 3(-1) = 3 + 2i$. Since both a and b are positive, iz must be in Quadrant I, and therefore at point E. The correct answer is (E).

HOW TO SCORE
PRACTICE TEST 1

When you take the real exam, the proctors will collect your test booklet and bubble sheet and send your bubble sheet to a processing center where a computer looks at the pattern of filled-in ovals on your bubble sheet and gives you a score. We couldn't include even a small computer with this book, so we are providing this more primitive way of scoring your exam.

Determining Your Score

STEP 1 Using the answer key, determine how many questions you got right and how many you got wrong on the test. Remember: Questions that you do not answer don't count as either right answers or wrong answers.

STEP 2 List the number of right answers here.

(A) _____

STEP 3 List the number of wrong answers here. Now divide that number by 4. (Use a calculator if you're feeling particularly lazy.)

(B) _____ ÷ 4 = (C) _____

(A) _____ − (C) _____ = _____

STEP 4 Subtract the number of wrong answers divided by 4 from the number of correct answers. Round this score to the nearest whole number. This is your raw score.

STEP 5 To determine your real score, take the number from Step 4 and look it up in the left column of the Score Conversion Table on the next page; the corresponding score on the right is your score on the exam.

PRACTICE TEST 1
SCORE CONVERSION TABLE

Raw Score	Scaled Score	Raw Score	Scaled Score	Raw Score	Scaled Score
50	800	25	610	0	410
49	800	24	600	−1	400
48	800	23	600	−2	390
47	800	22	590	−3	370
46	800	21	580	−4	360
45	800	20	580	−5	350
44	800	19	570	−6	340
43	790	18	560	−7	340
42	780	17	560	−8	330
41	770	16	550	−9	330
40	760	15	540	−10	320
39	750	14	530	−11	310
38	740	13	530	−12	300
37	730	12	520		
36	710	11	510		
35	700	10	500		
34	690	9	490		
33	680	8	480		
32	670	7	480		
31	660	6	470		
30	650	5	460		
29	640	4	450		
28	630	3	440		
27	630	2	430		
26	620	1	420		

Part III
Content Review

Chapter 5
Algebra

On the SAT Subject Test Math 2, you will often be asked to work with variables. While you may be exceptionally skilled with variable manipulation and have a good idea how to approach these questions using the methods you've studied in math class, there are several common pitfalls that can trip up even strong math students. However, fear not! We'll provide you with techniques for tackling algebraic problems with greater efficiency, precision, and confidence. We'll also cover solving for x, inequalities, factoring, simultaneous equations, quadratics, and more!

(You may be wondering why algebra comes before "fundamentals." As you will see in the next chapter, many of our techniques that simplify algebra problems will also simplify problems about fundamental math concepts. Trust us!)

ALGEBRA ON THE SAT SUBJECT TEST MATH 2

Algebra questions will make up approximately 20% of the SAT Subject Test Math 2. Many of these questions can be best answered using the algebra rules reviewed in this chapter. Others are best approached using some of the test-taking techniques discussed in Chapter 2.

Definitions

Here are some algebraic terms that will appear on the SAT Subject Test Math 2. Make sure you're familiar with them. If the meaning of any of these vocabulary words keeps slipping your mind, add those words to your flash cards.

Variable	An unknown quantity in an equation represented by a letter, for example, x, y, or z.
Constant	An unchanging numerical quantity—either a number or a letter that represents a number, for example, 5, 7.31, a, b, or k.
Term	An algebraic unit consisting of constants and variables including any operation other than addition and subtraction such as $5x$ or $9x^2$.
Coefficient	In a term, the constant before the variable. In ax^2, a is the coefficient. In $7x$, 7 is the coefficient.
Polynomial	An algebraic expression consisting of more than one term joined by addition or subtraction. For example, $x^3 - 3x^2 + 4x - 5$ is a polynomial with four terms.
Binomial	A polynomial with exactly two terms, such as $(x - 5)$.
Quadratic	A quadratic expression is a polynomial with one variable whose largest exponent is a 2, for example, $x^2 - 5x + 6$ or $x^2 + 4$.
Root	A root of a polynomial is a value of the variable that makes the polynomial equal to zero. More generally, the roots of an equation are the values that make the equation true. Roots are also known as zeros, solutions, and x-intercepts.
Degree	The greatest exponent on a variable in a polynomial or function. For example, $f(x) = 3x^4 + 3x - 2$ is a function of the fourth degree.

SOLVING EQUATIONS

Some questions on the SAT Subject Test Math 2 will require you to solve a simple algebraic equation. These questions often present you with an algebraic equation hidden in a word problem. Setting up an equation from the information in the problem is the first step to finding a solution and is the step where mistakes are often made. The translation chart on page 121 is very useful for setting up equations for word problems.

An algebraic equation is an equation that contains at least one unknown—a variable. "Solving" for an unknown means figuring out its value. Generally, the way to solve for an unknown is to isolate the variable—that is, manipulate the equation until the unknown is alone on one side of the equals sign. Whatever's on the other side of the equals sign is the value of the unknown. Take a look at this example.

$$5(3x^3 - 16) - 22 = 18$$

In this equation, x is the unknown. To solve for x, you need to get x alone. You isolate x by using inverse operations to undo everything that's being done to x in the equation. If x is being squared, you need to take a square root; if x is being multiplied by 3, you need to divide by 3; if x is being decreased by 4, you need to add 4, and so on. The trick is to do these things in the right order. Basically, you should start with the operation that is the furthest from the x and work your way inwards toward the x. Whatever would be done last to the x (using PEMDAS) should be dealt with first, and whatever would be done first to the x should be dealt with last.

The other thing to remember is that any time you do something to one side of an equation, you've got to do it to the other side also. Otherwise you'd be changing the equation, and you're trying to rearrange it, not change it. In this example, you'd start by undoing the subtraction by using addition.

$$
\begin{array}{rl}
5(3x^3 - 16) - 22 & = 18 \\
+\,22 & +\,22 \\
5(3x^3 - 16) & = 40
\end{array}
$$

Then undo the multiplication by 5 by using division, saving what's in the parentheses for last.

$$
\begin{array}{rcc}
5\left(3x^3 - 16\right) & = & 40 \\
\div\,5 & & \div\,5 \\
3x^3 - 16 & = & 8
\end{array}
$$

Once you've gotten down to what's in the parentheses, continue inverting each operation, working inwards toward the x—first the subtraction, then the multiplication, and the exponent last.

$$
\begin{array}{rl}
3x^3 - 16 & = 8 \\
+\,16 & +\,16 \\
3x^3 & = 24 \\
\div\,3 & \div\,3 \\
x^3 & = 8 \\
\sqrt[3]{x^3} & = \sqrt[3]{8} \\
x & = 2
\end{array}
$$

At this point, you've solved the equation. You have found that the value of x must be 2. Another way of saying this is that 2 is the root of the equation $5(3x^3 - 16) - 22 = 18$. Equations containing exponents may have more than one root.

Equations which have more than one root are common when you have an equation with an even degree. For example,

$$3x^4 = 48$$

First, divide both sides by 3,

$$x^4 = 16$$

Then take the fourth root of each side. Because you're taking an even root of each side, you will end up with both a positive and negative value for x.

$$\sqrt[4]{x^4} = \pm \sqrt[4]{16} \; ; x = \pm 2$$

Solving Equations with Radicals

To solve equations with radicals, you work the equation the same way you work other equations. In order to eliminate the radical, you take both sides to the power of that radical. For example,

$$3\sqrt{4x} + 2 = 8$$

Start by subtracting 2 from both sides, then divide both sides by 3,

$$3\sqrt{4x} = 6 \; ; \sqrt{4x} = 2$$

Next, square both sides, then divide by 4,

$$4x = 4; \; x = 1$$

Note that you do not get both a positive and negative root when you are working radicals, since the radical symbol represents only the principal root, and thus radical equations will have only one solution.

Solving Equations with Absolute Value

The rules for solving equations with absolute value are the same. The only difference is that, because what's inside the absolute value signs can be positive or negative, you're solving for two different results.

Let's look at an example.

$$|x - 2| = 17$$

The absolute value symbol represents distance from 0, which is never negative. Both 17 and −17 are a distance of 17 from 0. You therefore know that in order for the absolute value of the expression inside the bars to equal 17, the expression itself must equal either 17 or −17. This results in two equations.

$$x - 2 = 17 \quad \text{or} \quad x - 2 = -17$$

Now simply solve both equations.

$$
\begin{array}{lcl}
x - 2 = 17 & \text{or} & x - 2 = -17 \\
\underline{+2 \quad +2} & \text{or} & \underline{+2 \quad +2} \\
x = 19 & \text{or} & x = -15
\end{array}
$$

And that's all there is to it!

DRILL 1: SOLVING EQUATIONS

Practice solving equations in the following examples. Remember that some equations may have more than one root. The answers can be found in Part IV.

1. If $\dfrac{\left(3x^2 - 7\right)}{17} = 4$, then $x =$

2. If $n^2 = 5n$, then $n =$

3. If $\dfrac{2a - 3}{3} = -\dfrac{1}{2}$, then $a =$

4. If $\dfrac{5s + 3}{3} = 21$, then $s =$

5. If $\dfrac{3\left(8x - 2\right) + 5}{5} = 4$, then $x =$

6. If $|2m + 5| = 23$, then $m =$

7. If $\left|\dfrac{r - 7}{5}\right| = 4$, then $r =$

8. If $\dfrac{3\sqrt{2x}}{x} = 4$, then $x =$

9. If $2\sqrt[3]{y} = 6y$ and $y \neq 0$, then $y =$

FACTORING AND DISTRIBUTING

When manipulating algebraic equations, you'll need to use the tools of factoring and distributing. These are simply ways of rearranging equations to make them easier to work with.

Factoring

Factoring algebraic expressions is exactly like factoring numbers—it means finding something that you can divide the expression by without leaving a remainder. When factoring an algebraic expression, you should always start by seeing if there is a common factor, which means something you can divide evenly out of each term of the expression. You then put the rest of the expression in parentheses, with the common factor on the outside. Here's an example.

$$x^3 - 5x^2 + 6x = 0$$

On the left side of this equation, every term contains at least one x—that is, x is a common factor of every term in the expression. That means you can factor out an x.

$$x^3 - 5x^2 + 6x = 0$$

$$x(x^2 - 5x + 6) = 0$$

The new expression has exactly the same value as the old one; it's just written differently, in a way that might make your calculations easier. Numbers as well as variables can be factored out, as seen in the example below.

$$11x^2 + 88x + 176 = 0$$

This equation is, at first glance, a bit of a headache. It'd be nice to get rid of that coefficient in front of the x^2 term. In a case like this, check the other terms and see if they share a common factor. In fact, in this equation, every term on the left side is a multiple of 11. Because 11 is a factor of each term, you can pull it out.

$$11x^2 + 88x + 176 = 0$$

$$11\left(x^2 + 8x + 16\right) = 0$$

$$x^2 + 8x + 16 = 0$$

$$\left(x + 4\right)^2 = 0$$

$$x = -4$$

As you can see, factoring can make an equation easier to solve.

Distributing

Distributing is factoring in reverse. When an entire expression in parentheses is being multiplied by some factor, you can "distribute" the factor into each term, and get rid of the parentheses. For example,

$$3x(4 + 2x) = 6x^2 + 36$$

On the left side of this equation the parentheses make it difficult to combine terms and simplify the equation. You can get rid of the parentheses by distributing.

$$3x(4 + 2x) = 6x^2 + 36$$

$$12x + 6x^2 = 6x^2 + 36$$

And suddenly, the equation is much easier to solve.

$$\begin{aligned} 12x + 6x^2 &= 6x^2 + 36 \\ -6x^2 \quad &-6x^2 \\ 12x &= 36 \\ x &= 3 \end{aligned}$$

DRILL 2: FACTORING AND DISTRIBUTING

Practice a little factoring and distributing in the following examples, and keep an eye out for equations that could be simplified by this kind of rearrangement. The answers can be found in Part IV.

3. If $(11x)(50) + (50x)(29) = 4,000$, then $x =$

   (A) 2,000
   (B)   200
   (C)   20
   (D)   2
   (E)   0.2

5. If $ab \neq 0$, $\dfrac{-3b(a+2)+6b}{-ab} =$

   (A) −3
   (B) −2
   (C)   0
   (D)   1
   (E)   3

22. If $x \neq -1$, $\dfrac{x^5 + x^4 + x^3 + x^2}{x^3 + x^2 + x + 1} =$

   (A) $4x^2$
   (B) x^2
   (C) $4x$
   (D) x
   (E) 4

30. If $x \neq 0$ and $x \neq -1$, then $(x^5 + 2x^4 + x^3)^{-1} =$

(A) $\dfrac{2}{x^3(x^2 + x + 1)}$

(B) $-x^3(x+1)^2$

(C) $\dfrac{1}{2x^{12}}$

(D) $\dfrac{1}{x^3(x^2 + 1)}$

(E) $\dfrac{1}{x^3(x+1)^2}$

PLUGGING IN

Plugging In is a technique for turning algebra questions into simpler arithmetic questions while at the same time preventing errors. It works on questions in which there are variables or unknown quantities that cannot be calculated, and therefore can be replaced with numerical values of your choosing. Here's an example.

1. The use of a neighborhood car wash costs n dollars for a membership and p cents for each wash. If a membership includes a bonus of 4 free washes, which of the following reflects the cost, in dollars, of getting a membership at the car wash and washing a car q times, if q is greater than 4 ?

(A) $100n + pq - 4p$

(B) $n + 100pq - 25p$

(C) $n + pq - \dfrac{p}{25}$

(D) $n + \dfrac{pq}{100} - \dfrac{p}{25}$

(E) $n + \dfrac{p}{100} - \dfrac{q}{4}$

Here's How to Crack It

In this problem you see a lot of variables in the question and in the answer choices. That's a big clue!

> When you see variables in the answer choices, PLUG IN!

Let's try Plugging In with this problem. We'll start with *n*, the membership fee. Since this problem doesn't give us enough information to calculate the value of *n*, you can create our own value.

Plug in an easy number like 3, so that a membership costs $3.00.

Then, plug in a number for *p*, the charge per wash. Since this number is in cents, and we'll need to convert it to dollars in the answers, choose a number that can be converted easily to dollars, like 200. Let's make *p* = 200, so a wash costs $2.00.

Last, let's say that *q*, the number of washes, is 5. That's as easy as it gets. With 4 free washes, you're paying for only 1.

Then, just work out the answer to the question using your numbers. How much does it cost for a membership and 5 washes? Well, that's $3.00 for a membership, 4 washes free, and 1 wash for $2.00. The total is $5.00. That means that if you plug your numbers into the answer choices, the right answer should give you 5. We call that your target number—the number you are looking for in the answer choices. Put a double circle around your target number, so that it stands out from all the other numbers you've written down. It looks like a bull's-eye that you're trying to hit.

> **To Number or Not to Number?**
> Let's say you walk into a candy store. The store is selling certain pieces of candy for 5 cents and 10 cents each. You want to get 3 pieces of the 5 cent candy and 6 pieces of the 10 cent candy. You give the cashier a $5 bill. What's your change?
>
> Ok, now let's say you walk into a candy store that for some reason doesn't like numbers and is selling certain pieces of candy for *x* cents and *y* cents each. You want to get *m* pieces of the *x* cent candy and *n* pieces of the *y* cent candy. You give the cashier a $*z* bill. What's your change?
>
> Which problem would be easier to solve? The one with the numbers! Numbers make everything easier. So why bother with variables when you don't have to?

> **A Big Clue**
> There will be times when the College Board will give you questions that include variables and the phrase "in terms of" (for example, "in terms of *x*"). This is a big clue that you can plug in. Cross off the phrase "in terms of *x*," because you don't need it to solve the problem.

When you plug *n* = 3, *p* = 200, and *q* = 5 into the answer choices, the only answer choice that gives you 5 is (D). That means you've hit your target number, and you're done.

Let's look at a problem without variables.

3. The size of an art collection is tripled, and then 70 percent of the collection is sold. Acquisitions then increase the size of the collection by 10 percent. The size of the art collection is then what percent of its size before these three changes?

(A) 240%
(B) 210%
(C) 111%
(D) 99%
(E) 21%

Here's How to Crack It

Here's another question in which you aren't given numbers. In this case, you don't know the original size of the art collection. Instead of variables, though, the question and answers contain percents. This is another sign that you can plug in whatever numbers you like. Because you're working with percentages, 100 is a good number to plug in—it'll make your math easier.

You start with a collection of 100 items. It's tripled, meaning it increases to 300. Then it's decreased by 70%. Remember that percent changes are always made to the current value, so the size of the collection will decrease by 210 to leave 90. Then, finally, it increases by 10%. That's an increase of 9, for a final collection size of 99. Since the collection began at 100, it's now at 99% of its original size. The answer is (D). It doesn't matter what number you choose for the original size of the collection—you'll always get the right answer. The trick to choosing numbers is picking ones that make your math easier.

Take a look at one last (challenging) problem.

50. If x dollars are invested at y percent annual interest, and $0 < x < 10{,}000$ and $y > 0$, then in how many years will the value of the investment equal $10,000 ?

(A) $\log x + \log (1 + 0.01y)$

(B) $\dfrac{\log (1 + 0.01y)}{4 - \log x}$

(C) $\dfrac{4 \log x}{\log (1 + 0.01y)}$

(D) $\dfrac{4 - \log x}{\log (0.01y)}$

(E) $\dfrac{4 - \log x}{\log (1 + 0.01y)}$

Here's How to Crack It

The answer choices with logarithms make this problem look extra intimidating. This problem deals with repeated percent change, but the variables in the question mean you can plug in numbers to make life easier. If you make $y = 100$ then each year the value of the investment doubles. If you make $x = 2,500$, then after 1 year the investment is worth 5,000 and after 2 years the investment is worth 10,000. Therefore, 2 is your target; circle it. Now you can plug in 2,500 for x and 100 for y in each answer, eliminating answers that do not equal 2. The only answer that equals 2 is (E).

Remember to Plug In!

1. See variables in the question and answers? You can plug in!
2. Assign a numerical value to each variable. Pick numbers that make the math easy.
3. Work the problem until you get a numerical answer. Circle it twice; that's the target.
4. Plug in your numbers to each answer choice, eliminating every answer which doesn't match your target. Always check every answer choice with variables!

The idea behind Plugging In is that if the question contains variables which aren't given and can't be calculated, you can use whichever value you like (provided it meets any constraints the problem gives), and the problem and correct answer choice will always have to yield the same result. This allows you to proceed in a straightforward way through what may be truly messy algebra. Just choose your values, consistently use them throughout the problem, and see which answer choice they lead you to.

Occasionally, more than one answer choice will produce the target number. This often occurs when the question is looking for an exception, or something that "must be true." When that happens, eliminate the answer choices that didn't work out, and plug in some different kinds of numbers. Some numbers you might try are odd and even integers, positive and negative numbers, fractions, 0, 1 or –1, and really big or really small numbers, like 1,000 or –1,000. The new numbers will produce a new target number. Use this new target number to eliminate the remaining incorrect answer choices. If you find yourself having to plug in more than twice, look at the numbers you're choosing to make sure you're not using numbers that are too similar!

When using Plugging In, keep a few simple rules in mind:

- Avoid plugging in 1 or 0, which often makes more than one answer choice produce the same number. For the same reason, avoid plugging in numbers that appear in the answer choices—they're more likely to cause several answer choices to produce your target number.
- Plug in numbers that make your math easy—2, 3, and 5 are often good choices. Multiples of 100 are good in percentage questions, and multiples of 60 are good in questions dealing with seconds, minutes, and hours.

Plugging In can be an incredibly useful technique. By plugging in numbers, you're able to simplify complex algebra, avoid errors, and gain access to questions that might have appeared too difficult at first glance.

Plugging In is often safer because questions are often designed so that a mistake in the algebra will result in one of the incorrect answer choices. When your answer matches one of the choices, you think it must be right. Very tempting. Furthermore, all of the answer choices appear very similar in algebraic form, but become much more distinct when turned into numerical values using Plugging In. Often you'll be able to approximate to eliminate numbers that are obviously too big or too small, without doing a lot of calculation, and that will save you lots of time!

It is strongly recommended that you become comfortable with Plugging In. As you will see throughout this book, Plugging In often turns a challenging problem into a piece of cake. It can be tempting to continue doing the problems the way you've always done them, but remember that Plugging In is a brand new skill, and that means it takes practice to become strong at it. The Math 2 Subject Test can challenge even those with already exceptional math skills, and you'll want all the tools you can get to help you reach the best score possible.

DRILL 3: PLUGGING IN

Try solving the following practice questions by plugging in. Remember to check all your answer choices, and plug in a second set of numbers if more than one answer choice produces your target number. The answers can be found in Part IV.

1. The price of an item in a store is p dollars. If the tax on the item is t%, what is the total cost in dollars of n such items, including tax?

(A) npt

(B) $npt + 1$

(C) $\dfrac{np(t+1)}{100}$

(D) $100n(p + pt)$

(E) $\dfrac{np(t+100)}{100}$

2. Vehicle A travels at x miles per hour for x hours. Vehicle B travels a miles per hour faster than Vehicle A, and travels b hours longer than Vehicle A. Vehicle B travels how much farther than Vehicle A, in miles?

(A) $x^2 - ab$
(B) $a^2 + b^2$
(C) $ax + bx + ab$
(D) $x^2 + abx + ab$
(E) $2x^2 + (a + b)x + ab$

4. For any real number n, $|5-n|-|n-5| =$

(A) -2
(B) -1
(C) 0
(D) 1
(E) 2

8. If Company A builds a skateboards per week, and Company B builds b skateboards per day, then in m weeks, Company A builds how many more skateboards than Company B ?

(A) $7bm$

(B) $m(a - 7b)$

(C) $7(ma - mb)$

(D) $7m(a - b)$

(E) $\dfrac{m(a-b)}{7}$

12. If $a > 3$ and $b < 3$, then which of the following could be true?

   I. $a - b > 3$

  II. $a + b < 3$

 III. $|a+b| < 3$

(A) I only
(B) III only
(C) I and II only
(D) II and III only
(E) I, II, and III

18. For all real numbers, $x^3 < y^3$. Which of the following must be true?

  I. $x < y$

  II. $x^2 < y^2$

  III. $|x| < |y|$

  (A) I only
  (B) III only
  (C) I and II only
  (D) II and III only
  (E) I, II, and III

35. An empty bus picks up a passengers at its first stop. 3 more passengers get on at the second stop. The bus then picks up an average of b passengers over the next c stops without any passengers leaving the bus. One-third of the passengers depart the bus at the third-to-last stop. If no more passengers get on the bus and all of the passengers get off the bus by the last stop, then what is the average number of passengers leaving the bus on the last two stops?

  (A) $a + bc + 3$

  (B) $\dfrac{a + bc + 3}{3}$

  (C) $\dfrac{a + bc + 6}{3}$

  (D) $\dfrac{2(a + bc + 3)}{3}$

  (E) $a + bc + 1$

48. If $x^2 = -|y|$ and $y \neq 0$, which of the following must be true?
  (A) x is real.
  (B) x is irrational.
  (C) x is an integer.
  (D) x is imaginary.
  (E) $x = i$

PLUGGING IN THE ANSWERS (PITA)

Plugging In the Answers (PITA) is another approach to solving algebra questions. As you've just seen, Plugging In is useful on questions whose answer choices contain variables, percentages, fractions, or ratios—not actual numbers. PITA, on the other hand, is useful on questions with answer choices that contain actual numbers.

Answer choices are arranged in numerical order—usually from least to greatest. You can use this to your advantage by combining PITA and POE.

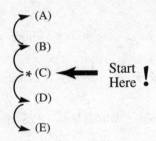

To use PITA on an algebra question, take (C), the middle answer choice, and stick it back into the problem. If it makes all of the statements in the question true, then it's the right answer. If it doesn't, eliminate (C) and try another answer choice. Usually, you'll know from your experience with (C) whether you want to try a smaller or larger answer choice. If (C) is too small, you can eliminate the smaller two choices and try again with the remaining two.

Like Plugging In, PITA can open doors for you when you're unsure how to approach a question with algebra. Also, like Plugging In, it can eliminate errors that often occur when writing an equation, such as sign changes. Particularly at the tough end of the SAT Subject Test Math 2, where you're getting into hard material, Plugging In and PITA can enable you to solve problems that would otherwise stump you.

Let's take a look at a PITA example.

EXCEPTION:
If a question asks for the greatest or least possible value, start with the greatest or least answer, respectively, rather than with (C).

2. A duck travels from point A to point B. If the duck flies $\frac{3}{4}$ of the way, walks $\frac{1}{9}$ of the way, and swims the remaining 10 kilometers of her trip, what is the total distance in kilometers traveled by the duck?

(A) 36
(B) 45
(C) 56
(D) 72
(E) 108

Here's How to Crack It
To use PITA on this question, you'd start with (C). The answer choices represent the quantity asked for in the question—in this case, the total distance traveled by the duck. Always be aware of what the answer choices represent and of what question you're answering. Choice (C), therefore, means that the duck traveled a total distance of 56 kilometers. Follow this information through the problem.

The duck flies $\frac{3}{4}$ of the way. $\frac{3}{4}$ of 56 is 42 kilometers.

The duck walks $\frac{1}{9}$ of the way. $\frac{1}{9}$ of 56 is 6.22 kilometers.

That makes 48.22 kilometers, which leaves 7.78 kilometers in the trip.

BUT the duck swims 10 kilometers!

That means that (C) isn't the right answer. It also tells you that you need a longer trip to fit in all that flying, walking, and swimming; move down to (D), the next largest answer, and try again. At this point, you can also eliminate (A), (B), and (C) because they are too small.

The duck flies $\frac{3}{4}$ of the way. $\frac{3}{4}$ of 72 is 54 kilometers.

The duck walks $\frac{1}{9}$ of the way. $\frac{1}{9}$ of 72 is 8 kilometers.

That makes 62 kilometers, which leaves 10 kilometers in the trip.

And THAT'S exactly how far the duck swims, 10 kilometers. Right answer.

You Should Try PITA Whenever
- the question asks for an actual value, and the answer choices are all numbers arranged in increasing or decreasing order
- you have the bizarre urge to translate a word problem into a complicated algebraic equation
- you find yourself reading a long, convoluted story about some number, and you don't even know what the number is
- you have no idea how to solve the problem

Generally, you won't have to try more than three answer choices when using PITA thanks to POE—and sometimes, the first answer you try, (C), will be correct. Keep your eyes open for PITA opportunities on the SAT Subject Test Math 2, particularly when you run into an algebra question that you're not sure how to solve.

If, after you plug in (C), you're not sure which way to go in the answer choices, don't haggle for too long. Just eliminate (C), pick a direction, and go! If you go the wrong way, you'll know pretty quickly, and then you can head the other way.

DRILL 4: PLUGGING IN THE ANSWERS (PITA)

Solve the following questions by using PITA. Remember to start with (C), the middle answer choice. The answers can be found in Part IV.

1. Matt has 4 more hats than Aaron and half as many hats as Michael. If the three together have 24 hats, how many hats does Michael have?

   (A)   7
   (B)   9
   (C) 12
   (D) 14
   (E) 18

2. A shipment of 3,200 items is divided into 2 portions so that the difference between the portions is one-half of their average. What is the ratio of the smaller to the larger portion?

   (A) 1:2
   (B) 1:3
   (C) 2:5
   (D) 3:5
   (E) 5:8

12. Three distinct positive integers have a sum of 15 and a product of 45. What is the largest of these integers?

   (A)   1
   (B)   3
   (C)   5
   (D)   9
   (E) 15

40. If the volume of a cylinder with height x and diameter x is equal to the surface area of a sphere with radius x, then what is the value of x ?

   (A)   1
   (B) $\sqrt{2}$
   (C)   2
   (D)   4
   (E) 16

INEQUALITIES

Inequalities can be treated just like equations in almost every way. You can add, subtract, multiply, and divide on both sides of the inequality sign. And you still solve by isolating the variable. There is only one major difference between solving an equation and solving an inequality.

Reading Inequality Signs

Here's how you should read the four basic inequality signs:

$a < b$	a is less than b
$a > b$	a is greater than b
$a \leq b$	a is less than or equal to b
$a \geq b$	a is greater than or equal to b

> Whenever you multiply or divide both sides of an inequality by a negative, flip the inequality sign.

Multiplying or dividing across an inequality by a negative flips the signs of all of the terms in the inequality. The inequality sign itself must also flip.

$$-1(4n - 20 > -3n + 15) \qquad\qquad -1(x \geq 5)$$

$$-4n + 20 < 3n - 15 \qquad\qquad -x \leq -5$$

This rule becomes a little more complicated when you are multiplying or dividing by a variable. For example, when you attempt to solve $\dfrac{x}{y} > 3$, if you multiply both sides by y, you don't know whether the result is $x > 3y$ or $x < 3y$ because you do not know whether y is positive or negative. Be careful in these cases, as this rule often shows up in questions which ask what "must be true."

Similarly, when you solve an inequality with an even exponent or absolute value, remember to include both positive and negative outcomes. In an inequality, you need to flip the sign when expressing the negative outcomes.

$$a^2 \geq 25 \text{ becomes } a \geq 5 \text{ or } a \leq -5$$

$$y^4 < 81 \text{ becomes } -3 < y < 3$$

$$|x + 2| > 5 \text{ becomes } x > 3 \text{ or } x < -7$$

Often Plugging In or Plugging In the Answers is the best way to deal with questions involving variables and inequalities.

---

3. If $x^3 + 3x^2 + 3x + 3 \geq 2$, then which of the following is true?

   (A) $x \neq 0$
   (B) $x \geq -1$
   (C) $x \leq -1$
   (D) $x \geq 2$
   (E) $x \leq 2$

Here's How to Crack It

You can plug in to the inequality and then eliminate answer choices. Pick a number that is true for some answer choices but false for others. Next, plug in that number into the original inequality. If the number makes the inequality true, eliminate answer choices that exclude that number. If the number makes the inequality false, eliminate answer choices that include that number.

Here, start with $x = 3$, which is included in (A), (B), and (D), and excluded in (C) and (E). When you plug in $x = 3$ in the original inequality, you get $3^3 + 3(3)^2 + 3(3) + 3 \geq 2$, or $66 \geq 2$. This is true, so $x = 3$ must be included in your answer. Eliminate (C) and (E). Next, make $x = 0$, which is included in (B) and excluded from (A) and (D). When you plug in $x = 0$ into the original inequality, you get $0^3 + 3(0)^2 + 3(0) + 3 \geq 2$, or $3 \geq 2$. This is true, so $x = 0$ must be included in your answer. Eliminate (A) and (D) and choose (B).

DRILL 5: INEQUALITIES

Practice solving inequalities in the following exercises. The answers can be found in Part IV.

1. If $\dfrac{6(5-n)}{4} \leq 3$, then _____

2. If $\dfrac{r+3}{2} < 5$, then _____

3. If $\dfrac{4(1-x)+9}{3} \leq 5$, then _____

4. If $8(3x + 1) + 4 < 15$, then _____

5. If $23 - 4t \geq 11$, then _____

6. If $4n - 25 \leq 19 - 7n$, then _____

7. If $-5(p+2) < 10p - 13$, then _____

8. If $\dfrac{23s+7}{10} \geq 2s + 1$, then _____

9. If $-3x - 16 \leq 2x + 19$, then _____

10. If $\dfrac{14s-11}{9} \geq s - 1$, then _____

11. If $\left| \dfrac{x+2}{3} \right| \leq 2$, then _____

12. If $\dfrac{z^4+2}{3} > 6$, then _____

WORKING WITH RANGES

Inequalities are also used when discussing the range of possible values a variable could equal. Sometimes you'll see an algebraic phrase in which there are two inequality signs. These are called ranges. Your variable can be any number within a range of numbers. For example: $2 < x < 10$. This means that x can be any number between, but not equal to, 2 and 10. Let's look at this next example:

> At a certain amusement park, anyone under the age of 12 is not allowed to ride the Stupendous Megacoaster. Anyone over the age of 60 is also prohibited due to health concerns. If x is the age of a rider of the Stupendous Megacoaster, what is the range of the possible values of x?

The end values of the range are obviously 12 and 60. But are 12 and 60 included in the ranges themselves, or not? If you read carefully, you'll see that only those under 12 or over 60 are barred from riding the Megacoaster. If you're 12 or 60, you're perfectly legal. The range of possible values of x is therefore given by $12 \le x \le 60$. Noticing the difference between "greater than" and "greater than or equal to" is crucial to many range questions.

You can manipulate ranges in a couple of ways. You can add and subtract ranges, as long as their inequality signs point the same way. You can also multiply or divide across a range to produce new information, as long as you obey that basic rule of inequalities—flip the sign if you multiply or divide by a negative number.

DRILL 6: WORKING WITH RANGES

The answers can be found in Part IV.

> If the range of possible values for x is given by $-5 < x < 8$, find the range of possible values for each of the following:
>
> 1. $-x$: _____
> 2. $4x$: _____
> 3. $x + 6$: _____
> 4. $(2 - x)$: _____
> 5. $\dfrac{x}{2}$: _____

Adding Ranges

Occasionally, a question on the SAT Subject Test Math 2 will require you to add, subtract, or multiply ranges. Take a look at this example:

> If $3 < a < 10$ and $-6 < b < 3$, what is the range of possible values of $a + b$?

Here, the range of $(a + b)$ will be the sum of the range of a and the range of b. One way to do this is to list out the four ways you can combine the endpoints of the two ranges. To do this, take the smallest a and add it to the smallest b. Then, add the smallest a to the biggest b. Then add the biggest a to the smallest b. Finally, take the biggest a and add it to the biggest b. The biggest and smallest results you get will be the endpoints of the range of $(a + b)$. Watch!

$$3 + -6 = -3$$
$$3 + 3 = 6$$
$$10 + -6 = 4$$
$$10 + 3 = 13$$

The smallest number you found is -3, and the biggest is 13, so the range of possible values looks like the following:

$$-3 < a + b < 13$$

Subtracting Ranges

To subtract one range from another, combine the endpoints just as you did when adding ranges, but in this case, subtract the four combinations of endpoints.

Make sure you're subtracting in the order the question asks you to. Let's look at this example.

If $-4 < a < 5$ and $2 < b < 12$, then what is the range of possible values of $a - b$?

This time, take the smallest a and subtract the smallest b. Then, find the smallest a minus the biggest b, and so on.

$$-4 - 2 = -6$$
$$-4 - 12 = -16$$
$$5 - 2 = 3$$
$$5 - 12 = -7$$

So the range you're looking for is

$$-16 < a - b < 3$$

Multiplying Ranges

To multiply ranges, follow the same steps, but multiply the endpoints. Let's try one.

If $-3 < f < 4$ and $-7 < g < 2$, then what is the range of possible values of fg ?

These are the four possible products of the bounds of *f* and *g*.

$$(-3)(-7) = 21 \qquad\qquad (-3)(2) = -6$$

$$(4)(-7) = -28 \qquad\qquad (4)(2) = 8$$

The greatest of these values is 21 and the least is –28. So the range of possible values of *fg* is

$$-28 < fg < 21$$

Ranges Using Absolute Value and Inequalities

The College Board can sometimes use inequalities and absolute value to express a range. Consider the following:

> Aaron must weigh between 70 and 80 kilograms to be eligible to wrestle in this week's tournament. If Aaron is eligible to wrestle and weighs *a* kilograms, which of the following expresses the range of the possible values of *a* ?

You could express this as discussed earlier: $70 < a < 80$. However, you can also use absolute value to show the same information. Remember the definition of absolute value is "distance from zero." You can apply this to Aaron's situation by first finding the midpoint: $\frac{70+80}{2} = 75$. Then, find the distance from the midpoint to either end: $80 - 75 = 5$. In other words, the range of Aaron's possible weights is a distance of less than 5 from 75. The absolute value of the difference between two values is the definition of the distance between them, so the absolute value of the difference between Aaron's actual weight and 75 must be less than 5, or in math $|a - 75| < 5$. Understanding this way of thinking about ranges can be helpful in many questions.

Another approach to these questions is to plug in. If you plug in on these questions, it's a good idea to try numbers that both do and do not satisfy the given conditions. When the number you plug in does satisfy the conditions, eliminate any choices that are false when that number is plugged in. When the number you plug in does not satisfy the conditions, eliminate any choices that are true when that number in plugged in. While this may seem counterintuitive, it can sometimes help make POE more efficient.

DRILL 7: MORE WORKING WITH RANGES

Try the following range questions. The answers can be found in Part IV.

1. If $-2 \le a \le 7$ and $3 \le b \le 9$, then what is the range of possible values of $b - a$?

2. If $2 \le x \le 11$ and $6 \ge y \ge -4$, then what is the range of possible values of $x + y$?

3. If $-3 \le n \le 8$, then what is the range of possible values of n^2?

4. If $0 < x < 5$ and $-9 < y < -3$, then what is the range of possible values of $x - y$?

5. If $-3 \le r \le 10$ and $-10 \le s \le 3$, then what is the range of possible values of $r + s$?

6. If $-6 < c < 0$ and $13 < d < 21$, then what is the range of possible values of cd?

7. If $|3 - x| \le 4$, then what is the range of possible values of x?

8. If $|2a + 7| \ge 13$, then what is the range of possible values of a?

DIRECT AND INVERSE VARIATION

Direct and indirect variation are specific relationships between quantities that tell you how the quantities change with respect to each other. Quantities that vary directly are said to be in *proportion* or *proportional*. Quantities that vary indirectly are said to be *inversely proportional*.

Direct Variation

If x and y vary directly, this can be said in several ways: x and y are in proportion; x and y change proportionally; or x varies directly as y. All of these descriptions come down to the same thing: x and y increase and decrease together. Specifically, they mean that the quantity $\frac{x}{y}$ will always have the same numerical value. That's all there is to it. Take a look at a question based on this idea.

A Great Way to Remember

To remember direct variation, think "direct means divide." So in order to solve, you set up a proportion with a fraction on each side of the equation. Just solve for the one number you don't know. There are two formulas associated with direct variation that may be familiar to you. They are $\frac{y_1}{x_1} = \frac{y_2}{x_2}$ or $y = kx$, where k is a constant.

3. If n varies directly as m, and n is 3 when m is 24, then what is the value of n when m is 11 ?

(A) 1.375
(B) 1.775
(C) 1.95
(D) 2.0
(E) 2.125

Here's How to Crack It

To solve the problem, use the definition of direct variation: $\dfrac{n}{m}$ must always have the same numerical value. Set up a proportion.

$$\frac{3}{24} = \frac{n}{11}$$

Solve by cross-multiplying and isolating n.

$$24n = 33$$
$$n = 33 \div 24$$
$$n = 1.375$$

And that's all there is to it. The correct answer is (A).

Opposites Attract

A great way to remember indirect or inverse variation is that direct and inverse variation are opposites. What's the opposite of division? Multiplication! So set up an inverse variation as two multiplication problems on either side of an equation. There are two formulas associated with indirect variation that may be familiar to you. They are $x_1 y_1 = x_2 y_2$ or $y = \dfrac{k}{x}$, where k is a constant.

Inverse Variation

If x and y vary inversely, this can be said in several ways as well: x and y are in inverse proportion; x and y are inversely proportional; or x varies indirectly as y. All of these descriptions come down to the same thing: x increases when y decreases, and x decreases when y increases. Specifically, they mean that the quantity xy will always have the same numerical value.

Take a look at this question based on inverse variation.

1. If a varies inversely as b, and $a = 3$ when $b = 5$, then what is the value of a when $b = 7$?

(A)   2.14
(B)   2.76
(C)   3.28
(D)   4.2
(E)   11.67

Here's How to Crack It

To answer the question, use the definition of inverse variation. That is, the quantity ab must always have the same value. Therefore, you can set up this simple equation.

$$3 \times 5 = a \times 7$$
$$7a = 15$$
$$a = 15 \div 7$$
$$a = 2.142857$$

So the correct answer is (A).

DRILL 8: DIRECT AND INVERSE VARIATION

Try these practice exercises using the definitions of direct and inverse variation. The answers can be found in Part IV.

2 If a varies inversely as b, and $a = 3$ when $b = 5$, then what is the value of a when $b = x$?

(A) $\dfrac{3}{x}$

(B) $\dfrac{5}{x}$

(C) $\dfrac{15}{x}$

(D) $3x$

(E) $3x^2$

3. If n varies directly as m, and $n = 5$ when $m = 4$, then what is the value of n when $m = 5$?

(A) 4.0
(B) 4.75
(C) 5.5
(D) 6.25
(E) 7.75

9. If p varies directly as q, and $p = 3$ when $q = 10$, then what is the value of p when $q = 1$?

(A) 0.3
(B) 0.43
(C) 0.5
(D) 4.3
(E) 4.33

11. If y varies directly as x^2, and $y = 24$ when $x = 3.7$, what is the value of y when $x = 8.3$?

    (A) 170.67
    (B) 120.77
    (C) 83.23
    (D) 64.00
    (E) 53.83

26. If the square of x varies inversely with the cube root of the square of y, and $y = 8$ when $x = \dfrac{1}{2}$, then what is the value of x when $y = \dfrac{1}{2}$?

    (A) 0.630
    (B) 1
    (C) 1.587
    (D) 1.260
    (E) 8

39. If the cube root of the sum of x and 2 varies inversely with the square of y, and $x = 6$ when $y = 3$, then what is the value of x when $y = 6$?

    (A) −1.875
    (B) 0.125
    (C) 0.5
    (D) 3
    (E) 18

WORK AND TRAVEL QUESTIONS

Word problems dealing with work and travel tend to cause a lot of mistakes, because the relationships among distance, time, and speed—or among work-rate, work, and time—sometimes confuse test-takers. When working with questions about travel, just remember this:

> distance = rate × time

When working with questions about work being done, remember this:

> work done = rate of work × time

Look Familiar?
If these two formulas seem the same, it's because they are. In the distance equation, the distance being covered is the work being done. Don't worry about learning too many equations; generally speaking, the few you'll need are more useful than their wording indicates.

DRILL 9: WORK AND TRAVEL QUESTIONS

Answer the following practice questions using these formulas. The answers can be found in Part IV.

1. A factory contains a series of water tanks, all of the same size. If Pump 1 can fill 12 of these tanks in a 12-hour shift, and Pump 2 can fill 11 tanks in the same time, then how many tanks can the two pumps fill, working together, in 1 hour?

   (A) 0.13
   (B) 0.35
   (C) 1.92
   (D) 2.88
   (E) 3.33

2. A projectile travels 227 feet in one second. If there are 5,280 feet in 1 mile, then which of the following best approximates the projectile's speed in miles per hour?

   (A) 155
   (B) 170
   (C) 194
   (D) 252
   (E) 333

5. A train travels from Langston to Hughesville and back in 5.5 hours. If the two towns are 200 miles apart, what is the average speed of the train in miles per hour?

   (A) 36.36
   (B) 72.73
   (C) 109.09
   (D) 110.10
   (E) 120.21

10. Jules can make m muffins in s minutes. Alice can make n muffins in t minutes. Which of the following gives the number of muffins that Jules and Alice can make together in 30 minutes?

   (A) $\dfrac{m+n}{30st}$

   (B) $\dfrac{30(m+n)}{st}$

   (C) $30(mt + ns)$

   (D) $\dfrac{30(mt+ns)}{st}$

   (E) $\dfrac{mt+ns}{30st}$

28. Samantha is running a race that is x meters. She runs the first 40% of the race at y meters per second and the remainder of the race at z meters per second. How long, in seconds, does it take for Samantha to finish the race?

(A) $\dfrac{x(0.4z+0.6y)}{yz}$

(B) $\dfrac{x(0.4y+0.6z)}{yz}$

(C) $x(0.4y+0.6z)$

(D) $0.24xyz$

(E) $\dfrac{0.4y+0.6z}{x}$

Average Speed

The "average speed" question is a special type of travel question. Here's what a basic "average speed" question might look like.

Won't Get Fooled Again

If an answer choice looks too good to be true, be skeptical. Finding the average of two averages is more than just averaging the two together, but knowing this allows you to eliminate (C), as it is a trap answer.

5. Roberto travels from his home to the beach, driving at 30 miles per hour. He returns along the same route at 50 miles per hour. If the distance from Roberto's house to the beach is 10 miles, then what is Roberto's average speed for the round-trip in miles per hour?

(A) 32.5
(B) 37.5
(C) 40.0
(D) 42.5
(E) 45.0

The easy mistake to make on this question is to simply choose (C), the average of the two speeds. Average speed isn't found by averaging speeds, however. Instead, you have to use this formula:

$$\text{average speed} = \frac{\text{total distance}}{\text{total time}}$$

The total distance is easy to figure out—10 miles each way is a total of 20 miles. Total time is a little trickier. For that, you have to use the "distance = rate × time" formula. Here, it's useful to rearrange the equation to read as follows:

$$\text{time} = \frac{\text{distance}}{\text{rate}}$$

On the way to the beach, Roberto traveled 10 miles at 30 mph, which took 0.333 hours, according to the formula. On the way home, he traveled 10 miles at 50 mph, which took 0.2 hours. That makes 20 miles in a total of .533 hours. Plug those numbers into the average-speed formula, and you get an average speed of 37.5 mph. The answer is (B).

Here's a general tip for "average speed" questions: On any round-trip in which the traveler moves at one speed heading out and another speed returning, the traveler's average speed will be a little lower than the average of the two speeds.

Look Familiar?
This formula may look familiar to you. That's because it's taken from our Average Pie. Another way to work with average speed questions is to use the Average Pie, in which the total becomes the total distance and the numbers of things becomes the time. So it would look like this:

DRILL 10: AVERAGE SPEED
Try these "average speed" questions. The answers can be found in Part IV.

7. Alexandra jogs from her house to the lake at 12 miles per hour and jogs back by the same route at 9 miles per hour. If the path from her house to the lake is 6 miles long, what is her average speed in miles per hour for the round-trip?

   (A) 11.3
   (B) 11.0
   (C) 10.5
   (D) 10.3
   (E) 10.1

11. A truck travels 50 miles from Town S to Town T in 50 minutes, and then immediately drives 40 miles from Town T to Town U in 40 minutes. What is the truck's average speed in miles per hour, from Town S to Town U ?

   (A) 1
   (B) 10
   (C) 45
   (D) 60
   (E) 90

25. Ben travels a certain distance at 25 miles per hour and returns across the same distance at 50 miles per hour. What is his average speed in miles per hour for the round-trip?

    (A) 37.5
    (B) 33.3
    (C) 32.0
    (D) 29.5
    (E) It cannot be determined from the information given.

49. Amy and Bob stand 250 m apart. Simultaneously, Amy begins walking 5 m/s directly toward Bob, Bob begins walking 2 m/s toward Amy, and their dog Charlie begins running 13 m/s from Amy toward Bob. When Charlie arrives at Bob, Charlie immediately turns around and heads back toward Amy at the same speed. Charlie continues running back and forth until Amy and Bob meet. How far does Charlie run by the time Amy and Bob meet?

    (A)   35.71 m
    (B)   269.23 m
    (C)   464.29 m
    (D)   650.00 m
    (E) 2875.00 m

That Nasty Phrase "In Terms Of"

Remember how we had you cross off the phrase "in terms of" when you plugged in because it doesn't help you at all? Well, solving x "in terms of" y for simultaneous equations doesn't help either. It takes too much time and there is too much room for error to solve in terms of one variable and then put that whole thing into the other equation. And much of the time, that's unnecessary because we don't care what the values of the individual variables are!

SIMULTANEOUS EQUATIONS

It's possible to have a set of equations that can't be solved individually but can be solved in combination. A good example of such a set of equations would be

$$4x + 2y = 18$$
$$x + y = 5$$

You can't solve either equation by itself. But you can if you put them together. This is called simultaneous equations. A simple method to solve many of these questions is to stack the equations one above the other and then add or subtract, depending on what you're looking for, which will often be an algebraic expression. For example, the question that contains the two equations you were given wants to know what the value of $10x + 6y$ is. Do you need to know x or y? No! You just need to know $10x + 6y$. Let's try adding the two equations.

$$4x + 2y = 18$$
$$+x + y = 5$$
$$\overline{5x + 3y = 23}$$

Did adding help? It may not look like it, but it actually did. Notice that the left hand side of the equation is half of $10x + 6y$. By multiplying both sides of the resulting equation by 2, you arrive at $10x + 6y = 46$, making 46 the correct answer. What you'll often find on these sorts of questions is that adding or subtracting the equations will give you either the answer itself or something that is a useful step along the way.

Here's another example of a system of simultaneous equations as they might appear on an SAT Subject Test Math 2 question. Try it.

4. If x and y are real numbers such that $3x + 4y = 10$ and $2x - 4y = 5$, then what is the value of x ?

$$\begin{array}{r} 3x + 4y = 10 \\ + \quad 2x - 4y = 5 \\ \hline 5x = 15 \\ x = 3 \end{array}$$

> **Add It Up**
> Do you notice how adding brings you close to what the question is asking for?

In the question above, instead of solving to find a third equation, you need to find one of the variables. Your job doesn't change: Stack 'em; then add or subtract. This will be the case with most simultaneous equations questions. Every once in a while you may want to multiply or divide one equation by a number before you add or subtract.

Try another one. Solve it yourself before checking the explanation.

2. If $12a - 3b = 131$ and $5a - 10b = 61$, then what is the value of $a + b$?

This time adding didn't work, did it? Let's go through and see what subtraction does.

$$\begin{array}{r} 12a - 3b = 131 \\ -1(5a - 10b) = -1(61) \\ \hline 12a - 3b = 131 \\ -5a + 10b = -61 \\ \hline 7a + 7b = 70 \\ a + b = 10 \end{array}$$

> **Avoid Subtraction Mistakes**
> If adding doesn't work and you want to try subtracting, first multiply one of the equations by −1, then add. That way you ensure that you don't make any calculation errors along the way.

Practice can help you develop a better sense of whether adding or subtracting will be more helpful. Sometimes it may be necessary to multiply one of the equations by a convenient factor to make terms that will cancel out properly. For example,

1. If $4n - 8m = 6$, and $-5n + 4m = 3$, then $n =$

$$4n - 8m = 6$$
$$-5n + 4m = 3$$

Here, neither adding nor subtracting will combine these two equations very usefully. However, things look a little brighter when the second equation is multiplied by 2.

$$4n - 8m = 6$$
$$-10n + 8m = 6$$

$$2(-5n + 4m = 3)$$
$$-6n = 12$$
$$n = -2$$

Occasionally, a simultaneous equation can be solved only by *multiplying* all of the pieces together. This will generally be the case only when the equations themselves involve multiplication alone, not the kind of addition and subtraction that the previous equations contained. Take a look at this example.

# of Equations = # of Variables

We've been talking about two equations, two variables, but it doesn't stop there. A good rule of thumb is, if the number of equations is equal to the number of variables, you can solve the equations. So count 'em and don't get discouraged!

$$ab = 3 \qquad bc = \frac{5}{9} \qquad ac = 15$$

34. If the above statements are true, what is one possible value of abc ?

    (A) 5.0
    (B) 8.33
    (C) 9.28
    (D) 18.54
    (E) 25.0

Here's How to Crack It

This is a tough one. No single one of the three small equations can be solved by itself. In fact, no two of them together can be solved. It takes all three to solve the system, and here's how it's done.

Where's the Trap?

Remember that a number 34 is a difficult question. What do you notice about (E)?

$$ab \times bc \times ac = 3 \times \frac{5}{9} \times 15$$

$$aabbcc = 25$$

$$a^2 b^2 c^2 = 25$$

Once you've multiplied all three equations together, all you have to do is take the square roots of both sides, and you've got values for abc.

$$a^2 b^2 c^2 = 25$$

$$abc = 5, -5$$

And so (A) is the correct answer.

DRILL 11: SIMULTANEOUS EQUATIONS

Try answering the following practice questions by solving equations simultaneously. The answers can be found in Part IV.

17. If $a + 3b = 6$, and $4a - 3b = 14$, $a =$

    (A) −4
    (B) 2
    (C) 4
    (D) 10
    (E) 20

27. If $xyz = 4$ and $y^2z = 5$, what is the value of $\dfrac{x}{y}$?

    (A) 20.0
    (B) 10.0
    (C) 1.25
    (D) 1.0
    (E) 0.8

28. If $2x - 7y = 12$ and $-8x + 3y = 2$, which of the following is the value of $x - y$?

    (A) 12.0
    (B) 8.0
    (C) 5.5
    (D) 1.0
    (E) 0.8

$$ab = \frac{1}{8},\ bc = 6,\ ac = 3$$

33. If all of the above statements are true, what is one possible value of abc ?

    (A) 3.75
    (B) 2.25
    (C) 2.0
    (D) 1.5
    (E) 0.25

35. If $\sqrt{abc} = 7$ and $\sqrt[3]{ab^2c} = 8$, then what is the value of b^{-4} ?

    (A) 8.389×10^{-5}
    (B) 9.159×10^{-3}
    (C) 0.0957
    (D) 10.449
    (E) 11,920.529

FOIL METHOD

A binomial is an algebraic expression that has two terms (pieces connected by addition or subtraction). FOIL is a method for multiplying two binomials together.

The letters of FOIL stand for

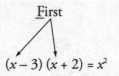

$$(x - 3)(x + 2) = x^2$$

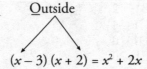

$$(x - 3)(x + 2) = x^2 + 2x$$

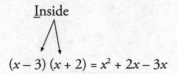

$$(x - 3)(x + 2) = x^2 + 2x - 3x$$

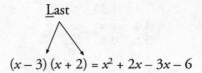

$$(x - 3)(x + 2) = x^2 + 2x - 3x - 6$$

Suppose you wanted to do the following multiplication:

$$(x + 5)(x - 2)$$

You would multiply the two *first* terms together, $(x)(x) = x^2$.
And then the *outside* terms, $(x)(-2) = -2x$.
And then the *inside* terms, $(5)(x) = 5x$.
And finally the two *last* terms, $(5)(-2) = -10$.

String the four products together and simplify them to produce an answer.

$$x^2 - 2x + 5x - 10$$

$$x^2 + 3x - 10$$

And that's the product of $(x + 5)$ and $(x - 2)$.

General Polynomial Multiplication

You may need to find the product of polynomials in which one or both polynomials have more than two terms. One way of dealing with such problems is to distribute one polynomial into the other and combine like terms. For example,

$$(x^3 + 2x - 3)(x^2 - 5x + 7)$$

Multiply the second polynomial by each term in the first polynomial.

$$x^3(x^2 - 5x + 7) + 2x(x^2 - 5x + 7) - 3(x^2 - 5x + 7) =$$
$$(x^5 - 5x^4 + 7x^3) + (2x^3 - 10x^2 + 14x) + (-3x^2 + 15x - 21)$$

Don't forget to distribute the negative when you multiply by –3. On the SAT Subject Test Math 2, be careful with negatives when you are multiplying polynomials! Next, list the terms in order from largest exponent to smallest.

$$x^5 - 5x^4 + 7x^3 + 2x^3 - 10x^2 - 3x^2 + 14x + 15x - 21$$

You should have a number of terms equal to the product of the number of terms in your polynomials (in this case, 3 · 3 = 9 terms). Last, combine like terms.

$$x^5 - 5x^4 + 9x^3 - 13x^2 + 29x - 21$$

DRILL 12: FOIL

Practice using FOIL and general polynomial multiplication on the following problems. The answers can be found in Part IV.

1. $(x - 2)(x + 11) =$
2. $(b + 5)(b + 7) =$
3. $(x - 3)(x - 9) =$
4. $(2x - 5)(x + 1) =$
5. $(n^2 + 5)(n - 3) =$
6. $(3a + 5)(2a - 7) =$
7. $(x - 3)(x - 6) =$
8. $(c - 2)(c + 9) =$
9. $(d + 5)(d - 1) =$
10. $(z^2 + 2)(z^2 - 5z + 22) =$
11. $(3x^2 - 2x + 5)(6x^2 + 4x - 2) =$

FACTORING QUADRATICS

An expression, such as $x^2 + 3x + 10$, is a quadratic polynomial. A quadratic is an expression that fits into the general form $ax^2 + bx + c$, with a, b, and c as constants. Remember that sometimes you won't see a bx or c term when b or c is equal to 0. An equation in general quadratic form looks like this:

General Form of a Quadratic Equation

$$ax^2 + bx + c = 0$$

Often, the best way to solve a quadratic equation is to factor it into two binomials—basically FOIL in reverse. Let's take a look at the quadratic you worked with in the previous section, and the binomials that are its factors.

$$x^2 + 3x - 10 = (x + 5)(x - 2)$$

Notice that the coefficient of the quadratic's middle term (3) is the sum of the constants in the binomials (5 and –2), and that the third term of the quadratic (–10) is the product of those constants. That relationship between a quadratic expression and its factors will always be true. To factor a quadratic, look for a pair of constants whose sum equals the coefficient of the middle term, and whose product equals the last term of the quadratic. Suppose you had to solve this equation:

$$x^2 - 6x + 8 = 0$$

Your first step would be to factor the quadratic polynomial. That means looking for a pair of numbers that add up to –6 and multiply to 8. Because their sum is negative but their product is positive, you know that the numbers are both negative. And there's only one pair of numbers that fits the bill, –2 and –4.

$$x^2 - 6x + 8 = 0$$

$$(x - 2)(x - 4) = 0$$

Since zero multiplied by anything is equal to zero, this equation will be true whether $(x - 2) = 0$ or $(x - 4) = 0$. Therefore,

$$x = \{2, 4\}$$

Two and four are therefore called the zeros of the equation. They are also known as the roots or solutions of the equation.

Once a quadratic is factored, it's easier to solve for x. The product of the binomials can be zero only if one of the binomials is equal to zero—and there are only two values of x that will make one of the binomials equal to zero (2 and 4). The equation is solved.

DRILL 13: FACTORING QUADRATICS

Solve the following equations by factoring the quadratic polynomials. Write down all of the roots of each equation (values of the variable that make the equations true). The answers can be found in Part IV.

1. $a^2 - 3a + 2 = 0$
2. $d^2 + 8d + 7 = 0$
3. $x^2 + 4x - 21 = 0$
4. $3x^2 + 9x - 30 = 0$
5. $2x^2 + 40x + 198 = 0$

6. $p^2 + 10p = 39$
7. $c^2 + 9c + 20 = 0$
8. $s^2 + 4s - 12 = 0$
9. $x^2 - 3x - 4 = 0$
10. $n^4 - 3n^2 - 10 = 0$

Special Quadratic Identities

There are a few quadratic expressions that are very useful to memorize for the SAT Subject Test Math 2, since they show up frequently and can help make factoring more straightforward.

$$(x + y)^2 = x^2 + 2xy + y^2$$

$$(x - y)^2 = x^2 - 2xy + y^2$$

$$(x + y)(x - y) = x^2 - y^2$$

Here are some examples of these quadratic identities in action.

1. $n^2 + 10n + 25 = (n + 5)(n + 5) = (n + 5)^2$
2. $r^2 - 16 = (r + 4)(r - 4)$
3. $n^2 - 4n + 4 = (n - 2)(n - 2) = (n - 2)^2$

But knowing these quadratic identities will do more for you than just allow you to factor some expressions quickly. The test includes questions based specifically on these identities. Since the identities are built into the framework of the problem, they are an excellent tool to have on hand, and will make the problem more straightforward to solve. Here's an example.

———————◯———————

26. If $a + b = 7$, and $a^2 + b^2 = 37$, then what is the value of ab ?

(A)   6
(B)   12
(C)   15
(D)   22
(E)   30

Here's How to Crack It

Algebraically, this is a tough problem to crack. You can't divide $a^2 + b^2$ by $a + b$ and get anything useful. In fact, most of the usual algebraic approaches to questions like these don't work here. Even plugging the answer choices back into the question (PITA) isn't very helpful. What you can do is recognize that the question is giving you all of the pieces you need to build the quadratic identity: $(x + y)^2 = x^2 + 2xy + y^2$. To solve the problem, rearrange the identity a little and plug in the values given by the question.

$$(a + b)^2 = a^2 + b^2 + 2ab$$
$$(7)^2 = 37 + 2ab$$
$$49 = 37 + 2ab$$
$$12 = 2ab$$
$$6 = ab$$

And presto, the answer appears. It's not easy to figure out what a or b is specifically—and you don't need to. Just find the value asked for in the question. Remember that this method relied on recognizing the components of the identity in the question, so it's very important to commit them to memory.

Rationalizing Denominators Using $x^2 - y^2$

One particularly useful way to use the special quadratic identity $x^2 - y^2$, which is called the difference of squares, is when you need to rationalize away a radical in a denominator with addition or subtraction. For example,

$$\frac{2n}{1 + \sqrt{n}}$$

You cannot simply multiply the fraction by $\dfrac{\sqrt{n}}{\sqrt{n}}$, as you would need to distribute the $\sqrt{n}$ to both terms in the denominator, leaving you no further along. Instead, you can use the difference of squares quadratic identity and instead multiply the fraction by $\dfrac{1 - \sqrt{n}}{1 - \sqrt{n}}$.

$$\left(\frac{2n}{1 + \sqrt{n}}\right)\left(\frac{1 - \sqrt{n}}{1 - \sqrt{n}}\right) = \frac{2n(1 - \sqrt{n})}{1 - n}$$

This eliminates the radical in the denominator of the fraction by using the quadratic identity.

DRILL 14: SPECIAL QUADRATIC IDENTITIES

Try solving the following questions using the quadratic identities, and take note of the clues that tell you when the identities will be useful. The answers can be found in Part IV.

3. If $n - m = -3$ and $n^2 - m^2 = 24$, then which of the following is the sum of n and m ?

   (A) −8
   (B) −6
   (C) −4
   (D) 6
   (E) 8

5. If $x + y = 3$ and $x^2 + y^2 = 8$, then $xy =$

   (A) 0.25
   (B) 0.5
   (C) 1.5
   (D) 2.0
   (E) 2.25

10. If the sum of two nonzero integers is 9 and the sum of their squares is 36, then what is the product of the two integers?

    (A) 9.0
    (B) 13.5
    (C) 18.0
    (D) 22.5
    (E) 45.0

39. $\dfrac{4x}{2x - 4\sqrt{2x}} =$

    (A) $2x - 4\sqrt{2x}$

    (B) $2 - \sqrt{2x}$

    (C) $8x^2 - 16x\sqrt{2x}$

    (D) $\dfrac{2(x + 2\sqrt{2x})}{x - 8}$

    (E) $\dfrac{2(x - 2\sqrt{2x})}{x + 8}$

THE QUADRATIC FORMULA

Unfortunately, not all quadratic equations can be factored by the reverse-FOIL method. The reverse-FOIL method is practical only when the roots of the equation are integers. Sometimes, however, the roots of a quadratic equation will be non-integer decimal numbers, and sometimes a quadratic equation will have no real roots at all. Consider the following quadratic equation:

$$x^2 - 7x + 8 = 0$$

There are no integers that add up to –7 and multiply to 8. This quadratic cannot be factored in the usual way. To solve this equation, it's necessary to use the quadratic formula—a formula that produces the root or roots of any equation in the general quadratic form $ax^2 + bx + c = 0$.

The Quadratic Formula

$$x = \frac{-b \pm \sqrt{b^2 - 4ac}}{2a}$$

The a, b, and c in the formula refer to the coefficients of an expression in the form $ax^2 + bx + c$. For the equation $x^2 - 7x + 8 = 0$, $a = 1$, $b = -7$, and $c = 8$. Plug these values into the quadratic formula and you get the roots of the equation.

$$x = \frac{-(-7) + \sqrt{(-7)^2 - 4(1)(8)}}{2(1)} \qquad x = \frac{-(-7) - \sqrt{(-7)^2 - 4(1)(8)}}{2(1)}$$

$$x = \frac{7 + \sqrt{49 - 32}}{2} \qquad x = \frac{7 - \sqrt{49 - 32}}{2}$$

$$x = \frac{7 + \sqrt{17}}{2} \qquad x = \frac{7 - \sqrt{17}}{2}$$

$$x = 5.56 \qquad x = 1.44$$

So the equation $x^2 - 7x + 8 = 0$ has two real roots, 5.56 and 1.44.

It's possible to tell quickly, without going all the way through the quadratic formula, how many roots an equation has. The part of the quadratic formula under the radical, $b^2 - 4ac$, is called the *discriminant*. The value of the discriminant gives you the following information about a quadratic equation:

- If $b^2 - 4ac > 0$, then the equation has two distinct real roots.
- If $b^2 - 4ac = 0$, then the equation has one distinct real root and is a perfect square. Actually, it has two identical real roots, which is also called a "double root."
- If $b^2 - 4ac < 0$, then the equation has no real roots. Both of its roots are imaginary.

DRILL 15: THE QUADRATIC FORMULA

In the following exercises, first use the discriminant to find how many roots each equation has and whether those roots are real or imaginary. Next, use the quadratic formula to find the root or roots of each of the following. To find imaginary roots, remember that $\sqrt{-1} = i$ (see Chapter 12 on imaginary numbers). The answers can be found in Part IV.

1. $x^2 - 7x + 5 = 0$

2. $3a^2 - 3a + 7 = 0$

3. $s^2 - 6s + 4 = 0$

4. $x^2 - 2 = 0$

5. $n^2 + 5n + 6.25 = 0$

6. $x^2 + 9 = 0$

7. $x^2\sqrt{3} + 12x\sqrt{5} - 8\sqrt{7}$

8. $x^2\sqrt{5} + x\sqrt{2} + 8\sqrt{13}$

GRAPHING CALCULATOR TO THE RESCUE!

On the TI-84, there are tools you can use to solve certain tricky algebra questions. For many problems with one variable, graphing the equation and using one of the following tools can be much easier (and safer!) than solving the problem algebraically.

Finding Real Roots Using the Zero Function

You can use the zero function under the CALC menu to find the zeroes of a function. For example, let's say you wanted to find the roots of $f(x) = \dfrac{x^5 - 3x^3 + 2x}{x - 3}$, when $x \neq 3$. Input the function under the Y= menu (be careful using parentheses with the fraction). Next, press 2ND->TRACE to access the CALC menu, and choose 2: zero. The calculator will graph the function and lead you to this screen.

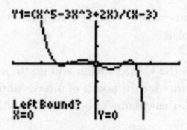

If you can't see the graph clearly, use the WINDOW function and change the Xmax, Xmin, Ymax, and Ymin values. Now, to select the first zero, use the arrows to select a point to the left of the first zero and hit ENTER. This sets the "left bound." Then move the cursor to a point to the right of the first zero but before the second zero and hit ENTER to select the "right bound." Once you've selected the right bound you find yourself at this screen.

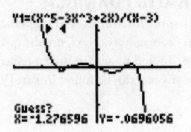

Move the cursor to the leftmost zero and hit ENTER.

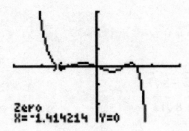

You find that $f(x) = 0$ at $(-1.414, 0)$. Repeat this procedure for the second and third zeroes. Occasionally, you will not find an exact zero; sometimes the y-value will be something vanishingly small. This is due to how the TI series creates graphs (by calculating a series of y-values based on a series of x-values); however, for the purposes of the SAT Subject Test Math 2, "close enough" will get you down to one multiple-choice response.

Finding Points of Intersection Using the Intersect Function

You can use the intersect function under the CALC menu to find the points of intersection of two graphs. This is useful when you want to find the solutions of two equations or functions that have only one variable. For example, let's say you wanted to find the points of intersection of $2x^3 - 10x + 6$ and $\frac{x}{2} + 2$. First, put each function into the Y= menu.

Next, use 2ND->ZOOM to access the FORMAT menu and make sure that CoordOn and ExprOn are enabled.

Go to 2ND->TRACE to access the CALC menu, and go to 5: intersect. Your calculator will graph both functions; if you cannot see the points of intersection, resize your window using the WINDOW function. Once your calculator has finished graphing the functions, you will see the following screen.

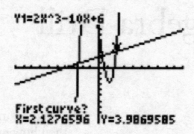

You can use the up and down arrows to change which function you choose as the first function. The function is listed at the top of the screen. Once you've selected the correct function, press ENTER and you will be prompted to select the second function. Once again, you can choose any function that you have under the "Y=" menu. Press ENTER and you will see the following.

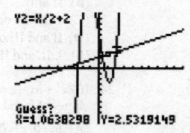

Your cursor will follow the function you identified as the "second curve." Trace that function until you are near the leftmost point of intersection, then press ENTER.

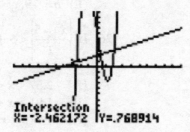

You've found the point of intersection to be approximately (–2.46, 0.77). This is one of the solutions to these equations. To find the other solutions, repeat the process starting from CALC-> intersect and select the other points of intersection in the last step.

Comprehensive Algebra Drill

The answers can be found in Part IV.

4. If $\dfrac{a^2+2x}{3}=5$ and $a^2+2=\dfrac{7x}{5}$, then what is the value of x?

    (A) 2.24
    (B) 3
    (C) 3.82
    (D) 5
    (E) 28.33

8. For which of the following values of k does $x^2+3.5x+k=0$ have one distinct, real root?

    (A) –3.5
    (B) –1.75
    (C) 3.0625
    (D) 6.125
    (E) 7

10. If $x+\sqrt[3]{x}=30$, then what is the value of x?

    (A) 3.107
    (B) 17.578
    (C) 25
    (D) 27
    (E) 27,000

14. If y subtracted from $4x$ is the cube root of 2, and $3x$ subtracted from $2y$ is the square of 3, then what is the sum of x and y?

    (A) –28.14
    (B) –10.26
    (C) 5.73
    (D) 10.26
    (E) 28.41

16. If the maximum value of a quadratic function is –2, then how many distinct real roots COULD the function have?

    I. 0
    II. 1
    III. 2

    (A) I only
    (B) II only
    (C) I and III only
    (D) II and III only
    (E) I, II, and III

24. If $2x^2+bx+c=0$, then for which of the following values of b and c are there no real values of x?

    (A) $b=0,\,c=0$
    (B) $b=-6,\,c=4$
    (C) $b=-8,\,c=8$
    (D) $b=3,\,c=1$
    (E) $b=-9,\,c=11$

26. If $\left|\dfrac{x^3+5}{2}\right|<6$, then

    (A) $-2.57<x<1.91$
    (B) $-1.91<x<2.57$
    (C) $-1.710<x<1.91$
    (D) $x<-1.91$ or $x>2.57$
    (E) $x<-2.57$ or $x>1.91$

36. For how many real values of x does $2x^4-5x^3+x^2-6x+9=0$?

    (A) 5
    (B) 4
    (C) 3
    (D) 2
    (E) 1

40. If $-3 < a < 4$, and $-2 < b < 2$, then what is the range of $(a+b)^2$?

   (A) $0 \le (a+b)^2 < 36$

   (B) $25 < (a+b)^2 < 36$

   (C) $-25 < (a+b)^2 < 36$

   (D) $-36 < (a+b)^2 < 25$

   (E) $0 < (a+b)^2 < 36$

46. If $x \ne \pm 2$, then $\dfrac{x^3 - 2x^2 + 4x - 8}{x^4 - 16} =$

   (A) $\dfrac{1}{x+2}$

   (B) $\dfrac{1}{x-2}$

   (C) $\dfrac{1}{x}$

   (D) $\dfrac{1}{x^2 - 4}$

   (E) $x - 2$

49. If $f(x) = x^4 + x^3 - 5x^2 + 2$ and $g(x) = 2x + 3$, which of the following is true?

   (A) $f(x) = g(x)$ for exactly 4 values of x.
   (B) $f(x) = g(x)$ for exactly 3 values of x.
   (C) $g(x) = 0$ for exactly 4 values of x.
   (D) $f(x) = 0$ for exactly 3 values of x.
   (E) $f(x) \ne g(x)$ for any value of x when
        $-2 < x < 2$.

Summary

○ Plugging In is a great way to sidestep the landmines that appear on the test.

○ You can plug in whenever
  • you see variables, percents, or fractions (without an original amount) in the answers
  • you're tempted to write and then solve an algebraic equation
  • you see the phrase "in terms of" in the question

○ PITA when you have numbers in the answers but don't know where to start or you are still tempted to write an algebraic equation. Don't forget to start with (C)!

○ Inequalities get solved just like equations, except that when you multiply or divide by a negative number, remember to flip the sign.

○ When combining ranges, remember to write out all four combinations of the endpoints of the ranges.

○ Absolute value questions often have two answers. Write out and solve both equations created by the absolute value.

○ Direct and indirect variation questions ask for the relationships between variables:
  • Direct: as x goes up, y goes up. Direct means divide. So you'll have an equation with two fractions.
  • Indirect: as x goes up, y goes down. Indirect (also known as inverse) means multiply. So you'll have an equation with two quantities being multiplied.

○ Work and travel questions often require either the rate equation: distance = rate × time (or work done = rate of work × time), or the Average Pie, which can be used to find average speed.

○ Simultaneous equation questions rarely require solving one variable in terms of another. Just stack 'em and add or subtract to find what you need. Remember that you can multiply or divide before or after you add or subtract to get to what you want.

○ The general form for a quadratic equation is $ax^2 + bx + c = 0$. To find the factors, you can reverse FOIL the equation. There are three special quadratics that you should keep an eye out for to save time and brainpower. They are:

- $(x + y)^2 = x^2 + 2xy + y^2$
- $(x - y)^2 = x^2 - 2xy + y^2$
- $(x + y)(x - y) = x^2 - y^2$

○ If you have a quadratic equation that you can't factor, try using the quadratic formula.

$$x = \frac{-b \pm \sqrt{b^2 - 4ac}}{2a}$$

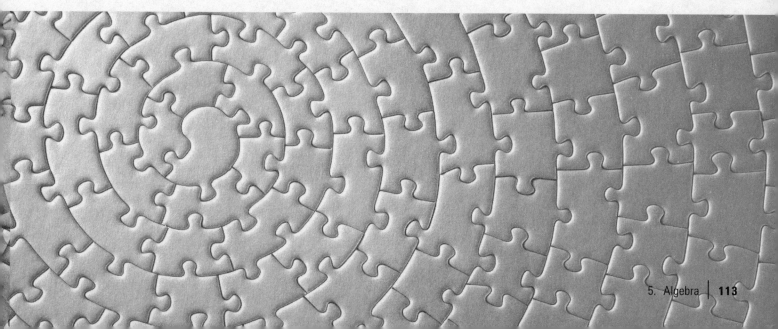

Chapter 6
Fundamentals

This chapter will cover some of the basic math rules you will need on the SAT Subject Test Math 2. These rules include some basic definitions, order of operations, averages, and exponents. This chapter will also give you techniques to help you conquer some of these concepts. Finally, this chapter will help you use your calculator more effectively on the SAT Subject Test Math 2.

Throughout this chapter you will encounter questions that use variables. As you saw in the last chapter, Plugging In makes many of these questions much easier. Many students (especially high-scorers) resist Plugging In, but remember that Plugging In is not only easier than doing the algebra on most problems, but also it's often faster and more accurate!

DEFINITIONS

There are a number of mathematical terms that will be thrown around freely on the test, and you'll want to recognize and understand them. Here are some of the most common terms.

Rational vs. Irrational

All rational numbers will simplify to fractions. An easy way to determine if a number is rational with the TI-84 is to use the MATH->FRAC function. If the number is rational, your calculator will show a fraction equivalent to your result. This function is also useful for finding fractional equivalents.

Integer	Positive and negative whole numbers and zero; NOT fractions or decimals.
Prime Number	An integer that has exactly two distinct factors: itself and 1. All prime numbers are positive; the smallest prime number is 2. 2 is also the only even prime number. 1 is not prime.
Rational Number	All positive and negative integers, fractions, and terminating or repeating decimal numbers; technically, any number that can be expressed as a fraction of two integers—which means everything except numbers containing weird radicals (such as $\sqrt{2}$), π, or e.
Irrational Number	Any number that does not end or repeat (in other words, any number that isn't rational). This includes all numbers with radicals that can't be simplified, such as $\sqrt{2}$ (perfect squares with radicals, such as $\sqrt{16}$ don't count because they can be simplified to integers, such as 4). Also, all numbers containing π or e. Note that repeating decimals such as .33333… are rational (they're equivalent to fractions, such as $\frac{1}{3}$).
Real Number	Any number on the number line; everything except imaginary or complex numbers.
Imaginary Number	The square roots of negative numbers, that is, any numbers containing i, which represents $\sqrt{-1}$.
Complex Number	A number that combines real and imaginary numbers, in the form $a + bi$, where $i = \sqrt{-1}$.
Consecutive Numbers	The members of a set listed in order, without skipping any; consecutive integers: –3, –2, –1, 0, 1, 2; consecutive positive multiples of 3: 3, 6, 9, 12; consecutive prime numbers: 2, 3, 5, 7, 11.
Distinct Numbers	Numbers that are different from each other.
Sum	The result of addition.
Difference	The result of subtraction.
Product	The result of multiplication.
Quotient	The result of division.

Remainder	The integer left over after dividing two numbers. For example, when 17 is divided by 2, the remainder is 1. Remember: On the SAT Subject Test Math 2, a remainder is ALWAYS an integer.
Reciprocal	The result when 1 is divided by a number. For example, the reciprocal of $\frac{3}{4}$ is $\frac{4}{3}$, and the reciprocal of 16 is $\frac{1}{16}$. The reciprocal is also the number to the −1 power. The product of a number and its reciprocal is always 1.
Positive Difference	Just what it sounds like—the number you get by subtracting the lesser of two numbers from the greater. You can also think of it as the distance between two numbers on the number line.
Absolute Value	The distance from zero. If you get a negative result after working what's in the brackets, make it positive.
Arithmetic Mean	The average of a list of values; also simply referred to as the "mean." Find by determining the sum of all the elements in the list, then dividing by the number of elements.
Median	The middle value in a list when arranged in consecutive order; in a list with an even number of members, the average of the *two* middle values.
Mode	The value that occurs most often in a set. If no value appears more often than all the others in a set, then that set has no mode. If multiple values appear the most often, then that set has multiple modes.
Factor	An integer which evenly divides into another integer. For example, the factors of 12 are 1, 2, 3, 4, 6, and 12.
Multiple	The product of a given integer and another integer. For example, the first four positive integer multiples of 12 are 12, 24, 36, and 48.
Even Number	An integer divisible by 2. The units digit will be 0, 2, 4, 6, or 8.
Odd Number	An integer not divisible by 2. The units digit will be 1, 3, 5, 7, or 9.
Positive	Any number greater than 0.
Negative	Any number less than 0.

At the beginning of each chapter in this book, you may see additional definitions that pertain to the material in that chapter. Every time you see such definitions listed, be sure that you know them well. One way to memorize the definitions is to make flash cards for them.

DOING ARITHMETIC

This chapter deals with the basic manipulations of numbers: averages, word problems, exponents, and so on. Most of these operations can be greatly simplified by the use of a calculator, so you should practice them with your calculator in order to increase your speed and efficiency. Remember the points about calculator use from Chapter 2, however. If you use your calculator incorrectly, you'll get questions wrong. If you use it on every question without thinking, it will slow you down. Keep your calculator near at hand, but think before you use it.

Order of Operations

You remember the Order of Operations, right? You might remember this as PEMDAS (or Please Excuse My Dear Aunt Sally) or BEMDAS. This is the order you must use to correctly solve an arithmetic problem. PEMDAS stands for Parentheses (or Brackets, in the case of BEMDAS), Exponents (and roots), Multiplication and Division, Addition and Subtraction. When using PEMDAS, it's important to remember that exponents and roots should be calculated from left to right, just as multiplication, division, addition, and subtraction should be. You can think of PEMDAS in the following way:

Pretty Print
Most graphing calculators can display calculations the way that they would be written by hand (for example, using a horizontal bar with a numerator above and a denominator below to represent a fraction). This feature is called Pretty Print. For some calculators, such as the TI-84, it is necessary to download an application to enable this feature. For other calculators, you need to enable Pretty Print in the settings. Either way, we recommend enabling this for the SAT Subject Test Math 2: doing so makes it easier to check if you've made a mistake, which is valuable!

PEMDAS
Parentheses and brackets
Exponents and roots
Multiplication and **D**ivision
Addition and **S**ubtraction

PEMDAS and Your Calculator

The safest way to do multi-step problems like this on a calculator is one step at a time.

On scientific and graphing calculators, it's possible to type complex expressions into your calculator all at once and let your calculator do the work of grinding out a number. But in order for your calculator to produce the right answer, the expression must be entered in exactly the right way—and that takes an understanding of the order of operations.

For example, the expression $\dfrac{2\sqrt{3^3 - 2}}{5}$ would have to be typed into some calculators this way:

$$(2\ \sqrt{}(3\ \wedge\ 3 - 2))/5 =$$

On other calculators, it would have to look like the following:

$$(2(3^{\wedge}3 - 2)^{\wedge}(1/2))/5 =$$

Any mistake in either pattern would produce an incorrect answer. On other calculators, the equation might have to be entered in still another way. If you intend to make your calculator do your work for you, check your calculator's operating manual, and practice. In general, use lots of parentheses to make sure the calculator does the arithmetic in the right order. If you use too many parentheses, the calculator will still give you the right answer, but if you don't use enough, you may get the wrong answer. And remember, the safest way to use your calculator is one step at a time.

DRILL 1: PEMDAS AND YOUR CALCULATOR

Check your PEMDAS skills by working through the following complicated calculations with your calculator. The answers can be found in Part IV.

1. $0.2 \times \left[\dfrac{15^2 - 75}{6} \right] =$

2. $\dfrac{5\sqrt{6^3 - 20}}{2} =$

3. $\sqrt{\dfrac{(7^2 - 9)(0.375 \times 16)^2}{10}} =$

4. $\sqrt{5\left[(13 \times 18) + \sqrt{121} \right]} =$

5. $\sqrt{\dfrac{2025^{0.5}}{0.2} - \dfrac{5}{\frac{1}{3}}} =$

6. $\dfrac{\sqrt[3]{8^2 + \left(10^2 - (13(3)) \right)}}{\sqrt[4]{5^2 - \sqrt{81}}}$

7. $\dfrac{\dfrac{4 + 2\sqrt{3}}{12 + 6\sqrt{2}}}{\dfrac{2 - \sqrt{2}}{4 - 2\sqrt{3}}}$

FRACTIONS, DECIMALS, AND PERCENTAGES

On arithmetic questions, you will often be called upon to change fractions to decimals, or decimals to percentages, and so on. Be careful whenever you change the form of a number.

You turn fractions into decimals by doing the division represented by the fraction bar.

$$\frac{1}{8} = 1 \div 8 = 0.125$$

To turn a decimal number into a fraction, count the number of decimal places (digits to the right of the decimal point) in the number. Then place the number over a 1 with the same number of zeros, get rid of the decimal point, and reduce.

$$0.125 = \frac{125}{1000} = \frac{25}{200} = \frac{1}{8}$$

Decimals and percentages are essentially the same. The difference is the percent sign (%), which means "÷ 100." To turn a decimal into a percentage, just move the decimal point two places to the right, and add the percent sign.

$$0.125 = 12.5\%$$

To turn percentages into decimals, do the reverse; get rid of the percent sign and move the decimal point two places to the left.

$$0.3\% = 0.003$$

It's important to understand these conversions, and to be able to do them in your head as much as possible. Don't rely on the percent key on your calculator; it's far too easy to become confused and use it when converting in the wrong direction.

Watch out for conversions between percentages and decimals—especially ones involving percentages with decimal points already in them (such as 0.15%). Converting these numbers is simple, but this step is still the source of many careless errors.

If you are given a decimal or percentage and want a fraction, on the TI-80 series (such as the TI-84) you can use the MATH->FRAC function. Input the number as a decimal, then use the MATH key. Select the first function, FRAC, and your calculator will output the fractional equivalent. Take our last example:

$$0.003 \to MATH \to FRAC \to \frac{3}{1000}$$

This function will always give you the most reduced form. The function will also display improper fractions if the result is greater than 1 or less than −1. For example,

$$-215 \div 125 = -1.72 \to MATH \to FRAC \to -\frac{43}{25}$$

Word Problem Translations

Most of the common careless errors made in answering math questions are made in the very first step: reading the question. All your skill in arithmetic does you no good if you're not solving the right problem, and all the power of your calculator can't help you if you've entered the wrong equation. Reading errors are particularly common in word problems.

The safest way to extract equations from long-winded word problems is to translate, word for word, from English to math. All of the following words have direct math equivalents:

English	Math
what what fraction how many	x, y, etc. (a variable)
a, an	1 (one)
percent	$\div 100$
of	• (multiplied by)
is, are, was, were	=
per	• (multiplied by) or $\div$ (divided by)
out of	$\div$ (divided by)
x is how much more than y	$x - y$
x is how many times (more than) y	$x \div y$
x is how much less than y	$y - x$

Don't Get Tripped Up
Start writing your multiplication sign as a dot, not an ×, if you haven't already. Using an × can get very confusing, especially if your variable is an x. Make it easy and don't trip yourself up!

Using this table as a guide, you can translate any English sentence in a word problem into an equation. Here's an example.

3. If the bar of a barbell weighs 15 pounds, and the entire barbell weighs 75 pounds, then the weight of the bar is what percent of the weight of the entire barbell?

The question at the end of the problem can be translated into

$$15 = \frac{x}{100} \bullet 75$$

Solve this equation, and the question is answered. You'll find that x is equal to 20, and 20% is the correct answer.

DRILL 2: WORD PROBLEM TRANSLATION

For each of the following exercises, translate the information in English into an equation and solve. The answers can be found in Part IV.

Word for Word
Use the English to math conversion chart to translate each word into math.

1. 6.5 is what percent of 260?

2. If there are 20 honors students at Pittman High and 180 students at the school in all, then the number of honors students at Pittman High is what percentage of the total number of students?

3. Thirty percent of 40 percent of 25 marbles is how many marbles?

4. What is the square root of one-third of 48?

5. The square root of what positive number is equal to one-eighth of that number?

6. The cube of x is how much less than the cube root of the sum of one-half y and z?

7. x is the nth root of the sum of 2 and the square of 3.

Percent Change

"Percent change" is a way of talking about increasing or decreasing a number. The percent change is just the amount of the increase or decrease, expressed as a percentage of the starting amount.

For example, if you took a $100.00 item and increased its price by $2.00, that would be a 2% change, because the amount of the increase, $2.00, is 2% of the original amount, $100.00. On the other hand, if you increased the price of a $5.00 item by the same $2.00, that would be a 40% increase—because $2.00 is 40% of $5.00. If you ever lose track of your numbers when computing a percent change, just use this formula:

$$\% \, \text{Change} = \frac{\text{Difference}}{\text{Original}} \times 100\%$$

Whenever you work with percent change, be careful not to confuse the *amount of the change* with the total *after* you've worked out the percent change. Just concern yourself with the original amount and the amount of the increase or decrease. The new total doesn't matter.

DRILL 3: PERCENT CHANGE

Test your understanding of percent change with the following practice questions. The answers can be found in Part IV.

2. A 25-gallon addition to a pond containing 150 gallons constitutes an increase of approximately what percent?

   (A) 14.29%
   (B) 16.67%
   (C) 17.25%
   (D) 20.00%
   (E) 25.00%

3. The percent decrease from 5 to 4 is how much less than the percent increase from 4 to 5 ?

   (A) 0%
   (B) 5%
   (C) 15%
   (D) 20%
   (E) 25%

Your Calculator Is Your Friend
Here's a great place to test out how you're putting equations in your calculator.

4. Nicoletta deposits $150.00 in her savings account. If this deposit represents a 12 percent increase in Nicoletta's savings, then how much does her savings account contain after the deposit?

   (A) $1,100.00
   (B) $1,250.00
   (C) $1,400.00
   (D) $1,680.00
   (E) $1,800.00

18. If $f(x) = \frac{1}{3}x + 2$ and $n > 0$, then what is the percent increase from $f(n)$ to $f(2n)$ when $n = 3$?

   (A) 25%

   (B) $33\frac{1}{3}\%$

   (C) 50%

   (D) $66\frac{2}{3}\%$

   (E) 300%

Percent change can show up in many different contexts on the SAT Subject Test Math 2. Here is one common way that the College Board uses percent change in a problem.

The Change-up, Change-down

A classic trick question will ask you what happens if you increase something by a percent and then decrease it by the same percent, as follows:

9. The price of a bicycle that usually sells for $250.00 is marked up 30 percent. If this new price is subsequently discounted by 30 percent, then the final price of the bicycle is

(A) $200.50
(B) $216.75
(C) $227.50
(D) $250.00
(E) $265.30

Here's How to Crack It

The easy mistake on this problem type is to assume that the price (after increasing by 30% and then decreasing by 30%) has returned to $250.00, the original amount. Nope! It doesn't actually work out that way, as you'll see if you try it step by step. First, you increase the original price by 30%.

$$\$250.00 + \left(\frac{30}{100} \times \$250.00 \right) =$$

$$\$250.00 + \$75.00 =$$

$$\$325.00$$

Then, discount this price by 30%.

$$\$325.00 - \left(\frac{30}{100} \times \$325.00 \right) =$$

$$\$325.00 - \$97.50 =$$

$$\$227.50$$

The answer is (C). As you can see, the final amount isn't equal to the starting amount. The reason for the difference is that you're increasing the price by 30% of the starting number, and then decreasing by 30% of a *different* number—the new, higher price. The changes will never be of the same *amount*—just the same percent. You end up with a number smaller than your starting number, because the decrease was bigger than the increase. In fact, if you'd done the decrease *first* and then the increase, you would still have gotten the same number, $227.50.

Remember this tip whenever you increase a quantity by a percent and then *decrease* by the same percent. Your final result will always be a bit smaller than your original amount. The same thing is true if you *decrease* a quantity by a percent and then increase by the same percent. You'll get a number a bit lower than your starting number.

Repeated Percent Change

On one common question type you'll have to work with percent change and exponents together. Occasionally, you'll be required to increase or decrease something by a percent again and again. Such questions often deal with growing populations or bank accounts collecting interest. Here's an example.

25. Ruby had $1,250.00 in a bank account at the end of 1990.
    If Ruby deposits no further money in the account, and the
    money in the account earns 5 percent interest every year, then
    to the nearest dollar, how much money will be in the account
    at the end of 2000 ?

    (A) $1,632.00
    (B) $1,786.00
    (C) $1,875.00
    (D) $2,025.00
    (E) $2,036.00

Here's How to Crack It

The easy mistake here is to find 5% of the original amount, which in this case would be $62.50. Add $62.50 for each of the ten years from 1990 to 2000 and you've got an increase of $625.00,

right? Wrong. That would give you a final total of $1,875.00, but that's not the right answer. Here's the problem—the interest for the first year is $62.50, which is 5% of $1,250. But that means that now there's $1,312.50 in the bank account, so the interest for the second year will be something different. As you can see, this could get messy.

Here's the easy way. The first year's interest can be computed like any ordinary percent change, by adding the percent change to the original amount.

> **Remember to Keep an Eye Out for Traps**
> Notice that $1,875.00 is in the answers. Remember that the College Board *loves* to put in numbers that look familiar to you. You'll see partial answers; you'll see answers to a question that wasn't even asked. Always remember to keep an eye out for answers that you can eliminate.

$$\$1,250.00 + \left(\frac{5}{100} \times \$1,250.00\right) = \text{total after one year}$$

But there's another way to write that. Just factor out the $1,250.00.

$$\$1,250.00 \times \left(1 + \frac{5}{100}\right) = \text{total after one year}$$

$$\$1,250.00 \times (1.05) = \text{total after one year}$$

You can get the total after one year by converting the percent change to a decimal number, adding 1, and multiplying the original amount by this number. To get the total after two years, just multiply by that number again.

$$\$1,250.00 \times (1.05) \times (1.05) = \text{total after two years}$$

And so on. So, to figure out how much money Ruby will have after 10 years, all you have to do is multiply her original deposit by 1.05, 10 times. That means multiplying Ruby's original deposit by 1.05 to the 10th power.

$$\$1,250.00 \times (1.05)^{10} = \text{total after 10 years}$$

$$\$1,250.00 \times 1.629 = \text{total after 10 years}$$

$$\$2,036.25 = \text{total after 10 years}$$

So, to the nearest dollar, Ruby will have $2,036.00 after 10 years. The answer is (E).

There's a simple formula you can use to solve repeated percent-increase problems.

$$\textbf{Final amount} = \text{Original} \times (1 + \text{Rate})^{\text{number of changes}}$$

The formula for repeated percent-decrease problems is almost identical. The only difference is that you'll be subtracting the percentage change from 1 rather than adding it.

$$\textbf{Final amount} = \text{Original} \times (1 - \text{Rate})^{\text{number of changes}}$$

Just remember that you've got to convert the rate of change (like an interest rate) from a percentage to a decimal number.

Here's another one. Try it yourself, and then check the explanation below.

28. The weight of a bar of hand soap decreases by 2.5 percent each time it is used. If the bar weighs 100 grams when it is new, what is its weight in grams after 20 uses?

    (A) 50.00
    (B) 52.52
    (C) 57.43
    (D) 60.27
    (E) 77.85

Here's How to Crack It

You've got all of your starting numbers. The original amount is 100 grams, and the rate of change is 2.5%, or 0.025 (remember to subtract it, because it's a decrease). You'll be going through 20 decreases, so the exponent will be 20. This is how you'd plug these numbers into the formula.

Final amount	$= 100 \times (1 - 0.025)^{20}$
	$= 100 \times (0.975)^{20}$
	$= 100 \times (0.60269)$
Final amount	$= 60.27$

The answer is (D). This is an excellent example of a question type that is difficult if you've never seen it before, and easy if you're prepared for it. Memorize the repeated percent-change formulas and practice using them.

> **To Memorize or Not to Memorize?**
> So, at this point, you're probably starting to get nervous about how many formulas we're giving you and how much you have to memorize. But remember that we're also showing you how to get there. Formulas are designed to save you time. If you ever can't remember a formula, you can still figure out how to do the problem. Notice for repeated percent change, you *can* do it the long way and still get to the right answer accurately. And don't forget your techniques like approximation and POE...and there's still more to come!

DRILL 4: REPEATED PERCENT CHANGE

Try the following practice questions. The answers can be found in Part IV.

20. At a certain bank, savings accounts earn 5 percent interest per year. If a savings account is opened with a $1,000.00 deposit and no further deposits are made, how much money will the account contain after 12 years?

    (A) $1,166.67
    (B) $1,333.33
    (C) $1,600.00
    (D) $1,795.86
    (E) $12,600.00

25. In 1900, the population of Malthusia was 120,000. Since then, the population has increased by exactly 8 percent per year. What was the population in the year 2000?

    (A) 216,000
    (B) 2,599,070
    (C) 1,080,000
    (D) 5.4×10^7
    (E) 2.6×10^8

28. In 1995, Ebenezer Bosticle created a salt sculpture that weighed 2,000 pounds. If this sculpture loses 4 percent of its mass each year to rain erosion, what is the last year in which the statue will weigh more than 1,000 pounds?

    (A) 2008
    (B) 2009
    (C) 2011
    (D) 2012
    (E) 2013

40. A savings bond pays 2.5 percent interest per year. In approximately how many years will the value of the savings bond be twice the original value?

    (A) 3
    (B) 22
    (C) 25
    (D) 28
    (E) 40

Ways to Remember
Remember that in order to find the average, you divide the total by the number of things. Think of the horizontal line in the Average Pie as one big division bar!

AVERAGES

The SAT Subject Test Math 2 uses average in a variety of ways. Remember, the average is the sum of all the values divided by the number of values you're adding up. Looking at this definition, you can see that every average involves three quantities: the total, the number of things being added, and the average itself.

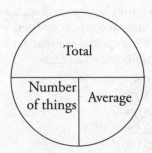

The chart above is called an Average Pie. It's The Princeton Review way of organizing the information found in an average problem. Cover up the "average" section with your thumb. In order to find the average, you divide the total by the "number of things." Now cover up the "number of things" section. You can find it by dividing the total by the average. Finally, you can find the total by multiplying the number of things by the average.

When you encounter averages on the SAT Subject Test Math 2, you will be given two of the three pieces of the pie. Finding the missing piece will be the key to solving most of these questions.

DRILL 5: AVERAGES

Test your understanding of averages with the following questions. The answers can be found in Part IV.

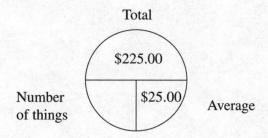

1. People at a dinner paid an average of $25.00 each. The total bill for dinner was $225.00.

   What else do you know? _____

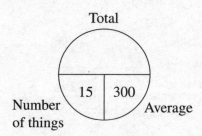

2. The average fruit picker on Wilbury Ranch picked 300 apples on Tuesday. There are 15 fruit pickers at Wilbury Ranch.

   What else do you know? _____

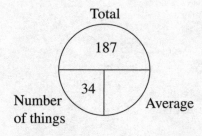

3. If the 34 students in the chess club lie down end to end, they would form a line 187 feet long.

   What else do you know? _____

Multiple Average Questions

The Average Pie becomes most useful when you're tackling a multiple-average question—one that requires you to manipulate several averages in order to find an answer. Here's an example.

17. Sydney's average score on the first 5 math tests of the year was 82. If she ended the year with a math test average of 88, and a total of 8 math tests were administered that year, what was her average on the last three math tests?

(A) 99.5
(B) 98.75
(C) 98.0
(D) 96.25
(E) 94.0

Here's How to Crack It

In this question, there are three separate averages to deal with: Sydney's average on the first five tests, her average on the last three tests, and her final average for all eight. In order to avoid confusion, take these one at a time. Draw the first Average Pie.

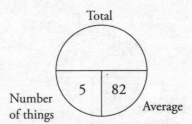

You have the number of things and the average, so you can find the total. You know that Sydney's total for the first test is 410. Fill in that information and draw another pie. For your second pie, the question tells you that Sydney's average on all 8 tests was 88, so you can multiply those numbers to find the total of her 8 scores, or 704. Fill in your second Average Pie below.

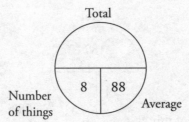

Since you know the total of all 8 tests and the total of the first 5 tests, you can figure out the total of the last three tests.

$$704 - 410 = 294$$

Draw one last pie, using the information that you have.

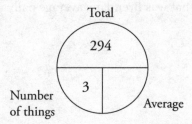

As it turns out, Sydney averaged a 98 on her last three math tests; so the answer is (C).

———————————○———————————

Multiple-average questions are never terribly difficult. Just draw an Average Pie every time you see the word *average* in the question. Organization is everything on these questions. It's easy to make careless errors if you get your numbers scrambled, so make sure you label the parts of the Average Pie. Notice that you can always add or subtract totals and numbers of things, but you can never add or subtract averages.

DRILL 6: MULTIPLE AVERAGE QUESTIONS

Try these problems. The answers can be found in Part IV.

18. At a charity fund-raiser, the average of the first 19 donations is $485.00. In order for the average of the first 20 donations to be $500.00, what must the amount of the twentieth donation be, in dollars?

(A) $300
(B) $515
(C) $650
(D) $785
(E) $800

20. During the first 20 days of September, the Tribune received an average of 4 complaint letters per day. During the last 10 days of September, the Tribune received an average of 7 complaint letters per day. What was the Tribune's average number of complaint letters per day for the entire month of September?

(A) 5.0
(B) 5.33
(C) 5.67
(D) 6.0
(E) 6.25

21. Over a year, Brendan sold an average of 12 umbrellas per day on rainy days, and an average of 3 umbrellas per day on clear days. If the weather was rainy one day in five, and this was not a leap year, what was Brendan's average daily umbrella sales for the year?

   (A) 4.8
   (B) 5.2
   (C) 6.75
   (D) 7.3
   (E) 9.0

42. Nathalie's average score on her first n tests was x. Her average on the next 3 tests was 20% greater than x. What was her average for all the tests?

   (A) x

   (B) $\dfrac{n+3}{x(n-3.6)}$

   (C) $\dfrac{1.2x(n+3)}{n}$

   (D) $\dfrac{n(x+3)}{n+3.6}$

   (E) $\dfrac{x(n+3.6)}{n+3}$

IRRATIONAL NUMBERS

Numbers that are not equivalent to any integer or any fraction with integers in the numerator and denominator are *irrational numbers*. Irrational numbers occur when one takes a root of a number and that root cannot be simplified into an integer. For example, $\sqrt{2} = 1.4142...$, so it is irrational. However, $\sqrt{\dfrac{9}{4}} = \dfrac{3}{2}$, so it is rational. In addition, the special numbers e and π are irrational: their decimals do not repeat, and they cannot be reduced to a simple fraction.

DRILL 7: IRRATIONAL NUMBERS

Try these problems. The answers can be found in Part IV.

33. Which of the following is irrational?

    (A) $\dfrac{\pi}{(\pi+1)^2}$

    (B) $\dfrac{\pi^2+2\pi+1}{(\pi+1)^2}$

    (C) $\log_\pi 1$

    (D) $\log_\pi (\pi^3)$

    (E) $\dfrac{\pi}{2\pi}$

35. If x is a prime number, then which of the following is NOT irrational?

    (A) $\sqrt{\dfrac{1}{x}}$

    (B) ex

    (C) $\ln{(e^{\frac{1}{x}})}$

    (D) $x^{\frac{2}{3}}$

    (E) e^{2x}

EXPONENTS

An exponent is a simple way of expressing repeated multiplication. You can think of 5^3, for example, as $5 \times 5 \times 5$. In this exponential expression, 5 is referred to as the "base," while 3 is the "exponent." Sometimes a third number is also present, called a "coefficient." In the expression $4b^2$, b is the base, 2 is the exponent, and 4 is the coefficient. Here, b is being squared, but the coefficient, 4, is not affected by the exponent.

For certain SAT Subject Test Math 2 questions, you'll need to do some algebraic calculations using exponents. To work with exponents in equations, you just need to remember a few basic rules.

Multiplying Exponential Terms When Bases Are the Same

It is fairly straightforward to multiply exponential terms when the bases are the same. Keep the same base, and add the exponents of the terms to find the new exponent.

$$n^3 \times n^5 = n^8 \qquad\qquad 3 \times 3^4 = 3^5$$

If coefficients are present, simply multiply the coefficients.

$$2b \times 3b^5 = 6b^6 \qquad\qquad \frac{1}{2}c^3 \times 6c^5 = 3c^8$$

Dividing Exponential Terms When Bases Are the Same

Dividing exponential terms is as straightforward as multiplying. Keep the same base, and subtract the exponents of the terms to find the new exponent.

$$x^8 \div x^6 = x^2 \qquad\qquad 7^5 \div 7 = 7^4$$

If coefficients are present, simply divide the coefficients.

$$6b^5 \div 3b = 2b^4 \qquad\qquad 5a^8 \div 3a^2 = \frac{5}{3}a^6$$

Rules for Exponents
To remember these rules, use MADSPM.
[Multiply Add]
[Divide Subtract]
[Power Multiply]

Multiplying and Dividing Exponential Terms When Exponents Are the Same

If you are multiplying or dividing terms which have different bases but have the same exponents, you can perform the operation on the bases without changing the exponent. You do so by putting the bases in a shared parenthesis to the same exponent. In other words, the bases will change, but the exponent will remain the same.

For multiplication,

$$3^3 \times 5^3 = 15^3 \qquad\qquad x^8 y^8 = (xy)^8$$

For division,

$$33^2 \div 3^2 = \left(\frac{33}{3}\right)^2 = 11^2 \qquad\qquad x^{20} \div y^{20} = \left(\frac{x}{y}\right)^{20}$$

Adding and Subtracting When Bases and Exponents Are the Same

You can add and subtract terms with the same bases and exponents the same way you can add or subtract coefficients with simple variables.

$$2a^3 + a^3 = 3a^3 \qquad\qquad 5x^2 - 4x^2 = x^2$$

If the bases or exponents are different, you cannot directly add or subtract the terms. However, you may be able to factor.

Adding and Subtracting When Bases and Exponents Are NOT the Same

If the bases and exponents are not the same, you may be able use the distributive property to factor. Find the largest common factor (of both the exponents and variables), divide by that factor and bring it to the front of a parenthesis.

$$2x^2 y + 4y = 2y(x^2 + 2) \qquad\qquad 5ab^3 - 3a^2 b = ab(5b^2 - 3a)$$

This is particularly useful on the SAT Subject Test Math 2 when you have fractions. In many cases you will need to factor the numerator and/or denominator of a fraction and then reduce.

$$\frac{3x^3 + 6x^2 y}{2x^2 + 4xy} = \frac{3x^2(x + 2y)}{2x(x + 2y)} = \frac{3x}{2}$$

Note that in some cases there may be values of x that make the original denominator equal zero (in our last example, when $x = 0$ or $y = -\dfrac{x}{2}$), but that don't make the simplified denominator equal zero. This will be relevant when you are asked to find limits (see Chapter 12).

Raising Powers to Powers

When an exponential term is raised to another power, the exponents are multiplied.

$$(x^2)^8 = x^{16} \qquad\qquad (7^5)^4 = 7^{20}$$

If there is a coefficient included in the term, then the coefficient is also raised to that power.

$$(3c^4)^3 = 27c^{12} \qquad\qquad (5g^3)^2 = 25g^6$$

Using these rules, you should be able to manipulate exponents wherever you find them.

_n_th roots on the TI-84

Under the "MATH" menu, function 5 is "$\sqrt[x]{y}$." To take any root of a number, you type the root you want, then MATH->5 (or scroll down to the $\sqrt[x]{y}$ function), then ENTER. For example, to find $\sqrt[5]{243}$, you would type "5 $\sqrt[x]{y}$ 243." PrettyPrint will help ensure you're entering the desired root and not multiplying by the square root!

ROOTS

Roots are exponents in reverse. For example, $4 \times 4 = 16$. That means that $4^2 = 16$. It also means that $\sqrt{16} = 4$. Square roots are by far the most common roots on the SAT Subject Test Math 2. The square root of a number is simply whatever you would square to get that number.

You may also encounter other roots: cube roots, fourth roots, fifth roots, and so on. Each of these roots is represented by a radical with a number attached, like $\sqrt[3]{x}$, which means the cube root of x. Roots of higher degrees work just as square roots do. The expression $\sqrt[4]{81}$, for example, equals 3—the number that you'd raise to the 4th power to get 81. Similarly, $\sqrt[5]{32}$ is the number that, raised to the 5th power, equals 32—in this case, 2.

When the number under a radical has a factor whose root is an integer, then the radical can be *simplified*. This means that the root can be pulled out. For example, $\sqrt{48}$ is equal to $\sqrt{16 \times 3}$. Because 16 is a perfect square, its root can be pulled out, leaving the 3 under the radical sign, as $4\sqrt{3}$. That's the simplified version of $\sqrt{48}$.

The Principal Idea

Remember how both 2 and –2 raised to the 4th power equal 16? Well, for the SAT Subject Test Math 2, a radical refers only to the *principal* root of an expression. When there is only one root, that's the principal root. An example of this is $\sqrt[3]{27}$. The only root of this expression is 3. When you have both a positive *and* a negative root, the positive root is considered to be the principal root and is the only root symbolized by the radical sign. So, even though $2^4 = 16$ and $(-2)^4 = 16$, $\sqrt[4]{16}$ means 2 only, and not –2.

Working with Roots

The rules for manipulating roots when they appear in equations are the same as the rules for manipulating exponents. Roots can be combined by addition and subtraction only when they are roots of the same order and roots of the same number.

$$3\sqrt{5} - \sqrt{5} = 2\sqrt{5} \qquad\qquad 3\sqrt[3]{x} + 2\sqrt[3]{x} = 5\sqrt[3]{x}$$

Roots can be multiplied and divided freely as long as all the roots are of the same order—all square roots, or all cube roots, and so on. The answer must also be kept under the radical.

$$\sqrt{a} \times \sqrt{b} = \sqrt{ab} \qquad\qquad \sqrt[3]{24} \div \sqrt[3]{3} = \sqrt[3]{8} = 2$$

$$\sqrt{18} \times \sqrt{2} = \sqrt{36} = 6 \qquad\qquad \sqrt[4]{5} \div \sqrt[4]{2} = \sqrt[4]{\frac{5}{2}}$$

Be sure to memorize these rules before working with roots.

Fractional Exponents

A fractional exponent is a way of raising a number to a power and taking a root of the number at the same time. The number on top is the normal exponent. The number on the bottom is the root—you can think of it as being in the "root cellar."

So, in order to raise a number to the $\frac{2}{3}$ power, you would square the number and then take the cube root of your result. You could also take the cube root first and then square the result—it doesn't matter which one you do first, as long as you realize that 2 is the exponent and 3 is the order of the root.

Remember that an exponent of 1 means the number itself, so $x^{\frac{1}{2}}$ is equal to $\sqrt{x}$, the square root of x to the first power. Knowing this will help you handle roots with your calculator. For example, $17^{\frac{1}{3}}$ can be entered into your calculator as 17^(1/3).

$$27^{\frac{1}{3}} = \sqrt[3]{27} = 3 \qquad\qquad b^{\frac{5}{2}} = \sqrt{b^5}$$

$$8^{\frac{2}{3}} = \sqrt[3]{8^2} = \sqrt[3]{64} = 4 \qquad\qquad x^{\frac{4}{3}} = \sqrt[3]{x^4}$$

> **Calculator Tip**
> Some scientific calculators have an exponent key that looks like y^x, x^y, or x^n instead of ^.

Using Fractional Exponents to Combine Unlike Roots

Earlier you learned about combining terms under the radical when multiplying two terms under the same radical. You can use fractional roots to combine terms that are under *different* radicals as well. For example,

$$\sqrt{x} \cdot \sqrt[3]{y}$$

You know that $\sqrt{x} = x^{\frac{1}{2}}$ and $\sqrt[3]{y} = y^{\frac{1}{3}}$. If you make these terms over a common denominator, then the terms will be under the same root.

$$x^{\frac{1}{2}} = x^{\frac{3}{6}} \text{ and } y^{\frac{1}{3}} = y^{\frac{2}{6}}, \text{ so } \sqrt{x} \cdot \sqrt[3]{y} = x^{\frac{3}{6}} y^{\frac{2}{6}}$$

Using your exponent rules, you can factor out $\frac{1}{6}$ from the exponents.

$$x^{\frac{3}{6}} y^{\frac{2}{6}} = (x^3 y^2)^{\frac{1}{6}} = \sqrt[6]{x^3 y^2}$$

SPECIAL EXPONENTS

There are some exponents on the SAT Subject Test Math 2 that you've got to treat a little differently. The following are some unusual exponents with which you should be familiar.

Zero

Any number (except zero) raised to the power of zero is equal to 1, no matter what you start with. It's a pretty simple rule.

$$5^0 = 1 \qquad\qquad x^0 = 1$$

One

Any number raised to the first power is itself—it doesn't change. In fact, ordinary numbers, written without exponents, are numbers to the first power. You can think of them as having an invisible exponent of 1. That's useful when using the basic exponent rules you've just reviewed. It means that $(x^4 \div x)$ can be written as $(x^4 \div x^1)$, which can prevent confusion when you're subtracting exponents.

$$x = x^1 \qqua\qquad 4^1 = 4$$

Negative Exponents

Treat a negative exponent exactly like a positive exponent, with one extra step. After you have applied the exponent, flip the number over—that is, you turn the number into its reciprocal.

$$a^{-4} = \frac{1}{a^4} \qquad\qquad 3^{-2} = \frac{1}{3^2} = \frac{1}{9}$$

$$x^{-1} = \frac{1}{x} \qquad\qquad \left(\frac{2}{3}\right)^{-1} = \frac{3}{2}$$

The negative sign works the same way on fractional exponents. First, you apply the exponent as you would if it were positive, and then flip it over.

$$x^{-\frac{1}{2}} = \frac{1}{\sqrt{x}} \qquad\qquad a^{-\frac{3}{2}} = \frac{1}{\sqrt{a^3}}$$

MORE IMPORTANT EXPONENT STUFF

There are a few important things to remember about the effects of exponents on various numbers:

- A positive number raised to any power remains positive. No exponent can make a positive number negative.
- A negative number raised to an odd power remains negative.
- A negative number raised to an even power becomes positive.

In other words, anything raised to an odd power keeps its sign. If a^3 is negative, then a is negative; if a^3 is positive, then a is positive. A term with an odd exponent has only one root. For example, if $a^3 = -27$, there's only one value of a that makes it true: $a = -3$.

On the other hand, anything raised to an even power becomes positive, regardless of its original sign. This means that an equation with an even exponent has two roots. For example, if $b^2 = 25$, then b has two possible values: 5 and –5. It's important to remember that two roots exist for any equation with an even exponent (the only exception is when $b^2 = 0$, in which case b can equal only 0, and b^2 has only one root).

Another important point to remember on the SAT Subject Test Math 2 is that radicals only refer to *principal* roots. If you are taking the odd root of a number, the principal root is the sole root: $\sqrt[3]{8} = 2$ only and $\sqrt[3]{-8} = -2$ only. However, when you are taking the even root of a number, the principal root is the positive root. For example, 2 and –2 to the fourth power both equal 16. However, on the SAT Subject Test Math 2, $\sqrt[4]{16} = 2$ only.

When dealing with fractional exponents, keep in mind what they represent and how you would express them with a radical. The numerator of the exponent would become the exponent under the radical; therefore, a real base number raised to an exponent with an even numerator will always be positive, whereas a negative base number raised to an exponent with an odd numerator will remain negative and a positive base number raised to an exponent with an odd numerator will remain positive. For example, $(-4)^{\frac{2}{3}} = \sqrt[3]{(-4)^2} = \sqrt[3]{16}$ because -4^2 equals positive 16. However, $(-3)^{\frac{3}{5}} = \sqrt[5]{(-3)^3} = \sqrt[5]{-27}$ because $(-3)^3$ equals negative 27.

In addition, in a fractional exponent the denominator would be expressed as the radical, so if the denominator is even and the numerator is odd, then a negative base will be imaginary (as you will be taking the even root of a negative number). For example, $(-2)^{\frac{1}{2}} = \sqrt{-2} = i\sqrt{2}$. However, an even numerator will always result in a positive number (as discussed above) and therefore will NOT be imaginary. Furthermore, as you saw earlier, an odd denominator will always be real if the base is real, even if it is negative (since you can take the odd root of a negative number). For more information about imaginary numbers, see Chapter 12.

DRILL 8: EXPONENTS

In the following exercises, find the roots of the exponential expressions given. Specify whether each expression has no real roots, one real root, two real roots, or infinitely many real roots. The answers can be found in Part IV.

1. $b^3 = 27; b =$
2. $x^2 = 121; x =$
3. $n^5 = 32; n =$
4. $c^2 = 10; c =$
5. $x^4 = 81; x =$
6. $x^3 = -8; x =$
7. $d^6 = 729; d =$
8. $n^0 = 1$ (for $n \neq 0$); $n =$

Now try some multiple-choice questions. In the following exercises, expand the exponential expressions. Where the bases are numbers, find the numerical values of the expressions. The answers to these drills can be found in Part IV.

9. $4^{\frac{3}{2}} =$

   (A) 2.52
   (B) 3.64
   (C) 8.00
   (D) 16.00
   (E) 18.67

10. $x^{-\frac{3}{4}} =$

    (A) $-\sqrt[5]{x} \cdot x^4$

    (B) $-\dfrac{x^3}{x^4}$

    (C) $\dfrac{x^4}{x^3}$

    (D) $\dfrac{1}{\sqrt[4]{x^3}}$

    (E) $-\sqrt[4]{x^3}$

11. $\left(\dfrac{2}{3}\right)^{-2} =$

    (A) 2.25
    (B) 1.67
    (C) 0.44
    (D) −1.50
    (E) −0.44

12. $\left(\dfrac{1}{a}\right)^{-\frac{1}{3}} =$

(A) $-\dfrac{1}{\sqrt[3]{a}}$

(B) $\sqrt[-3]{a}$

(C) $\dfrac{1}{a^3}$

(D) $-a^3$

(E) $\sqrt[3]{a}$

13. $5^{\frac{2}{3}} =$

(A) 2.92
(B) 5.00
(C) 6.25
(D) 8.67
(E) 11.18

14. $\left(-\dfrac{5}{6}\right)^0 =$

(A) −1.2
(B) −0.8
(C) 0.0
(D) 1.0
(E) 1.2

Comprehensive Fundamentals Drill

The answers can be found in Part IV.

1. $\dfrac{\sqrt[3]{\sqrt{3}+4(2+\sqrt[3]{5})}}{\sqrt{49+3(2+9)}} =$

   (A) 0.281
   (B) 0.477
   (C) 0.528
   (D) 1.223
   (E) 1.496

2. If x and y are odd integers, which of the following must be even?

   (A) $\dfrac{x}{y}$

   (B) $\dfrac{x^2 y}{y}$

   (C) $\dfrac{x+y}{2}$

   (D) $x^{\frac{1}{2}} y^{\frac{1}{2}}$

   (E) $(x+1)(y-1)$

10. "The cube root of the sum of one-third m and n is the cube of one-third of the sum of m and n" is equivalent to which of the following?

    (A) $\dfrac{(m+n)^3}{3} = \sqrt[3]{\dfrac{m}{3}+n}$

    (B) $\left(\dfrac{m+n}{3}\right)^3 = \sqrt[3]{\dfrac{m}{3}+n}$

    (C) $\left(\dfrac{m+n}{3}\right)^3 = \dfrac{\sqrt[3]{m+n}}{3}$

    (D) $\dfrac{(m+n)^3}{3} = \dfrac{\sqrt[3]{m+n}}{3}$

    (E) $\left(\dfrac{m+n}{3}\right)^3 = \sqrt[3]{\dfrac{m+n}{3}}$

15. $\sqrt{x^3 y^5} \cdot \sqrt[3]{x^2 y} =$

    (A) $x^2 y^2 \sqrt[6]{xy^3}$

    (B) $x^2 y^2 \sqrt[6]{xy^5}$

    (C) $xy\sqrt[6]{x^2 y^5}$

    (D) $xy\sqrt[5]{y}$

    (E) $x^5 y^6 \sqrt[5]{xy}$

18. If the average of a, b, c, d, and e is 86, the average of a, b, and c is 84, and the average of c, d, and e is 82, what is the value of c ?

    (A) 68
    (B) 83
    (C) 85
    (D) 98
    (E) It cannot be determined from the information given.

20. If the surface area of cube A is x, and the surface area of cube B is $4x$, then the volume of cube B is what percent greater than the volume of cube A ?

    (A) $\dfrac{x}{100}\%$

    (B) $4x\%$

    (C) 400%

    (D) 700%

    (E) 800%

23. $\dfrac{x^4+3x^3}{2x^5+6x^4}+\dfrac{x^3y+2x^2y}{2x^4y+4x^3y}=$

(A) $x+y$

(B) x

(C) $\dfrac{1}{x}$

(D) $\dfrac{1}{2x}$

(E) $\dfrac{1}{x(x+y)}$

35. Paul buys a boat worth \$4,395. Every year, the boat loses 10% of its value. If x is an integer, what is the least value of x for which the boat is worth less than \$2,000 after x years?

(A) 1
(B) 5
(C) 7
(D) 8
(E) 9

37. If x, y, and z are consecutive negative integers, then which of the following COULD be false?

(A) $\dfrac{xyz}{2}$ is an integer.

(B) $\dfrac{xyz}{3}$ is an integer.

(C) $\dfrac{xyz}{4}$ is an integer.

(D) xyz is negative.

(E) $yz > x$

43. A gardener wishes to make 400 mL of a solution of plant food with a concentration of 45%. She will make the solution by mixing x mL of an 80% solution and y mL of a 30% solution. What is the value of x ?

(A) 30
(B) 70
(C) 120
(D) 180
(E) 320

45. If x is an integer greater than 3, the average of set A which contains x elements is y, and the average of 3 elements of set A is z, then what is the average of the other elements in set A ?

(A) $xy - 3z$

(B) $(xy - 3z)(x - 3)$

(C) $\dfrac{x}{y} - 3z$

(D) $\dfrac{x - 3z}{y}$

(E) $\dfrac{xy - 3z}{x - 3}$

Summary

o Many SAT Subject Test Math 2 questions require you to be comfortable with the definitions of various terms. If you don't know a term, make a flashcard and memorize it!

o Make sure you know PEMDAS and apply it to EVERY question with multiple operations! Functions questions in particular can be tricky with respect to order of operations!

o There are two formulas for percent change:
  • The basic formula for percent change is

$$\%\,\text{Change} = \frac{\text{Difference}}{\text{Original}} \times 100\%$$

  • The formula for repeated percent change is Final = Original × (1 ± Rate)$^{\text{# of changes}}$. If it's a repeated percent increase, you add Rate. If it's a decrease, you subtract Rate.

o If you have a question that asks for the average, mean, or arithmetic mean, use the Average Pie.

o Irrational numbers are numbers which CANNOT be simplified into a fraction using only integers. If you have a TI-80 series calculator, you can use MATH->FRAC whenever you want to know the fraction equivalent of a decimal.

o Remember the rules for exponents: MADSPM. Roots are the inverse operation of exponents; you can express roots either with the radical sign or with fractional exponents. You can use fractional exponents to combine terms with different roots.

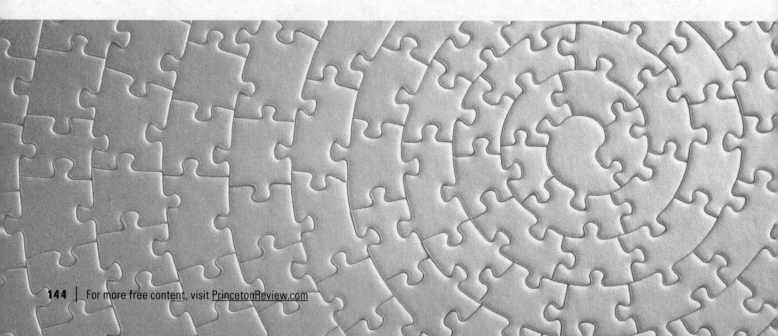

o   Special exponents:
  •   Any number, except 0, raised to the 0 power is 1.
  •   Raising a number to the first power does not change the number.
  •   A negative exponent means take the reciprocal of the number (divide 1 by the number), and then apply the exponent.
  •   Fractional exponents are a way of writing exponents and roots together: the top of the fraction is the exponent and the bottom of the fraction is the root.

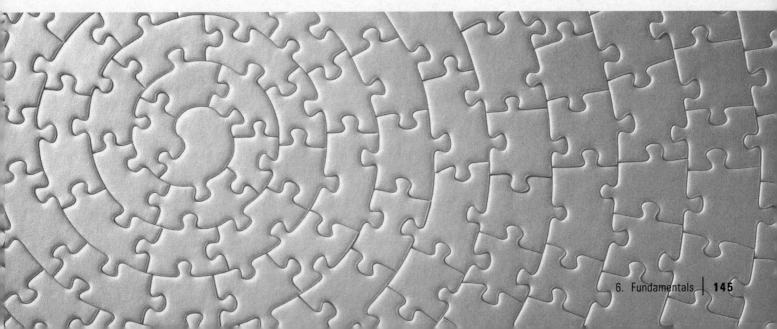

Chapter 7
Plane and Solid Geometry

Plane (2-dimensional) geometry is not directly tested on the SAT Subject Test Math 2. However, concepts from plane geometry are often important to answering questions, especially in solid and coordinate geometry, so it's important that you are comfortable and familiar with this material. Solid (3-dimensional) geometry is tested on approximately three questions on the SAT Subject Test Math 2. These questions can be tough to visualize at first, so practice and start drawing some figures!

DEFINITIONS

Here are some geometry definitions and symbols which appear on the SAT Subject Test Math 2. Be sure you know all of these; if you are not 100% comfortable with any of these, make flashcards and memorize them!

Line	A "line" in plane geometry is perfectly straight and extends infinitely in both directions. Line AB may be represented with $\overleftrightarrow{AB}$.
Line Segment	A line segment is a section of a line—still perfectly straight, but having limited length. It has two endpoints. Line segment AB may be represented with $\overline{AB}$.
Ray	A ray has one endpoint and extends infinitely in one direction. Ray AB may be represented with $\overrightarrow{AB}$.
Bisector	Any line that cuts a line segment, angle, or polygon exactly in half. It *bisects* another shape.
Midpoint	The point that divides a line segment into two equal halves.
Equidistant	Having equal distance from two different things.
Plane	A "plane" in plane geometry is a perfectly flat surface that extends infinitely in two dimensions.
Complementary Angles	Angles whose measures add up to 90 degrees.
Supplementary Angles	Angles whose measures add up to 180 degrees.
Straight Angle	An angle equal to 180 degrees; a straight line.
Parallel Lines	Lines that run in exactly the same direction—they are separated by a constant distance, never growing closer together or farther apart. Parallel lines never intersect. "Line AB is parallel to line BC" may be represented by the expression $\overleftrightarrow{AB} \parallel \overleftrightarrow{CD}$.
Perpendicular Lines	Lines which intersect at a 90 degree angle. Perpendicular lines AB and CD may be represented by the expression $\overleftrightarrow{AB} \perp \overleftrightarrow{CD}$.
Polygon	A flat shape formed by straight line segments, such as a rectangle or triangle.
Regular Polygon	A polygon that has all equal sides and angles. For example, equilateral triangles and squares are regular.
Triangle	A polygon with three sides. The sum of the angles of a triangle is 180 degrees.
Isosceles Triangle	A triangle with at least two equal sides. The angles opposite the equal sides are also equal.

Equilateral Triangle	A triangle with three equal sides and three equal angles. Each angle is equal to 60 degrees.
Right Triangle	A triangle with one 90 degree angle. The sides adjacent to the right angle are called legs, and the side opposite the right angle is known as the hypotenuse.
Similar Triangles	Triangles that have angles equal to one another. The corresponding sides of the triangles are proportional. For example, if $\Delta ABC \sim \Delta XYZ$, then $\dfrac{AB}{XY} = \dfrac{BC}{YZ} = \dfrac{AC}{XZ}$.
Quadrilateral	A four-sided polygon. The sum of the angles of a quadrilateral is 360 degrees.
Parallelogram	A quadrilateral that has opposite sides that are parallel and equal. Opposite angles of a parallelogram are equal, and the sum of any two adjacent angles is 180 degrees.
Rectangle	A parallelogram with four 90 degree angles. The diagonals of a rectangle are equal.
Square	A rectangle with four equal sides.
Trapezoid	A quadrilateral with two parallel sides.
Isosceles Trapezoid	A trapezoid in which the non-parallel sides are equal. The two angles adjacent to a parallel line are equal, and the two angles adjacent a non-parallel line add up to 180 degrees.
Altitude	A vertical line drawn from the polygon's base to the opposite vertex. Altitudes are always drawn perpendicular to the base.
Perimeter	The sum of the lengths of a polygon's sides.
Radius	A line segment extending from the center of a circle to a point on that circle.
Arc	A portion of a circle's edge. Arc AB may be represented with $\overarc{AB}$.
Chord	A line segment connecting two distinct points on a circle.
Sector	A portion of a circle's area between two radii, like a slice of pie.
Inscribed	A shape that is *inscribed* in another shape is placed inside that shape with the tightest possible fit. For example, a circle inscribed in a square is the largest circle that can be placed inside that square. The two shapes will touch at points, but they'll never overlap.

Circumscribed	A *circumscribed* shape is drawn around another shape with the tightest fit possible. For example, a circle circumscribed around a square is the smallest circle that can be drawn around that square. The two shapes will touch at points, but they'll never overlap.
Tangent	Something that is *tangent* to a curve touches that curve at only one point without crossing it. A shape may be "internally" or "externally" tangent to a curve, meaning that it may touch the inside or outside of the curve.
Central Angle (of a circle)	An angle at the center of the circle with each ray comprising a radius. The central angle is proportional to the arc and sector it creates: $$\frac{\text{central angle}}{360} = \frac{\text{arc length}}{\text{circumference}} = \frac{\text{sector area}}{\text{total area}}$$
Inscribed Angle (of a circle)	An angle formed by joining points A and B on a circle with point P, also on the circle. The angle measurement of $\angle APB$ will remain constant when point P moves within the arc AB. If $\overline{AB}$ is a diameter, then $\angle APB$ = 90 degrees. If $\overline{AP}$ = $\overline{BP}$ in a circle with center O, then central angle $\angle AOB = 2(\angle APB)$.
Tangent Line (to a circle)	A line that intersects the circle at exactly one point and is perpendicular to the radius. If $\overleftrightarrow{AC}$ is tangent to the circle with center O at point B, then $\overleftrightarrow{AC} \perp \overline{OB}$.

PLANE GEOMETRY FORMULAS

As discussed earlier, plane geometry is not directly tested on the SAT Subject Test Math 2. However, many solid and coordinate geometry questions require you to use plane geometry. Be sure you know the following formulas; make flashcards for the unknown or unfamiliar!

Parallel Lines Intersected by a Transversal	If you have two parallel lines intersected by a third line (known as a transversal), the following rules apply: all big angles are equal, all small angles are equal, and any big angle plus any small angle equals 180 degrees.
Sum of Angles in a Polygon	$180(s - 2)$, where s is the number of sides. Or, remember that a triangle has 180 degrees, and you add 180 degrees for each additional side.

Measure of Each Angle in a Regular Polygon	$\dfrac{180(s-2)}{s}$, where s is the number of sides.
Proportionality of Triangles	In any triangle, the largest side is opposite the largest angle, the middle side is opposite the middle angle, and the smallest side is opposite the smallest angle.
Third Side Rule	In any triangle, any side must be greater than the difference of the other two sides but less than the sum of those sides. For instance, in triangle $\triangle ABC$, if $\overline{AB}$ = 5 and $\overline{BC}$ = 7, then $2 < \overline{AC} < 12$.
Area of a Triangle	$\dfrac{1}{2}bh$, where b is perpendicular to h (not necessarily a side of the triangle OR within the triangle).
Area of a Triangle Using Trigonometry	$\dfrac{1}{2}ab\sin\theta$, where a and b are the sides of the triangle, and θ is the angle between a and b.
Area of an Equilateral Triangle	$\dfrac{s^2\sqrt{3}}{4}$
Pythagorean Theorem	$a^2 + b^2 = c^2$, where a and b are the legs of a right triangle, and c is the hypotenuse.
45-45-90 Right Triangle	Also known as an isosceles right triangle. If each leg is s, then the hypotenuse is $s\sqrt{2}$. Often tested as the diagonal of a square.
30-60-90 Right Triangle	If the side opposite the 30 degree angle is s, then the side opposite the 60 is $s\sqrt{3}$, and the hypotenuse is $2s$. Often used to find the height of an equilateral triangle.
Area of a Parallelogram	bh, where h is the height (which is a line segment perpendicular to the base) and b is the base.
Area of a Parallelogram Using Trigonometry	$ab\sin\theta$, where a and b are adjacent sides of the parallelogram, and θ is the angle in between a and b.
Area of a Rectangle	lw
Area of a Square	s^2
Area of a Square Using the Diagonal	$\dfrac{d^2}{2}$

Area of a Trapezoid	$\left(\dfrac{b_1 + b_2}{2}\right)h$, where b_1 and b_2 are the parallel sides, and h is the distance between the parallel sides. You can also break a trapezoid into a rectangle and two triangles if you forget the formula (but it's best to memorize!).
Circumference of a Circle	$2\pi r$ or πd
Area of a Circle	πr^2
CArd	Mnemonic for circle relationships: Circumference = $2\pi r$ or πd; Area = πr^2; radius = $\dfrac{d}{2}$; and diameter = $2r$.

PRISMS

Prisms are three-dimensional figures that have two parallel bases that are polygons. Cubes and rectangular solids are examples of prisms that the College Board often asks about. In general, the volume of a prism is given by the following formula:

> **Volume of a Prism**
>
> $V = Bh$

Area and Volume

In general, the volume of a shape involves the area of the base, often referred to as B, and the height, or h, of the solid.

In this formula, B represents the area of either base of the prism (the top or the bottom), and h represents the height of the prism (perpendicular to the base). The formulas for the volume of a rectangular solid, a cube, and a cylinder all come from this basic formula.

RECTANGULAR SOLIDS

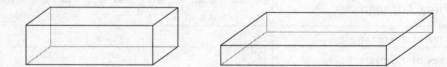

A rectangular solid is simply a box; the College Board also sometimes calls it a rectangular prism. It has three distinct dimensions: *length*, *width*, and *height*. The volume of a rectangular solid (the amount of space it contains) is given by this formula:

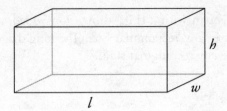

Volume of a Rectangular Solid

$$V = lwh$$

The surface area (*SA*) of a rectangular solid is the sum of the areas of all of its faces. A rectangular solid's surface area is given by the formula below.

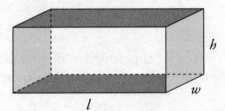

Surface Area of a Rectangular Solid

$$SA = 2lw + 2wh + 2lh$$

The volume and surface area of a solid make up the most basic information you can have about that solid (volume is tested more often than surface area). You may also be asked about *lengths* within a rectangular solid—edges and diagonals. The dimensions of the solid give the lengths of its edges, and the diagonal of any *face* of a rectangular solid can be found using the Pythagorean Theorem. There's one more length you may be asked about—the long diagonal (or space diagonal) that passes from corner to corner through the center of the box. The length of the long diagonal is given by this formula:

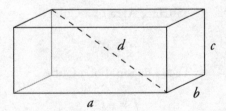

Long Diagonal of a Rectangular Solid (Super Pythagorean Theorem)

$$a^2 + b^2 + c^2 = d^2$$

This is the Pythagorean Theorem with a third dimension added, and it works just the same way. This formula will work in any rectangular box. The long diagonal is the longest straight line that can be drawn inside any rectangular solid.

CUBES

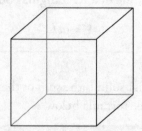

A cube is a rectangular solid that has the same length in all three dimensions. All six of its faces are squares. This simplifies the formulas for volume, surface area, and the long diagonal.

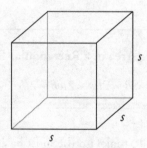

Volume of a Cube

$$V = s^3$$

Surface Area of a Cube

$$SA = 6s^2$$

Face Diagonal of a Cube

$$f = s\sqrt{2}$$

Long Diagonal of a Cube

$$d = s\sqrt{3}$$

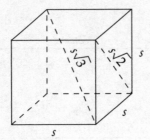

CYLINDERS

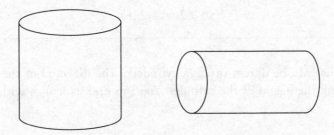

A cylinder is like a prism but with a circular base. It has two important dimensions—radius and height. Remember that volume is the area of the base times the height. In this case, the base is a circle. The area of a circle is πr^2. So the volume of a cylinder is $\pi r^2 h$.

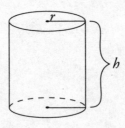

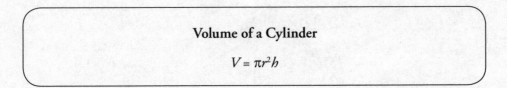

Volume of a Cylinder

$$V = \pi r^2 h$$

The surface area of a cylinder is found by adding the areas of the two circular bases to the area of the rectangle you'd get if you unrolled the side of the cylinder. That boils down to the following formula:

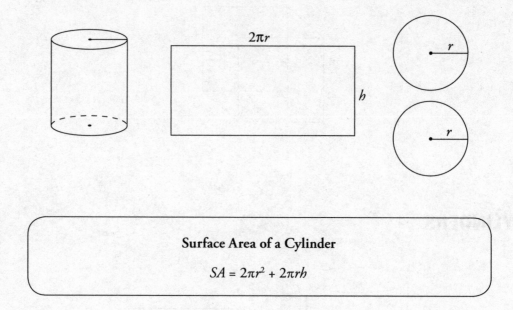

Surface Area of a Cylinder

$$SA = 2\pi r^2 + 2\pi rh$$

The longest line that can be drawn inside a cylinder is the diagonal of the rectangle formed by the diameter and the height of the cylinder. You can find its length with the Pythagorean Theorem.

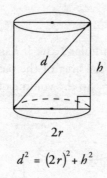

$$d^2 = (2r)^2 + h^2$$

CONES

If you take a cylinder and shrink one of its circular bases down to a point, then you have a cone. A cone has three significant dimensions which form a right triangle—its radius, its height, and its *slant height,* which is the straight-line distance from the tip of the cone to a point on the edge of its base. The formulas for the volume and surface area of a cone are given in the information box at the beginning of the SAT Subject Test Math 2. The formula for the volume of a cone is pretty straightforward.

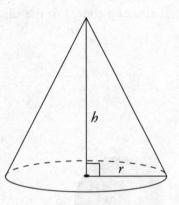

> ### Volume of a Cone
>
> $$V = \frac{1}{3}\pi r^2 h$$

But you have to be careful computing *surface area* for a cone using the formula provided by the College Board. The formula at the beginning of the SAT Subject Test Math 2 is for the *lateral area* of a cone—the area of the sloping sides—not the complete surface area. It doesn't include the circular base. Here's a more useful equation for the surface area of a cone.

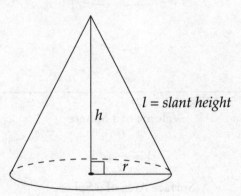

Connect the Dots
Notice that the volume of a cone is just one-third of the volume of a circular cylinder. Make memorizing easy!

Surface Area of a Cone

$$SA = \pi r l + \pi r^2$$

If you want to calculate only the lateral area of a cone, just use the first half of the above formula—leave the πr^2 off.

SPHERES

A sphere is simply a hollow ball. It can be defined as all of the points in space at a fixed distance from a central point. The one important measure in a sphere is its radius. The formulas for the volume and surface area of a sphere are given to you at the very beginning of the SAT Subject Test Math 2. That means that you don't need to have them memorized, but here they are anyway:

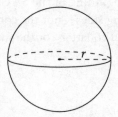

Volume of a Sphere

$$V = \frac{4}{3}\pi r^3$$

Surface Area of a Sphere

$$SA = 4\pi r^2$$

The intersection of a plane and a sphere always forms a circle unless the plane is *tangent* to the sphere, in which case the plane and sphere touch at only one point.

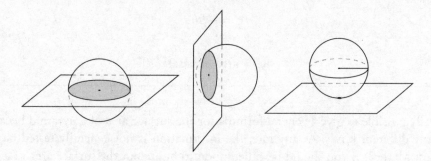

PYRAMIDS

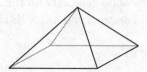

A pyramid is a little like a cone, except that its base is a polygon instead of a circle. Pyramids don't show up often on the SAT Subject Test Math 2. When you do run into a pyramid, it will almost always have a rectangular base. Pyramids can be pretty complicated solids, but for the purposes of this test, a pyramid has just two important measures—the area of its base and its height. The height of a pyramid is the length of a line drawn straight down from the pyramid's tip to its base. The height is perpendicular to the base. The volume of a pyramid is given by this formula.

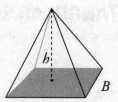

> **Connect the Dots**
> Notice that the volume of a pyramid is just one-third of the volume of a prism. Make memorizing easy!

Volume of a Pyramid

$$V = \frac{1}{3} Bh$$

(B = area of base)

It's not really possible to give a general formula for the surface area of a pyramid because there are so many different kinds. At any rate, the information is not generally tested on the SAT Subject Test Math 2. If you should be called upon to figure out the surface area of a pyramid, just figure out the area of each face using polygon rules, and add them up.

TRICKS OF THE TRADE

Here are some common ways the College Board likes to use solid geometry on the SAT Subject Test Math 2. As you will see, many of these questions test concepts you know (including plane geometry!) in unfamiliar ways.

Triangles in Rectangular Solids

Many questions about rectangular solids are actually testing triangle rules. Such questions generally ask for the lengths of the diagonals of a box's faces, the long diagonal of a box, or other lengths. These questions are usually solved using the Pythagorean Theorem and the Super Pythagorean Theorem that finds a box's long diagonal (see the section on Rectangular Solids).

DRILL 1: TRIANGLES IN RECTANGULAR SOLIDS

Here are some practice questions using triangle rules in rectangular solids. The answers can be found in Part IV.

17. What is the length of the longest line that can be drawn in a cube of volume 27 ?

    (A) 3.0
    (B) 4.2
    (C) 4.9
    (D) 5.2
    (E) 9.0

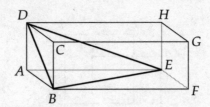

22. In the rectangular solid shown, if $AB = 4$, $BC = 3$, and $BF = 12$, what is the perimeter of triangle EDB ?

    (A) 27.33
    (B) 28.40
    (C) 29.20
    (D) 29.50
    (E) 30.02

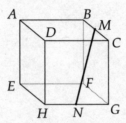

25. In the cube above, M is the midpoint of BC, and N is the mid-point of GH. If the cube has a volume of 1, what is the length of MN ?

    (A) 1.23
    (B) 1.36
    (C) 1.41
    (D) 1.73
    (E) 1.89

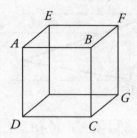

41. In the cube shown above with side length s, what is the area of the plane inside the cube defined by D, E, and G?

(A) $s^2\sqrt{3}$

(B) $\dfrac{s^2\sqrt{3}}{2}$

(C) $\dfrac{s^2\sqrt{3}}{4}$

(D) s^2

(E) $\dfrac{s^2}{2}$

Volume Questions

Many solid geometry questions test your understanding of the relationship between a solid's volume and its other dimensions—sometimes including the solid's surface area. To solve these questions, just plug the numbers you're given into the solid's volume formula.

DRILL 2: VOLUME

Try the following practice questions. The answers can be found in Part IV.

1. The volume and surface area of a cube are equal. What is the length of an edge of this cube?
   (A) 1
   (B) 2
   (C) 4
   (D) 6
   (E) 9

2. A cube has a surface area of $6x$. What is the volume of the cube?

(A) $x^{\frac{2}{3}}$

(B) $x^{\frac{3}{2}}$

(C) $6x^2$

(D) $36x^2$

(E) x^3

10. A rectangular solid has a volume of 30, and its edges have integer lengths. What is the greatest possible surface area of this solid?

(A) 62
(B) 82
(C) 86
(D) 94
(E) 122

15. The water in Allegra's swimming pool has a depth of 7 feet. If the area of the pentagonal base of the pool is 150 square feet, then what is the volume, in cubic feet, of the water in her pool?

(A)   57
(B)   50
(C) 1,050
(D) 5,250
(E) It cannot be determined from the information given.

26. A sphere has a radius of r. If this radius is increased by b, then the surface area of the sphere is increased by what amount?

(A) b^2
(B) $4\pi b^2$
(C) $8\pi rb + 4\pi b^2$
(D) $8\pi rb + 2rb + b^2$
(E) $4\pi r^2 b^2$

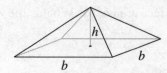

35. If the pyramid shown has a square base with edges of length b, and $b = 2h$, then which of the following is the volume of the pyramid?

    (A) $\dfrac{h^3}{3}$

    (B) $\dfrac{4h^3}{3}$

    (C) $4h^3$

    (D) $8h^2 - h$

    (E) $\dfrac{8h^3 - 4h}{3}$

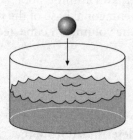

42. A sphere of radius 1 is totally submerged in a cylindrical tank of radius 4, as shown. The water level in the tank rises a distance of h. What is the value of h ?

    (A) 0.072
    (B) 0.083
    (C) 0.096
    (D) 0.108
    (E) 0.123

Inscribed Solids

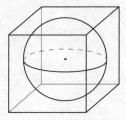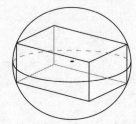

Some questions on the SAT Subject Test Math 2 will be based on spheres inscribed in cubes or cubes inscribed in spheres (these are the most popular inscribed shapes). Occasionally you may also see a rectangular solid inscribed in a sphere, or a cylinder inscribed in a rectangular box, etc. The trick to these questions is always figuring out how to get from the dimensions of one of the solids to the dimensions of the other.

Following are a few basic tips that can speed up your work on inscribed solids questions.

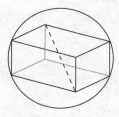

- When a cube or rectangular solid is inscribed in a sphere, the long diagonal of that solid is equal to the diameter of the sphere.

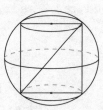

- When a cylinder is inscribed in a sphere, the sphere's diameter is equal to the diagonal of the rectangle formed by the cylinder's heights and diameter.

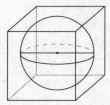

- When a sphere is inscribed in a cube, the diameter of the sphere is equal to the length of the cube's edge.

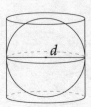

- If a sphere is inscribed in a cylinder, both solids have the same diameter.

Most inscribed solids questions fall into one of the preceding categories. If you run into a situation not covered by these tips, just look for the way to get from the dimensions of the inner shape to those of the external shape, or vice versa.

DRILL 3: INSCRIBED SOLIDS

Here are some practice inscribed solids questions. The answers can be found in Part IV.

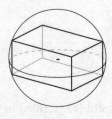

17. A rectangular solid is inscribed in a sphere as shown. If the dimensions of the solid are 3, 4, and 6, then what is the radius of the sphere?

    (A) 2.49
    (B) 3.91
    (C) 4.16
    (D) 5.62
    (E) 7.81

19. A cylinder is inscribed in a cube with an edge of length 2. What volume of space is enclosed by the cube but not by the cylinder?

    (A) 1.41
    (B) 1.56
    (C) 1.72
    (D) 3.81
    (E) 4.86

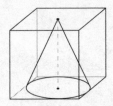

25. A cone is inscribed in a cube of volume 1 in such a way that its base is inscribed in one face of the cube. What is the volume of the cone?

    (A) 0.21
    (B) 0.26
    (C) 0.33
    (D) 0.42
    (E) 0.67

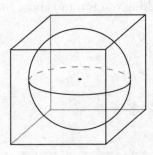

37. Cube *A* has a volume of 1,000. Sphere *S* is inscribed inside Cube *A*. Cube *B* (not shown) is inscribed inside Sphere *S*. What is the surface area of Cube *B* ?

    (A)   5.774
    (B)   33.333
    (C) 192.450
    (D) 200
    (E) 600

Solids Produced by Rotation

Three types of solids can be produced by the rotation of simple two-dimensional shapes—spheres, cylinders, and cones. Questions about solids produced by rotation are generally fairly simple; they usually test your ability to visualize the solid generated by the rotation of a flat shape. Sometimes, rotated solids questions begin with a shape in the coordinate plane—that is, rotated around one of the axes or some other line. Practice will help you figure out the dimensions of the solid from the dimensions of the original flat shape.

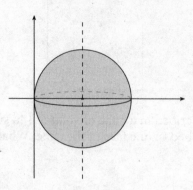

A sphere is produced when a circle is rotated around its diameter. This is an easy situation to work with, as the sphere and the original circle will have the same radius. Find the radius of the circle, and you can figure out anything you want to about the sphere.

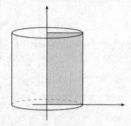

A cylinder is formed by the rotation of a rectangle around a central line *or* one edge.

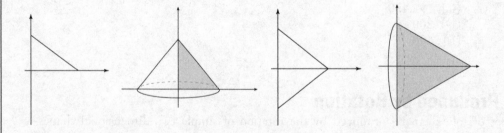

A cone is formed by rotating a right triangle around one of its legs (think of it as spinning the triangle) or by rotating an isosceles triangle around its axis of symmetry. Another way of thinking about it is if you spun the triangle in the first figure above around the *y*-axis (so you're rotating around the leg that's sitting on the *y*-axis) you would get the second figure. Likewise, if you spun the third figure above around the *x*-axis (so you're rotating around the axis of symmetry), you would end up with the fourth figure.

DRILL 4: ROTATIONAL SOLIDS

Try these rotated solids questions for practice. The answers can be found in Part IV.

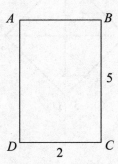

19. What is the volume of the solid generated by rotating rectangle *ABCD* around *AD* ?

    (A) 15.7
    (B) 31.4
    (C) 62.8
    (D) 72.0
    (E) 80.0

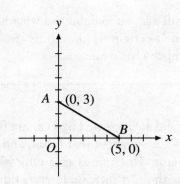

29. If the triangle created by *OAB* is rotated around the *x*-axis, what is the volume of the generated solid?

    (A) 15.70
    (B) 33.33
    (C) 40.00
    (D) 47.12
    (E) 78.54

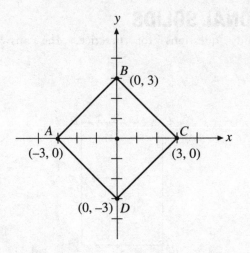

40. What is the volume generated by rotating square *ABCD* around the *y*-axis?

    (A) 24.84
    (B) 28.27
    (C) 42.66
    (D) 56.55
    (E) 84.82

Changing Dimensions

Some solid geometry questions will ask you to figure out what happens to the volume of a solid if all of its lengths are increased by a certain factor or if its area doubles, and so on. To answer questions of this type, just remember a basic rule.

> When the lengths of a solid are increased by a certain factor, the surface area of the solid increases by the square of that factor, and the volume increases by the cube of that factor. This rule is true only when the solid's shape doesn't change—its length must increase in *every* dimension, not just one. For that reason, cubes and spheres are most often used for this type of question because their shapes are constant.

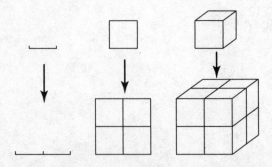

In the illustration on the previous page, a length is doubled, which means that the corresponding area is 4 times as great, and the volume is 8 times as great. If the length had been tripled, the area would have increased by a factor of 9, and the volume by a factor of 27.

DRILL 5: CHANGING DIMENSIONS

Try these practice questions. The answers can be found in Part IV.

3. If the radius of sphere A is one-third as long as the radius of sphere B, then the volume of sphere A is what fraction of the volume of sphere B ?

(A) $\dfrac{1}{3}$

(B) $\dfrac{1}{4}$

(C) $\dfrac{1}{9}$

(D) $\dfrac{1}{12}$

(E) $\dfrac{1}{27}$

5. A rectangular solid with length l, width w, and height h has a volume of 24. What is the volume of a rectangular solid with length $\dfrac{l}{2}$, width $\dfrac{w}{2}$, and height $\dfrac{h}{2}$?

(A) 18
(B) 12
(C) 6
(D) 3
(E) 2

10. If the surface area of a cube is increased by a factor of 2.25, then its volume is increased by what factor?

(A) 1.72
(B) 3.38
(C) 4.50
(D) 5.06
(E) 5.64

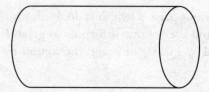

33. The volume of the cylinder shown above is x. If the radius of the cylinder is doubled and the height is halved, then which of the following is the volume of the new cylinder?

(A) $\dfrac{x}{2}$

(B) x

(C) $2x$

(D) x^2

(E) $\dfrac{x^2}{2}$

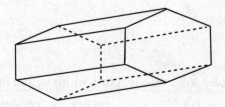

46. In the regular hexagonal prism shown above, if the lengths and widths of the rectangular faces were doubled and the hexagonal faces changed accordingly, then the resulting volume would be how many times the original volume?

(A) 64
(B) 32
(C) 8
(D) 4
(E) 2

Comprehensive Plane and Solid Geometry Drill

The answers can be found in Part IV.

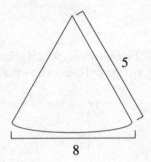

3. What is the volume of the cone above?

   (A) 50.265
   (B) 83.776
   (C) 150.796
   (D) 201.062
   (E) 251.327

14. A square has vertices (0, 3), (6, 0), (3, 9), and (9, 6). If the coordinates of all points are tripled, then the area of the resulting square is how many times greater than the original?

    (A) 1.732
    (B) 3
    (C) 6
    (D) 9
    (E) 27

19. An equilateral triangle is located in the coordinate plane with vertices (3, 3), (3, 9) and (8.169, 6). Which of the following could be a fourth point added to the triangle to create a parallelogram?

    I.   (8.196, 12)
    II. (8.196, 0)
    III. (−2.196, 6)

    (A) I only
    (B) I and II only
    (C) II only
    (D) II and III only
    (E) I, II, and III

25. A prism has hexagonal bases and 6 rectangular sides. How many edges does this prism have?

    (A) 6
    (B) 12
    (C) 18
    (D) 19
    (E) 24

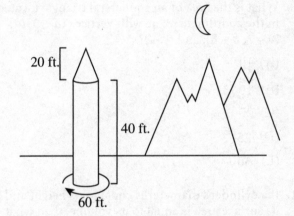

26. A wizard's tower (shown above) is comprised of a cylinder 40 feet high and 60 feet around topped with a cone of the same circumference that is 20 feet high. If the wizard's tower is to be painted with a paint which covers 100 square feet per gallon, how many gallons of paint will be required to paint the tower?

    (A)   6.649
    (B)   24.000
    (C)   30.649
    (D) 113.097
    (E) 664.884

32. A sphere and a cone have equal volumes. If the radius of the sphere is x, the radius of the cone is y, and the height of the cone is x, then what is the value of x?

(A) $\dfrac{y}{2}$

(B) $\dfrac{y^2}{2}$

(C) y

(D) $2y$

(E) $\sqrt{y}$

38. What is the area of an equilateral triangle located in the coordinate plane with vertices $(a + 3, b)$, $(a - 3, b + 8)$, and (c, d)?

(A) 10

(B) $10\sqrt{3}$

(C) 25

(D) $25\sqrt{3}$

(E) $50\sqrt{3}$

41. If a cylinder's diameter is equal to its height and its surface area is equal to its volume, then what is the greatest distance between two points within the cylinder?

(A) 3

(B) $3\sqrt{2}$

(C) 6

(D) $6\sqrt{2}$

(E) It cannot be determined from the information given.

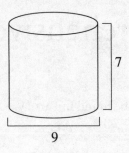

45. Which of the following, when rotated around AB, would create the cylinder shown above?

(A)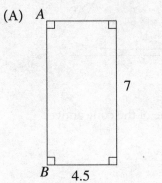

(B)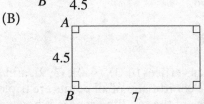

(C)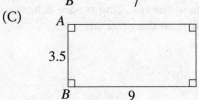

(D)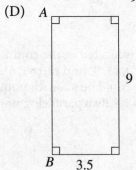

(E)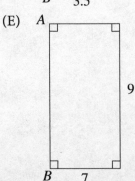

48. A parallelogram is located in the polar coordinate system with vertices $(0, 0)$, $(2, \frac{\pi}{6})$, $(4, 0)$, and (r, θ). What is the area of the parallelogram?

    (A) 0.073
    (B) 4
    (C) 4.619
    (D) 5.819
    (E) 6.928

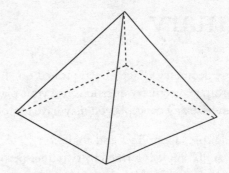

50. The pyramid above has a square base. If each edge of the pyramid is s, then what is the height of the pyramid?

    (A) $\dfrac{s\sqrt{2}}{2}$

    (B) $s\sqrt{2}$

    (C) s

    (D) $\dfrac{s^2}{2}$

    (E) $\dfrac{\sqrt{s}}{2}$

Summary

○ Plane geometry is not directly tested on the SAT Subject Test Math 2. However, many solid and coordinate geometry questions test your plane geometry knowledge, so make sure you work on and memorize any concepts you may have forgotten!

○ Some rules about lines and angles:
- A 90° angle is formed by two lines perpendicular to each other.
- There are 180° in a line.
- When two straight lines intersect, the angles created opposite each other are equal. The adjacent angles (two angles beside each other along the same straight line) have a sum of 180°.

○ When parallel lines are transected by a third line, big angles and small angles are created. All the big angles are equal, all the small angles are equal, and a big plus a small equals 180°.

○ Some rules about triangles:
- The sum of the angles in a triangle is 180°.
- The longest side of a triangle is across from the largest angle. The smallest side of a triangle is across from the smallest angle. Equal sides are across from equal angles.
- Isosceles triangles have at least two equal sides and two equal angles. Equilateral triangles have three equal sides and three equal angles.
- The third side rule states that the length of any side of a triangle must be between the sum and the difference of the other two sides.
- The area of a triangle is $A = \dfrac{1}{2}bh$. The height must be perpendicular to the base.

○ The area of a triangle may also be found using $A = \dfrac{1}{2}ab\sin\theta$, where a and b are the measures of two side lengths and θ is the angle between those sides.

○ Right triangles are triangles with one 90° angle. The Pythagorean Theorem states that, in a right triangle, $a^2 + b^2 = c^2$, where c is the hypotenuse of the triangle and a and b are the two legs.

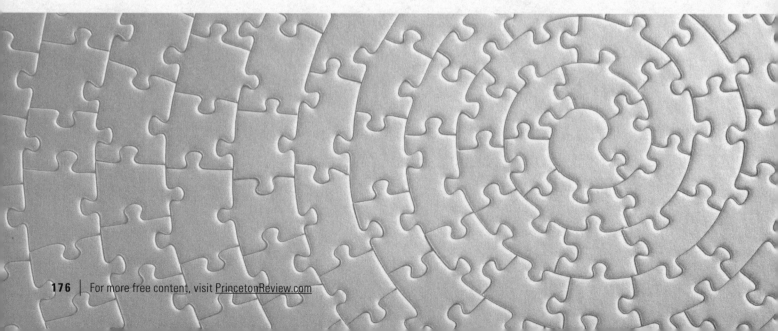

o Special right triangles are helpful in simplifying the math. They often provide an easier route to the correct solution than using the Pythagorean Theorem, so look closely for opportunities to use them. The following is a list of special right triangles:

- There are some Pythagorean triplets that are helpful to commit to memory. They are 3:4:5, 5:12:13, 7:24:25, and any multiples of these as well.

- The sides of a 45°-45°-90° triangle have a very specific ratio: $x : x : x\sqrt{2}$, where x is the length of each leg.

- The sides of a 30°-60°-90° triangle have a very specific ratio: $x : x\sqrt{3} : 2x$, where x is the length of the shorter leg.

o Similar triangles have the same angle measures. The corresponding sides and heights of similar triangles are proportional.

o Quadrilaterals are four-sided figures. The sum of the angles in a quadrilateral is 360°.

- Parallelograms have two sets of equal, parallel lines. The area of a parallelogram is $A = bh$, where the base is perpendicular to the height.

- You can also find the area of a parallelogram using $A = ab \sin \theta$, where a and b are the measures of two adjacent sides and θ is the measure of an angle of the parallelogram.

- Rectangles are parallelograms with four right angles.

- Squares are rectangles with four equal sides.

- Trapezoids are four-sided figures whose top and bottom are parallel but different in length. The area of a trapezoid is $A = \left(\dfrac{b_1 + b_2}{2} \right) h$, where b_1 is one base and b_2 is the other.

o The sum of the angles of an n-sided polygon is $(n - 2) \times 180°$.

o Here are some things to remember about a circle:

- A circle contains a total of 360°.

- The radius is the distance from the center of the circle to any point on the circle.

- The diameter is a straight line drawn from one point on a circle through the center to another. Its length is twice the radius.

- The circumference of the circle is the distance around the circle. You can think of it as the perimeter of the circle. Its formula is $C = \pi d$. You may also know it as $C = 2\pi r$.

- The formula for the area of a circle is $A = \pi r^2$.

- A sector is a slice of pie of the circle. The part of the circumference that the sector contains is called an arc and is in the same proportion to the circumference as the angle of the sector is to 360°.
- A central angle is an angle whose vertex is the center of the circle. An inscribed angle has its vertex on the circle and its two endpoints on the circle. Its angle is half of what the central angle is to those same two endpoints.
- Any angle inscribed in a semicircle is a right angle.
- A line tangent to the circle touches the circle in only one place and is always perpendicular to the radius drawn to the point of tangency.

○ For the purposes of the SAT Subject Test Math 2, prisms are 3-dimensional figures with two equal, parallel bases. The bases can be any shape from plane geometry.

○ The volume of a prism is the area of the base, often referred to as B, times the height, h.

○ Let's talk rectangular prisms:
- The formula for the volume of a rectangular prism is $V = lwh$.
- The formula for the surface area of a rectangular solid is $SA = 2lw + 2wh + 2lh$. Think about painting the outside of the figure. Find the area of each side.
- The Super Pythagorean Theorem, which is helpful in solving questions about the diagonal of a rectangular prism, is $a^2 + b^2 + c^2 = d^2$.

○ Let's talk cubes. Remember that a cube is just a rectangular prism whose length, width, and height are equal. If you forget a formula, just use the rectangular prism formula!
- The volume of a cube is $V = s^3$.
- The surface area of a rectangular solid is $SA = 6s^2$.

○ Let's talk cylinders. A cylinder is a prism whose bases are circles.
- The volume of a cylinder is $V = \pi r^2 h$.
- The surface area of a rectangular solid is $SA = 2\pi r^2 + 2\pi rh$. If you forget this, remember that you're just painting the outside. So you'll need the area of two circles and the area of the other piece, which, when rolled out (like a roll of paper towels), is a rectangle whose sides are the circumference of the circle and the height.

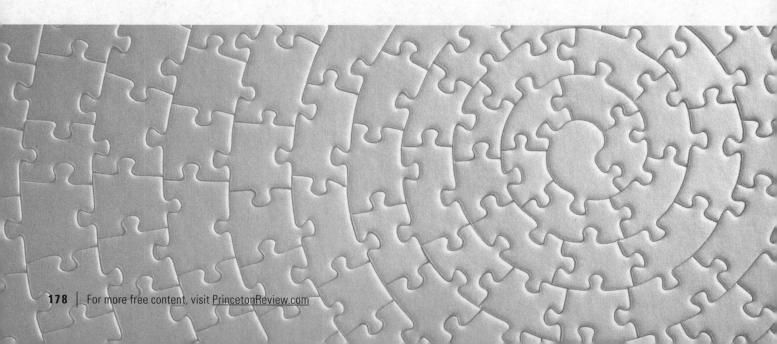

o   A cone is similar to a cylinder except that one of its bases is merely a point.

- The formula for the volume of a cone is $V = \dfrac{1}{3}\pi r^2 h$, where the height must be perpendicular to the base.

- The formula for the surface area of a cone is $SA = \pi r l + \pi r^2$, where l is the slant height.

o   A sphere is a hollow ball.

- The formula for the volume of a sphere is $V = \dfrac{4}{3}\pi r^3$.

- The formula for the surface area of a cone is $SA = 4\pi r^2$.

o   Pyramids are like cones, but the base is a plane geometry shape. The formula for the volume of a pyramid is $V = \dfrac{1}{3}Bh$.

o   Inscribed figures always have a line or curve that connects the inner figure to the outer figure.

o   Questions about solids produced by rotation usually test your ability to visualize the solid created by the rotation of a flat shape.

Chapter 8
Coordinate
Geometry

About 6 questions on the SAT Subject Test Math 2 will deal with coordinate geometry. Topics range from simple lines, distance, and midpoints to hyperbolas and three-dimensional, spatial coordinate geometry. This chapter will cover all the formulas and concepts you will need to know in order to tackle these problems.

DEFINITIONS

Here are some geometry terms that appear on the SAT Subject Test Math 2. Make sure you're familiar with them. If the meaning of any of these vocabulary words keeps slipping your mind, add that word to your flash cards.

Coordinate Plane	A system of two perpendicular axes used to describe the position of a point using a pair of coordinates—also called the *rectangular coordinate system* or the *Cartesian plane*.
Slope	For a straight line, the ratio of vertical change to horizontal change.
***x*-axis**	The horizontal axis of the coordinate plane.
***y*-axis**	The vertical axis of the coordinate plane.
Origin	The intersection of the *x*- and *y*-axes, with coordinates $(0, 0)$.
***x*-intercept**	The *x*-coordinate of the point at which a line or other function intersects the *x*-axis. These values are also known as *zeros, roots,* or *solutions.* At the *x*-intercept, $y = 0$.
***y*-intercept**	The *y*-coordinate of the point at which a line or other function intersects the *y*-axis. At the *y*-intercept, $x = 0$.

THE COORDINATE PLANE

> **The Coordinate Plane**
>
> The coordinate plane is a perfectly flat surface that extends an infinite distance in two dimensions. Oh, and it doesn't exist. It's just an abstract idea, a way of seeing mathematical relationships visually.

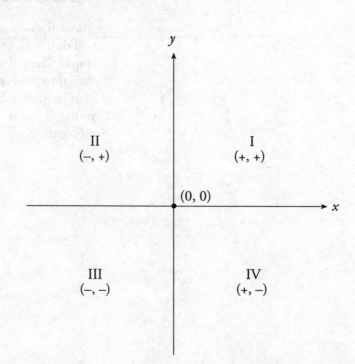

As you recall from school, the coordinate plane has two perpendicular axes, the (horizontal) *x*-axis and the (vertical) *y*-axis. The intersection of the axes is the origin, which has coordinates (0, 0). *Coordinates* show the placement of a point on the plane. The *x*-coordinate measures horizontal distance from the *y*-axis; positive values are to the right of the *y*-axis, whereas negative values are to the left. Similarly, the *y*-coordinate measures distance from the *x*-axis: positive values are above the *x*-axis, negative values below. By convention, coordinates are given in the form (*x*, *y*).

The axes also divide the coordinate plane into four quadrants. Quadrant I is the upper-right quadrant (where both the *x*- and *y*-coordinates are positive), and the quadrants are numbered counter-clockwise from quadrant I.

DRILL 1: THE COORDINATE PLANE

On the coordinate plane below, match each coordinate pair to the corresponding point on the graph and identify the quadrant in which the point is located. The answers can be found in Part IV.

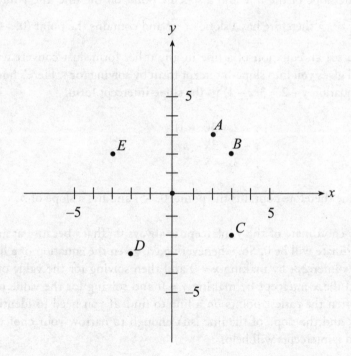

1. (–3, 2) Point _____, Quadrant _____
2. (2, 3)   Point _____, Quadrant _____
3. (3, –2) Point _____, Quadrant _____
4. (–2, –3) Point _____, Quadrant _____
5. (3, 2)   Point _____, Quadrant _____

THE EQUATION OF A LINE

While most coordinate geometry questions on the SAT Subject Test Math 2 involve more complicated functions, some questions will require you to know the equation of a line. The most common form in which the equation of a line appears on the SAT Subject Test Math 2 is the slope-intercept form.

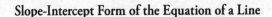

> **Slope-Intercept Form of the Equation of a Line**
>
> $$y = mx + b$$

This equation is probably an old friend. To recap, m and b are constants: m is the slope (discussed in the next section) and b is the y-intercept.

When a linear equation is in standard form, $Ax + By = C$, you won't need to convert to slope-intercept form to find the slope or y-intercept. The slope will be $-\dfrac{A}{B}$ and the y-intercept will be $\dfrac{C}{B}$.

An equation in this form might look like: $y = \dfrac{2}{3}x - 4$. So $m = \dfrac{2}{3}$ and $b = -4$.

Let's talk a little about the y-intercept. This is the y-coordinate of the point at which the line intersects the y-axis. So, the slope-intercept formula of a line gives you the slope of the line and a specific point on the line, the y-intercept. The line $y = \dfrac{2}{3}x - 4$ therefore has a slope of $\dfrac{2}{3}$ and contains the point $(0, -4)$.

If you see an equation of a line in any other form, just convert what the College Board gives you into slope-intercept form by solving for y. Here's how you'd convert the equation $y + 2 = 3(x - 1)$ to the slope-intercept form.

$$y + 2 = 3(x - 1)$$
$$y + 2 = 3x - 3$$
$$y = 3x - 5$$

The line therefore contains the point $(0, -5)$ and has a slope of 3.

Notice that the x-coordinate of the y-intercept is always 0. That's because at any point on the y-axis, the x-coordinate will be 0. So, whenever you're given the equation of a line in any form, you can find the y-intercept by making $x = 0$ and then solving for the value of y. In the same way, you can find the x-intercept by making $y = 0$ and solving for the value of x. The x- and y-intercepts are often the easiest points on a line to find. If you need to identify the graph of a linear equation, and the slope of the line isn't enough to narrow your choices down to one, finding the x- and y-intercepts will help.

To graph a line, simply plug a couple of x-values into the equation of the line, and plot the coordinates that result. The y-intercept is generally the easiest point to plot. Often, the y-intercept and the slope are enough to graph a line accurately enough or to identify the graph of a line.

DRILL 2: THE EQUATION OF A LINE

Try the following practice questions. The answers can be found in Part IV.

1. If a line of slope 0.6 contains the point (3, 1), then it must also contain which of the following points?

   (A) (−2, −2)
   (B) (−1, −4)
   (C) (0, 0)
   (D) (2, −1)
   (E) (3, 4)

2. The line $y - 1 = 5(x - 1)$ contains the point $(0, n)$. What is the value of n ?

   (A) 0
   (B) −1
   (C) −2
   (D) −3
   (E) −4

4. What is the slope of the line whose equation is $2y - 13 = -6x - 5$?

   (A) −5
   (B) −3
   (C) −2
   (D) 0
   (E) 3

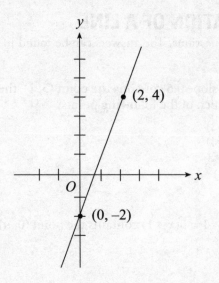

6. If the line $y = mx + b$ is graphed above, then which of the following statements is true?

    (A) $m < b$

    (B) $m = b$

    (C) $2m = 3b$

    (D) $2m + 3b = 0$

    (E) $m = \dfrac{2b}{3}$

Slope

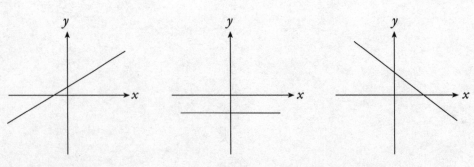

Figure 1   Figure 2   Figure 3

Often, slope is all you need to match the equation of a line to its graph. To begin with, it's easy to distinguish positive slopes from negative slopes. A line with a positive slope is shown in Figure 1 above; it goes uphill from left to right. A line with zero slope is shown in Figure 2; it's horizontal, and neither rises nor falls. A line with a negative slope is shown in Figure 3; it goes downhill from left to right.

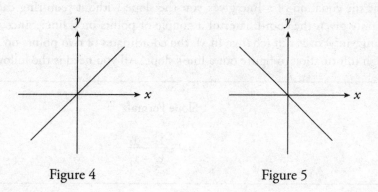

Figure 4   Figure 5

A line with a slope of 1 rises at a 45° angle, as shown in Figure 4. A line with a slope of −1 falls at a 45° angle, as shown in Figure 5.

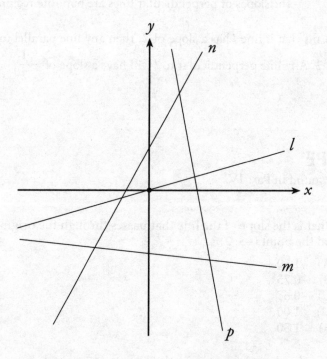

Because a line with a slope of 1 or −1 forms a 45° angle with either axis, you can figure out even more about a line's slope by comparing that line's slope to a 45° angle. Lines that are closer to horizontal have fractional slopes. Lines that are closer to vertical have slopes greater than 1 or less than −1. On the graph above, for example, line *l* has a positive fractional slope. Line *m* has a negative fractional slope. Line *n* has a positive slope greater than 1. Line *p* has a negative slope less than −1. Estimating slope can be a valuable time-saver.

You Have Two Points, You Have It All!
Using the slope formula, you can figure out the slope of any line given only two points on that line—which means that you can figure out the complete equation of the line. Just find the line's slope and plug the slope and one point's coordinates into the point-slope equation of a line.

Remember that the equation of a line gives you the slope without requiring calculation. But what if you're only given the coordinates of a couple of points on a line? Since the slope of a line is rise (change in *y*) over run (change in *x*), the coordinates of two points on a line provide you with enough information to figure out a line's slope. All you need is the following formula:

> **Slope Formula**
>
> $$m = \frac{y_2 - y_1}{x_2 - x_1}$$

Slopes can also help you determine the relationship between lines in a coordinate plane.

Flip It!
Opposite reciprocal means flip the number over and reverse the sign.

- The slopes of parallel lines are identical.
- The slopes of perpendicular lines are opposite reciprocals.

That means that if line *l* has a slope of 2, then any line parallel to *l* will also have a slope of 2. Any line perpendicular to *l* will have a slope of $-\frac{1}{2}$.

DRILL 3: SLOPE

The answers can be found in Part IV.

1. What is the slope of the line that passes through the origin and the point (−3, 2) ?

   (A) −1.50
   (B) −0.75
   (C) −0.67
   (D) 1.00
   (E) 1.50

5. Lines *l* and *m* are perpendicular lines that intersect at the origin. If line *l* passes through the point (2, −1), then line *m* must pass through which of the following points?

   (A) (0, 2)
   (B) (1, 3)
   (C) (2, 1)
   (D) (3, 6)
   (E) (4, 0)

13. Which of the following could be the graph of
    $2(y + 1) = -6(x - 2)$?

(A)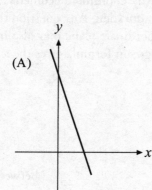

(B)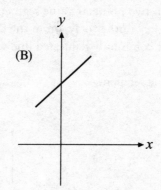

(C)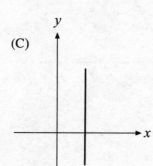

(D)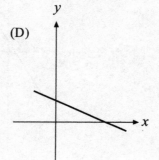

(E)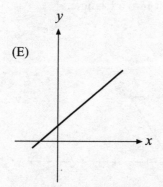

37. Line f and line g are perpendicular lines with slopes of x and
    y, respectively. If $xy \neq 0$, which of the following are possible
    values of $x - y$?

    I. 0.8
    II. 2.0
    III. 5.2

    (A) I only
    (B) I and II only
    (C) I and III only
    (D) II and III only
    (E) I, II, and III

Line Segments

A line by definition goes on forever—it has infinite length. Coordinate geometry questions may also ask about line *segments*, however. Any coordinate geometry question asking for the distance between two points is a line segment question. Any question that draws or describes a rectangle, triangle, or other polygon in the coordinate plane may also involve line segment formulas. The most commonly requested line segment formula gives the length of a line segment.

Let's look at a line segment.

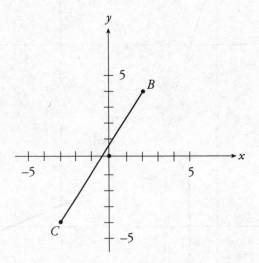

If you want to find the length of $\overline{BC}$, turn it into a triangle.

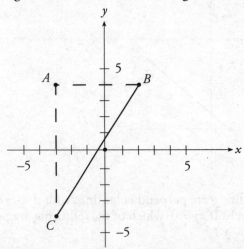

We've added in point A to illustrate the point. You know how to find the hypotenuse of a triangle, right? Pythagorean Theorem! It's easy to find the distance from A to B, just count across. The distance is 5. The distance between A and C is 8. Using the Pythagorean Theorem, we can fill in $5^2 + 8^2 = 89$. So the length of $\overline{BC}$ is $\sqrt{89}$. If you ever forget the distance formula, remember: all you have to do is make a triangle. After all, that's how the distance formula was created in the first place!

> **The Distance Formula**
>
> For the two points (x_1, y_1) and (x_2, y_2),
>
> $$d = \sqrt{(x_2 - x_1)^2 + (y_2 - y_1)^2}$$

Now let's take a look at the same triangle we were working with and use the distance formula.

How Did We Get There?

Look carefully at the distance formula. Notice anything familiar? If you square both sides, it's just the Pythagorean Theorem!

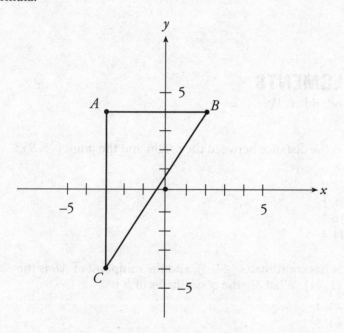

The coordinates of B are $(2, 4)$. The coordinates of C are $(-3, -4)$. If you plug these coordinates into the distance formula, you get

$$d = \sqrt{(2 - (-3))^2 + (4 - (-4))^2}$$
$$d = \sqrt{(5)^2 + (8)^2}$$
$$d = \sqrt{25 + 64}$$
$$d = \sqrt{89}$$
$$d = 9.434$$

Notice that you would get the same answer by counting the vertical distance between B and C (8) and the horizontal distance between B and C (5), and using the Pythagorean Theorem to find the diagonal distance.

The other important line segment formula is used to find the coordinates of the middle point of a line segment with endpoints (x_1, y_1) and (x_2, y_2).

Another Way to Think About It
The midpoint formula finds the average of the x-coordinates and the average of the y-coordinates.

Coordinates of the Midpoint of a Line Segment

For the two points (x_1, y_1) and (x_2, y_2),

$$M = \left(\frac{x_1 + x_2}{2}, \frac{y_1 + y_2}{2} \right)$$

The midpoint and distance formulas used together can answer any line segment question.

DRILL 4: LINE SEGMENTS

The answers can be found in Part IV.

2. What is the distance between the origin and the point (−5, 9) ?

(A) 5.9
(B) 6.7
(C) 8.1
(D) 10.3
(E) 11.4

6. Point A has coordinates (−4, 3), and the midpoint of AB is the point (1, −1). What are the coordinates of B ?

(A) (−3, 4)
(B) (−4, 5)
(C) (4, −5)
(D) (5, −4)
(E) (6, −5)

12. Which of the following points is farthest from the point (2, 2) ?

(A) (8, 8)
(B) (−6, 2)
(C) (4, −6)
(D) (−5, −3)
(E) (9, 4)

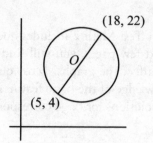

28. What is the area of the circle with center *O* shown above?

(A) 11.102
(B) 22.204
(C) 69.756
(D) 123.250
(E) 387.201

LINEAR INEQUALITIES

A linear inequality looks just like a linear equation, except that an inequality sign replaces the equals sign. They are graphed just as lines are graphed, except that the "greater than" or "less than" is represented by shading above or below the line. If the inequality is a "greater than or equal to" or "less than or equal to," then the line itself is included and is drawn as a solid line. If the inequality is a "greater than" or "less than," then the line itself is not included; the line is drawn as a dotted line, and only the shaded region is included in the inequality. Take a look at some examples.

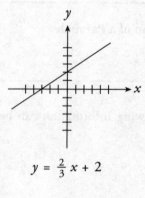

$y = \frac{2}{3}x + 2$

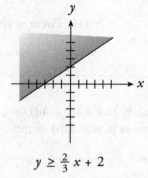

$y \geq \frac{2}{3}x + 2$

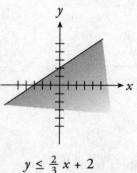

$y \leq \frac{2}{3}x + 2$

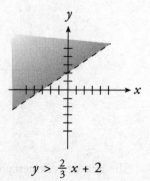

$y > \frac{2}{3}x + 2$

GENERAL EQUATIONS

In addition to lines, the SAT Subject Test Math 2 includes questions on other shapes graphed in the coordinate plane. On the next few pages, you will find equations for these shapes and information on how the equations affect the graphs. Most questions that the College Board will ask are simply testing your knowledge of the basic features of these equations and graphs. Remember that for every equation, solutions for (x, y) correspond to points on the graph.

The Parabola

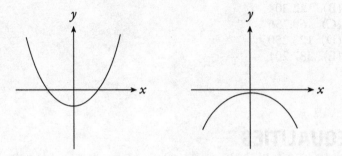

A parabola takes the form of a single curve opening either upward or downward, becoming increasingly steep as you move away from the center of the curve. Parabolas are the graphs of *quadratic* functions, which were discussed in Chapter 5. The equation of a parabola can come in two forms. Here is the one that will make you happiest on SAT Subject Test Math 2.

Vertex Form of the Equation of a Parabola

$$y = a(x - h)^2 + k$$

In this formula, *a, h,* and *k* are constants. The following information can be taken from the equation of a parabola in standard form:

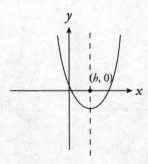

The axis of symmetry of the parabola is the line $x = h$.

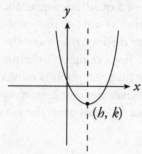

The vertex of the parabola is the point (h, k).

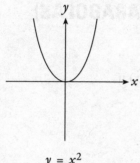

$y = x^2$

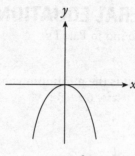

$y = -x^2$

If a is positive, the parabola opens upward. If a is negative, the parabola opens downward.

> **General Form of the Equation of a Parabola**
>
> $$y = ax^2 + bx + c$$

In this formula, a, b, and c are constants. The following information can be taken from the equation of a parabola in general form:

- The axis of symmetry of the parabola is the line $x = -\dfrac{b}{2a}$.

- The x-coordinate of the parabola's vertex is $-\dfrac{b}{2a}$. The y-coordinate of the vertex is whatever you get when you plug $-\dfrac{b}{2a}$ into the equation as x.

- The y-intercept of the parabola is the point $(0, c)$.

- If a is positive, the parabola opens upward. If a is negative, the parabola opens downward.

Déjà Vu?
This equation may look familiar. It turns out that quadratic equations are equations of parabolas. It's all connected.

Since a parabola is simply the graph of a quadratic equation, the quadratic formula can be used to find the roots (x-intercepts or zeros), if any, of the parabola. The discriminant, or $b^2 - 4ac$, can be used to determine how many distinct real roots the quadratic has, which is the number of x-intercepts the parabola has. For example, if the discriminant is 0, you know that the parabola has one root, which means that the graph is tangent to the x-axis at the vertex of the parabola. If the discriminant is positive, the graph intercepts the x-axis at two points. If the discriminant is negative, the parabola does not cross the x-axis.

DRILL 5: GENERAL EQUATIONS (PARABOLAS)

The answers can be found in Part IV.

21. What is the minimum value of $f(x)$ if
$f(x) = x^2 - 6x + 8$?

(A) -3
(B) -2
(C) -1
(D) 0
(E) 2

22. What are the coordinates of the vertex of the
parabola defined by the equation $y = \dfrac{1}{2}x^2 + x + \dfrac{5}{2}$?

(A) $(-2, 4)$
(B) $(-1, 2)$
(C) $(1, 2)$
(D) $(2, 4)$
(E) $(2, -4)$

25. At which of the following x-values does the
parabola defined by $y = (x - 3)^2 - 4$ cross the x-axis?

(A) -3
(B) 3
(C) 4
(D) 5
(E) 9

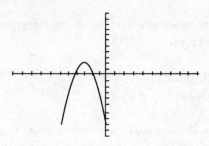

36. Which of the following could be the equation of the graph above?

(A) $y = -(x-3)^2 + 2$

(B) $y = -(x+3)^2 + 2$

(C) $y = -(x-3)^2 - 2$

(D) $y = -(x+3)^2 - 2$

(E) $y = (x+3)^2 + 2$

The Circle

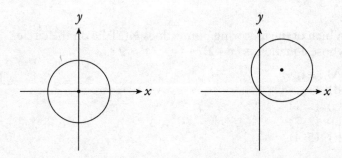

The circle is that round shape you know and love. It's also probably the College Board's favorite nonlinear shape in the coordinate plane. Below is the formula for a circle.

Standard Form of the Equation of a Circle

$$(x - h)^2 + (y - k)^2 = r^2$$

In this formula, h, k, and r are constants. The following information can be learned from the equation of a circle in standard form:

- The center of the circle is the point (h, k).
- The length of the circle's radius is r.

And that's all there is to know about a circle. Once you know its radius and the position of its center, you can sketch the circle yourself or identify its graph easily. It's also a simple matter to estimate the radius and center coordinates of a circle whose graph is given, and make a good guess at the equation of that circle. One last note: if the circle's center is the origin, then $(h, k) = (0, 0)$. This greatly simplifies the equation of the circle.

> **Equation of a Circle with Center at Origin**
>
> $$x^2 + y^2 = r^2$$

DRILL 6: GENERAL EQUATIONS (CIRCLES)
The answers can be found in Part IV.

18. Which of the following points does NOT lie on the circle whose equation is $(x - 2)^2 + (y - 4)^2 = 9$?

    (A) $(-1, 4)$
    (B) $(-1, -1)$
    (C) $(2, 1)$
    (D) $(2, 7)$
    (E) $(5, 4)$

20. Points S and T lie on the circle with equation $x^2 + y^2 = 16$. If S and T have identical y-coordinates but distinct x-coordinates, then which of the following is the distance between S and T ?

    (A) 4.0
    (B) 5.6
    (C) 8.0
    (D) 11.3
    (E) It cannot be determined from the information given.

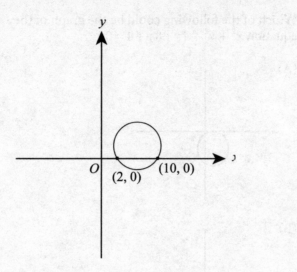

45. Which of the following equations could represent the circle shown in the figure above?

(A) $x^2 + y^2 - 14x - 8y + 40 = 0$
(B) $x^2 + y^2 - 14x + 8y + 40 = 0$
(C) $x^2 + y^2 - 12x - 6y + 20 = 0$
(D) $x^2 + y^2 - 10x + 8y + 16 = 0$
(E) $x^2 + y^2 + 4x - 6y - 12 = 0$

50. Which of the following could be the graph of the equation $x^2 + y^2 + 4x + 8y + 4 = 0$?

(A)

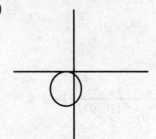

(B)

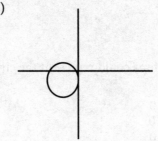

(C)

(D)

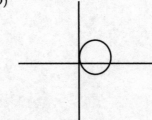

(E)

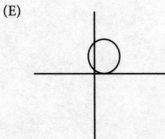

The Ellipse

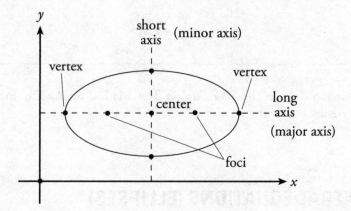

An ellipse has a center like a circle, but since it's squashed a little flatter than a circle; it has no constant radius. Instead, an ellipse has two *vertices* (the plural of *vertex*) at the ends of its long axis, and two *foci* (the plural of *focus*), points within the ellipse. The foci of an ellipse are important to the definition of an ellipse. The distances from the two foci to a point on the ellipse always add up to the same number for every point on the ellipse. This is the formula for an ellipse.

General Equation of an Ellipse

$$\frac{(x-h)^2}{a^2} + \frac{(y-k)^2}{b^2} = 1$$

In this formula, *a*, *b*, *h*, and *k* are constants. The following information can be learned from the equation of an ellipse in standard form:

> The center of an ellipse is the point (*h*, *k*).
> The width of the ellipse is 2*a*, and the height is 2*b*.

An ellipse can be longer either horizontally or vertically. If the constant under the $(x - h)^2$ term is larger than the constant under the $(y - k)^2$ term, then the major axis of the ellipse is horizontal. If the constant under the $(y - k)^2$ term is bigger, then the major axis is vertical. Like that of a circle, the equation for an ellipse becomes simpler when it's centered at the origin, and (*h*, *k*) = (0, 0).

Equation of an Ellipse with Center at Origin

$$\frac{x^2}{a^2} + \frac{y^2}{b^2} = 1$$

The few ellipses that show up on the SAT Subject Test Math 2 are usually in this simplified form; they are centered at the origin.

DRILL 7: GENERAL EQUATIONS (ELLIPSES)

The answers can be found in Part IV.

15. How long is the major axis of the ellipse with a formula of $\frac{x^2}{16} + \frac{y^2}{25} = 1$?

    (A) 1
    (B) 4
    (C) 5
    (D) 8
    (E) 10

40. Which of the following points is the center of the ellipse whose formula is $\frac{(x+5)^2}{9} + \frac{(y-3)^2}{4} = 1$?

    (A) $\left(\frac{25}{9}, -\frac{9}{4}\right)$

    (B) $\left(-\frac{5}{9}, \frac{3}{4}\right)$

    (C) $(-5, 3)$

    (D) $(25, -9)$

    (E) $(9, 16)$

45. Which of the following could be the graph of the

equation $\frac{x^2}{16} + y^2 = 1$?

(A)

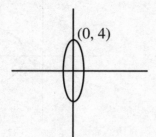

(B)

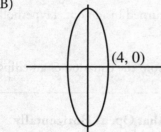

(C)

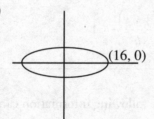

(D)

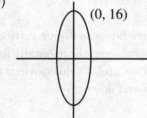

(E)

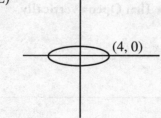

The Hyperbola

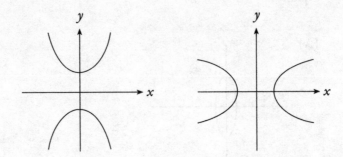

A hyperbola is essentially an ellipse turned inside-out. Hyperbolas are infrequently tested on the SAT Subject Test Math 2.

The equation of a hyperbola differs from the equation of an ellipse only by a sign.

Equation of a Hyperbola That Opens Horizontally

$$\frac{(x-h)^2}{a^2} - \frac{(y-k)^2}{b^2} = 1$$

In this formula, *a*, *b*, *h*, and *k* are constants. The following information can be learned from the equation of a hyperbola in standard form:

The hyperbola's center is the point (h, k).

Like an ellipse, a hyperbola can be oriented either horizontally or vertically. If the *y*-term is negative, as it is in the equation above, then the curves open horizontally (to the right and left). However, if the *x*-term is negative—that is, the *x*, *h*, and *a* values switch places with the *y*, *k*, and *b* values—then the curves open vertically (up and down):

Equation of a Hyperbola That Opens Vertically

$$\frac{(y-k)^2}{b^2} - \frac{(x-h)^2}{a^2} = 1$$

Like that of an ellipse, a hyperbola's equation becomes simpler when it is centered at the origin, and $(h, k) = (0, 0)$.

Equation of a Hyperbola with Center at Origin

$$\frac{x^2}{a^2} - \frac{y^2}{b^2} = 1$$

The few hyperbolas that show up on the SAT Subject Test Math 2 are usually in this simplified form; they are centered at the origin.

DRILL 8: GENERAL EQUATIONS (HYPERBOLAS)

Try these hyperbola questions. The answers can be found in Part IV.

38. The hyperbola $\dfrac{(x+4)^2}{9} - \dfrac{(y+5)^2}{4} = 1$ has its center at which of the following points?

    (A) $(-9, -4)$
    (B) $(-4, -5)$
    (C) $(4, 5)$
    (D) $(9, -4)$
    (E) $(16, 25)$

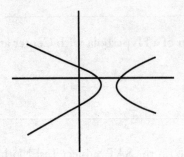

45. Which of the following could be the equation of the hyperbola above?

(A) $\dfrac{(x-4)^2}{4} - \dfrac{(y+2)^2}{4} = 1$

(B) $\dfrac{(y-4)^2}{4} - \dfrac{(x+2)^2}{4} = 1$

(C) $\dfrac{(x+4)^2}{4} - \dfrac{(y-2)^2}{4} = 1$

(D) $\dfrac{(y+2)^2}{4} - \dfrac{(x-4)^2}{4} = 1$

(E) $\dfrac{(x-4)^2}{4} + \dfrac{(y+2)^2}{4} = 1$

TRIAXIAL COORDINATES: THINKING IN 3D

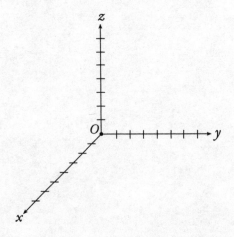

On the SAT Subject Test Math 2, you may run into a twist on the coordinate plane—a coordinate *space*. A third dimension can be added to the coordinate plane by introducing a third axis (often referred to as the z-axis) that passes through the origin at right angles to both the x-axis and the y-axis. While the x- and y-axes define the location of a point in a plane, the x-, y-, and z-axes define the location of a point in a three-dimensional space.

Such a system of three axes is called a *three-dimensional coordinate system,* a *triaxial coordinate system,* or a *coordinate space.* Sometimes it's not called anything at all; the College Board will simply show you a diagram of a three-dimensional graph, or a set of triple coordinates, and expect you to understand what you're seeing. The coordinates of a point in three dimensions are given in this form: (*x, y, z*). The point (3, 4, 5) is located 3 units along the *x*-axis, 4 units along the *y*-axis, and 5 units along the *z*-axis. Always check the labels on the axes if you're given a diagram, because there's no firm convention about which axis is pictured in which position.

If you are given two points in 3-D, (x_1, y_1, z_1) and (x_2, y_2, z_2), then the distance, *d*, between them is given by the following formula:

Distance in a Three-Dimensional Space

$$d = \sqrt{(x_2 - x_1)^2 + (y_2 - y_1)^2 + (z_2 - z_1)^2}$$

Most of the three-dimensional coordinate questions on the SAT Subject Test Math 2 require you to calculate a distance between two points in a 3-D coordinate system. Just use the formula.

Connect the Dots
This formula is equivalent to the Super Pythagorean Theorem: $a^2 + b^2 + c^2 = d^2$.

DRILL 9: TRIAXIAL COORDINATES

Try the following questions involving triaxial coordinates. The answers can be found in Part IV.

14. What is the distance between the origin and the point (5, 6, 7) ?

(A)   4.24
(B)   7.25
(C)   10.49
(D)   14.49
(E)   18.00

19. Sphere *O* has a radius of 6, and its center is at the origin. Which of the following points is NOT inside the sphere?

(A) (–3, 5, 1)
(B) (–4, –4, 3)
(C) (5, –2, 2)
(D) (4, 1, –4)
(E) (2, –4, –3)

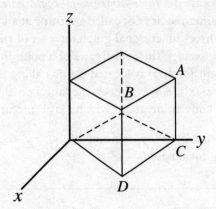

37. A cube is located in the *xyz*-coordinate system shown above. If *A* is located at (0, 7.071, 5), then which of the following are the coordinates of *B* ?

    (A) (0, 5, 7.071)
    (B) (0, 3.536, 5)
    (C) (3.536, 5, 5)
    (D) (3.536, 3.536, 5)
    (E) (7.071, 5, 5)

Comprehensive Coordinate Geometry Drill

The answers can be found in Part IV.

1. What is the x-intercept of the line containing the points $(19, 7)$ and $(-4, 18)$?

    (A) $(33.636, 0)$
    (B) $(-33.636, 0)$
    (C) $(370, 0)$
    (D) $(0.478, 0)$
    (E) $(0, 48)$

2. What is the slope of a line perpendicular to the line defined by the equation $4x + 7y = 23$?

    (A) -4

    (B) $-\dfrac{4}{7}$

    (C) $\dfrac{7}{4}$

    (D) $\dfrac{23}{7}$

    (E) 4

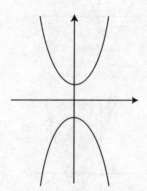

5. Which of the following could be the equation of the graph shown above?

    (A) $y = x^2 + 4$

    (B) $y = -x^2 - 4$

    (C) $\dfrac{x^2}{4} - \dfrac{y^2}{4} = 1$

    (D) $\dfrac{y^2}{4} - \dfrac{x^2}{4} = 1$

    (E) $\dfrac{x^2}{4} + \dfrac{y^2}{4} = 1$

12. What are the coordinates of the vertex of the parabola defined by the equation $y = -3x^2 + 5x - 11$?

    (A) $(0, -11)$
    (B) $(0.833, -8.917)$
    (C) $(0.833, -11)$
    (D) $(2.557, 0)$
    (E) $(-0.891, 0)$

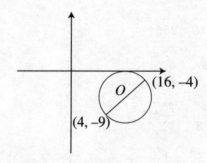

18. What is the equation of the circle with center O ?

    (A) $(x - 10)^2 + (y + 6.5)^2 = 42.25$

    (B) $(x + 10)^2 + (y - 6.5)^2 = 42.25$

    (C) $(x - 10)^2 + (y + 6.5)^2 = 6.5$

    (D) $(x + 10)^2 + (y - 6.5)^2 = 6.5$

    (E) $(x - 20)^2 + (y + 13)^2 = 42.25$

22. Triangle ABC lies in the xy-coordinate system. Point A is located at $(-2, 4)$. Point B is located at $(0.5, 12)$. Point C is located at $(7, -5)$. What is the distance between the midpoint of $\overline{AB}$ and point C ?

    (A) 8.381
    (B) 12.728
    (C) 14.424
    (D) 15.134
    (E) 229.063

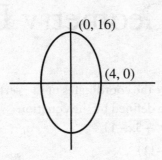

(0, 16)

(4, 0)

25. Which of the following could be the equation of the graph shown above?

(A) $\dfrac{x^2}{16}+\dfrac{y^2}{256}=1$

(B) $\dfrac{x^2}{4}+\dfrac{y^2}{16}=1$

(C) $\dfrac{x^2}{8}+\dfrac{y^2}{32}=1$

(D) $\dfrac{x^2}{64}+\dfrac{y^2}{1024}=1$

(E) $\dfrac{x^2}{256}+\dfrac{y^2}{16}=1$

28. Which of the following is the graph of $y \le (x-2)^2 - 3$?

(A)

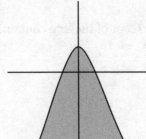

(B)

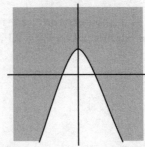

(C)

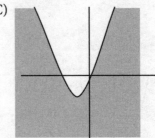

(D)

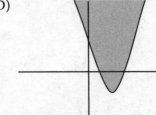

(E)

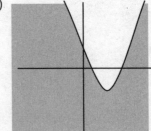

36. Which of the following points is on the *y*-axis and equidistant from (0, 2) and (6, 0) ?

(A) (3, 1)
(B) (0, –8)
(C) (0, 1)
(D) (0, 3)
(E) (0, 8)

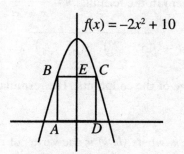

$f(x) = -2x^2 + 10$

Note: Figure not drawn to scale.

42. In the figure above, rectangle *ABCD* intersects the function *f(x)* at points *B* and *C*. Point *E* is located at (0, 3.5). What is the area of rectangle *ABCD* ?

(A)   1.803
(B)   3.250
(C)   3.606
(D)   6.310
(E)   12.619

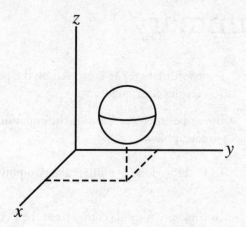

49. A sphere with radius 5 and center (5, 7, 6) is shown in the triaxial coordinate system above. Which of the following is NOT a point on the sphere?

(A)   (0, 7, 6)
(B)   (5, 2, 6)
(C)   (5, 3, 3)
(D)   (5, 4, 10)
(E)   (2, 7, 9)

Summary

○ The coordinate plane is created by the perpendicular intersection of the *x*- and *y*-axis. This intersection creates four quadrants.

○ The slope-intercept form of the equation of a line is $y = mx + b$. The slope of the line is *m* and the *y*-intercept is *b*.

○ To find the slope of a line, take two points on the line and put them in the formula $m = \dfrac{y_2 - y_1}{x_2 - x_1}$.

○ The distance formula comes from the Pythagorean Theorem. It is $d = \sqrt{\left(x_2 - x_1\right)^2 + \left(y_2 - y_1\right)^2}$.

○ To find the coordinates of the midpoint of a line, take the average of the endpoints. The formula is $M = \left(\dfrac{x_1 + x_2}{2}, \dfrac{y_1 + y_2}{2} \right)$.

○ The general form of the equation of a parabola is $y = a(x - h)^2 + k$, where (h, k) is the vertex of the parabola. The general form of a parabola is a quadratic equation: $y = ax^2 + bx + c$. Use the general form to find the axis of symmetry, the vertex, and whether the parabola opens up or down.

○ The general form of the equation of a circle is $(x - h)^2 + (y - k)^2 = r^2$, where (h, k) is the center of the circle.

○ The general form of the equation of an ellipse is $\dfrac{\left(x - h\right)^2}{a^2} + \dfrac{\left(y - k\right)^2}{b^2} = 1$, where (h, k) is the center of the ellipse.

○ The general form of the equation of a hyperbola is $\dfrac{\left(x - h\right)^2}{a^2} - \dfrac{\left(y - k\right)^2}{b^2} = 1$, where (h, k) is the center of the hyperbola.

○ The 3-D coordinate plane has 3 axes, *x*, *y*, and *z*. The formula for the distance of a line in three-dimensional space is

$$d = \sqrt{\left(x_2 - x_1\right)^2 + \left(y_2 - y_1\right)^2 + \left(z_2 - z_1\right)^2}$$

Chapter 9
Trigonometry

Trigonometry on the SAT Subject Test Math 2 runs the gamut from completing triangles using SOHCAHTOA to trigonometric identities, Law of Sines and Law of Cosines, and polar coordinates. If you wish to succeed on this test, master these concepts!

DEFINITIONS

Here are some basic definitions that you will need to know for the SAT Subject Test Math 2. Make sure you're familiar with them. If the meaning of any of these vocabulary words keeps slipping your mind, add that word to your flash cards.

Acute Angle	An angle whose measure in degrees is between 0 and 90, exclusive.
Obtuse Angle	An angle whose measure in degrees is between 90 and 180, exclusive.
Theta	The Greek letter θ (pronounced thay-tuh) is a variable, just like x and y, used to represent the measure of an angle in trigonometry.
arc–	Prefix added to trigonometric functions, meaning *inverse*.

THE BASIC FUNCTIONS

The basis of trigonometry is the relationship between the parts of a right triangle. When you know the measure of one of the acute angles in a right triangle, you know all the angles in that triangle. For example, if you know that a right triangle contains a 20° angle, then you know all three angles—the right triangle must have a 90° angle, and because there are 180° in a triangle, the third angle must measure 70°. You don't know the lengths in the triangle, but you know its shape and its proportions.

A right triangle that contains a 20° angle can have only one shape, though it can be any size. The same is true for a right triangle containing any other acute angle. That's the fundamental idea of trigonometry. Once you know the measure of an acute angle in a right triangle, you know that triangle's proportions.

Similar Right Triangles

Remember that similar triangles have the same angles. So, any right triangle that contains a 20° angle will be similar to all other right triangles with a 20° angle.

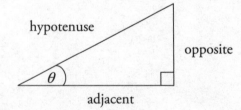

The three basic functions in trigonometry—the sine, cosine, and tangent—are ways of expressing proportions in a right triangle (that's the ratio of one side to another). They may sound familiar to you. Or maybe you've heard of a little phrase called SOHCAHTOA?

Let's break it down.

SOHCAHTOA

$$\sin = \frac{opposite}{hypotenuse} \qquad \cos = \frac{adjacent}{hypotenuse} \qquad \tan = \frac{opposite}{adjacent}$$

Sine

The sine of an angle is the ratio of the opposite side to the hypotenuse. The sine function of an angle θ is abbreviated $\sin \theta$.

Cosine

The cosine of an angle is the ratio of the adjacent side to the hypotenuse. The cosine function of an angle θ is abbreviated $\cos \theta$.

Tangent

The tangent of an angle is the ratio of the opposite side to the adjacent side. The tangent function of an angle θ is abbreviated $\tan \theta$.

These three functions form the basis of everything else in trigonometry. All of the more complicated functions and rules in trigonometry can be derived from the information contained in SOHCAHTOA.

> **It's All About Proportions**
> A trigonometric function of any angle comes from the proportions of a right triangle containing that angle. For any given angle, there is only one possible set of proportions.

What Can Your Calculator Do For You?

As you likely know, your calculator has the values of the basic functions programmed into it. The names of these functions are abbreviated "sin," "cos," and "tan."

Before using your calculator on a trigonometry problem, be sure to check whether your calculator is in the proper mode, either degrees or radians. Most questions on the SAT Subject Test Math 2 will be in degrees, but questions in radians come up as well. On a TI-80 series calculator, such as the TI-84, press the MODE button; the option to change from radians to degrees is the third option.

If you press the trigonometric function followed by the measure of the angle (in the proper units), your calculator will provide the value at that angle ($\frac{opposite}{hypotenuse}$ for sine, etc.).

$$\sin 30° = 0.5$$

$$\cos \frac{\pi}{6} = 0.866$$

$$\tan 30° = 0.577$$

If you know the value of the function but need to solve for the angle given, you can use the inverse function, indicated either with a superscript of –1 on the function (such as $\sin^{-1}$) or the prefix *arc-* (such as arcsin). On the TI-84, the inverse functions are accessed by pressing the 2ND button followed by the function. Radians are typically expressed as fractions using π, so if you are finding radians, take your decimal result and divide by π. Next, use MATH->FRAC to find the fractional value of the angle, then add π in the numerator. This trick only works if you use actual values (no rounding; mode in FLOAT on the TI-84).

$$\sin^{-1} 0.5 = 30° \text{ or } \arcsin 0.5 = 30°$$

$$\cos^{-1} 0.866 = 0.524 ; \frac{0.524}{\pi} = 0.167 = \frac{1}{6} \text{ , so } \cos^{-1} 0.866 = \frac{\pi}{6}$$

$$\tan^{-1} 0.577 = 30°$$

Note that inverse functions on your calculator will give you the SMALLEST value of the angle which is equal to the function. This can matter in Unit Circle and Radian questions and when you are using Law of Sines.

DRILL 1: TRIG FUNCTIONS IN RIGHT TRIANGLES

Use the definitions of the sine, cosine, and tangent to fill in the requested quantities in the following triangles. The answers can be found in Part IV.

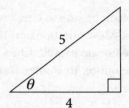

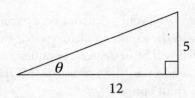

Special Right Triangles

Be on the lookout for special right triangles on trigonometry questions!

1. $\sin \theta =$ _____

    $\cos \theta =$ _____

    $\tan \theta =$ _____

2. $\sin \theta =$ _____

    $\cos \theta =$ _____

    $\tan \theta =$ _____

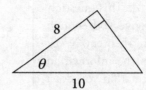

3. $\sin \theta =$ _____

   $\cos \theta =$ _____

   $\tan \theta =$ _____

4. $\sin \theta =$ _____

   $\cos \theta =$ _____

   $\tan \theta =$ _____

Completing Right Triangles

Questions on the SAT Subject Test Math 2 may ask you to find an unknown side or angle of a right triangle using the basic trigonometric functions. For example,

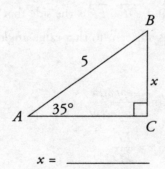

   $x =$ _____

Because we're dealing with the hypotenuse and the side that is opposite the angle, the best definition to use is sine.

$$\sin = \frac{opposite}{hypotenuse}$$

$$\sin 35° = \frac{x}{5}$$

$$5(\sin 35°) = x$$

$$5(0.5736) = x$$

$$2.8679 = x$$

$\overline{BC}$ of $\triangle ABC$ therefore has a length of 2.87.

> **The Unknown**
>
> In triangle *ABC,* you know only two quantities—the length of *AB* and the measure of $\angle A$. This question, unlike previous examples, doesn't give you enough information to use the Pythagorean Theorem. What you need is an equation that relates the information you have (*AB* and $\angle A$) to the information you don't have (*x*). Use the SOHCAHTOA definitions to set up an equation. Solve that equation, and you find the value of the unknown.

You can use a similar technique to find the measure of an unknown angle in a right triangle. For example,

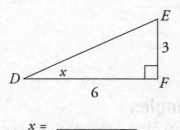

$x =$ _____

In triangle *DEF*, you know $\overline{EF}$ and $\overline{DF}$. $\overline{EF}$ is the side that is opposite the angle we're looking for, and $\overline{DF}$ is the side that is adjacent to that same angle. So the best definition to use is tangent.

$$\tan = \frac{opposite}{adjacent}$$

$$\tan x = \frac{EF}{FD}$$

$$\tan x = \frac{3}{6}$$

$$\tan x = 0.5$$

To solve for *x*, take the *inverse tangent* of both sides of the equation. On the left side, that just gives you *x*. The result is the angle whose tangent is 0.5.

$$\tan^{-1}(\tan x) = \tan^{-1}(0.5)$$

$$x = 26.57°$$

The measure of $\angle D$ is therefore 26.57°.

DRILL 2: COMPLETING TRIANGLES

Use the techniques you've just reviewed to complete the following triangles. The answers can be found in Part IV.

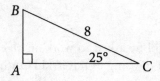

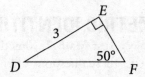

1. $AB =$ _____

    $CA =$ _____

    $\angle B =$ _____

2. $EF =$ _____

    $FD =$ _____

    $\angle D =$ _____

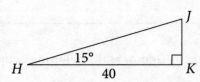

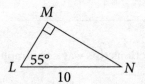

3. $HJ =$ _____

    $JK =$ _____

    $\angle J =$ _____

4. $LM =$ _____

    $MN =$ _____

    $\angle N =$ _____

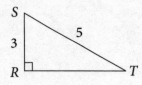

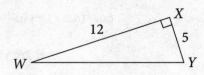

5. $TR =$ _____

   $\angle S =$ _____

   $\angle T =$ _____

6. $YW =$ _____

   $\angle W =$ _____

   $\angle Y =$ _____

TRIGONOMETRIC IDENTITIES

On the SAT Subject Test Math 2, sometimes you will be asked to work an algebraic problem using trigonometry. These questions often boil down to using SOHCAHTOA in a handful of clever ways.

Often, the way to simplify equations that are mostly made up of trigonometric functions is to express the functions as follows:

$$\sin = \frac{O}{H} \qquad \cos = \frac{A}{H} \qquad \tan = \frac{O}{A}$$

Writing trig functions this way can simplify trig equations, as the following example shows

$$\frac{\sin x}{\cos x} =$$

$$\frac{O}{H} \div \frac{A}{H} =$$

$$\frac{O}{A} = \tan x$$

Working with trig functions this way lets you simplify expressions. The equation above is actually a commonly used *trigonometric identity*. You should memorize this, as it can often be used to simplify equations.

$$\frac{\sin x}{\cos x} = \tan x$$

Here's the breakdown of another frequently used trigonometric identity.

$$\sin^2 \theta + \cos^2 \theta =$$

$$(\sin \theta)(\sin \theta) + (\cos \theta)(\cos \theta) =$$

$$\left(\frac{O}{H}\right)\left(\frac{O}{H}\right) + \left(\frac{A}{H}\right)\left(\frac{A}{H}\right) =$$

$$\frac{O^2}{H^2} + \frac{A^2}{H^2} =$$

$$\frac{O^2 + A^2}{H^2} = 1$$

That last step may seem a little baffling, but it's really simple. This equation is based on a right triangle, in which O and A are legs of the triangle, and H is the hypotenuse. Consequently you know that $O^2 + A^2 = H^2$. That's just the Pythagorean Theorem. That's what lets you do the last step, in which $\frac{O^2 + A^2}{H^2} = 1$. This completes the second commonly used identity that you should memorize.

$$\sin^2 \theta + \cos^2 \theta = 1$$

In addition to memorizing these two identities, you should practice working algebraically with trig functions in general. Some questions may require you to use the SOHCAHTOA definitions of the trig functions; others may require you to use the two identities you've just reviewed. Take a look at these examples.

20. If $\sin x = 0.707$, then what is the value of $(\sin x) \times (\cos x) \times (\tan x)$?

(A)   1.0
(B)   0.707
(C)   0.5
(D)   0.4
(E)   0.207

Here's How to Crack It

This is a tricky question. To solve it, simplify that complicated trigonometric expression. Writing in the SOHCAHTOA definitions works just fine, but in this case it's even faster to use one of those identities.

$$(\sin x) \cdot (\cos x) \cdot (\tan x) =$$
$$(\sin x) \cdot (\cos x) \cdot \left(\frac{\sin x}{\cos x}\right) =$$
$$(\sin x) \cdot (\sin x) =$$
$$\sin^2 x =$$

Now it's a simpler matter to answer the question. If $\sin x = 0.707$, then $\sin^2 x = 0.5$. The answer is (C).

Take a look at this one.

---

21. If $\sin a = 0.4$, and $1 - \cos^2 a = x$, then what is the value of x?

(A) 0.8
(B) 0.6
(C) 0.44
(D) 0.24
(E) 0.16

Here's How to Crack It

Here again, the trick to the question is simplifying the complicated trig expression. Since $\sin^2 \theta + \cos^2 \theta = 1$, you can rearrange any of those terms to rephrase it. Using the second trig identity, you can quickly take these steps.

$$1 - \cos^2 a = x$$
$$\sin^2 a = x$$
$$(0.4)^2 = x$$
$$x = 0.16$$

And that's the answer. Choice (E) is correct.

Let's look at another problem.

38. If $\dfrac{(\sin x)(\cos x)}{\tan x} = 0.345$, then $\sin^2 x =$

(A) -0.655
(B) -0.345
(C) 0.345
(D) 0.655
(E) 1

Here's How to Crack It

You know that $\tan x = \dfrac{\sin x}{\cos x}$, so you can rework the problem.

$$\dfrac{(\sin x)(\cos x)}{\dfrac{\sin x}{\cos x}} = 0.345.$$

If you multiply by the reciprocal of the denominator, you get

$$(\sin x)(\cos x)\left(\dfrac{\cos x}{\sin x}\right) = 0.345$$

$$\cos^2 x = 0.345.$$

Now, to get to $\sin^2 x$, you need to replace $\cos^2 x$ with $1 - \sin^2 x$.

$$1 - \sin^2 x = 0.345$$

$$-\sin^2 x = -0.655$$

$$\sin^2 x = 0.655$$

The answer is (D).

Plugging In on Trigonometric Algebra

As you saw in the Algebra chapter, Plugging In is a powerful tool on many SAT Subject Test Math 2 problems. This is also true for problems dealing with trigonometric identities: just plug in for the unknown angle.

When you plug in on these problems, choose a value for x or θ which gives unique values for sin, cos, and tan. Avoid multiples of 45 (such as 45, 90, or 180) if you're in degrees or multiples of $\frac{\pi}{4}$ in radians.

Try one more problem.

——————————○——————————

26. $\dfrac{\sin x \cos x}{1 - \cos^2 x} =$

    (A) $\sec x$
    (B) $\sin^2 x$
    (C) $\cos x$
    (D) $\tan x$
    (E) $\cot x$

Here's How to Crack It

Make sure your calculator is in degrees mode and make $x = 20$. Use your calculator to find the value of the expression (remember that to find $\cos^2 20°$ you need to find $\cos 20°$ and then square the result).

$$\frac{\sin 20° \cos 20°}{1 - \cos^2 20°} = \frac{(0.342)(0.940)}{1 - (0.940)^2} = \frac{0.321}{0.117} = 2.744$$

Now, you can plug in $x = 20°$ to each answer choice and find the choice which equals 2.747. You don't need to check (B) and (C), as they cannot be greater than 1. Also remember that sec $x = \dfrac{1}{\cos x}$ and cot $x = \dfrac{1}{\tan x}$. The only choice which is close to 2.744 is (E).

(Note: you may have noticed that $1 - \cos^2 x = \sin^2 x$, which lets you cancel sin x from the numerator and denominator, leaving you with $\dfrac{\cos x}{\sin x}$, which is cot x. However, when you DON'T notice these things, or have a moment of bafflement on the test, Plugging In can get you to the answer.)

——————————○——————————

Now, use what you've learned about SOHCAHTOA and trigonometric identities to simplify the trigonometric expressions in the following problems.

DRILL 3: TRIGONOMETRIC IDENTITIES

Try the following practice questions. The answers can be found in Part IV.

10. $(1 - \sin x)(1 + \sin x) =$

   (A) $\cos x$
   (B) $\sin x$
   (C) $\tan x$
   (D) $\cos^2 x$
   (E) $\sin^2 x$

16. $\dfrac{\tan x \cos x}{\sin x} =$

   (A) $\dfrac{1}{\tan x}$

   (B) $\dfrac{1}{\cos x}$

   (C) 1

   (D) $\cos^2 x$

   (E) $\tan x$

24. $\dfrac{1}{\cos x} - (\sin x)(\tan x) =$

   (A) $\cos x$
   (B) $\sin x$
   (C) $\tan x$
   (D) $\cos^2 x$
   (E) $\sin^2 x$

38. $\dfrac{\tan x - \sin x \cos x}{\tan x} =$

   (A) $1 - \cos x$
   (B) $1 - \sin x$
   (C) $\tan x + 1$
   (D) $\cos^2 x$
   (E) $\sin^2 x$

45. $\dfrac{(1 + \sin \theta)(1 - \sin \theta)}{\sin^4 \theta + 2 \sin^2 \theta \cos^2 \theta + \cos^4 \theta} =$

   (A) 1

   (B) 0.5

   (C) $\sin^2 \theta$

   (D) $\cos^2 \theta$

   (E) $\sin \theta \cos \theta$

The Other Trig Functions

On the SAT Subject Test Math 2, you may run into the *other* three trigonometric functions—the cosecant, secant, and cotangent. These functions are abbreviated $\csc\theta$, $\sec\theta$, and $\cot\theta$, respectively, and they are simply the reciprocals of the three basic trigonometric functions you've already reviewed.

Here's how they relate.

$$\csc\theta = \frac{1}{\sin\theta} \qquad \sec\theta = \frac{1}{\cos\theta} \qquad \cot\theta = \frac{1}{\tan\theta} = \frac{\cos\theta}{\sin\theta}$$

You can also express these functions in terms of the sides of a right triangle—just by flipping over the SOHCAHTOA definitions of the three basic functions.

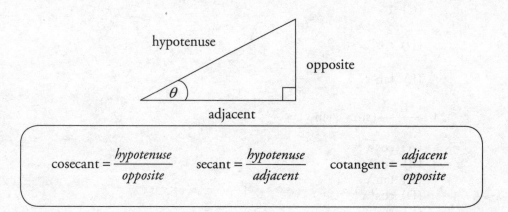

$$\text{cosecant} = \frac{hypotenuse}{opposite} \qquad \text{secant} = \frac{hypotenuse}{adjacent} \qquad \text{cotangent} = \frac{adjacent}{opposite}$$

These three functions generally show up in algebra-style questions, which require you to simplify complex expressions containing trig functions. The goal is usually to get an expression into the simplest form possible, one that contains no fractions. Such questions are like algebra-style questions involving the three basic trig functions; the only difference is that the addition of three more functions increases the number of possible forms an expression can take. For example,

$$(\cos x)(\cot x) + (\sin^2 x \csc x) =$$

$$(\cos x)(\frac{\cos x}{\sin x}) + (\sin^2 x)(\frac{1}{\sin x}) =$$

$$\frac{\cos^2 x}{\sin x} + \frac{\sin^2 x}{\sin x} =$$

$$\frac{\cos^2 x + \sin^2 x}{\sin x} =$$

$$\frac{1}{\sin x} =$$

$$\csc x$$

The entire expression (cos *x*)(cot *x*) + (sin² *x* csc *x*) is therefore equivalent to a single trig function, the cosecant of *x*. That's generally the way algebraic trigonometry questions work on the SAT Subject Test Math 2.

DRILL 4: OTHER TRIG FUNCTIONS

Simplify each of these expressions to a single trigonometric function. Keep an eye out for the trigonometric identities reviewed on pages 220, 221, and 226; they'll still come in handy. The answers can be found in Part IV.

19. $\sec^2 x - 1 =$

(A) $\sin x \cos x$
(B) $\sec^2 x$
(C) $\cos^2 x$
(D) $\sin^2 x$
(E) $\tan^2 x$

23. $\dfrac{1}{\sin x \cot x} =$

(A) $\cos x$
(B) $\sin x$
(C) $\tan x$
(D) $\sec x$
(E) $\csc x$

24. $\sin x + (\cos x)(\cot x) =$

(A) $\csc x$
(B) $\sec x$
(C) $\cot x$
(D) $\tan x$
(E) $\sin x$

38. $\dfrac{(\sec x + \tan x)(\sec x - \tan x)}{(\sec x + 1)(\sec x - 1)} =$

(A) 1
(B) $\csc^2 x$
(C) $\sin x \cos x$
(D) $\tan^2 x$
(E) $\cot^2 x$

GRAPHING TRIGONOMETRIC FUNCTIONS

There are two common ways to represent trigonometric functions graphically—on the *unit circle*, or on the coordinate plane (you'll get a good look at both methods in the coming pages). Both of these graphing approaches are ways of showing the repetitive nature of trigonometric functions. All of the trig functions (sine, cosine, and the rest) are called *periodic* functions. That simply means that they cycle repeatedly through the same values.

The Unit Circle

Do Not Adjust Your Math Book
Some of the images of the unit circle on the next several pages are not drawn to scale. This reflects something you'll find on the SAT Subject Test itself: given a choice between the math and the illustration, always trust the math.

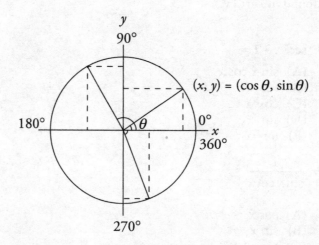

This is the unit circle. It looks a little like the coordinate plane; in fact, it *is* the coordinate plane, or at least a piece of it. The circle is called the *unit circle* because it has a radius of 1 (a single unit). This is convenient because it makes trigonometric values easy to figure out. The radius touching any point on the unit circle is the hypotenuse of a right triangle. The length of the horizontal leg of the triangle is the cosine (which is therefore the *x*-coordinate) and the length of the vertical leg is the sine (which is the *y*-coordinate). It works out this way because sine = opposite ÷ hypotenuse, and cosine = adjacent ÷ hypotenuse; and here the hypotenuse is 1, so the sine is simply the length of the opposite side, and the cosine is simply the length of the adjacent side.

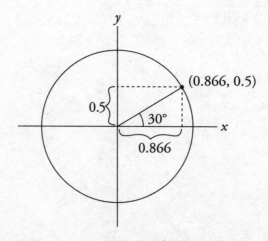

Suppose you wanted to show the sine and cosine of a 30° angle. That angle would appear on the unit circle as a radius drawn at a 30° angle to the positive *x*-axis (above). The *x*-coordinate of the point where the radius intercepts the circle is 0.866, which is the value of cos 30°. The *y*-coordinate of that point is 0.5, which is the value of sin 30°.

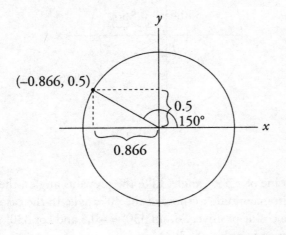

Now take a look at the sine and cosine of a 150° angle. As you can see, it looks just like the 30° angle, flipped over the *y*-axis. Its *y*-value is the same—sin 150° = 0.5—but its *x*-value is now *negative*. The cosine of 150° is −0.866.

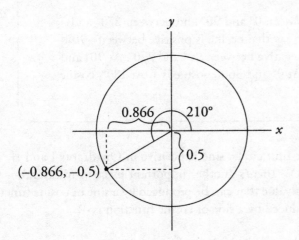

Here, you see the sine and cosine of a 210° angle. Once again, this looks just like the 30° angle, but this time flipped over the *x*- and *y*-axes. The sine of 210° is −0.5; the cosine of 210° is −0.866.

What Goes Around Comes Around

If you picked a certain angle and its sine, cosine, and tangent, and then slowly changed the measure of that angle, you'd see the sine, cosine, and tangent change as well. But after a while, you would have increased the angle by 360°—in other words, you would come full circle, back to the angle you started with, going counterclockwise. The new angle, equivalent to the old one, would have the same sine, cosine, and tangent as the original. As you continued to increase the angle's measure, the sine, cosine, and tangent would cycle through the same values all over again. All trigonometric functions repeat themselves every 360°. The tangent and cotangent functions actually repeat every 180°.

Thus, angles of 0° and 360° are mathematically equivalent. So are angles of 40° and 400°, or 360° and 720°. Any two angle measures separated by 360° are equivalent. For example, to find equivalent angles to 40°, you just keep adding 360°. Likewise, you can go around the unit circle *clockwise* by *subtracting* multiples of 360°. Some angles equivalent to 40° would thus be 40° − 360° = −320°, −680°, −1040°, and so on. In the next few sections, you'll see how that's reflected in the graphs of trigonometric functions.

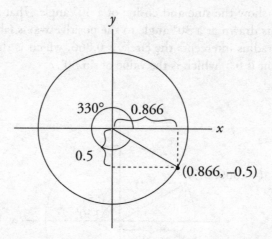

This is the sine and cosine of a 330° angle. Like the previous angles, the 330° angle has a sine and cosine equivalent in magnitude to those of the 30° angle. In the case of the 330° angle, the sine is negative and the cosine positive. So, sin 330° = −0.5 and cos 330° = 0.866. Notice that a 330° angle is equivalent to an angle of −30°.

Following these angles around the unit circle gives us some useful information about the sine and cosine functions.

- Sine is positive between 0° and 180° and negative between 180° and 360°. At 0°, 180°, and 360°, sine is zero. At 90°, sine is 1. At 270°, sine is −1.
- Cosine is positive between 0° and 90° and between 270° and 360°. (You could also say that cosine is positive between −90° and 90°.) Cosine is negative between 90° and 270°. At 90° and 270°, cosine is zero. At 0° and 360°, cosine is 1. At 180°, cosine is −1.

When these angles are sketched on the unit circle, sine is positive in Quadrants I and II, and cosine is positive in Quadrants I and IV. There's another important piece of information you can get from the unit circle. The biggest value that can be produced by a sine or cosine function is 1. The smallest value that can be produced by a sine or cosine function is −1.

Following the tangent function around the unit circle also yields useful information.

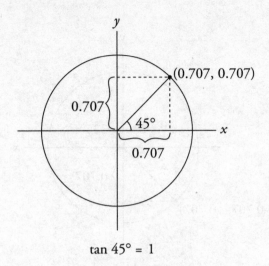

tan 45° = 1

The sine of 45° is $\frac{\sqrt{2}}{2}$, or 0.707, and the cosine of 45° is also $\frac{\sqrt{2}}{2}$, or 0.707. Since the tangent is the ratio of the sine to the cosine, that means that the tangent of 45° is 1.

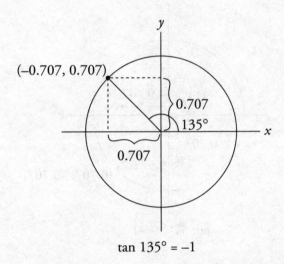

tan 135° = −1

The tangent of 135° is −1. Here the sine is positive, but the cosine is negative.

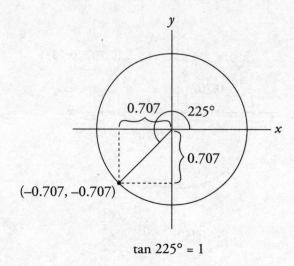

tan 225° = 1

The tangent of 225° is 1. Here the sine and cosine are both negative.

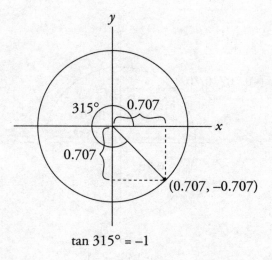

tan 315° = −1

The tangent of 315° is −1. Here the sine is negative, and the cosine is positive.

This is the pattern that the tangent function always follows. It's positive in Quadrants I and III and negative in Quadrants II and IV.

- Tangent is positive between 0° and 90° and between 180° and 270°.
- Tangent is negative between 90° and 180° and between 270° and 360°.

The unit circle is extremely useful for identifying equivalent angles (like 270° and −90°), and also for seeing other correspondences between angles, like the similarity between the 45° angle and the 135° angle, which are mirror images of one another on the unit circle.

A good way to remember where sine, cosine, and tangent are positive is to write the words of the phrase **A**ll **S**tudents **T**ake **C**alculus in Quadrants I, II, III, and IV, respectively, on the coordinate plane. The first letter of each word (**A S T C**) tells you which functions are positive in that quadrant. So **A**ll three functions are positive in Quadrant I, the **S**ine function is positive in Quadrant II, the **T**angent function is positive in Quadrant III, and the **C**osine function is positive in Quadrant IV.

DRILL 5: THE UNIT CIRCLE

Make simple sketches of the unit circle to answer the following questions about angle equivalencies. The answers can be found in Part IV.

18. If $\sin 135° = \sin x$, then x could equal

   (A) $-225°$
   (B) $-45°$
   (C) $225°$
   (D) $315°$
   (E) $360°$

21. If $\cos 60° = \cos n$, then n could be

   (A) $30°$
   (B) $120°$
   (C) $240°$
   (D) $300°$
   (E) $360°$

26. If $\sin 30° = \cos t$, then t could be

   (A) $-30°$
   (B) $60°$
   (C) $90°$
   (D) $120°$
   (E) $240°$

30. If $\tan 45° = \tan x$, then which of the following could be x ?

   (A) $-45°$
   (B) $135°$
   (C) $225°$
   (D) $315°$
   (E) $360°$

36. If $0° \le \theta \le 360°$ and $(\sin \theta)(\cos \theta) < 0$, which of the following gives the possible values of θ ?

   (A) $0° \le \theta \le 180°$
   (B) $0° \le \theta \le 180°$ or $270° \le \theta \le 360°$
   (C) $0° < \theta < 90°$ or $180° < \theta < 270°$
   (D) $90° < \theta < 180°$ or $270° < \theta < 360°$
   (E) $0° < \theta < 180°$ or $270° < \theta < 360°$

40. Which of the following are equivalent to cot 40° ?

    I. cot 220°

    II. cot 130°

    III. $\dfrac{\cos 400°}{\sin 400°}$

    (A) I only
    (B) II only
    (C) III only
    (D) I and II only
    (E) I and III only

Degrees and Radians

On the SAT Subject Test Math 2, you may run into an alternate means of measuring angles. This alternate system measures angles in *radians* rather than degrees. One degree is defined as $\dfrac{1}{360}$ of a full circle. One radian, on the other hand, is the measure of an angle that intercepts an arc exactly as long as the circle's radius. Since the circumference of a circle is 2π times the radius, the circumference is about 6.28 times as long as the radius, and there are about 6.28 radians in a full circle.

Because a number like 6.28 isn't easy to work with, angle measurements in radians are usually given in multiples or fractions of π. For example, there are exactly 2π radians in a full circle. There are π radians in a semicircle. There are $\dfrac{\pi}{2}$ radians in a right angle. Because 2π radians and 360° both describe a full circle, you can relate degrees and radians with the following proportion:

$$\frac{\text{degrees}}{360} = \frac{\text{radians}}{2\pi}$$

To convert degrees to radians, just plug the number of degrees into the proportion and solve for radians. The same technique works in reverse for converting radians to degrees. The figures below show what the unit circle looks like in radians, compared to the unit circle in degrees.

Radians

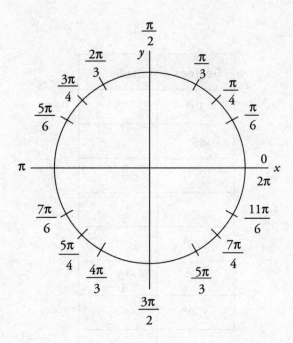

Degrees

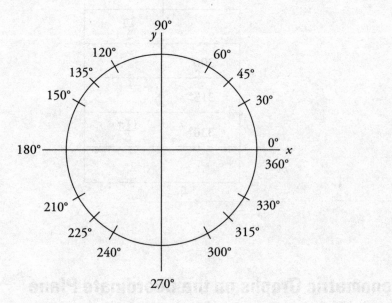

DRILL 6: DEGREES AND RADIANS

Fill in the following chart of radian–degree equivalencies. The answers can be found in Part IV.

Degrees	Radians
30°	
45°	
	$\dfrac{\pi}{3}$
	$\dfrac{\pi}{2}$
120°	
	$\dfrac{3\pi}{4}$
150°	
	π
	$\dfrac{5\pi}{4}$
240°	
	$\dfrac{3\pi}{2}$
300°	
315°	
330°	$\dfrac{11\pi}{6}$
	2π

Trigonometric Graphs on the Coordinate Plane

In a unit-circle diagram, the *x*-axis and *y*-axis represent the horizontal and vertical components of an angle, just as they do on the coordinate plane. The angle itself is represented by the angle between a certain radius and the positive *x*-axis. Any trigonometric function can be represented on a unit-circle diagram.

When a single trigonometric function is graphed, however, the axes take on different meanings. The *x*-axis represents the value of the angle; this axis is usually marked in radians. The *y*-axis represents a specific trigonometric function of that angle. For example, here is the coordinate plane graph of the *sine* function.

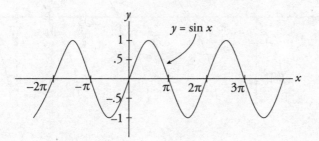

Periodic Repetitions
Trigonometric functions are called *periodic functions*. The *period* of a function is the distance a function travels before it repeats. A periodic function will repeat the same pattern of values forever. As you can see from the graph, the period of the sine function is 2π radians, or 360°.

Compare this graph to the unit circle on page 228. A quick comparison will show you that both graphs present the same information. At an angle of zero, the sine is zero; at a quarter circle ($\frac{\pi}{2}$ radians, or 90°), the sine is 1; and so on.

Here is the graph of the *cosine* function.

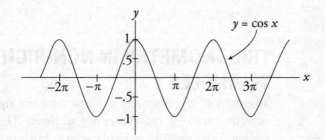

Make Things Easier
Because the sine and cosine curves have the same shape and size, you can focus on memorizing the facts for just one of them.

Notice that the cosine curve is identical to the sine curve, only shifted to the left by $\frac{\pi}{2}$ radians, or 90°. The cosine function also has a period of 2π radians.

Finally, here is the graph of the *tangent* function.

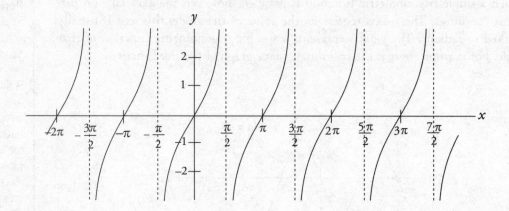

This function, obviously, is very different from the others. First, the tangent function has no upper or lower limit, unlike the sine and cosine functions, which produce values no higher than 1 or lower than –1. Second, the tangent function has *asymptotes*. These are values on the *x*-axis at which the tangent function does not exist; they are represented by vertical dotted lines. Finally, the tangent function has a period of π radians.

It's important to be able to recognize the graphs of the three basic trigonometric functions. You'll find more information about these functions and their graphs in the following chapter on functions.

The Undefined Tangent

It's easy to see why the tangent function's graph has asymptotes, if you recall the definition of the tangent.

$$\tan\theta = \frac{\sin\theta}{\cos\theta}$$

A fraction is undefined whenever its denominator equals zero. At any value where the cosine function equals zero, therefore, the tangent function is undefined—it doesn't exist. As you can see by comparing the cosine and tangent graphs, the tangent has an asymptote wherever the cosine function equals zero.

TRIGONOMETRY IN NON-RIGHT TRIANGLES

The rules of trigonometry are based on the right triangle, as you've seen in the preceding sections. Right triangles are *not*, however, the only places you can use trigonometric functions. There are a couple of powerful rules relating angles and lengths that you can use in *any* triangle. There are only two basic laws you need to know—the Law of Sines and the Law of Cosines.

The Law of Sines

The Law of Sines can be used to complete the dimensions of a triangle about which you have partial information. This is what the law says:

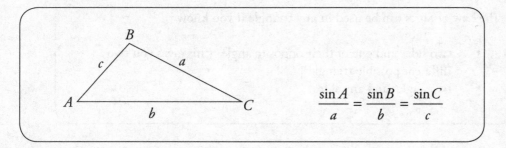

$$\frac{\sin A}{a} = \frac{\sin B}{b} = \frac{\sin C}{c}$$

Please Explain
In English, this law means that the sine of each angle in a triangle is related to the length of the opposite side by a constant proportion. Once you figure out the proportion relating the sine of one angle to the opposite side, you know the proportion for every angle.

Let's take a look at an example.

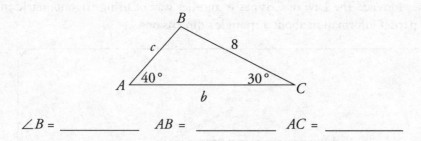

$\angle B =$ _____ $AB =$ _____ $AC =$ _____

In this triangle, you know only two angles and one side. Immediately, you can fill in the third angle, knowing that there are 180° in a triangle. Then, you can fill in the missing sides using the Law of Sines. Write out the proportions of the Law of Sines, filling in the values you know.

We Know, We Know
Yes, 0.643 ÷ 8 rounds to 0.0804, but if you keep the value of sin 40° in your calculator and divide by 8, you'll get 0.0803.

$$\frac{\sin 40°}{8} = \frac{\sin 110°}{b} = \frac{\sin 30°}{c}$$

$$\frac{0.643}{8} = \frac{0.940}{b} = \frac{0.5}{c}$$

$$0.0803 = \frac{0.940}{b} = \frac{0.5}{c}$$

At this point, you can set up two individual proportions and solve them individually for b and c, respectively.

$$0.0803 = \frac{0.940}{b} \qquad\qquad 0.0803 = \frac{0.5}{c}$$

$$b = \frac{0.940}{0.0803} \qquad\qquad c = \frac{0.5}{0.0803}$$

$$b = 11.70 \qquad\qquad c = 6.23$$

The length of *AB* is therefore 6.23, and the length of *AC* is 11.70. Now you know every dimension of triangle *ABC*.

The Law of Sines can be used in any triangle if you know

- two sides and one of their opposite angles (this gives you two different possible triangles)
- two angles and any side

The Law of Cosines

When you don't have the information necessary to use the Law of Sines, you may be able to use the Law of Cosines instead. The Law of Cosines is another way of using trigonometric functions to complete partial information about a triangle's dimensions.

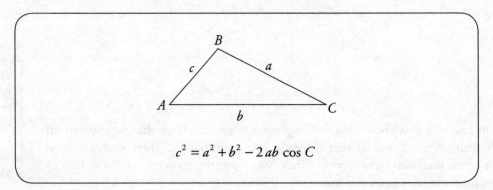

$$c^2 = a^2 + b^2 - 2ab \cos C$$

The Law of Cosines is a way of completing the dimensions of any triangle. You'll notice that it looks a bit like the Pythagorean Theorem. That's basically what it is, with a term added to the end to compensate for non-right angles. If you use the Law of Cosines on a right triangle, the "$2ab \cos C$" term becomes zero, and the law becomes the Pythagorean Theorem. The Law of Cosines can be used to fill in unknown dimensions of a triangle when you know any three of the quantities in the formula.

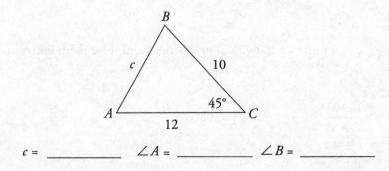

$c =$ _____ $\angle A =$ _____ $\angle B =$ _____

In this triangle, you know only two sides and an angle—the angle between the known sides. That is, you know a, b, and C. In order to find the length of the third side, c, just fill the values you know into the Law of Cosines, and solve.

$$c^2 = a^2 + b^2 - 2ab \cos C$$
$$c^2 = (10)^2 + (12)^2 - 2(10)(12) \cos 45°$$
$$c^2 = 100 + 144 - 240(0.707)$$
$$c^2 = 74.3$$
$$c = 8.62$$

The length of AB is therefore 8.62. Now that you know the lengths of all three sides, just use the Law of Sines to find the values of the unknown angles, or re-arrange the Law of Cosines to put the other unknown angles in the C position, and solve to find the measures of the unknown angles.

> The Law of Cosines can be used in any triangle if you know
>
> - all three sides; or
> - two sides and the angle between them

DRILL 7: NON-RIGHT TRIANGLES

In the following practice exercises, use the Law of Sines and the Law of Cosines to complete the dimensions of these non-right triangles. The answers can be found in Part IV.

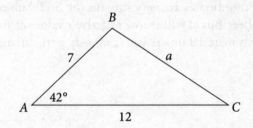

1. $a = $ _____ $\angle B = $ _____ $\angle C = $ _____

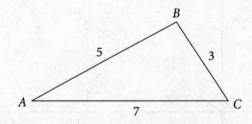

2. $\angle A = $ _____ $\angle B = $ _____ $\angle C = $ _____

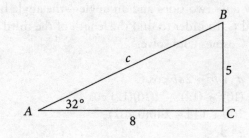

3. $c =$ _____ $\angle B =$ _____ $\angle C =$ _____

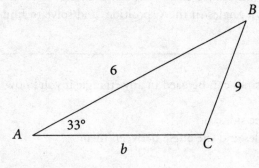

4. $b =$ _____ $\angle B =$ _____ $\angle C =$ _____

POLAR COORDINATES

Polar coordinates are another way of describing the position of a point on the coordinate plane. Questions involving polar coordinates are very rare on the SAT Subject Test Math 2, and it's even less likely that the College Board will throw negative r values at you. In other words, don't spend too much time on this material unless you're already a trigonometry wizard.

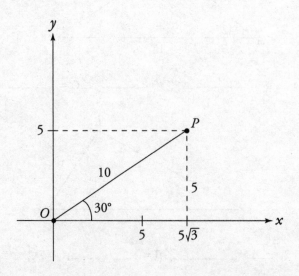

In the previous figure, the position of point P can be described in two ways. In standard rectangular coordinates, you would count across from the origin to get an x-coordinate and up from the origin to get a y-coordinate. (Remember: these x and y distances can be regarded as legs of a right triangle. The hypotenuse of the triangle is the distance between the point and the origin.) Rectangular coordinates consist of a horizontal distance and a vertical distance, and take the form (x, y). In rectangular coordinates, point P would be described as $\left(5\sqrt{3}, 5\right)$.

Polar coordinates consist of the distance, r, between a point and the origin, and the angle, θ, between that segment and the positive x-axis. Polar coordinates thus take the form (r, θ). The angle θ can be expressed in degrees, but is more often expressed in radians. In polar coordinates, therefore, P could be described as $(10, 30°)$ or $\left(10, \dfrac{\pi}{6}\right)$.

As you saw in the unit circle, there's more than one way to express any angle. For any angle, there is an infinite number of equivalent angles that can be produced by adding or subtracting 360° (or 2π, if you're working in radians) any number of times. Therefore, there is an infinite number of equivalent polar coordinates for any point. Point P, at $(10, 30°)$, can also be expressed as $(10, 390°)$, or $\left(10, \dfrac{13\pi}{6}\right)$. You can continually produce equivalent expressions by adding or subtracting 360° (or 2π).

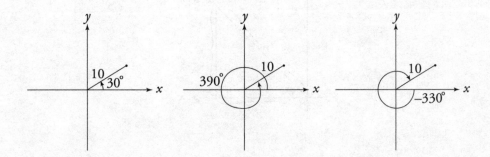

There's still another way to produce equivalent polar coordinates. The distance from the origin—the r in (r, θ)—can be negative. This means that once you've found the angle at which the hypotenuse must extend, a negative distance extends in the *opposite* direction, 180° away from the angle. Therefore, you can also create equivalent coordinates by increasing or decreasing the angle by 180° and flipping the sign on the distance. The point P at $(10, 30°)$ or $\left(10, \dfrac{\pi}{6}\right)$ could also be expressed as $(-10, 210°)$ or $\left(-10, \dfrac{7\pi}{6}\right)$. Other equivalent coordinates can be generated by pairing equivalent angles with these negative distances.

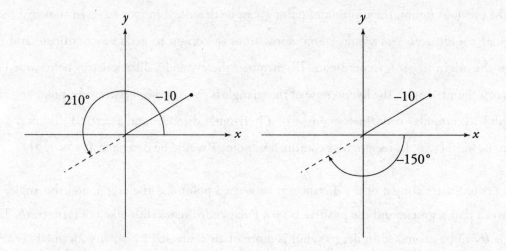

Converting Coordinates

Converting rectangular coordinates to polar coordinates and vice versa is simple. You just use the trigonometry techniques reviewed in this chapter.

Given a point (r, θ) in polar form, you can find its rectangular coordinates by drawing a right triangle such as the following:

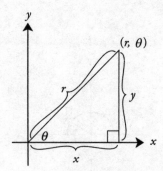

From this picture, using SOHCAHTOA and the Pythagorean Theorem, you can see the following relationships:

$$\cos \theta = \frac{x}{r}; \quad \sin \theta = \frac{y}{r}; \quad \tan \theta = \frac{y}{x}; \quad x^2 + y^2 = r^2; \quad \theta = \tan^{-1}\left(\frac{y}{x}\right)$$

Therefore, to go from Cartesian coordinates to polar coordinates, you use the Pythagorean Theorem and the inverse of tangent to solve.

$$(x, y) \rightarrow (r, \theta) \qquad r = \sqrt{x^2 + y^2} \qquad \theta = \tan^{-1}\left(\frac{y}{x}\right)$$

Be careful when finding θ, as the College Board is fond of using equivalent angles (consult the unit circle discussed earlier in this chapter).

You can also use sine and cosine to convert from polar coordinates to an (x, y) pair.

$$(r, \theta) \rightarrow (x, y) \qquad x = r\cos\theta \qquad y = r\sin\theta$$

DRILL 8: POLAR COORDINATES

Try the following practice questions about polar coordinates. The answers can be found in Part IV.

39. Which of the following rectangular coordinate pairs is equivalent to the polar coordinates $\left(6, \frac{\pi}{3}\right)$?

    (A) (0.5, 1.7)
    (B) (2.6, 5.2)
    (C) (3.0, 5.2)
    (D) (4.2, 4.8)
    (E) (5.2, 15.6)

42. The point $\left(7, \frac{3\pi}{4}\right)$ in polar coordinates is how far from the x-axis?

    (A) 3.67
    (B) 4.95
    (C) 5.25
    (D) 6.68
    (E) 16.71

$$A = \left(6, \frac{\pi}{3}\right) \qquad B = \left(6, \frac{5\pi}{3}\right) \qquad C = (3, 2\pi)$$

45. The points A, B, and C in polar coordinates define which of the following?

    (A) A point
    (B) A line
    (C) A plane
    (D) A three-dimensional space
    (E) None of these

50. Which of the following is the area of the triangle defined by the polar coordinates $(2, \frac{\pi}{2})$, $(8, \frac{\pi}{6})$, and $(8, \frac{5\pi}{6})$?

    (A)   3.141
    (B)   6.928
    (C)   13.856
    (D)   15.708
    (E)   27.713

Comprehensive Trigonometry Drill

The answers can be found in Part IV.

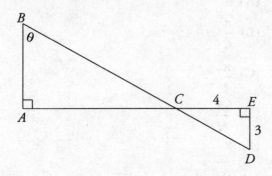

7. In the figure above, if $\overline{CE} = 4$ and $\overline{DE} = 3$, then what is the value of $\sin \theta$?

    (A) 0.014
    (B) 0.6
    (C) 0.75
    (D) 0.8
    (E) 1.333

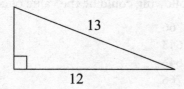

10. If x is the smallest angle in the triangle above, then what is the value of $\sec x$?

    (A) $\dfrac{13}{12}$

    (B) $\dfrac{13}{5}$

    (C) $\dfrac{12}{5}$

    (D) $\dfrac{12}{13}$

    (E) $\dfrac{5}{12}$

13. If $(1 - \sin x)(1 + \sin x) = 0.165$, then what is the value of $\tan^2 x$?

    (A) 0.198
    (B) 0.835
    (C) 1.517
    (D) 2.303
    (E) 5.061

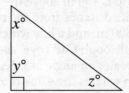

Note: Figure not drawn to scale.

20. In the figure above, which of the following must be true?

    I. $\sec x = \csc z$
    II. $x = z$
    III. $\sin x < \tan x$

    (A) I only
    (B) II only
    (C) I and III only
    (D) II and III only
    (E) I, II, and III

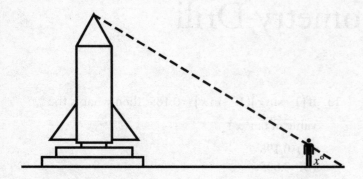

25. Carl (pictured above) is standing near a rocket. Carl's eyes are 1.6 m above ground level. If the rocket's tip is 150 m above the ground, the minimum safe distance from the rocket when it launches is 500 m, and a line which passes from the ground, through Carl's eye, and to the tip of the rocket creates an angle of x degrees with the ground, then what is the value of x which ensures that Carl is a safe distance from the rocket?

(A) 0.005
(B) 0.999
(C) 16.531
(D) 16.669
(E) 16.867

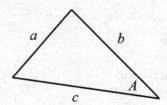

34. In the triangle above, if $a = \sqrt{20}$, $b = 7$, and $c = 9$, then what is the value of sec A ?

(A) 0.488
(B) 0.873
(C) 1.145
(D) 2.050
(E) 29.189

35. If $0 \le x \le \pi$, then for what value of x does

$$\sin\left(x + \frac{\pi}{6}\right) = \cos x \,?$$

(A) 0

(B) $\dfrac{\pi}{6}$

(C) $\dfrac{\pi}{4}$

(D) $\dfrac{5\pi}{6}$

(E) π

40. $(-8, 6)$ in the xy-coordinate system is equal to which of the following polar coordinates?

(A) $(-0.644, 10)$
(B) $(10, 2.214)$
(C) $(10, -0.644)$
(D) $(-10, 0.644)$
(E) $(-10, 5.640)$

45. If csc $\theta = -1.556$ and $-90° \le \theta \le 90°$, then which of the following could be the value of cos θ ?

(A) -0.766
(B) -0.643
(C) 0.643
(D) 0.766
(E) 1.556

47. If $\sin^2\left(\dfrac{\pi}{x}\right) + \sin^2\left(\dfrac{\pi}{y}\right) + \sin^2\left(\dfrac{\pi}{z}\right) = 2.345$, then

$$\cos^2\left(\dfrac{\pi}{x}\right) + \cos^2\left(\dfrac{\pi}{y}\right) + \cos^2\left(\dfrac{\pi}{z}\right) =$$

(A) -2.345
(B) -0.655
(C) 0.655
(D) 0.809
(E) 2.345

48. If $\dfrac{\pi}{2} < x < \pi$ and sin $x = 0.782$, then what is

cos $3x$?

(A) -1.870
(B) -0.901
(C) 0.705
(D) 0.789
(E) 0.901

Summary

o Memorize SOHCAHTOA. It's your best friend. $sin = \dfrac{opp}{hyp}$, $cos = \dfrac{adj}{hyp}$, and $tan = \dfrac{opp}{adj}$. Tan is

also equal to $\dfrac{sin}{cos}$. The College Board will test these with trigonometric identity questions.

o You can use the inverse of a function on your calculator to find the angle when you know the value of the corresponding trigonometric function.

o The unit circle is a circle on the coordinate plane with a radius of 1. You can use Pythagorean Theorem, SOHCAHTOA, and the fact that if you draw a line from the origin to any point on the circle and create a triangle, the hypotenuse will always be 1.

o The reciprocals of the trig functions are cosecant, secant, and cotangent. Their relation to the trig

functions are: $\csc\theta = \dfrac{1}{\sin\theta}$, $\sec\theta = \dfrac{1}{\cos\theta}$, and $\cot\theta = \dfrac{1}{\tan\theta}$.

o Radians are just another way to measure angles. The relationship between degrees and radians is

$\dfrac{degrees}{360} = \dfrac{radians}{2\pi}$.

o Use **All S**tudents **T**ake **C**alculus (ASTC) to remember which trig functions are positive in each quadrant.

o The graphs of trigonometric functions are periodic functions. Know what each graph looks like.

o For non-right triangles, there are two important laws. In a triangle with sides a, b, and c and cor-

responding angles A, B, and C, the Law of Sines says that $\dfrac{\sin A}{a} = \dfrac{\sin B}{b} = \dfrac{\sin C}{c}$; and the Law of Cosines

says that $c^2 = a^2 + b^2 - 2ab \cos C$.

- Polar coordinates use the distance, r, between a point and the origin, and the angle θ, which can be written in degrees or radians. A point in polar coordinates would be (r, θ).

- To convert from polar coordinates to xy-coordinates, remember the following: $x = r \cos \theta$, $y = r \sin \theta$.

- To convert from xy-coordinates to polar coordinates, remember the following: $r = \sqrt{x^2 + y^2}$, and $\theta = \tan^{-1}\left(\dfrac{y}{x}\right)$. Also remember to look for equivalent angles if your result for $\tan^{-1}\left(\dfrac{y}{x}\right)$ isn't given as an answer.

Chapter 10
Functions

On the SAT Subject Test Math 2 you will be asked many different questions about functions. Some questions will use strange symbols; these are called algebraic functions. Most of these questions will ask you to plug values into the functions.

However, most of the function questions you will see will use standard function notation ($f(x)$). You will be asked questions about compound functions, inverse functions, and more. As you will see, Plugging In is often the best approach to these questions.

Finally, you will see questions that ask you to analyze the graph of a function. Some questions may simply ask whether a given graph is actually a function. Other questions will ask about symmetry or transformations of a graph. You will see various ways of approaching these questions in this chapter.

DEFINITIONS

Here are some terms concerning algebraic functions that appear on the SAT Subject Test Math 2. Make sure you're familiar with them. If the meaning of any of these vocabulary words keeps slipping your mind, add that word to your flash cards.

Domain	The set of values that may be put into a function.
Range	The set of values that can be produced by a function.
Even Function	A function for which $f(x) = f(-x)$—even functions are symmetrical across the y-axis.
Odd Function	A function for which $-f(x) = f(-x)$—odd functions have origin symmetry, which means that they are the same when reflected across the origin.
Root	Values in a function's domain at which the function equals zero—a root is also called a *zero, solution,* or *x-intercept* of a function.
Degree	The sum of the exponents in an algebraic term—the degree of a polynomial is the highest degree of any term in the polynomial.
Asymptote	A line that the graph of a function approaches but never reaches.
Period	In periodic functions, the distance traveled by the function before it repeats itself.
Frequency	The number of times a graph repeats itself in a given distance; the reciprocal of the function's period.
Amplitude	In a periodic function, half the difference between the least and greatest values of the function.
Nonnegative	The values of a function that are greater than or equal to zero.

WEIRD SYMBOLS AS FUNCTIONS

If you see a question using symbols that you've never seen before, it is a function question. The College Board will try to frighten you with weird characters, but as long as you can follow the directions and plug in, you'll have little trouble with these questions.

---

1. If $\Diamond a \Diamond = a^2 - 5a + 4$, then $\Diamond 6 \Diamond =$

   (A) 6
   (B) 8
   (C) 10
   (D) 12
   (E) 14

Here's How to Crack It

Answer this question by plugging 6 into the definition of the function everywhere *a* is found.

$$(6)^2 - 5(6) + 4 =$$

$$36 - 30 + 4 =$$

$$10$$

The answer is (C).

Don't be confused if a question requires you to plug something strange into a function. Just follow the instructions, and the answer will become clear.

---

3. If $\&y = y^2 - 6$, then which of the following equals $\&(y + 6)$?

    (A) y^2
    (B) $y^2 - 36$
    (C) $2y - 36$
    (D) $y^2 + 12y + 30$
    (E) $y^2 + 12y + 42$

Here's How to Crack It

To find the answer, just plug in a number. Let's pick $y = 2$.

That means we want to find the value of $\&(2 + 6)$, which is $\&8$. Plugging 8 into the definition gives us

$$(8)^2 - 6 = 58$$

Now just plug in 2 for *y* in the answer choices to see which one becomes 58, your target number. Choice (D) is the correct answer.

DRILL 1: WEIRD SYMBOLS AS FUNCTIONS

Practice your techniques on the following function questions. The answers can be found in Part IV.

19. If $[x] = -\left|x^3\right|$, then $[4] - [3] =$

    (A) −91
    (B) −37
    (C)   1
    (D) 37
    (E) 91

20. If ¥c is defined as $5(c - 2)^2$, then ¥5 + ¥6 =

    (A) ¥7
    (B) ¥8
    (C) ¥9
    (D) ¥10
    (E) ¥11

$$\$a = \begin{cases} a \text{ if } a \text{ is even} \\ -a \text{ if } a \text{ is odd} \end{cases}$$

21. \$1 + \$2 + \$3 ... \$100 + \$101 =

    (A) −151
    (B) −51
    (C)   0
    (D)   50
    (E)   51

FUNCTIONS USING STANDARD NOTATION

On many questions, the College Board will also give you functions with letters, such as f and g, that look like the ones you've probably studied in school. A function is a type of relation between two sets of numbers called the domain and range of the function. Specifically, a function is a relation in which every element in the domain corresponds to only one element in the range; for every x in the function, there is only one possible $f(x)$ (or y, on a graph).

The most basic function questions test only your understanding of functions and the algebra required to work with them. Here are some examples of basic functions.

$$f(x) = \left|x^2 - 16\right| \qquad g(x) = \frac{1}{4}(x - 2)^3$$

$$t(a) = a(a - 6) + 8 \qquad p(q) = \frac{3 - q}{q}$$

The best way to think of function is that it's like a machine. It spits out a different result depending on what you put into it. As long as you follow the directions of the machine, it will spit out the right response for you. The test may bring up a couple of phrases: independent variable and dependent variable. The *independent variable* is what you put into the machine. You could put anything in; it doesn't rely on anything, so it's *independent*. The *dependent variable* is what your machine spits out. What it is depends on what's put into the machine. That's why it's the *dependent variable*. On a graph, the independent variable is on the *x*-axis and the dependent variable is on the *y*-axis.

When questions ask you to work with algebraic functions, you'll be required to do one of two things: plug numbers into a function and get a numerical answer, or plug variables into a function and get an algebraic answer. For example, given the function $g(x) = (x + 2)^2$, you could run into two types of questions.

$f(x) = y$
Sometimes it helps to think of $f(x)$ as being equal to y. Both are the result you get when you put a number into the equation.

1. If $g(x) = (x + 2)^2$, what is the value of $g(4)$?

   (A) 8
   (B) 12
   (C) 16
   (D) 36
   (E) 64

Here's How to Crack It

Answering this question is a simple matter of plugging 4 into the function, and simplifying $(4 + 2)^2$ to get 36.

Here, on the other hand, is an algebraic version of the same question.

3. If $g(x) = (x + 2)^2$, then $g(x + 2) =$

   (A) $x^2 + 4$
   (B) $x^2 + 6$
   (C) $x^2 + 4x + 4$
   (D) $x^2 + 4x + 6$
   (E) $x^2 + 8x + 16$

The Rare Occasion

There are a few unusual function types that you should be prepared for. It is possible, for example, for elements in the domain to consist of more than one value, like this:

$$f(a, b) = \frac{a^2 + b^2}{ab}$$

$$g(x, y) = (x + 2)^2 - (y - 2)^2$$

In each of these functions, an element in the domain is a pair of values. Functions of this kind are fairly rare on the SAT Subject Test Math 2, but you may run into one. Although they're unusual, they're not difficult. Simply treat them like ordinary functions—to calculate the value of $f(3, 4)$, for example, simply take the values 3 and 4 and plug them into the definition of the function in the positions of *a* and *b*, respectively (you get $\frac{25}{12}$).

Here's How to Crack It

To solve this question, just plug in a number for x. Let's pick $x = 3$, and plug that into $g(x + 2)$. You need to find $g(3 + 2) = g(5)$, which is $(5 + 2)^2 = 49$, our target number. Now, plug $x = 3$ into the answer choices, to see which one turns into 49. Choice (E) is the correct answer.

You may also have to work with a *split function*—sometimes called a *piecewise function*. A split function is one that has different definitions, depending on some condition that is part of the function. Here are a couple of examples of split functions.

$$y(x) = \begin{cases} x^2, & x > 0 \\ 1, & x = 0 \\ -x^2, & x < 0 \end{cases} \qquad f(x) = \begin{cases} 5x, & \text{if } x \text{ is odd} \\ 4x, & \text{if } x \text{ is even} \end{cases}$$

Functions of this type are fairly self-explanatory. It's just necessary to check the conditions of the function before plugging values in to make sure you're using the right function definition.

DRILL 2: FUNCTIONS USING STANDARD NOTATION

Practice working with functions in the following questions. The answers can be found in Part IV.

1. If $f(x) = x^2 - x^3$, then $f(-1) =$

    (A) −2
    (B) −1
    (C) 0
    (D) 1
    (E) 2

3. If $f(z) = \sqrt{z^2 + 8z}$, then how much does $f(z)$ increase as z goes from 7 to 8 ?

    (A) 0.64
    (B) 1.07
    (C) 2.96
    (D) 3.84
    (E) 5.75

11. If $g(t) = t^3 + t^2 - 9t - 9$, then $g(3) =$

    (A) −9
    (B) 0
    (C) 9
    (D) 27
    (E) 81

14. If $f(x, y) = \dfrac{xy}{x+y}$, which of the following is equal to $f(3, -6)$?

 (A) −48
 (B)   −6
 (C)   3
 (D)   6
 (E)   18

15. If $h(x) = x^2 + x - 2$, and $h(n) = 10$, then n could be which of the following?

 (A) −4
 (B) −3
 (C) −1
 (D)   1
 (E)   2

19. The function f is given by $f(x) = x \cdot [x]$, where $[x]$ is defined to be the greatest factor of x that does not equal x. What is $f(75)$?

 (A)   25
 (B)   225
 (C)   625
 (D) 1,125
 (E) 1,875

$$g(x) = \begin{cases} 2|x| & \text{if } x \le 0 \\ -|x| & \text{if } x > 0 \end{cases}$$

20. What is the value of $g(-y)$ if $y = 3$?

 (A) −6.0
 (B) −3.0
 (C) −1.5
 (D)   1.5
 (E)   6.0

$$f(x, y) = \begin{cases} \dfrac{xy^2}{2} & \text{if } xy \text{ is even} \\ \dfrac{x^2 y}{2} & \text{if } xy \text{ is odd} \\ \dfrac{1}{xy} & \text{otherwise} \end{cases}$$

37. $f(2,3) + f(0.5,4) =$

 (A)   6.5
 (B)   9.167
 (C)   9.5
 (D) 10
 (E) 13

COMPOUND FUNCTIONS

Compound functions combine functions by using the output of one function as the input of the other. The first thing to remember about compound functions is order of operations: you do what's in the parentheses first. For example,

f∘g?

Sometimes the College Board will use the notation $f \circ g$. This notation means that the second function is inside the parentheses; in other words, $f \circ g = f(g(x))$. In either case, you work from right to left.

$$f(x) = x^3 + 2 \qquad\qquad g(x) = x^2$$

$$f(g(x)) = (x^2)^3 + 2 = x^6 + 2 \text{ BUT } g(f(x)) = (x^3 + 2)^2 = x^6 + 4x^3 + 4$$

As you can see, for most compound functions, the order in which the functions apply matters *greatly* in what the result will be!

Luckily, on the SAT Subject Test Math 2, there are many techniques that can greatly simplify compound function questions. In particular, Plugging In works very well on these types of questions. Read on to see examples of different ways the College Board will use compound functions on this test.

Plugging In Values Given by The College Board

The simplest compound function questions on the SAT Subject Test Math 2 are the questions in which you are given the number to plug in to the function. These questions often have wrong answers that misuse negative numbers or violate order of operations. For example,

$$f(x) = x^2 + 10x + 3 \qquad\qquad g(x) = \frac{1}{\sqrt{x + 22}}$$

$$g(f(x)) = \frac{1}{\sqrt{x^2 + 10x + 25}}$$

The expression $g(f(x))$ is a compound function made up of the functions $f(x)$ and $g(x)$. As with any algebraic expression with parentheses, you start with the innermost part. To find $g(f(x))$ for any x, calculate the value of $f(x)$, and plug that value into $g(x)$. The result is $g(f(x))$. Like questions based on simple algebraic functions, compound-function questions come in two flavors—questions that require you to plug numbers into compound functions and do the arithmetic, and questions that require you to plug terms with variables into compound functions and find an algebraic answer. Here's an example.

$$f(x) = x^2 + 10x + 3$$
$$g(x) = \frac{1}{\sqrt{x + 22}}$$

16. What is the value of $g(f(-4))$?

   (A) 0.11
   (B) 1.00
   (C) 2.75
   (D) 5.41
   (E) 6.56

Here's How to Crack It

To find the value of $g(f(-4))$, just plug -4 into $f(x)$; you should find that $f(-4) = -21$. Then, plug -21 into $g(x)$. You should find that $g(-21) = 1$. The correct answer is (B).

---○---

The other answers in this problem illustrate how the College Board anticipates where you can mess up. For example, if you use 4 instead of -4 in $f(x)$, you find $f(4) = 59$, and $g(59) = 0.11$, which is (A). If, however, you were to reverse order of operations and find $f(g(-4))$, you would find an answer of 5.41, which is (D).

PITA and Compound Functions

Another relatively simple type of compound function question asks you to find the inside function when you're given the outside function and a value for the compound function. Despite the use of compound function notation, these questions are really the same as normal function notation questions; they just look more complicated. In these cases, Plugging In the Answers is the best approach.

---○---

12. If $f(x) = 4x - 2$ and $f(g(x)) = 10$, then $g(x) =$

(A) 2

(B) 3

(C) 10

(D) $4x + 2$

(E) $\dfrac{x+2}{4}$

Here's How to Crack It

This question is looking for a value that, when put into $f(x)$, gives a result of 10. The question just happens to call that "something" $g(x)$. You know that one of the five answer choices must work, so plug in the answers. Choices (D) and (E) contain variables; therefore, plugging those answers into $f(x)$ will result in an answer choice with variables. You want $f(g(x)) = 10$, with no variables, so eliminate (D) and (E). Choice (B) is the middle choice of those that remain, so plug 3 into $f(x)$: $f(3) = 4(3) - 2 = 10$. This matches what the question says, so choose (B).

---○---

Finding the Algebraic Expression of a Compound Function

A more complicated way that the College Board tests compound functions is by asking for the algebraic expression of a compound function. Luckily, the SAT Subject Test Math 2 is a multiple-choice test, so you don't have to come up with the expression yourself. Instead, you can (and should) plug in a value for x and turn these questions into ones like question 12 above. Try an example.

$$f(x) = x^2 + 10x + 3$$

$$g(x) = \frac{1}{\sqrt{x+22}}$$

21. For all $x > -5$, which of the following is $g(f(x))$?

(A) $\dfrac{1}{x-5}$

(B) $\dfrac{1}{x+5}$

(C) $\sqrt{x^2 + 10x + 3}$

(D) $\dfrac{1}{x^2 + 10x + 3}$

(E) $\dfrac{1}{(x+5)^2}$

Here's How to Crack It

Instead of doing lots of messy algebra, just pick an easy number to plug in for x. Let's try $x = 3$. So you're looking for $g(f(3))$. Work from the inside out, $f(3) = 42$, so $g(f(3)) = g(42)$. When you plug 42 into g, you get $\dfrac{1}{8}$, the target number. Plugging $x = 3$ into the answer choices, you find that (B) hits that target.

Finding an Original Function When Given the Compound Function

A variation on asking for the algebraic function of a compound function is to ask for one of the original functions given the other original function and the compound function. As above, the best way to approach these questions is to plug in. However, you still need to respect order of operations and plug in accordingly. Here's an example.

50. If $f(x) = (x+2)^2 + 3$ and $f(g(x)) = \dfrac{7x^2 + 46x + 76}{x^2 + 6x + 9}$, then

    $g(x) =$

    (A) $x + 3$

    (B) $\dfrac{1}{x+3}$

    (C) $(x+2)^2 - 3$

    (D) $\left(\dfrac{2x+2}{x+3}\right)^2$

    (E) $\dfrac{7x^2 + 46x + 76}{x^2 + 6x + 9}$

Here's How to Crack It

Start by plugging in to the compound function. Make $x = 2$, so

$f(g(2)) = \dfrac{7(2)^2 + 46(2) + 76}{(2)^2 + 6(2) + 9} = 7.84$. Next, plug $x = 2$ into the answer choices to find the

possible values for $g(2)$.

(A) $\quad (2) + 3 = 5$

(B) $\quad \dfrac{1}{(2)+3} = 0.2$

(C) $\quad ((2)+2)^2 - 3 = 13$

(D) $\quad \left(\dfrac{2(2)+2}{(2)+3}\right)^2 = 1.44$

(E) $\quad \dfrac{7(2)^2 + 46(2) + 76}{(2)^2 + 6(2) + 9} = 7.84$

Remember that you're looking for the $g(2)$ that, put into $f(x)$, gives you the value of $f(g(2))$ you just found. Therefore, plug each value for $g(2)$ into the original $f(x)$, and find the one that equals 7.84.

Using "Y=" and "CALC->value" on function questions
For some function questions, you will find yourself trying many values of x in a given function. On the TI-84, you can save yourself a lot of work by using the "Y=" and "value" functions on your calculator. First, press the "Y=" button and input the function. Be careful with parentheses, especially with functions using fractions! Next, press "2ND" "TRACE" to access the "CALC" menu. The first option is "value"; select that option and input the x-value you are looking for. Your calculator will give you the value of $f(x)$ at that spot; type in another number to find another $f(x)$. If you get an error, simply resize the window using the "WINDOW" tool so you can see the point you're requesting.

(A) $\quad f(5) = (5+2)^2 + 3 = 52$

(B) $\quad f(0.2) = (0.2+2)^2 + 3 = 7.84$

(C) $\quad f(13) = (13+2)^2 + 3 = 228$

(D) $\quad f(1.44) = (1.44+2)^2 + 3 = 14.8336$

(E) $\quad f(7.84) = (7.84+2)^2 + 3 = 99.8256$

The answer is (B).

DRILL 3: COMPOUND FUNCTIONS

Practice working with compound functions in the following questions. The answers can be found in Part IV.

2. If $f(x) = 3x$ and $g(x) = x + 4$, what is the difference between $f(g(x))$ and $g(f(x))$?

    (A) 0
    (B) 2
    (C) 4
    (D) 8
    (E) 12

8. If $f(x) = |x| - 5$ and $g(x) = x^3 - 5$, what is $f(g(-2))$?

    (A) –18
    (B) –5
    (C)   0
    (D)   3
    (E)   8

9. If $f(x) = 5 + 3x$ and $f(g(x)) = 17$, then $g(x) =$

    (A) 3
    (B) 4
    (C) 56
    (D) $3 + 5x$
    (E) $5 + 3x$

$$f(x) = x^2 + 10x + 25$$

$$g(x) = \sqrt{x} + 4$$

16. For all $x > -5$, which of the following is $g(f(x))$?

    (A) $x - 1$
    (B) $x + 1$
    (C) $x + 7$
    (D) $x + 9$
    (E) $x^2 - 2x - 1$

$$f(x) = \sqrt{x}$$

$$g(x) = x^3 - 2$$

20. What is the positive difference between $f(g(3))$ and $g(f(3))$?

    (A) 0.7
    (B) 0.9
    (C) 1.8
    (D) 3.4
    (E) 6.8

22. If $f(x) = \log\left(\dfrac{x}{2}\right)$ and $f(g(x)) = 2$, then $g(x) =$

    (A)   0.01
    (B)   10
    (C)   20
    (D) 100
    (E) 200

35. If $f(x) = x^2 - 1$ and $f\left(g(x)\right) = \dfrac{1 - x^2}{x^2}$, then $g(x) =$

    (A) $\dfrac{x-1}{x}$

    (B) $\dfrac{1}{x}$

    (C) $\dfrac{1}{x^2}$

    (D) $\dfrac{1}{x-1}$

    (E) $2 - x$

INVERSE FUNCTIONS

Inverse functions are opposites—functions that undo each other. Here's a simple example.

$$f(x) = 5x \qquad f^{-1}(x) = \frac{x}{5}$$

Here, the function $f(x)$ multiplies x by 5. Its inverse, symbolized by $f^{-1}(x)$, divides x by 5. Any number put through one of these functions and then the other would come back to where it started. Here's a slightly more complex pair of inverse functions.

$$f(x) = 5x + 2 \qquad f^{-1}(x) = \frac{x-2}{5}$$

Here, the function $f(x)$ multiplies x by 5 and then adds 2. The inverse function $f^{-1}(x)$ does the opposite steps in reverse order, subtracting 2 and then dividing by 5. Let's add one more step.

$$f(x) = \frac{5x+2}{4} \qquad f^{-1}(x) = \frac{4x-2}{5}$$

Now, the function $f(x)$ multiplies x by 5, adds 2, and then divides by 4. The inverse function $f^{-1}(x)$ once again does the reverse; it multiplies by 4, subtracts 2, and then divides by 5. An inverse function always works this way; it does the opposite of each operation in the original function, in reverse order.

$f(g(x)) = x$

Compound functions and inverse functions are often used together in questions on the SAT Subject Test Math 2. It's characteristic of inverse functions that they have opposite effects—they undo each other. For that reason, whenever you see the statement $f(g(x)) = x$, you know that the functions $f(x)$ and $g(x)$ are inverse functions. When a value x is put through one function and then the other, it returns to its original value. That means that whatever changes $f(x)$ makes are undone by $g(x)$. The statement $f(g(x)) = x$ means that $g(x) = f^{-1}(x)$.

The typical inverse-function question gives you the definition of a function and asks you to identify the function's inverse.

---

30. If $f(x) = \dfrac{x}{4} + 3$ and $f(g(x)) = x$, which of the following is $g(x)$?

    (A) $x - \dfrac{3}{4}$

    (B) $x - 12$

    (C) $4x - 3$

    (D) $4x - 12$

    (E) $4(x + 12)$

Here's How to Crack It

In this question, the statement $f(g(x)) = x$ tells you that $f(x)$ and $g(x)$ are inverse functions. Finding $g(x)$, then, amounts to finding the inverse of $f(x)$. You could do this by picking out the function that does the opposite of the operations in $f(x)$, in reverse order; but there's an easier way. By definition, inverse functions undo each other. In practice, this means that if you plug an easy number into $f(x)$ and get a result, the inverse function will be the function that turns that result back into your original number.

For example, given the function $f(x)$, you might decide to plug in 8, a number that makes the math easy.

$$f(x) = \frac{x}{4} + 3$$

$$f(8) = \frac{8}{4} + 3$$

$$f(8) = 2 + 3$$

$$f(8) = 5$$

You find that $f(x)$ turns 8 into 5. The inverse function $g(x)$ will be the one that does the reverse—that is, turns 5 into 8. To find $g(x)$, plug 5 into each of the answer choices. The answer choice that gives you 8 will be the correct answer. In this case, the correct answer is (D).

> **Invert x and y**
>
> If it doesn't look like Plugging In will help you, another great way to find the inverse of a function is to switch x and y, or $f(x)$. So if the original function is $f(x) = 3x - 4$, move it all around. First replace $f(x)$ with y so you can see it all more easily. Now you have $y = 3x - 4$. Switch x and y: $x = 3y - 4$. Now solve for y; $x + 4 = 3y$; and $\frac{x+4}{3} = y$. As a final touch, replace y with $f^{-1}(x)$: $f^{-1}(x) = \frac{x+4}{3}$. And you now have the inverse of $f(x) = 3x - 4$.

DRILL 4: INVERSE FUNCTIONS

Practice your inverse-function techniques on these questions. The answers can be found in Part IV.

7. If $f(x) = \dfrac{4x - 5}{2}$ and $f(g(x)) = x$, then $g(x) =$

(A) $2x + \dfrac{5}{4}$

(B) $\dfrac{2x + 5}{4}$

(C) $x + \dfrac{5}{2}$

(D) $\dfrac{x}{4} + \dfrac{2}{5}$

(E) $\dfrac{5x + 2}{4}$

18. If $f(x) = 4x^2 - 12x + 9$ for $x \geq 0$, what is $f^{-1}(9)$?

   (A) 1
   (B) 3
   (C) 5
   (D) 12
   (E) 16

30. If $f(3) = 9$, then $f^{-1}(4) =$

   (A) −2
   (B) 0
   (C) 2
   (D) 16
   (E) It cannot be determined from the information given.

31. If $f(x) = \sqrt{\dfrac{x+2}{3}}$ and $f(g(x)) = x$, then $g(x) =$

   (A) x

   (B) $\dfrac{x^2 - 2}{3}$

   (C) $3x^2 - 2$

   (D) $3x^2 - 6$

   (E) $3(x - 2)^2$

DOMAIN AND RANGE

Some function questions will ask you to make statements about the domain and range of functions. With a few simple rules, it's easy to figure out what limits there are on the domain or range of a function.

Domain

The domain of a function is the set of values that may be put into a function without violating any laws of math. When you're dealing with a function in the $f(x)$ form, the domain includes all of the allowable values of x. Sometimes a function question will limit the function's domain in some way, like the following:

Domain

An easy way to think about it is that the domain is all the possible values of x.

For all integers n, $f(n) = (n - 2)\pi$. What is the value of $f(7)$?

In this function, the independent variable n is limited; n can be only an integer. The domains of most functions, however, are not obviously limited. Generally, you can put whatever number you want into a function; the domain of many functions is all real numbers. Only certain functions have domains that are mathematically limited. To figure out the limits of a function's domain, you need to use a few basic rules. Here are the laws that can limit a function's domain.

> ## Mathematical Impossibilities That Limit the Domain of a Function
>
> - **Values that result in a denominator of zero:** Any value that would make the denominator of a fraction equal zero must be excluded from the domain of the function.
> - **Any even root of a negative number (including square roots):** An even root of a negative number will give an imaginary result. Because domain requires real values for the function, any value that would result in taking the even root of a negative number must be excluded from the domain of the function.

Whenever a function contains a fraction, a square root, or another even-numbered root, it's possible that the function will have a limited domain. Look for any values that would make denominators zero, or even-numbered roots negative. Those values must be eliminated from the domain. Take a look at these examples.

$$f(x) = \frac{x+5}{x}$$

In this function, there is a variable in the denominator of a fraction. This denominator must not equal zero, so the domain of $f(x)$ is $x \neq 0$.

$$g(x) = \frac{x}{x+5}$$

Once again, this function has a variable in the denominator of a fraction. In this case, the value of x that would make the denominator equal zero is –5. Therefore, the domain of $g(x)$ is $x \neq -5$.

$$t(a) = 4\sqrt{a}$$

This function has a variable under a square root sign. The quantity under a square root sign must not be negative, so the domain of $t(a)$ is $a \geq 0$.

$$s(a) = 3\sqrt{10-a}$$

Here again, you have a function with a variable under a square root. This time, the values that would make the expression negative are values greater than 10; all of these values must be eliminated from the function's domain. The domain of $s(a)$ is therefore $a \leq 10$.

A function can involve both fractions and square roots. Always pay careful attention to any part of a function that could place some limitation on the function's domain. It's also possible to run into a function where it's not easy to see what values violate the denominator rule or the square root rule. Generally, factoring is the easiest way to make these relationships clearer. Here's an example.

$$f(x) = \frac{1}{x^3 + 2x^2 - 8x}$$

Here, you've got variables in the denominator. You know this is something to watch out for, but it's not obvious what values might make the denominator equal zero. To make it clearer, factor the denominator.

$$f(x) = \frac{1}{x\left(x^2 + 2x - 8\right)}$$

$$f(x) = \frac{1}{x(x + 4)(x - 2)}$$

Now, things are much clearer. Whenever quantities are being multiplied, the entire product will equal zero if any one piece equals zero. Any value that makes the denominator equal zero must be eliminated from the function's domain. In this case, the values 0, –4, and 2 all make the denominator zero. The domain of $f(x)$ is $x \neq -4, 0, 2$. Take a look at one more example.

$$g(x) = \sqrt{x^2 + 4x - 5}$$

Once again, you've got an obvious warning sign—variables under a radical. Any values of x that make the expression under the radical negative must be eliminated from the domain. But what values are those? Are there any? To make it clear, factor the expression.

$$g(x) = \sqrt{(x + 5)(x - 1)}$$

The product of two expressions can be negative only when one of the expressions is negative and the other positive. If both expressions are positive, their product is positive. If both expressions are negative, their product is still positive. So the domain of $g(x)$ must contain only values that make $(x + 5)$ and $(x - 1)$ both negative, both positive, or one equal to zero. The expression $(x + 5)$ is zero at $x = 5$ and negative when $x < -5$. The expression $(x - 1)$ is zero at $x = 1$ and negative when $x < 1$. Between –5 and 1, $(x - 1)$ is negative and $(x + 5)$ is positive. Therefore, the product of the two expressions will be negative when $-5 < x < 1$; this must be excluded from the domain of the function. All other real values of x are in the domain; therefore, the domain of $g(x)$ is $x \leq -5$ or $x \geq 1$.

Domain Notation

The domain of a function is generally described using the variable x. A function $f(x)$ whose domain includes only values greater than 0 and less than 24, could be described in the following ways:

> The domain of $f(x)$ is $\{0 < x < 24\}$.
> The domain of f is the set $\{x: 0 < x < 24\}$.

A function in the form $f(x)$ can be referred to either as $f(x)$ or simply as f.

Range

The range of a function is the set of possible values that can be produced by the function. When you're dealing with a function in the $f(x)$ form, the range consists of all the allowable values of $f(x)$. The range of a function, like the domain, is limited by a few laws of mathematics. Several of these laws are the same laws that limit the domain. Here are the major rules that limit a function's range.

> **Range**
> An easy way to think about it is that the range is all possible values of y. In the case of functions, the range is all the possible values of $f(x)$.

- An even exponent produces only nonnegative numbers. Any term raised to an even exponent must be positive or zero.
- The square root of a quantity represents only the positive root. Like even powers, a square root can't be negative. The same is true for other even-numbered roots ($\sqrt[4]{}$, $\sqrt[6]{}$, etc.).
- Absolute values produce only nonnegative values.

These three operations—even exponents, even roots, and absolute values—can produce only nonnegative values. Consider these three functions.

$$f(x) = x^4 \qquad f(x) = \sqrt{x} \qquad f(x) = |x|$$

These functions all have the same range, $\{f(x) \geq 0\}$. These are the three major mathematical operations that often limit the ranges of functions. They can operate in unusual ways. The fact that a term in a function must be nonnegative can affect the entire function in different ways. Take a look at the following examples.

$$f(x) = -x^4 \qquad f(x) = -\sqrt{x} \qquad f(x) = -|x|$$

Each of these functions once again contains a nonnegative operation, but in each case the sign is now flipped by a negative sign. The range of each function is now $\{f(x) \leq 0\}$. In addition to being flipped by negative signs, ranges can also be slid upward or downward by addition and subtraction. Take a look at these examples.

$$f(x) = x^4 - 5 \qquad f(x) = \sqrt{x} - 5 \qquad f(x) = |x| - 5$$

Each of these functions contains a nonnegative operation that is then decreased by 5. The range of each function is consequently also decreased by 5, becoming $\{f(x) \geq -5\}$. Notice the pattern: a nonnegative operation has a range of $\{f(x) \geq 0\}$. When the sign of the nonnegative operation is flipped, the sign of the range also flips. When a quantity is added to the operation, the same quantity is added to the range. These changes can also be made in combination.

$$g(x) = \frac{-x^2 + 6}{2}$$

In this function, the sign of the nonnegative operation is flipped, 6 is added, and the whole thing is divided by 2. As a result, the range of $g(x)$ is $\{g(x) \leq 3\}$. The range of x^2, which is $\{y: y \geq 0\}$, has its sign flipped, is increased by 6, and is then divided by 2.

Range Notation

Ranges can be represented in several ways. If the function $f(x)$ can produce values between -10 and 10, then a description of its range could look like any of the following:

- The range of $f(x)$ is given by $\{f: -10 < f(x) < 10\}$.
- The range of $f(x)$ is $\{-10 < f(x) < 10\}$.
- The range of $f(x)$ is the set $\{y: -10 < y < 10\}$.

Solving a Range Question

Now that you've learned about ranges, let's try out a question. Take a look at the following example.

13. If $f(x) = \left| -x^2 - 8 \right|$ for all real numbers x, then which of the following sets is the range of f?

(A) $\{y: y \geq -8\}$
(B) $\{y: y > 0\}$
(C) $\{y: y \geq 0\}$
(D) $\{y: y \leq 8\}$
(E) $\{y: y \geq 8\}$

Range and POE

As with many problems on the SAT Subject Test Math 2, range problems are often best handled using Process of Elimination. Here are a few tips to help you eliminate answer choices on these problems:

- Look for negative values. Remember that even exponents, even roots, and absolute value must always be nonnegative.
- Similarly, a negative in front of any of the above makes that part of the expression always not positive.
- Plugging In often works great! Plug in a value for x, find $f(x)$, and eliminate any answer that doesn't include the result in its range.

Here's How to Crack It

Start out with what you know about the equation. Since the result of absolute value is a nonnegative number, you can eliminate (A) right away. Is there a maximum number that an absolute value creates? No. So you can also eliminate (D). Now look at x^2. We know that there's no maximum that x^2 can be, but there is a minimum. The smallest x^2 can be is 0. If $x^2 = 0$, then the result inside the absolute value sign would be –8. This means that, when $x = 0$, $f(x) = 8$. So the answer is (E). Now you may be thinking, but what about that negative sign?

Well, increasing the value of x would make $-x^2$ smaller, and that smaller number minus 8 would be even smaller. Then the absolute value would make all that negativity positive, which confirms that the least value of the function is 8.

Plugging In on Range Questions

Because all questions on the SAT Subject Test Math 2 are multiple-choice, you can always plug in and use POE on range questions. It may take a little longer, but it gives you a chance to score another point. So, if you're confused by the process of finding the range, or not sure what steps to take on a particular range question, plug in!

Let's take another look at question 13 on the previous page. If you plugged in $x = 3$, you would find that $f(3) = 17$. From that info you could eliminate (D). If you plugged in 0, you'd see that $f(0) = 8$. If you plugged in numbers less than 0, you'd see that $f(x)$ never gets smaller than 8. The answer is (E). You still get to the right answer!

Using Your Calculator to Solve a Range Question

You can also use your calculator to help you solve range questions. Let's take a look.

49. If $f(x) = \left| \dfrac{3x^2 - 4x - 5}{8} \right| - 7$, then what is the range of $f(x)$?

   (A) $\{y: y \geq -7.625\}$
   (B) $\{y: y \geq -7\}$
   (C) $\{y: y \geq -6.375\}$
   (D) $\{y: y \leq -7.625\}$
   (E) $\{y: y \geq 0\}$

Here's How to Crack It:

Without your calculator, you need to figure out if the quadratic in the numerator of the fraction has real roots (which would make the expression within the absolute value bracket potentially equal to zero) and go from there. With a graphing calculator, you can use the "Y=" function instead. On the TI-84, go to the "Y=" menu and input the function (note: absolute value can be found under MATH->NUM->abs). Be careful with parentheses, especially with the fraction and the absolute value!

Next, press 2ND->TRACE to access the CALC menu. You can use the third and fourth options, "minimum" and "maximum," to find local minimums and maximums on the graph. To find a minimum, set the "left bound" to the left of a minimum, "right bound" to the right, and "guess?" close to the minimum. Your calculator will find the lowest value of the function in that range. Note that often you will not get an exact minimum/maximum because of the way the calculator graphs the function (by calculating a series of points).

In this case, graphing the function gives you something like this.

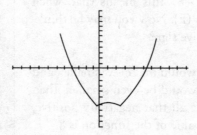

Because the function continues up to infinity, there is no maximum; eliminate (D). The function also clearly goes below the x-axis; eliminate (E). Now, you can see that you have two local minimums (to the left and to the right of the y-axis), so you need to check both with the minimum function. At both minimums, $y = -7$, so the range of the function is $y \geq -7$, (B).

FUNCTIONS WITHIN INTERVALS: DOMAIN MEETS RANGE

A question that introduces a function will sometimes ask about that function only within a certain interval. This interval is a set of values for the variable in the x position.

For example,

> If $f(x) = 4x - 5$ for [0, 10], then which of the following sets represents the range of f ?
> If $f(x) = 4x - 5$ for $0 \leq x \leq 10$, what is the range of f ?

Remember?
Don't forget that x represents the independent variable!

Be Careful
You have to be alert when domains or ranges are given in this notation, because it's easy to mistake intervals in this form for coordinate pairs. Tricky!

These two questions present the same information and ask the same question. The second version simply uses a different notation to describe the interval, or domain, in which $f(x)$ is being looked at.

The example given above also demonstrates the most common form of a function-interval question, in which you're given a domain for the function and asked for the range. Whenever the function has no exponents, finding the range is easy. Just plug the upper and lower extremes of the domain into the function. The results will be the upper and lower bounds of the range. In the example above, the function's range is the set $\{y : -5 \leq y \leq 35\}$.

The interval that you are given means that, for that particular question, you have a different set of values for the function's domain.

DRILL 5: DOMAIN AND RANGE

Practice your domain and range techniques on the following questions. The answers can be found in Part IV.

9. If $f(x) = \dfrac{1}{x^3 - x^2 - 6x}$, then which of the following sets is the domain of f?

    (A) $x \neq -2, 0, 3$
    (B) $x \neq 0$
    (C) $x > -2$
    (D) $x > 0$
    (E) $x > 3$

15. If $g(x) = \sqrt{x^2 - 4x - 12}$, then the domain of g is given by which of the following?

    (A) $x \geq -2$
    (B) $x \neq 3, 4$
    (C) $-2 \leq x \leq 6$
    (D) $-2 < x < 6$
    (E) $x \leq -2$ or $x \geq 6$

16. If $t(a) = \dfrac{a^2 + 5}{3}$, then which of the following sets is the range of t?

    (A) $t(a) \neq 0$
    (B) $t(a) \geq 0$
    (C) $t(a) \geq 0.60$
    (D) $t(a) \geq 1.67$
    (E) $t(a) \geq 2.24$

19. If $f(x) = 4x + 3$ for $-1 \leq x \leq 4$, then which of the following gives the range of f?

    (A) $-4 \leq f(x) \leq 7$
    (B) $-4 \leq f(x) \leq 19$
    (C) $-1 \leq f(x) \leq 7$
    (D) $-1 \leq f(x) \leq 19$
    (E) $1 \leq f(x) \leq 19$

28. If $f(x) = \dfrac{x^4 - 2}{3}$ for $[-3, 3]$, then what is the range

of $f(x)$?

(A) $f(x) \geq 0$
(B) $f(x) \geq -0.667$
(C) $f(x) = -27.333, 26.333$
(D) $-0.667 \leq f(x) \leq 81$
(E) $-0.667 \leq f(x) \leq 26.333$

GRAPHING FUNCTIONS

All of the function techniques covered in this chapter so far have dealt with the algebra involved in doing functions. Most of the function questions on the SAT Subject Test Math 2 will be algebra questions like the ones you've seen so far. However, there's another class of function questions that appears on the SAT Subject Test Math 2—graphical questions.

Graphical function questions require you to relate an algebraic function to the graph of that function in some way. Here are some of the tasks you might be required to do on a graphical function question:

- Match a function's graph with the function's domain or range.
- Match the graph of a function with the function's algebraic definition.
- Decide whether statements about a function are true or false, based on its graph.

None of these tasks is very difficult, as long as you're prepared for them. The next few pages will tell you everything you need to know.

Identifying Graphs of Functions

The most useful tool for identifying the graph of a function is the *vertical-line test*. Remember that a function is a relation of a domain and a range, in which each value in the domain matches up with only one value in the range. Simply put, there's only one $f(x)$, or y, for each x. Graphically, that means that any vertical line drawn through the x-axis can intersect a function only once. If you can intersect a graph more than once with a vertical line, it isn't a function. Here's the vertical-line test in action.

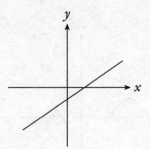

This is a function, because no vertical line can intersect it more than once. All straight lines are functions, with only one exception. A vertical line is not a function, because another vertical line would intersect it at an infinite number of points.

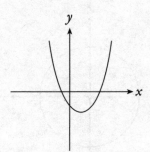

This is also a function. Any parabola that opens up or down is a function.

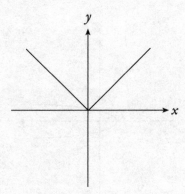

This is the graph of $y = |x|$, and it's a function as well.

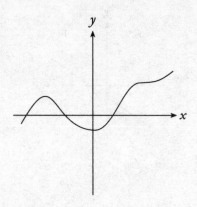

This complicated curve also passes the vertical-line test for functions.

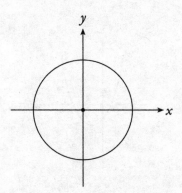

This is not a function; there are many places where a vertical line can intersect a circle twice.

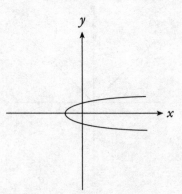

This isn't a function either. Although this graph is parabolic in shape, it fails the vertical-line test.

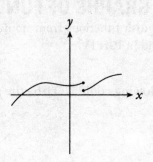

Nope. It's close, but there's one point where a vertical line can intersect this graph twice—it can't be a function.

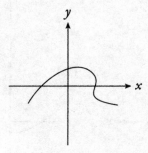

This curve is also not a function. It's possible to cross this curve more than once with one vertical line.

DRILL 6: IDENTIFYING GRAPHS OF FUNCTIONS

Use the vertical-line test to distinguish functions from nonfunctions in the following practice questions. The answers can be found in Part IV.

1. Which of the following could NOT be the graph of a function?

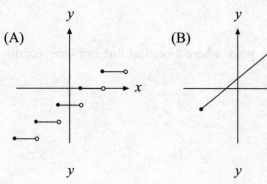

(A)

(B)

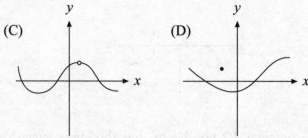

(C)

(D)

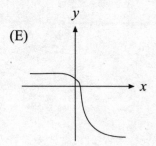

(E)

3. Which of the following could NOT be the graph of a function?

(A)
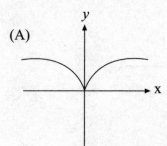

(B)
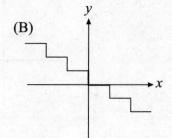

(C)
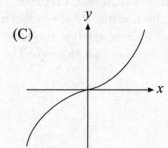

(D)
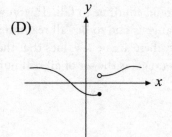

(E)
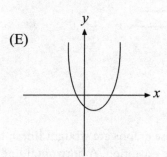

RANGE AND DOMAIN IN GRAPHS

The graph of a function gives important information about the function itself. You can generally state a function's domain and range accurately just by looking at its graph. Even when the graph doesn't give you enough information to state them exactly, it will often let you eliminate incorrect answers about the range and domain.

Take a look at the following graphs of functions and the information they provide.

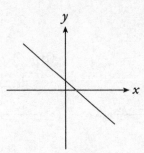

If you followed this line to the left, it would continue to rise forever. Likewise, if you followed it to the right, it would continue to fall. The range of this line (the set of *y*-values it occupies) goes on forever; the range is said to be "all real numbers." Because the line also continues to the left and right forever, there are no *x*-values that the line does not pass through. The domain of this function, like its range, is the set of all real numbers.

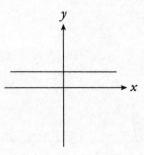

The same thing is true of all linear functions (whose graphs are straight lines); their ranges and domains include all real numbers. There's only one exception. A horizontal line extends forever to the left and right (through all *x*-values) but has only one *y*-value. Its domain is therefore all real numbers, while its range contains only one value.

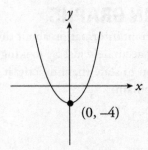

(0, −4)

The domain of this function is the set of all real numbers, because parabolas continue widening forever. Its range, however, is limited. The parabola extends upward forever, but never descends lower along the *y*-axis than *y* = −4. The range of this function is therefore $\{y: y \geq -4\}$.

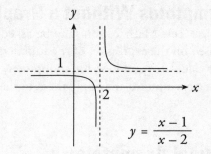

$$y = \frac{x-1}{x-2}$$

This function has two asymptotes. Asymptotes are lines that the function approaches but never reaches. They mark values in the domain or range at which the function does not exist or is undefined. The asymptotes on this graph mean that it's impossible for x to equal 2, and it's impossible for y to equal 1. The domain of $f(x)$ is therefore $\{x: x \neq 2\}$, and the range is $\{y: y \neq 1\}$.

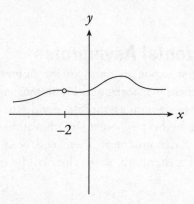

The hole in this function's graph means that there's an x-value missing at that point. The domain of any function whose graph sports a little hole like this one must exclude the corresponding x-value. The domain of this function, for example, would simply be $\{x: x \neq -2\}$.

To estimate range and domain based on a function's graph, just use common sense and remember these rules:

- If something about a function's shape will prevent it from continuing forever up and down, then that function has a limited range.
- If the function has a horizontal asymptote at a certain y-value, then that value is excluded from the function's range.
- If anything about a function's shape will prevent it from continuing forever to the left and right, then that function has a limited domain.
- If a function has a vertical asymptote or hole at a certain x-value, then that value is excluded from the function's domain.
- If you are asked to identify an asymptote, plug in very large positive and negative numbers for x or y and see what values the other variable approaches. Try 1, 1,000, –1, –1,000, etc.
- Sometimes you can use Plugging In the Answers (PITA) and see which values of x or y don't make sense in the equation.
- Graphing the function on your calculator may be the easiest approach.

We'll talk more about asymptotes in the next section.

Plugging In for Asymptotes

Plugging In works well on these questions. For instance, you can plug in the answers on vertical asymptote questions by using the denominator of the fraction in the function. If, when you plug in, the denominator equals 0, then you have an asymptote at that value of x!

On Horizontal Asymptote questions, plug in a very large or very small number (like 100,000 or –100,000) for x. The value of the function at that value of x should be very close to one of your answers; that answer is where an asymptote is.

Finding Asymptotes Without a Graph

On the SAT Subject Test Math 2, you may be asked to find the asymptotes of a given function based on the expression of the function. You can always graph such functions on your calculator and look for asymptotes, but it may be easier to know the rules for finding asymptotes and apply them to the given function.

Finding Vertical Asymptotes

In order for a function to have asymptotes (vertical or horizontal), the function must be expressed as a fraction. Finding a vertical asymptote is relatively straightforward. Set the denominator of the function equal to 0 and solve for x. There is a vertical asymptote at each value of x. Furthermore, the domain of the function must exclude those values of x.

Finding Horizontal Asymptotes

If the degree (largest exponent on x) of the numerator is equal to the degree of the denominator, there is a horizontal asymptote somewhere other than $y = 0$ (the x-axis). To find the horizontal asymptote, divide the coefficient of the leading term (the term with the highest exponent) of the numerator by the coefficient of the leading term of the denominator. There will be a horizontal asymptote when y equals that value. Furthermore, that value will be excluded from the range of the function.

If the degree of the denominator is greater than the degree of the numerator, there is a horizontal asymptote at $y = 0$ (the x-axis).

If the degree of the numerator is greater than the degree of the denominator, there is no horizontal asymptote. Instead, there will be a slant asymptote (which, luckily, is not tested on the SAT Subject Test Math 2).

Try an example.

---

32. Which of the following lines are asymptotes of

$$f(x) = \frac{3x^2 - 6x + 9}{x^2 - 2x + 1} \; ?$$

   I. $y = 3$
   II. $y = 0$
   III. $x = 1$

   (A) I only
   (B) II only
   (C) III only
   (D) I and III only
   (E) I, II, and III

Here's How to Crack It

Start by looking for vertical asymptotes. Set the denominator equal to zero and solve.

$$x^2 - 2x + 1 = 0$$

$$(x - 1)(x - 1) = 0$$

$$x = 1$$

Therefore, there is an asymptote at $x = 1$; eliminate (A) and (B). To find horizontal asymptotes, first look at the degrees of the numerator and denominator. The degrees are equal, so there will not be an asymptote at $y = 0$; eliminate (E). Because the degrees are equal, take the leading terms ($3x^2$ and x^2) and divide the coefficients (remember, the coefficient of x^2 is 1): $\frac{3}{1} = 3$, so there is an asymptote at $y = 3$, so eliminate (C) and choose (D).

DRILL 7: RANGE AND DOMAIN IN GRAPHS

Test your understanding of range and domain with the following practice questions. The answers can be found in Part IV.

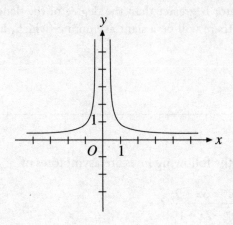

17. If the graph of $y = f(x)$ is shown above, which of the following could be the domain of f?

(A) $\{x : x \neq 0\}$

(B) $\{x : x > 0\}$

(C) $\{x : x \geq 0\}$

(D) $\{x : x > 1\}$

(E) $\{x : x \geq 1\}$

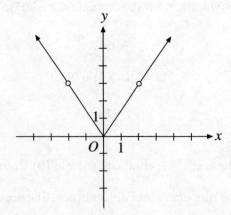

24. Which of the following could be the domain of the function graphed above?

(A) $\{x : x \neq 2\}$

(B) $\{x : -2 < x < 2\}$

(C) $\{x : x < -2 \text{ or } x > 2\}$

(D) $\{x : |x| \neq 2\}$

(E) $\{x : |x| > 2\}$

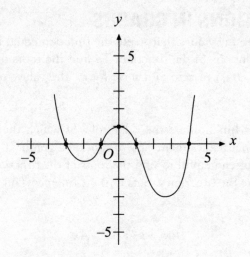

28. If $y = g(x)$ is graphed above, which of the following sets could be the range of $g(x)$?

    (A) $\{y : y \leq -1\}$

    (B) $\{y : y \geq -1\}$

    (C) $\{y : y \geq -3\}$

    (D) $\{y : -3 \leq y \leq -1\}$

    (E) $\{y : y \leq -3 \text{ or } y \geq -1\}$

37. Which of the following lines is an asymptote of the graph of $y = 3e^{-2x} + 5$?

    (A) $x = 0$
    (B) $x = -2$
    (C) $y = 5$
    (D) $y = 0$
    (E) $y = -6$

48. Which of the following lines is an asymptote of the graph of $y = \dfrac{1-x}{x-2}$?

    I. $x = 2$

    II. $y = -\dfrac{1}{2}$

    III. $y = -1$

    (A) I only
    (B) II only
    (C) III only
    (D) I and II only
    (E) I and III only

ROOTS OF FUNCTIONS IN GRAPHS

The roots of a function are the values that make the function equal to zero. Hence, the roots are also called zeros or solutions of the function. To find the roots of a function $f(x)$ algebraically, you simply set $f(x)$ equal to zero and solve for x. The values of x that you find are the roots of the function.

Graphically, the roots of a function are the values of x at which the graph crosses the x-axis, that is, the x-intercepts. That makes them easy to spot on a graph. If you are asked to match a function to its graph, it's often helpful to find the roots of the function using algebra; then it's a simple matter to compare the function's roots to the x-intercepts on the graph. Take a look at this function.

$$f(x) = x^3 + 3x^2 - 4x$$

If you factor it to find its roots, you get

$$f(x) = x(x + 4)(x - 1)$$

The roots of $f(x)$ are therefore $x = -4$, 0, and 1. You can expect the graph of $y = f(x)$ to cross the x-axis at those three x-values.

On the SAT Subject Test Math 2, you may be asked to find the roots of a nasty-looking function. Luckily the test is multiple-choice, so you can plug in the answers on those problems. Simply plug each answer choice into the function and find the answer which makes the function equal zero. Remember that the College Board rounds, so an answer choice that is very close to zero is likely to be correct.

DRILL 8: ROOTS OF FUNCTIONS IN GRAPHS

Try the following practice questions by working with the roots of functions. The answers can be found in Part IV.

16. Which of the following is a zero of
    $f(x) = 2x^2 - 7x + 5$?

    (A) 1.09
    (B) 1.33
    (C) 1.75
    (D) 2.50
    (E) 2.75

19. The function $g(x) = x^3 + x^2 - 6x$ has how many distinct roots?

    (A) 1
    (B) 2
    (C) 3
    (D) 4
    (E) It cannot be determined from the information
        given.

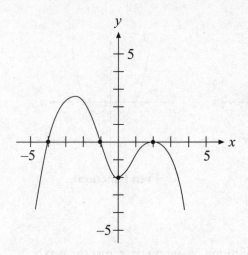

25. If the graph of $y = f(x)$ is shown above, which of the following sets represents all the roots of $f(x)$?

(A) $\{x = -2, 0, 2\}$

(B) $\{x = -4, -1, 0\}$

(C) $\{x = -1, 2\}$

(D) $\{x = -4, -1, 2\}$

(E) $\{x = -4, -1\}$

SYMMETRY IN FUNCTIONS

Symmetry Across the *y*-Axis (Even Functions)

Some questions on the SAT Subject Test Math 2 will ask about lines or points of symmetry of functions. The most common line of symmetry to be asked about is the *y*-axis. Imagine drawing a function symmetrically across the *y*-axis on a piece of paper.

If the paper were folded along the *y*-axis, the left and right halves of the graph would meet perfectly. Functions with symmetry across the *y*-axis are sometimes called even functions. This is because functions with only even exponents have this kind of symmetry, even though they are not the only even functions. Look at the following graphs of even functions.

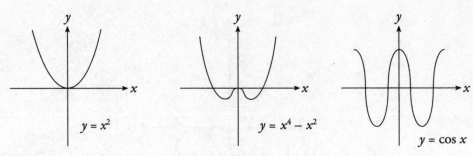

Even Functions

This is the algebraic definition of symmetry across the *y*-axis:

A function is symmetrical across the *y*-axis when

$$f(-x) = f(x)$$

This means that the negative and positive versions of any *x*-value produce the same *y*-value.

Origin Symmetry (Odd Functions)

A function has origin symmetry when one half of the graph is identical to the other half and reflected across the point (0, 0). Functions with origin symmetry are sometimes called odd functions, because functions with only odd exponents (as well as some other functions) have this kind of symmetry.

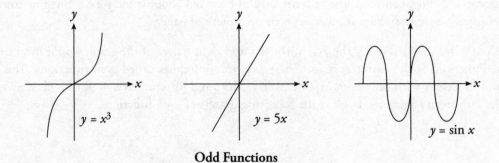

Odd Functions

This is the algebraic definition of origin symmetry:

A function has origin symmetry when

$$f(-x) = -f(x)$$

This means that the negative and positive versions of any x-value produce opposite y-values.

Symmetry Across the x-Axis

Some equations will produce graphs that are symmetrical across the x-axis. These equations can't be functions, however, because each x-value would then have to have two corresponding y-values. A graph that is symmetrical across the x-axis automatically fails the vertical-line test.

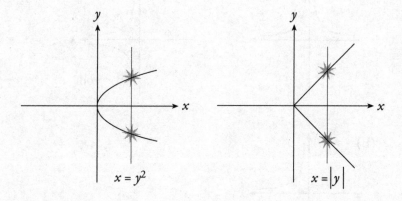

Questions asking about symmetry generally test basic comprehension of these definitions. It's also important to understand the connection between these algebraic definitions and the appearance of graphs with different kinds of symmetry.

DRILL 9: SYMMETRY IN FUNCTIONS

Try these practice questions. The answers can be found in Part IV.

6. Which of the following graphs is symmetrical with respect to the *x*-axis?

(A)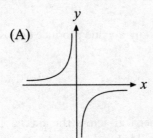

(B)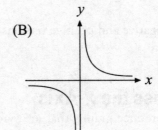

(C)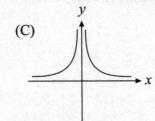

(D)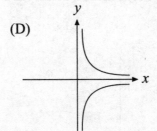

(E)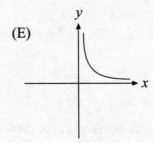

17. If an even function is one for which $f(x)$ and $f(-x)$ are equal, then which of the following is an even function?

(A) $g(x) = 5x + 2$

(B) $g(x) = x$

(C) $g(x) = \dfrac{x}{2}$

(D) $g(x) = x^3$

(E) $g(x) = -|x|$

30. If an odd function is one for which $f(-x) = -f(x)$, and $g(x)$ is an odd function, then which one of the following could be the graph of $g(x)$?

(A)

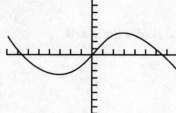

(B)

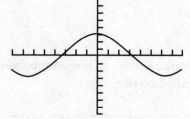

(C)

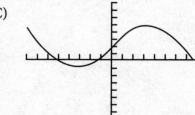

(D)

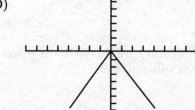

(E)

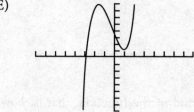

34. Which of the following is true for the function $f(x) = \left(\dfrac{x}{3}\right)^3$?

    I. $f(x)$ is even.
    II. $f(x)$ is odd.
    III. $f(x)$ is symmetrical across the x-axis.

(A) None of the above
(B) I only
(C) II only
(D) III only
(E) I, II, and III

Periodic Functions

A *periodic function* is a function that repeats a pattern of range values forever. Always look for a pattern when you're dealing with a periodic function.

Remember?
We also talked about periodic functions in the Trigonometry section.

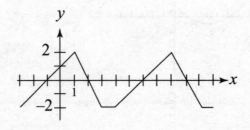

40. Two cycles of periodic function *f* are shown in the graph of $y = f(x)$ above. What is the value of $f(89)$?

(A) –2
(B) –1
(C)   0
(D)   1
(E)   2

Here's How to Crack It

In this question, we need to find the period of the function, that is, how many units along the x-axis the function covers before it repeats its range values. Find the pattern. From peak to peak, it goes from $x = 1$ to $x = 8$. This means that the function repeats itself every 7 units (the period is 7). Where does 89 fall in this pattern? Well, you want to take away multiples of 7 from 89, to find out an equivalent range value on the graph above. So, $f(89) = f(82) = f(75)$…and so on. Since $89 \div 7 = 12$ remainder 5, this means that $f(89) = f(5)$. From the graph, $f(5) = -1$, and the answer is (B).

Transformation of Function Graphs

When giving you a function question, the College Board may decide to fool around with the variable. Sometimes you'll be asked how this affects the graph of the function. For example, the College Board may show you $f(x)$ and ask you about the graph of $\left| f(x) \right|$. You can either plug in points or know the following rules.

In relation to $f(x)$:

- $f(x) + c$ is shifted upward c units in the plane.
- $f(x) - c$ is shifted downward c units in the plane.
- $f(x + c)$ is shifted to the left c units in the plane.
- $f(x - c)$ is shifted to the right c units in the plane.
- $-f(x)$ is flipped upside down over the x-axis.
- $f(-x)$ is flipped left-right over the y-axis.
- $\left| f(x) \right|$ is the result of flipping upward all of the parts of the graph that appear below the x-axis.
- $Cf(x)$ is stretched vertically when $C > 1$. Positive y-values become bigger and negative y-values become smaller.

- $\dfrac{f(x)}{C}$ or $\dfrac{1}{C} f(x)$ is stretched horizontally.

Of course, you may have to combine these rules. If so, plugging in some points may be the easiest way to go.

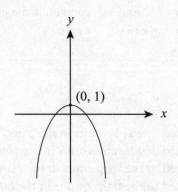

(0, 1)

31. The graph of $y = f(x)$ is shown above. Which of the following is the graph of $y = -f(x + 1)$?

(A)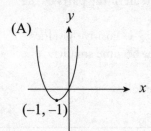

(−1, −1)

(B)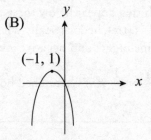

(−1, 1)

(C)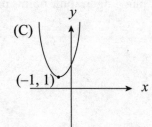

(−1, 1)

(D)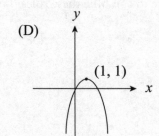

(1, 1)

(E)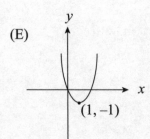

(1, −1)

Here's How to Crack It

To figure out what happens to the graph of $f(x)$, just use the rules above. The $x + 1$ inside the parentheses shifts the graph one unit to the left. If this were the final answer, the vertex would be at $(-1, 1)$. Now you have to take care of the negative sign outside the function. It reflects the entire function across the x-axis, so the vertex gets reflected to $(-1, -1)$ and the parabola opens upward. If you reflected first and then shifted to the left, you'd get the same result. The answer is (A).

Let's look at one more.

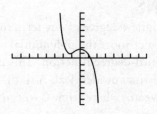

47. The graph of $f(x)$ is shown above. Which of the following could be the graph of $-3f(x) + 3$?

(A)   (B)

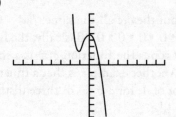 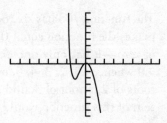

(C)   (D)

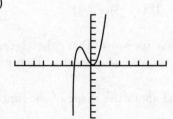 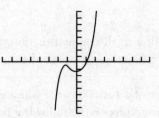

(E)

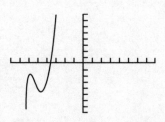

Here's How to Crack It

If the function is multiplied by –3, then it must be flipped across the x-axis and stretched vertically. Eliminate (A) and (B), because they are not flipped across the x-axis. If the function was stretched vertically, then the difference of the y-values between the local minimum at approximately $x = -1$ and the local maximum at $x = 0$ must increase (i.e., the points must be "stretched" apart). The graph of (D) has the same distance between the local minimums and maximums that the original has, so eliminate it. Adding 3 outside of the parentheses would move the graph up 3 units and not displace the graph to the left; eliminate (E) because the graph was moved off the y-axis and choose (C).

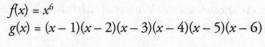

DEGREES OF FUNCTIONS

The degree of a polynomial is the highest degree of any term in the polynomial. The degree also determines at most how many distinct roots the polynomial will have. For example, the function $p(x) = x^3 - 4x^2 + 7x - 12$ is a third-degree function. This means that $p(x)$ has at most three distinct roots. These roots can be distinct or identical. A sixth-degree function can have at most 6 distinct roots. It can actually have anywhere from 0 to 6 distinct roots. Let's take a look at two sixth-degree functions.

$$f(x) = x^6$$
$$g(x) = (x - 1)(x - 2)(x - 3)(x - 4)(x - 5)(x - 6)$$

Math Vocab

Remember that *distinct* means *different*.

The function $f(x)$ has six roots, but they're all the same: $f(x) = 0$ when $x = 0$, which makes the function equal $0 \cdot 0 \cdot 0 \cdot 0 \cdot 0 \cdot 0$. Basically, the function has six roots of zero—it has only one *distinct* root. The function $g(x)$ has six distinct roots: $g(x) = 0$ when $x = 1, 2, 3, 4, 5,$ or 6. Another example is that a function might have four roots of 2, a root of 3, and a root of 4, for a total of three distinct roots. The equation of this function would look like

$$f(x) = (x - 2)^4(x - 3)(x - 4)$$

This is still a sixth-degree function, and it has six roots. That's the algebraic meaning of the degree of a function: It equals the maximum number of roots that the function has.

The degree of a function tells you a great deal about the shape of the function's graph. Take a look at the graphs on the following pages.

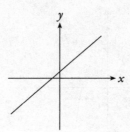

This is the graph of a first-degree function. All first-degree functions are linear functions, whose graphs are straight lines. A first-degree function has no extreme values—that is, it has no point which is higher or lower than all of the others.

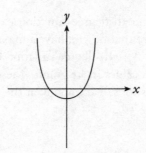

A second-degree function is usually a parabola. The function graphed above must be at least a second-degree function. A second-degree function has one extreme value, a maximum or minimum. This function's extreme value is a minimum.

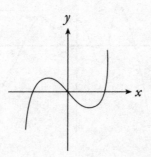

A third-degree function can have as many as two local extreme values. The function graphed on the previous page, which has a local maximum and a local minimum, must be at least a third-degree function. A "local" maximum (or minimum) means the values of the function are bigger (or smaller) than all of the surrounding values, but that the function may be bigger (or smaller) at some distant values of x.

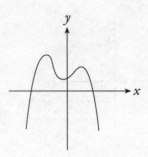

A fourth-degree function can have as many as three local extreme values. The function above has three extreme values, two local maxima and a local minimum between them. It must be at least a fourth-degree function.

By now, you should see the pattern. A fourth-degree function can have a maximum of three extreme values in its graph; a fifth-degree function can have a maximum of four extreme values in its graph. This pattern goes on forever. An nth-degree function has a maximum of n distinct roots and a maximum of $(n - 1)$ extreme values in its graph. These two rules are the basis of a number of SAT Subject Test Math 2 questions. Take a look at the following practice questions.

DRILL 10: DEGREES OF FUNCTIONS

The answers can be found in Part IV.

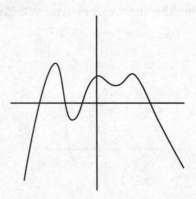

8. If the graph above shows $f(x)$, then $f(x)$ has how many distinct real roots?

(A) Three
(B) Four
(C) Five
(D) Six
(E) It cannot be determined from the information given.

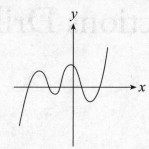

17. If the graph above is a portion of the graph of
    $y = f(x)$, then which of the following could be $f(x)$?

    (A) $ax + b$
    (B) $ax^2 + bx + c$
    (C) $ax^3 + bx^2 + cx + d$
    (D) $ax^4 + bx^3 + cx^2 + dx + e$
    (E) $ax^5 + bx^4 + cx^3 + dx^2 + ex + f$

20. If $g(x)$ is a fourth-degree function, then which of the following
    could be the definition of $g(x)$?

    (A) $g(x) = (x - 3)(x + 5)$
    (B) $g(x) = x(x + 1)^2$
    (C) $g(x) = (x - 6)(x + 1)(x - 5)$
    (D) $g(x) = x(x + 8)(x - 1)^2$
    (E) $g(x) = (x - 2)^3(x + 4)(x - 3)$

Fun with Functions

As noted at the beginning of the chapter, functions are perhaps the most heavily-tested concept on the SAT Subject Test Math 2. The techniques discussed in this chapter will help you crack the questions you will find on the test. The College Board likes to mix concepts and push limits on these questions, so be flexible in your approach, and if you're stuck, look for ways to use Plugging In or PITA!

Comprehensive Functions Drill

The answers can be found in Part IV.

1. If $x \Diamond y = x^2 y + 2xy - y$, then $3 \Diamond 1.5 =$

   (A) $1.5 \Diamond 3$
   (B) $2 \Diamond 3$
   (C) $3 \Diamond 2$
   (D) $0 \Diamond 21$
   (E) $21 \Diamond 0$

3. If $f(x) = \dfrac{x^2 + 3}{2}$ and $g(x) = \sqrt[3]{x}$ then

   $f(g(2.7)) =$

   (A) 1.392
   (B) 1.726
   (C) 2.469
   (D) 4.392
   (E) 5.145

5. If $g(x) = \dfrac{\sqrt[3]{x^2 - 2x + 3}}{\sqrt{x-3}}$, then what is the domain

   of $g(x)$?

   (A) $\{x : x \neq 3\}$
   (B) $\{x : x \neq -3\}$
   (C) $\{x : x \geq 3\}$
   (D) $\{x : x \leq 3\}$
   (E) $\{x : x > 3\}$

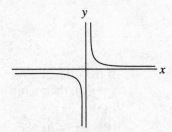

11. Which of the following are true about the function shown above?

    I. The function is even.
    II. The function is odd
    III. The function is symmetrical across the line $y = -x$.

    (A) I only
    (B) II only
    (C) III only
    (D) I and III only
    (E) II and III only

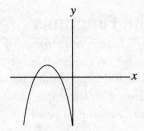

18. If the graph of $f(x)$ is shown above, and $g(x) = x^2$, then which of the following equations represents $f(x)$?

    (A) $f(x) = g(x + 3)^2 + 2$
    (B) $f(x) = g(x - 3)^2 + 2$
    (C) $f(x) = -g(x + 3)^2 - 2$
    (D) $f(x) = -g(x + 3)^2 + 2$
    (E) $f(x) = -g(x - 3)^2 + 2$

27. Which of the following functions has a vertical asymptote at $x = 3$?

(A) $f(x) = \dfrac{3x^2 + 4x}{x^2 + 9}$

(B) $f(x) = x^2 + 6x + 12$

(C) $f(x) = \dfrac{3x^2 + 4}{x^2 - 9}$

(D) $f(x) = \dfrac{x}{3x^3 + 2x - 4} \theta$

(E) $f(x) = 2x - 6$

$$f(x) = \begin{cases} x^2 - 3 & \text{if } x < -1 \\ e^x & \text{if } -1 \le x \le 1 \\ \ln x & \text{if } x > 1 \end{cases}$$

28. What is the value of $f(f(f(-2)))$?

(A) −2.718
(B) −2
(C) −1
(D) 1
(E) 2.718

32. If $x > 0$ and $f(x) = \dfrac{2}{x^2}$, then what is $f^{-1}(x)$?

(A) $\dfrac{\sqrt{2x}}{x}$

(B) $\dfrac{2}{x^2}$

(C) $\dfrac{\sqrt{x}}{2}$

(D) $\dfrac{2}{x}$

(E) $\dfrac{\sqrt{2}}{x}$

44. If $g(x) = x^2 - 1$ and $f(g(x)) = 2x^2$, then $f(x) =$

(A) $2x + 1$

(B) $2x + 2$

(C) $x\sqrt{2} + 1$

(D) $2x^2 - 1$

(E) $2x^2 - \dfrac{1}{2}$

45. If function $f(x)$ is periodic, then which of the following functions is NOT periodic?

(A) $\left| -f(x) \right|$

(B) $f(x + 2) + 2$

(C) $3f(x - 2)$

(D) $xf(x)$

(E) $\dfrac{1}{f(x)}$

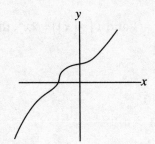

49. The graph of $f(x)$ is show above. If $f(g(x)) = x$, then which of the following could be the graph of $g(x)$?

(A)

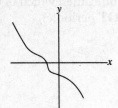

(B)

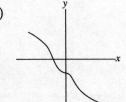

(C)

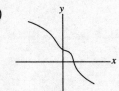

(D)

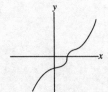

(E)

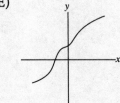

Summary

○ Algebraic functions are the functions with weird symbols. They tell you what to do. Just follow the directions of the function.

○ Mathematical functions relate two sets of numbers: the domain and the range. Think of it like a machine. You put in one number, and the machine spits out another number.

○ A compound function is a combination of two or more functions. It's like having two machines. You put your number in one machine, and you take the result from that and put it into the second machine.

○ Inverse functions are opposites. Here are a couple of specifics:
  • An example of what inverse functions do is the following: if you put 5 into your first machine and get 12, then you put 12 into the inverse of that machine, you'll get 5.
  • Inverse functions will be symbolized either by $f^{-1}(x)$, or $f(g(x)) = x$.
  • Inverse function questions can be solved either by Plugging In or by replacing $f(x)$ with y and switching x and y in the equation and solving.

○ Domain is all the possible values of x in a given function. These are the numbers you put into the function. They are independent.

○ Range is all the possible values of y (or $f(x)$) in a given function. These are the numbers you get out of the function. They are dependent.

○ In order to figure out if a graph is a function, use the vertical-line test. The line will touch only one point on the graph if the graph is a function.

○ When answering domain and range questions with graphs, take a look to see what values x can't be and what values y can't be.

○ Asymptotes are only possible in functions expressed as fractions. Vertical asymptotes are found by setting the denominator of the function equal to zero and solving for x.

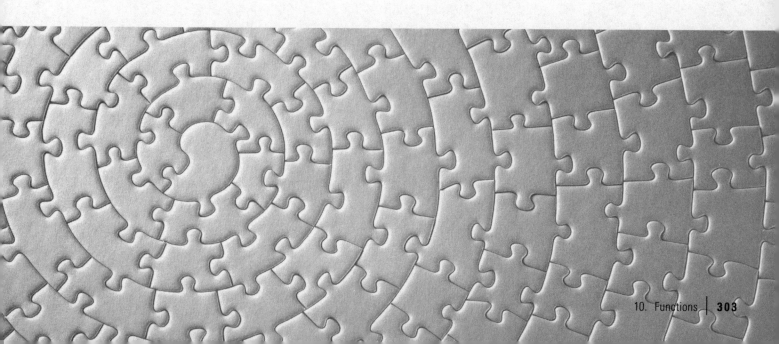

o   Horizontal asymptotes can only be present if the degree of the numerator is equal to the degree of the denominator. To find a horizontal asymptote, divide the coefficient of the leading term of the numerator by the coefficient of the leading term of the denominator. The function will have an asymptote at the point where y equals that quotient.

o   The roots of a function will make the function equal to 0 when you substitute them for the independent variable. Graphically, a function crosses the x-axis at its root values.

o   There are a few types of symmetry discussed in this chapter. An easy way to think about symmetry is this: if you physically folded your paper along the line of symmetry and all the points on both sides touched, the graph would be symmetrical along that line.
   •   A function is symmetrical across the y-axis when $f(-x) = f(x)$. This is called an even function.
   •   A function has origin symmetry when $f(-x) = -f(x)$. This is called an odd function.
   •   A graph that is symmetrical across the x-axis isn't a function, because it fails the vertical-line test.

o   You may see questions that ask about the movement of a function. If the number is outside the parentheses of the function, the graph shifts along the y-axis. If it is inside the parentheses, the graph shifts along the x-axis.

o   A periodic function is a function which repeats a pattern of range values forever.

o   The degree of a term is the sum of the exponents of the variables of that term. The degree of a function is the degree of the term with the highest degree in that function.

Chapter 11
Statistics and Sets

Questions that ask about statistics on the SAT Subject Test Math 2 deal with the arrangements and combinations of large groups, probability, overlapping groups, and statistical measures like mean, median, and mode. There are only about 2 or 3 questions about statistics and sets on the SAT Subject Test Math 2, so only focus on this chapter after you've mastered the material in previous chapters.

DEFINITIONS

Here are some terms dealing with sets and statistics that appear on the SAT Subject Test Math 2. Make sure you're familiar with them. If the meaning of any of these vocabulary words keeps slipping your mind, add that word to your flash cards.

Mean	An average—also called an arithmetic mean.
Median	The middle value in a list of numbers when the numbers are arranged in order. When there is an even number of values in the list, the median is the average of the two middle values.
Mode	The value that occurs most often in a list.
Range	The result when you subtract the smallest value from the largest value in a list.
Standard Deviation	A measure of how the data is spread apart.
Combination	A grouping of distinct objects in which order is not important.
Permutation	An arrangement of distinct objects in a definite order.

WORKING WITH STATISTICS

The science of statistics is all about working with large groups of numbers and trying to see patterns and trends in those numbers. To look at those numbers in different ways, statisticians use a variety of mathematical tools. And, just to keep you guessing, the College Board tests your knowledge of several of these tools. The three most commonly tested statistical measures are the mean, the median, and the mode.

Mean

The mean (or arithmetic mean) is simply the average of the elements of a set. To find the mean, divide the sum of the elements of the set by the number of elements in the set. On the SAT Subject Test Math 2, the Average Pie (see Chapter 6) is often the best way to approach these questions.

Median

The median is the middle value of a set. To find a set median, you must first put all of its elements in order. If the set has an odd number of elements, then there will be one value in the exact middle, which is the median value. If the set has an even number of elements, then there will be two middle values; the median value is the average of these two middle values.

Mode

The mode of a set is simply the value that occurs most often in that set. If there are multiple values which occur the most often, then that set has multiple modes. Many statistics questions require you to work with all three of these measures. The calculations involved are usually not very difficult. However, the real challenge of these questions is simply understanding these terms and knowing how to use them. Similarly, there are two more statistical terms that you may be required to know for certain questions—range and standard deviation.

Range

The range of a set is the positive difference between the set's highest and lowest values. You can also think of the range as the distance on the number line from the lowest to the highest value in the set. Remember that distances are always positive.

Stem-and-Leaf Plots and Boxplots

The College Board may ask you about a stem-and-leaf plot or a boxplot once in a while. The good news is that the questions are usually pretty simple if you understand the basic concepts.

Suppose that the members of a class earned these quiz scores: 65, 70, 70, 78, 80, 81, 84, 86, 89, 89, 93, 93, 93, 98, 100.

A stem-and-leaf plot would show the data like this.

```
 6 | 5
 7 | 0  0  8
 8 | 0  1  4  6  9  9
 9 | 3  3  3  8
10 | 0
```

The tens digits are listed vertically, and then each ones digit is listed horizontally. For example, the row that reads "7| 0 0 8" means "70, 70, 78." This forms a sort of bar graph, but we have actual numbers instead of bars.

A boxplot shows the data broken into quartiles. Using our fifteen quiz scores, this would be the boxplot.

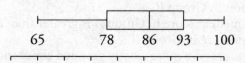

Each part of the boxplot represents 25% of the data. Here, 78 is the *first quartile*, or Q_1, 86 is the median (sometimes called the *second quartile*, or Q_2), and 93 is the *third quartile*, or Q_3. The only other thing you need to know is that the *interquartile range* is the range of the middle 50%: $Q_3 - Q_1$, or the width of the box. In this example, that's $93 - 78 = 35$.

How Far From the SD?
Some questions may ask you to figure out how many deviations above or below the mean a number is. In order to figure that out, find the difference between the mean and the number you're dealing with. Then divide it by the standard deviation.

Standard Deviation

The standard deviation of a set is a measure of the set's variation from its mean. A set composed of 10 identical values (having a range of 0) could have the same mean as a set with widely scattered values. The first list would have a much smaller standard deviation than the second.

Standard deviation comes up very infrequently on the SAT Subject Test Math 2. Computing a standard deviation is a long, annoying process that you will not be asked to endure. (Aren't you glad?) Just remember that the standard deviation is a measure of how far the typical value in a set is from the set's average. The bigger the standard deviation, the more widely dispersed the values are. The smaller the standard deviation, the more closely grouped the values in a set are around the mean. On some questions, you need to know how many standard deviations above or below the mean a certain value is. On other questions, drawing a rough sketch of the data will be enough.

DRILL 1: STATISTICS

Try the following practice questions using these statistical definitions. The answers can be found in Part IV.

11. List M contains ten elements whose sum is zero. Which of the following statements must be true?

   I. The mean of the elements in M is zero.
   II. The median of the elements in M is zero.
   III. The mode of the elements in M is zero.

   (A) None
   (B) I only
   (C) I and II only
   (D) II and III only
   (E) I, II, and III

35. The subjects in a research study are divided into Group A and Group B. Both groups are given the same test. The mean score in Group A is greater than that in Group B, but the standard deviation of scores in Group A is less than that in Group B. Which of the following must be true?

   (A) The range of scores in Group A is equal to the range of scores in Group B.
   (B) The median score in Group A is greater than the median score in Group B.
   (C) The scores are more closely grouped about the mean in Group A than in Group B.
   (D) The highest score in Group A is greater than the highest score in Group B.
   (E) The number of subjects in Group A is less than the number of subjects in Group B.

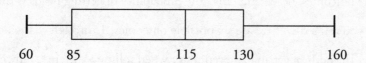

60   85   115   130   160

37. The above boxplot shows the test scores for incoming students at the Brainstorm Institute. Which of the following must be true about the test scores of the incoming students?

(A) The average (arithmetic mean) score of the bottom 50 percent of the incoming students is 50 points lower than the average score of the top 50 percent of incoming students.

(B) The interquartile range of the scores of the incoming students is equal to the range between the highest score and the median score of the incoming students.

(C) The range of all the scores of the incoming students is twice the interquartile range of the scores of the incoming students.

(D) The average (arithmetic mean) score of the incoming students is less than the median score of the incoming students.

(E) The average (arithmetic mean) score of the incoming students is equal to the median score of the incoming students.

PROBABILITY

Probability is a mathematical expression of the likelihood of an event. The basis of probability is simple. The likelihood of any event is discussed in terms of all of the possible outcomes. To express the probability of a given event, x, you would count the number of possible outcomes, count the number of outcomes that give you what you want, and arrange them in a fraction, like this:

$$\text{Probability of } x = \frac{\text{number of outcomes that are } x}{\text{total number of possible outcomes}}$$

Every probability must have a value between 0 and 1, inclusive. The largest a probability can be is 1. A probability of 1 indicates total certainty. The smallest a probability can be is 0, meaning that it's something that cannot happen. Most probabilities you'll be asked to find on the SAT Subject Test Math 2 are fractions between 0 and 1.

Not!
You can find the probability that something WILL NOT happen by subtracting the probability that it WILL happen from 1. For example, if the weather-person tells you that there is a 0.3 probability of rain today, then there must be a 0.7 probability that it won't rain, because $1 - 0.3 = 0.7$.

Figuring out the probability of any single event is usually simple. When you flip a coin, there are only two possible outcomes, heads and tails. The probability of getting heads is therefore 1 out of 2, or $\frac{1}{2}$. When you roll a die, there are six possible outcomes, 1 through 6; the odds of getting a 6 is therefore $\frac{1}{6}$. The odds of getting an even result when rolling a die are $\frac{1}{2}$ since there are three even results in six possible outcomes. Here's a typical example of a simple probability question.

2. A bag contains 7 blue marbles and 14 marbles that are not blue. If one marble is drawn at random from the bag, what is the probability that the marble is blue?

(A) $\frac{1}{7}$

(B) $\frac{1}{3}$

(C) $\frac{1}{2}$

(D) $\frac{2}{3}$

(E) $\frac{3}{7}$

Here's How to Crack It

Here, there are 21 marbles in the bag, 7 of which are blue. The probability that a marble chosen at random would be blue is therefore $\frac{7}{21}$, or $\frac{1}{3}$. The correct answer is (B).

Probability of Multiple Events

Some advanced probability questions require you to calculate the probability of more than one event. Here's a typical example.

8. If a fair coin is flipped three times, what is the probability that the result will be tails exactly twice?

(A) $\dfrac{1}{8}$

(B) $\dfrac{1}{5}$

(C) $\dfrac{3}{8}$

(D) $\dfrac{5}{8}$

(E) $\dfrac{2}{3}$

Here's How to Crack It

When the number of possibilities involved is small enough, the easiest and safest way to do a probability question like this is to write out all of the possibilities and count the ones that give you what you want. Here are all the possible outcomes of flipping a coin three times.

heads, heads, heads	tails, tails, tails
heads, heads, tails	tails, tails, heads
heads, tails, heads	tails, heads, tails
heads, tails, tails	tails, heads, heads

As you can see by counting, only three of the eight possible outcomes produce tails exactly twice. The chance of getting exactly two tails is therefore $\dfrac{3}{8}$. The correct answer is (C).

Sometimes, however, you'll be asked to calculate probabilities for multiple events when there are too many outcomes to write out easily. Consider, for example, this variation on an earlier question.

31. A bag contains 7 blue marbles and 14 marbles that are not blue. What is the probability that the first three marbles drawn at random from this bag will be blue?

(A) $\dfrac{1}{3}$

(B) $\dfrac{1}{9}$

(C) $\dfrac{1}{21}$

(D) $\dfrac{1}{38}$

(E) $\dfrac{1}{46}$

Here's How to Crack It

Three random drawings from a bag of 21 objects produce a huge number of possible outcomes. It's not practical to write them all out. To calculate the likelihood of three events combined, you need to take advantage of a basic rule of probability.

> The probability of multiple events occurring together is the product of the probabilities of the events occurring individually.

In order to calculate the probability of a series of events, calculate the odds of each event happening separately and multiply them together. This is especially important in processes like drawings, because each event affects the odds of following events. This is how you'd calculate the probability of those three marble drawings.

The first drawing is just like the simple question you did earlier; there are 7 blue marbles out of 21 total—a probability of $\dfrac{1}{3}$.

For the second drawing, the numbers are different. There are now 6 blue marbles out of a total of 20, making the probability of drawing another blue marble $\dfrac{6}{20}$, or $\dfrac{3}{10}$.

For the third drawing, there are now 5 blue marbles remaining out of a total of 19. The odds of getting a blue marble this time are $\dfrac{5}{19}$.

To calculate the odds of getting blue marbles on the first three random drawings, just multiply these numbers together.

$$\frac{1}{3} \times \frac{3}{10} \times \frac{5}{19} = \frac{1}{38}$$

The odds of getting three blue marbles are therefore $\frac{1}{38}$, and the answer is (D). This can also be expressed as a decimal, as 0.026. The College Board often asks for answers in decimal form on the SAT Subject Test Math 2, just to make sure you haven't forgotten how to push the little buttons on your calculator. Just bear with them.

Finally, you may be asked to find the probability of one of multiple independent events occurring. Here's an example.

38. The probability that Alan attends a party is $\frac{3}{7}$. The probability that Barry attends the same party is $\frac{4}{9}$. What is the probability that at least one of them attends the party?

(A) $\frac{12}{63}$

(B) $\frac{7}{16}$

(C) $\frac{4}{9}$

(D) $\frac{43}{63}$

(E) $\frac{55}{63}$

Here's How to Crack It

As with the last example, you cannot write out all the probabilities, especially because in this case the probabilities are given not as individual pieces, but already as fractions. Instead, use another rule of probabilities:

> Probability of an event occurring = 1 − probability of event not occurring

Therefore, if you can find the probability of neither Alan nor Barry attending the party, you can subtract that from one and find the probability that at least one of the two attends. The probability that Alan does not attend is $1 - \dfrac{3}{7} = \dfrac{4}{7}$, while the probability that Barry doesn't attend is $1 - \dfrac{4}{9} = \dfrac{5}{9}$. To find the probability that both of them do not attend, multiply: $\left(\dfrac{4}{7}\right)\left(\dfrac{5}{9}\right) = \dfrac{20}{63}$. Then, subtract $\dfrac{20}{63}$ from 1: $1 - \dfrac{20}{63} = \dfrac{43}{63}$, (D).

Your Calculator Knows Fractions
Your calculator can do all the heavy lifting of manipulating fractions for you. Simply solve the problem by dividing out each fraction (be sure to carry over answers using the ANS key). When you get to the last step, on the TI-84 you can press MATH->FRAC to convert a decimal answer into a fraction!

DRILL 2: PROBABILITY

Try the following practice questions about probability. The answers can be found in Part IV.

1. If the probability that it will rain is $\dfrac{5}{12}$, then what is the probability that it will NOT rain?

   (A) $\dfrac{7}{12}$

   (B) $\dfrac{5}{7}$

   (C) $\dfrac{12}{7}$

   (D) $\dfrac{12}{5}$

   (E) It cannot be determined from the information given.

3. In an experiment, it is found that the probability that a released bee will land on a painted target is $\frac{2}{5}$. It is also found that when a bee lands on the target, the probability that the bee will attempt to sting the target is $\frac{1}{3}$. In this experiment, what is the probability that a released bee will land on the target and attempt to sting it?

(A) $\frac{2}{15}$

(B) $\frac{1}{5}$

(C) $\frac{2}{5}$

(D) $\frac{1}{3}$

(E) $\frac{6}{5}$

Day	Daily Cookie Production	Number Burned
Monday	256	34
Tuesday	232	39
Wednesday	253	41

6. The chart above shows the cookie production at MunchCo for three days. What is the probability that a cookie made on one of these three days will be burned?

(A) $\frac{1}{26}$

(B) $\frac{2}{13}$

(C) $\frac{1}{7}$

(D) $\frac{3}{13}$

(E) It cannot be determined from the information given.

11. If two six-sided dice are rolled, each having faces numbered 1 to 6, what is the probability that the product of the two numbers rolled will be odd?

(A) $\dfrac{1}{6}$

(B) $\dfrac{1}{4}$

(C) $\dfrac{1}{3}$

(D) $\dfrac{1}{2}$

(E) $\dfrac{7}{12}$

30. In a basketball-shooting contest, if the probability that Heather will make a basket on any given attempt is $\dfrac{4}{5}$, then what is the probability that she will make at least one basket in three attempts?

(A) $\dfrac{12}{125}$

(B) $\dfrac{64}{125}$

(C) $\dfrac{124}{125}$

(D) 1

(E) $\dfrac{12}{5}$

45. A jar contains b blue marbles, r red marbles, and g green marbles. If two marbles are to be taken from the jar one at a time, then what is the probability that the first marble is blue and the second marble is red?

(A) $\dfrac{br}{\left(b+r+g\right)^2}$

(B) $\dfrac{b+r}{b+r+g}$

(C) $\dfrac{br}{\left(b+r+g\right)^2-1}$

(D) $\left(\dfrac{b}{b+r+g}\right)\left(\dfrac{r}{b+r+g-1}\right)$

(E) $1-\dfrac{g}{b^2+r^2+g^2}$

PERMUTATIONS, COMBINATIONS, AND FACTORIALS

Questions about permutations, combinations, and factorials are relatively rare on the SAT Subject Test Math 2. As with many of the topics from precalculus, most of these questions are not as hard as they look. Rather, these questions test your knowledge of these topics and your ability to work with them. Both permutations and combinations are simply ways of counting groups, whereas factorials are a mathematical operation which arises from permutations and combinations (though factorials may be tested separately from permutations and combinations on the SAT Subject Test Math 2).

Simple Permutations

A permutation is an arrangement of objects of a definite order. The simplest sort of permutation question might ask you how many different arrangements are possible for 6 different chairs in a row, or how many different 4-letter arrangements of the letters in the word FUEL are possible. Both of these simple questions can be answered with the same technique.

Just draw a row of boxes corresponding to the positions you have to fill. In the case of the chairs, there are six positions, one for each chair. You would make a sketch like the following:

Then, in each box, write the number of objects available to put into that box. Keep in mind that objects put into previous boxes are no longer available. For the chair-arranging example, there would be 6 chairs available for the first box; only 5 left for the second box; 4 for the third, and so on until only one chair remained to be put into the last position. Finally, just multiply the numbers in the boxes together, and the product will be the number of possible arrangements, or permutations.

$$\boxed{6}\ \boxed{5}\ \boxed{4}\ \boxed{3}\ \boxed{2}\ \boxed{1} = 720$$

There are 720 possible permutations of a group of 6 chairs. This number can also be written as "6!"—that's not a display of enthusiasm—the exclamation point means *factorial*. The number is read "six factorial," and it means $6 \cdot 5 \cdot 4 \cdot 3 \cdot 2 \cdot 1$, which equals 720. A factorial is simply the product of a series of integers counting down to 1 from the specified number. For example, the number 70! means $70 \cdot 69 \cdot 68 \ldots 3 \cdot 2 \cdot 1$.

The number of possible arrangements of any group with n members is simply $n!$. In this way, the number of possible arrangements of the letters in FUEL is 4!, because there are 4 letters in the group. That means $4 \cdot 3 \cdot 2 \cdot 1$ arrangements, or 24. If you sketched 4 boxes for the 4 letter positions and filled in the appropriate numbers, that's exactly what you'd get.

Advanced Permutations

Permutations get a little trickier when you work with smaller arrangements. For example, what if you were asked how many 2-letter arrangements could be made from the letters in FUEL? It's just a modification of the original counting procedure. Sketch 2 boxes for the 2 positions. Then fill in the number of letters available for each position. As before, there are 4 letters available for the first space, and 3 for the second. The only difference is that you're done after two spaces.

$$\boxed{4}\ \boxed{3} = 12$$

As you did before, multiply the numbers in the boxes together to get the total number of arrangements. You should find that there are 12 possible 2-letter arrangements from the letters in FUEL.

That's all there is to permutations. The box-counting procedure is the safest way to approach them. Just sketch the number of positions available, and fill in the number of objects available for each position, from first to last—then multiply those numbers together.

On to Combinations

Which One to Use?
Combination and permutation questions can be very similar in appearance. Always ask yourself carefully whether sequence is important in a certain question before you proceed.

Combinations differ from permutations in just one way. In combinations, order doesn't matter. A permutation question might ask you to form different numbers from a set of digits. Order would certainly matter in that case, because 135 is very different from 513. Similarly, a question about seating arrangements would be a permutation question, because the word "arrangements" tells you that order is important. So questions that ask about "schedules" or "orderings" require you to calculate the number of *permutations*.

Combination questions, on the other hand, deal with groupings in which order isn't important. Combination questions often deal with the selection of committees. Josh, Lisa, Andy isn't any different from Andy, Lisa, Josh, as far as committees go. In the same way, a question about the number of different 3-topping pizzas you could make from a 10-topping list would be a combination question, because the order in which the toppings are put on is irrelevant. Questions that refer to "teams" or "pairs" are therefore asking about the number of possible *combinations*.

Calculating Combinations

Calculating combinations is surprisingly easy. All you have to do is throw out duplicate answers that count as separate permutations, but not as separate combinations. For example, let's make a full-fledged combination question out of that pizza example.

pepperoni   sausage
meatballs   anchovies
green peppers   onion
mushrooms   garlic
tomato   broccoli

21. If a pizza must have 3 toppings chosen from the list above, and
    no topping may be used more than once on a given pizza, how
    many different kinds of pizza can be made?

    (A) 720
    (B) 360
    (C) 120
    (D) 90
    (E) 30

Here's How to Crack It

To calculate the number of possible combinations, start by figuring out the number of possible
permutations.

$$\boxed{10}\ \boxed{9}\ \boxed{8} = 720$$

That tells you that there are 720 possible 3-topping permutations that can be made from a list of
10 toppings. You're not done yet, though. Because this is a list of permutations, it contains many
arrangements that duplicate the same group of elements in different orders. For example, those
720 permutations would include these:

pepperoni, mushrooms, onion   mushrooms, onion, pepperoni
pepperoni, onion, mushrooms   onion, pepperoni, mushrooms
mushrooms, pepperoni, onion   onion, mushrooms, pepperoni

All six of these listings are different permutations of the same group. In fact, for every 3-
topping combination, there will be 6 different permutations. You've got to divide 720 by 6 to
get the true number of combinations, which is 120. The correct answer is (C).

So, how do you know what number to divide permutations by to get combinations? It's simple. For the 3-position question above, we divided by 6, which is 3!. That's all there is to it. To calculate a number of possible combinations, calculate the possible permutations first, and divide that number by the number of positions, factorial. Take a look at one more.

---

14. How many different 4-person teams can be made from a roster of 9 players?

(A) 3,024
(B) 1,512
(C) 378
(D) 254
(E) 126

Here's How to Crack It

This is definitely a combination question. Start by sketching 4 boxes for the 4 team positions.

Then fill in the number of possible contestants for each position, and multiply them together. This gives you the number of possible *permutations*.

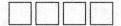 9 8 7 6 = 3,024

Finally, divide this number by 4! for the 4 positions you're working with. This gets rid of different permutations of identical groups. You divide 3,024 by 24 and get the number of possible combinations, 126. The correct answer is (E).

Using Your Calculator to Solve Permutations and Combinations

On the TI-84, you can quickly solve permutations and combinations using "nPr" (for permutations) and "nCr" (for combinations), found under the PRB submenu of the MATH menu.

To use these tools, first you need to determine the "*n*" and "*r*" values. For both, *n* is the total number of options you are choosing from, and *r* is the number of choices you are making. First, input your *n* value. Then, press MATH->PRB and select either the second (for permutations) or third (for combinations) option. Then enter your *r* value.

For example, let's say you have 15 dragon figurines and you want to display 7 of them in a row. To determine the number of ways you can make your display, use nPr (because order matters) and input the following into your calculator:

$$15 \text{ nPr } 7 = 32{,}432{,}400$$

Now, if you wanted to find the number of groups of 7 dragon figurines you could make from your collection, you would use nCr instead.

$$15 \text{ nCr } 7 = 6{,}435$$

In both cases, the approach of making slots and filling in the options will work. However, knowing how to use these calculator shortcuts can save you time, especially when you are dealing with bigger numbers on the SAT Subject Test Math 2.

Factorials

On the SAT Subject Test Math 2, the College Board occasionally asks you to calculate a factorial itself. If you try to do a factorial question in your head, you're likely to fall into one of the College Board's traps. Use your calculator and be careful.

18. $\dfrac{5!}{6! - 5!} =$

   (A) $\dfrac{1}{6!}$

   (B) $\dfrac{1}{6}$

   (C) $\dfrac{1}{5}$

   (D) 5

   (E) $\dfrac{5!}{6}$

For this question, just use your calculator. $5! = 120$ and $6! = 720$, so you have $\dfrac{120}{600} = \dfrac{1}{5}$. The answer is (C). It's supposed to be easy, but don't try to simplify this in your head. In this instance, every option is a potential trap, so take the time to be sure about your choice.

Factoring the Factorial

Sometimes numbers will be too bulky for your calculator, or you'll realize there's a faster way. You can factor factorials. Let's take another look at question 18 from the previous page. Notice that the denominator is $6! - 5!$. $6!$ is the same as $6 \cdot 5!$, which means you can factor $5!$ out of the denominator and you're left with $5!(6 - 1)$. Now you can cancel and you end up with $\dfrac{1}{5}$.

Let's try a harder problem.

―――――――――○―――――――――

44. $\dfrac{n!(n-1)!}{(n+1)!} =$

(A) $\dfrac{n(n+1)!}{n-1}$

(B) $n(n-1)!$

(C) $(n!)^2$

(D) $\dfrac{(n-1)!}{n+1}$

(E) $(n-1)! + n$

Here's How to Crack It

As you've seen throughout this book, Plugging In is a great way to make your life much easier. Make $n = 5$. Now the problem is $\dfrac{5!(5-1)!}{(5+1)!} = \dfrac{5!(4!)}{6!}$. Now, write out the factorials and cancel: $\dfrac{5 \times 4 \times 3 \times 2 \times 1(4 \times 3 \times 2 \times 1)}{6 \times 5 \times 4 \times 3 \times 2 \times 1} = \dfrac{4 \times 3 \times 2 \times 1}{6}$. Now you can multiply and you find that $\dfrac{4 \times 3 \times 2 \times 1}{6} = 4$. Plug 5 into each answer choice for n; only (D) equals 4.

―――――――――○―――――――――

DRILL 3: PERMUTATIONS, COMBINATIONS, AND FACTORIALS

Try the following practice questions about permutations, combinations, and factorials. The answers can be found in Part IV.

12. How many different 4-student committees can be chosen from a panel of 12 students?

    (A)   236
    (B)   495
    (C)   1,980
    (D)   11,880
    (E)   20,736

18. In how many different orders may 6 books be placed on a shelf?

    (A)   36
    (B)   216
    (C)   480
    (D)   720
    (E)   46,656

31. How many 7-person committees consisting of 4 females and 3 males may be assembled from a pool of 17 females and 12 males?

    (A)   523,600
    (B) 1,560,780
    (C) 1.26×10^7
    (D) 7.54×10^7
    (E) 7.87×10^9

49. If there are n available substitute teachers at a school and $n > 3$, then how many groups of 3 substitute teachers are available?

    (A) $n!$

    (B) $3(n!)$

    (C) $\dfrac{n!}{3}$

    (D) $\dfrac{n!}{(n-3)!}$

    (E) $\dfrac{n!}{6(n-3)!}$

GROUP QUESTIONS

Group questions are a very specific type of counting problem. They don't come up frequently on the SAT Subject Test Math 2, but when they do come up, they're easy pickings if you're prepared for them. If you're not, they can be a bit confusing. Here's a sample group question.

---○---

19. At Bedlam Music School, 64 students are enrolled in the gospel choir, and 37 students are enrolled in the handbell choir. Fifteen students are enrolled in neither group. If there are 100 students at Bedlam, how many students are enrolled in both the gospel choir and the handbell choir?

    (A) 12
    (B) 16
    (C) 18
    (D) 21
    (E) 27

Here's How to Crack It

As you can see, part of the difficulty of such problems lies in reading them—they're confusing. The other trick lies in the actual counting. If there are students in both the gospel choir and the handbell choir, then when you count the members of both groups, you're counting some kids twice—the kids who are in both groups. To find out how many students are in both groups, just use the group problem formula.

> **Group Problem Formula**
>
> Total = Group 1 + Group 2 + Neither − Both

For question 34, this formula gives you 100 = 64 + 37 + 15 − Both. Solve this, and you get Both = 16. The correct answer is (B).

---○---

The group problem formula will work for any group question with two groups. Just plug in the information you know, and solve for the piece that's missing.

DRILL 4: GROUP QUESTIONS

Use the group formula on the following practice questions. The answers can be found in Part IV.

10. At Buford Prep School, 253 students are enrolled in French, and 112 students are enrolled in Latin. 23 students are enrolled in both Latin and French. If there are 530 students at Buford Prep School, how many students are enrolled in neither French nor Latin?

    (A) 188
    (B) 342
    (C) 388
    (D) 484
    (E) 507

13. On the Leapwell gymnastics team, 14 gymnasts compete on the balance beam, 12 compete on the uneven bars, and 9 compete on both the balance beam and the uneven bars. If 37 gymnasts compete on neither the balance beam nor the uneven bars, how many gymnasts are on the Leapwell team?

    (A) 45
    (B) 51
    (C) 54
    (D) 63
    (E) 72

28. In a European tour group, $\frac{1}{3}$ of the tourists speak Spanish, $\frac{2}{5}$ of the tourists speak French, and $\frac{1}{2}$ of the tourists speak neither language. What fraction of the tourists in the tour group speak both Spanish and French?

    (A) $\frac{2}{15}$

    (B) $\frac{7}{30}$

    (C) $\frac{1}{3}$

    (D) $\frac{1}{2}$

    (E) $\frac{14}{15}$

Comprehensive Statistics and Sets Drill

The answers can be found in Part IV.

Scores on test A

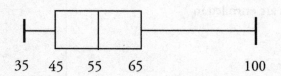

35   45   55   65   100

3. If 400 students took test A and their score distribution is shown above, then how many students scored between 65 and 100 on test A ?

(A) 25
(B) 45
(C) 75
(D) 100
(E) 140

```
3 | 0 0 0 1 1 2 2 2 8 9
4 | 0 5
5 | 1
6 | 1 7 8
7 | 2 2
8 | 8
9 | 0
```

4. What is the median of the data represented in the stem-and-leaf graph shown above?

(A) 30
(B) 39
(C) 39.5
(D) 48.95
(E) 60

Wallburn County Sewage Treatment Plant
E. coli bacteria count per 1 L, week of April 15th

Sunday, April 15th	1,222,430
Monday, April 16th	4,220
Tuesday, April 17th	654
Wednesday, April 18th	23,444
Thursday, April 19th	777,777
Friday, April 20th	22
Saturday, April 21st	43,221

14. In the chart above, for how many days was the *E. coli* bacteria count per 1 L within 30,000 of the mean count for the week?

(A) Zero
(B) One
(C) Two
(D) Three
(E) Four

15. Which of the following sets has the smallest standard deviation?

(A) {14, 14, 14, 14}
(B) {0, 2, 4}
(C) {–8, 0, 8, 16, 32}
(D) {–3, –2, –2, –1}
(E) {–500, 500}

16. 350 people bought popcorn, soda, or both at a movie theater. If 179 people bought popcorn and 57 people bought both popcorn and soda, how many more people bought only soda than bought only popcorn?

(A) 49
(B) 114
(C) 122
(D) 171
(E) 228

18. Don has a collection of 14 fedoras. Don wants to wear a different fedora to work every day this week, Monday through Friday. How many different ways could Don wear his fedoras to work this week?

(A)   2,002
(B)   240,240
(C)   537,824
(D)   17,297,280
(E)   105,413,504

23. A college radio station has 10 punk records, 6 crunk records, and 12 funk records. If three records are to be played in order at random without repeating any record, then what is the probability that a crunk, punk, and funk record are played in that order?

(A) $\dfrac{1}{21,952}$

(B) $\dfrac{45}{1,372}$

(C) $\dfrac{10}{273}$

(D) $\dfrac{5}{34}$

(E) $\dfrac{1}{3}$

27. The rules of a coed basketball league require that a team have 2 men and 3 women on the court at a time. If Team Awesome has 7 men and 5 women, then how many different groups of men and women can Team Awesome have on the court?

(A) $\dfrac{7!}{2!5!} \times \dfrac{5!}{3!2!}$

(B) $\dfrac{7!}{8!} \times \dfrac{5!}{4!}$

(C) $\dfrac{7!}{5!} \times \dfrac{5!}{2!}$

(D) $\dfrac{7!}{2!} \times \dfrac{5!}{3!}$

(E) $\dfrac{12!}{7!}$

32. The probability that Jerry wins his first fencing match is 0.57. The probability that Jerry wins his second fencing match is 0.94. What is the probability that Jerry wins at least one of these two fencing matches?

(A) 0.54
(B) 0.94
(C) 0.97
(D) 1.48
(E) 1.51

38. Laura Jane has a deck of 40 cards numbered 1–40. The first card she draws is numbered 8. Then she draws a second card and determines that the third card she draws will have a 50% chance of having a number between the first and second card she drew. What number was on Laura Jane's second card?

(A) 19
(B) 20
(C) 27
(D) 28
(E) 29

43. A jar contains 32 pennies, 21 nickels, and 22 dimes. If three coins are chosen at random, what is the probability that the combined value of those coins is greater than 6 cents? (Note: pennies are worth 1 cent, nickels are worth 5 cents, and dimes are worth 10 cents.)

(A) 0.0759
(B) 0.0777
(C) 0.1828
(D) 0.9223
(E) 0.9266

Summary

○ Statistics is about working with large groups of numbers and looking for patterns and trends in those numbers.
  • The mean is the average value of a set.
  • The median is the middle value of a set when the values of the set are in chronological order.
  • The mode is the value that occurs the most in a set.

○ Standard deviation is a measure of the set's variation from its mean. Don't worry about calculating standard deviation for the SAT Subject Test Math 2; instead, remember that the larger the standard deviation, the more spread out the elements are.

○ The range of a set is the positive difference between the highest and lowest values.

○ Probability is the number of ways to get what you want divided by the total number of possible outcomes.
  • The probability of multiple events occurring can be calculated either by writing them all out or by multiplying the individual probabilities together.
  • The probability of at least one event occurring is best found by finding the probability that none of the events occur and subtracting that result from one.

○ A permutation is the number of ways you can arrange objects in an order. To find a permutation, make slots for the number of things in your arrangement, put the number of possible options into each slot, and multiply.

○ A combination is the number of ways you can group objects. In other words, order doesn't matter. You start the same way as a permutation, but then divide by the factorial of the number of slots.

○ A factorial is found by multiplying the numbers between 1 and the number you're looking for: $4! = 4 \times 3 \times 2 \times 1$. Use your calculator; on the TI-84 the factorial is the fourth option under MATH->PRB.

○ Group questions require one formula: Total = Group 1 + Group 2 + Neither − Both

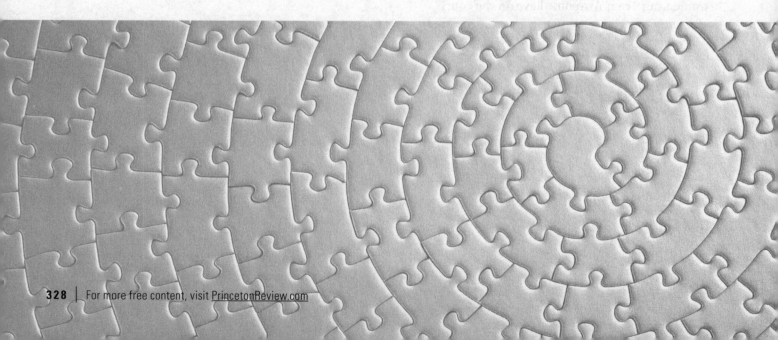

Chapter 12
Miscellaneous

This chapter covers the topics that you may or may not see on the SAT Subject Test Math 2. If you haven't yet mastered the preceding chapters, do so! If you're ready to take your score to the final level, however, then this is the chapter for you.

There are a LOT of topics covered in this chapter, and you will not see all of these topics on any given SAT Subject Test Math 2. However, remember that the scaling of this test will allow you to get a perfect score without answering every question correctly. Don't agonize over mastering every topic in this chapter; instead, focus on the topics you've seen before and see what you can pick up in the other areas.

LOGARITHMS

Exponents can also be written in the form of logarithms. For example, $\log_2 8$ represents the exponent that turns 2 into 8. In this case, the "base" of the logarithm is 2. It's easy to make a logarithmic expression look like a normal exponential expression. Here you can say $\log_2 8 = x$, where x is the unknown exponent that turns 2 into 8. Then you can rewrite the equation as $2^x = 8$. Notice that, in this equation, 2 is the base of the exponent, just as it was the base of the logarithm. Logarithms can be rearranged into exponential form using the following definition:

> **Definition of a Logarithm**
>
> $\log_b n = x \Leftrightarrow b^x = n$

A logarithm that has no written base is assumed to be a base-10 logarithm. Base-10 logarithms are called "common logarithms," and are so frequently used that the base is often left off. Therefore, the expression "log 1,000" means $\log_{10} 1{,}000$. Most calculations involving logarithms are done in base-10 logs. When you punch a number into your calculator and hit the "log" button, the calculator assumes you're using a base-10 log. There will be times when you're dealing with other bases.

Let's look at an example.

---

13. $\log_7 22 =$

   (A) 0.630
   (B) 0.845
   (C) 1.342
   (D) 1.588
   (E) 3.143

Here's How to Crack It

Your calculator may not have a button to input a different base into a logarithmic expression, so you'll need to do a couple of tricks to solve this. The expression given is the equivalent of $7^x = 22$ if you put x in for what $\log_7 22$ is equal to. At this point, you could plug in the answers for x and see which answer works in the above equation, but there's also another approach.

You can take the log (base 10) of both sides of the equation.

$$\log 7^x = \log 22$$

As you'll see on the next pages, the Power Rule lets you take the x in the exponent out of the expression and simply multiply the expression by x.

$$x \log 7 = \log 22$$

Now, to isolate x, you divide both sides by log 7:

$$x = \frac{\log 22}{\log 7} = 1.588$$

The answer is (D).

———————◯———————

Rather than going through all these steps each time you have a logarithm question with a weird base, you can simply remember the following formula:

> **Change of Base Formula**
>
> $$\log_B A = \frac{\log A}{\log B}$$

DRILL 1: LOGARITHMS

Test your understanding of the definition of a logarithm with the following exercises. The answers can be found in Part IV.

1. $\log_2 32 =$ _____   2. $\log_3 x = 4$: $x =$ _____

3. $\log 1000 =$ _____   4. $\log_b 64 = 3$: $b =$ _____

5. $x^{\log_x y} =$ _____   6. $\log_7 1 =$ _____

7. $\log_x x =$ _____   8. $\log_x x^{12} =$ _____

9. $\log 37 =$ _____   10. $\log 5 =$ _____

Logarithmic Rules

In addition to the simple questions you just did, you may need to manipulate equations with logarithms. There are three properties of logarithms that are often useful on the SAT Subject Test Math 2. These properties are very similar to the rules for working with exponents—which isn't surprising, because logarithms and exponents are the same thing. The first two properties deal with the logarithms of products and quotients.

> ## The Product Rule
>
> $$\log_b (xy) = \log_b x + \log_b y$$
>
> ## The Quotient Rule
>
> $$\log_b \left(\frac{x}{y} \right) = \log_b x - \log_b y$$

These rules are just another way of saying that when you multiply terms, you add exponents, and when you divide terms, you subtract exponents. Be sure to remember that when you use them, the logarithms in these cases all have the same base.

The third property of logarithms deals with the logarithms of terms raised to powers.

> ## The Power Rule
>
> $$\log_b (x^r) = r \log_b x$$

This means that whenever you take the logarithm of a term with an exponent, you can pull the exponent out and make it a coefficient.

$$\log (7^2) = 2 \log 7 = 2(0.8451) = 1.6902$$

$$\log_3 (x^5) = 5 \log_3 x$$

These logarithm rules are often used in reverse to simplify a string of logarithms into a single logarithm. Just as the product and quotient rules can be used to expand a single logarithm into several logarithms, the same rules can be used to consolidate several logarithms that are being added or subtracted into a single logarithm. In the same way, the power rule can be used backward to pull a coefficient into a logarithm, as an exponent. Take a look at how these rules can be used to simplify a string of logarithms with the same base.

$$\log 8 + 2 \log 5 - \log 2 =$$

$$\log 8 + \log 5^2 - \log 2 = \qquad (Power\ Rule)$$

$$\log 8 + \log 25 - \log 2 =$$

$$\log (8 \times 25) - \log 2 = \qquad (Product\ Rule)$$

$$\log 200 - \log 2 =$$

$$\log \left(\frac{200}{2} \right) = \qquad (Quotient\ Rule)$$

$$\log 100 = 2$$

DRILL 2: LOGARITHMIC RULES

In the following exercises, use the Product, Quotient, and Power rules of logarithms to simplify each logarithmic expression into a single logarithm with a coefficient of 1. The answers can be found in Part IV.

1. $\log 5 + 2 \log 6 - \log 9 =$
2. $2 \log_5 12 - \log_5 8 - 2 \log_5 3 =$
3. $4 \log 6 - 4 \log 2 - 3 \log 3 =$
4. $\log_4 320 - \log_4 20 =$
5. $2 \log 5 + \log 3 =$

Logarithms in Exponential Equations

Logarithms can be used to solve many equations that would be very difficult or even impossible to solve any other way. The trick to using logarithms in solving equations is to convert all of the exponential expressions in the equation to base-10 logarithms, or common logarithms. Common logarithms are the numbers programmed into your calculator's logarithm function. Once you express exponential equations in terms of common logarithms, you can run the equation through your calculator and get real numbers.

When using logarithms to solve equations, be sure to remember the meaning of the different numbers in a logarithm. Logarithms can be converted into exponential form using the definition of a logarithm provided at the beginning of this section.

Let's take a look at the kinds of tough exponential equations that can be solved using logarithms.

39. If $5^x = 2^{700}$, then what is the value of x?

This deceptively simple equation is practically impossible to solve using conventional algebra. Two to the 700th power is mind-bogglingly huge; there's no way to calculate that number. There's also no way to get x out of that awkward exponent position. This is where logarithms come in. Take the logarithm of each side of the equation.

$$\log 5^x = \log 2^{700}$$

Now use the Power Rule of logarithms to pull the exponents out.

$$x \log 5 = 700 \log 2$$

Then isolate x.

$$x = 700 \times \frac{\log 2}{\log 5}$$

Now use your calculator to get decimal values for log 2 and log 5, and plug them into the equation.

$$x = 700 \times \frac{0.3010}{0.6990}$$

$$x = 700 \times 0.4307$$

$$x = 301.47$$

And *voilà*, a numerical value for x. This is the usual way in which logarithms will prove useful on the SAT Subject Test Math 2. Solving tough exponent equations will usually involve taking the common log of both sides of the equation, and using the Power Rule to bring exponents down. Another method can be used to find the values of logarithms with bases other than 10, even though logarithms with other bases aren't programmed into your calculator. Here's an example.

25. What is the value of x if $\log_3 32 = x$?

You can't do this one in your head. The logarithm is asking, "What exponent turns 3 into 32?" Obviously, it's not an integer. You know that the answer will be between 3 and 4, because $3^3 = 27$ and $3^4 = 81$. That might be enough information to eliminate an answer choice or two, but it probably won't be enough to pick one answer choice. Here's how to get an exact answer.

$$x = \log_3 32$$

$$x = \frac{\log 32}{\log 3} \quad \textit{(Change of Base Formula)}$$

$$x = \frac{1.5051}{0.4771}$$

$$x = 3.1546$$

And there's the exact value of x.

DRILL 3: LOGARITHMS IN EXPONENTIAL EQUATIONS

In the following examples, use the techniques you've just seen to solve these exponential and logarithmic equations. The answers can be found in Part IV.

1. If $2^4 = 3^x$, then $x =$

2. $\log_5 18 =$

3. If $10^n = 137$, then $n =$

4. $\log_{12} 6 =$

5. If $4^x = 5$, then $4^{x+2} =$

6. $\log_2 50 =$

7. If $3^x = 7$, then $3^{x+1} =$

8. If $\log_3 12 = \log_4 x$, then $x =$

Natural Logarithms

On the SAT Subject Test Math 2, you may run into a special kind of logarithm called a natural logarithm. Natural logarithms are logs with a base of e, a constant that is approximately equal to 2.718.

The constant e is a little like π. It's a decimal number that goes on forever without repeating itself, and, like π, it's a basic feature of the universe. Just as π is the ratio of a circle's circumference to its diameter, no matter what, e is a basic feature of growth and decay in economics, physics, and even in biology.

The role of e in the mathematics of growth and decay is a little complicated. Don't worry about that, because you don't need to know very much about e for the SAT Subject Test Math 2. Just memorize a few rules and you're ready to go.

Natural logarithms are so useful in math and science that there's a special notation for expressing them. The expression $\ln x$ (which is read as "ell-enn x") means the log of x to the base e, or $\log_e x$. That means that there are three different ways to express a natural logarithm.

> Definitions of a Natural Logarithm
>
> $\ln n = x \iff \log_e n = x \iff e^x = n$

You can use the definitions of a natural logarithm to solve equations that contain an e^x term. Since e equals 2.718281828…, there's no easy way to raise it to a specific power. By rearranging the equation into a natural logarithm in "$\ln x$" form, you can make your calculator do the hard work for you. Here's a simple example.

19. If $e^x = 6$, then $x =$

 (A) 0.45
 (B) 0.56
 (C) 1.18
 (D) 1.79
 (E) 2.56

Calculator Tip
On some scientific calculators, you'll punch in 6 first, and then hit the "ln x" key

Here's How to Crack It

The equation in the question, $e^x = 6$, can be converted directly into a logarithmic equation using the definition of a logarithm. It would then be written as $\log_e 6 = x$, or $\ln 6 = x$. To find the value of x, just hit the "LN" key on your calculator and punch in 6. You'll find that $x = 1.791759$. The correct answer is (D).

Logarithm as Inverse Operation

Another way to approach logarithm questions is to understand that logarithms are an operation that can be inverted. In the same way that you use addition to undo subtraction, multiplication to undo division, and the cube root to undo a cube when solving an equation, you can use logarithms to invert unwanted bases and vice versa. For example, what would you do to solve the following equation?

$$x + 3 = 7$$

You would subtract 3, the inverse operation of adding 3, from both sides, in order to isolate the x and get $x = 4$.

What do you do when you have the following equation instead?

$$2^x = 8$$

You can either apply a rule that you've memorized in order to rewrite the equation using logs, or you can respond exactly as you did to the equation above, by using inverse operations. Here, you can take a log base 2 of both sides to invert the exponent with base of 2, thus isolating the x. Always remember when doing this that the base of the log must match the base you wish to cancel.

$$\log_2(2^x) = \log_2(8)$$

Since the log base 2 and an exponent with base of 2 are inverse operations, you can now cancel them, leaving you with

$$x = \log_2 8$$

Similarly, when you have an equation with an unwanted logarithm, you can give a base to both sides and cancel in the same way.

$$\log_3 x = 4$$

becomes

$$3^{\log_3 x} = 3^4$$

Once again, the base and the logarithm cancel, leaving you with

$$x = 3^4$$

While this may seem challenging at first, it truly is identical to any other pair of operations you've been inverting and canceling all along, and it can be a useful method for approaching logarithm questions that might otherwise be baffling on test day.

Plugging In, PITA, and Logarithms

Because many logarithm questions involve algebraic manipulation, you can use Plugging In or PITA on most of these questions. Typically, this approach is faster than using the logarithmic rules. Be sure to remain flexible in your approach and look for the most efficient way to do each problem.

Graphing Logarithmic and Exponential Functions

For the SAT Subject Test Math 2, you may also have to know the shapes of some basic graphs associated with natural logs.

Here they are

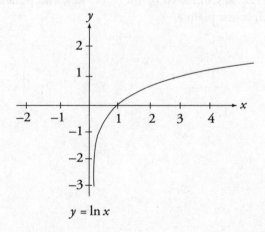

$$y = \ln x$$

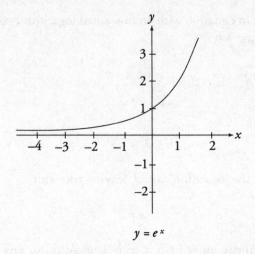

$y = e^x$

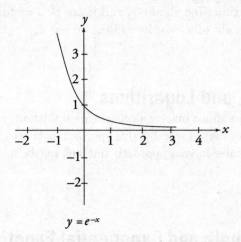

$y = e^{-x}$

Finally, some questions may require you to estimate the value of e to answer a question. Just remember that $e \approx 2.718$. If you forget the value of e, you can always get your calculator to give it to you. Just hit the "2ND" key followed by the "LN" key, and punch in 1. The result will be e to the first power, which is just plain e.

DRILL 4: NATURAL LOGARITHMS

The answers can be found in Part IV.

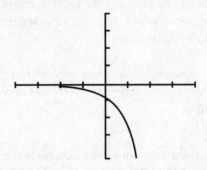

8. If the graph above shows $f(x)$, then which of the following could be $f(x)$?

   (A) $\ln x$
   (B) $-\ln x$
   (C) e^x
   (D) e^{-x}
   (E) $-e^x$

18. If $e^z = 8$, then $z =$

    (A) 1.74
    (B) 2.08
    (C) 2.35
    (D) 2.94
    (E) 3.04

23. If set $M = \{\pi, e, 3\}$, then which of the following shows the elements in set M in descending order?

    (A) $\{\pi, e, 3\}$
    (B) $\{e, 3, \pi\}$
    (C) $\{\pi, 3, e\}$
    (D) $\{3, \pi, e\}$
    (E) $\{3, e, \pi\}$

38. If $6e^{\frac{n}{3}} = 5$, then what is the value of n ?

    (A) −0.55
    (B) −0.18
    (C)   0.26
    (D)   0.64
    (E)   1.19

40. If $\ln 1.5x = 1.5$, then $x =$

    (A) 0
    (B) 0.270
    (C) 0.405
    (D) 2.988
    (E) 4.481

VISUAL PERCEPTION

Some questions on the SAT Subject Test Math 2 ironically do not appear to test mathematical skills in any conventional sense of the phrase. One type of non-mathematical question on the test is the visual perception question, which asks you to visualize (that is, draw) a picture of a situation described in two or three dimensions.

The best technique for such questions is to draw your best representation of the situation described and use that as a guide in eliminating answers. You don't have to be a great artist, but a simple diagram will go a long way.

17. Which of the following equations describes the set of points equidistant from the lines described by the equations $y = 2x + 7$ and $y = 2x + 1$?

   (A) $y = 4x + 8$
   (B) $y = 4x + 6$
   (C) $y = 2x + 8$
   (D) $y = 2x + 6$
   (E) $y = 2x + 4$

This is asked in words because if there were a picture, it would be too easy. So make it easier by drawing a picture.

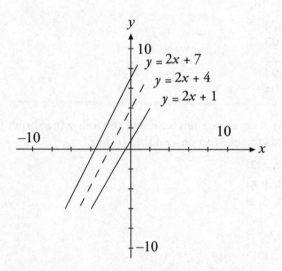

If you draw points halfway between the two lines, you get another line. It's parallel to the other two, so its slope is 2; eliminate (A) and (B), and it's halfway between the two, so its y-intercept is halfway between 7 and 1. That's a y-intercept of 4, so (E) is the answer.

Now try another.

36. Which of the following CANNOT be the result of the intersection of a cube and a plane?

(A) A point
(B) A line
(C) A triangle
(D) A square
(E) A pentagon

Here's How to Crack It

This question is asking you to imagine the intersection of a two-dimensional object and a three-dimensional object. It can help to think of the plane as static and to imagine how you can manipulate the cube in relation to the plane to find the answer.

You can create a point by intersecting the two objects at a vertex of a cube.

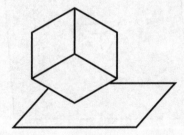

Therefore, you can eliminate (A). Similarly, using the edge of the cube creates a line.

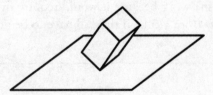

Eliminate (B).

Let's skip (C) for the moment, because (D) is easier. A square is created by simply intersecting one face of the cube with the plane.

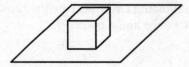

Eliminate (D).

To create a triangle, you would need to have three line segments which intersect at three vertices. If you were to "push" the corner of the cube through the plane, the three faces adjacent to that vertex would each have a line segment where the plane intersects that face. Those three line segments would each meet at the edge of the cube.

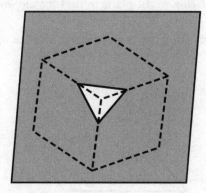

You have three intersecting line segments; therefore, you have a triangle, so eliminate (C) and choose (E).

(Note that the pentagon doesn't work because it would require five line segments. You cannot join five straight line segments from a cube if they all have to be on the same plane.)

DRILL 5: VISUAL PERCEPTION

Try the following practice questions about visual perception. The answers can be found in Part IV.

12. Lines *l*, *m*, *n*, and *o* are all distinct lines which lie in the same plane. If line *l* is perpendicular to line *m*, line *m* is parallel to line *o*, and line *o* is perpendicular to line *n*, which of the following must be true?

    I. Line *l* is parallel to line *n*.
    II. Line *n* is perpendicular to line *l*.
    III. Line *n* is parallel to line *m*.

    (A) I only
    (B) II only
    (C) III only
    (D) I and III only
    (E) I, II, and III

30. Which of the following could be the number of circles created by the intersection of a sphere and a cube?

    I. 5
    II. 6
    III. 7

    (A) I only
    (B) II only
    (C) III only
    (D) I and II only
    (E) I and III only

47. Circles *A* and *B* (not shown) lie in a plane and have the same center. The radius of circle *A* is twice that of circle *B*. Points *X*, *Y*, and *Z* are on the circumference of circle *A*. What is the maximum number of distinct non-overlapping regions of nonzero area that can be formed by the circumferences of circles *A* and *B* and chords *XY* and *YZ* ?

    (A) Two
    (B) Four
    (C) Six
    (D) Seven
    (E) Eight

SEQUENCES

The typical SAT Subject Test Math 2 has one question dealing with arithmetic or geometric sequences. Once you understand the basic concepts behind these sequences, these questions are pretty straightforward.

Arithmetic Sequences

The smarty-pants people at the College Board define an arithmetic sequence as "one in which the difference between successive terms is constant." Real human beings just say that an arithmetic sequence is what you get when you pick a starting value and add the same number again and again.

Here are some sample arithmetic sequences.

$$\{a_n\} = 1, 7, 13, 19, 25, 31,\ldots$$
$$\{b_n\} = 3, 13, 23, 33, 43, 53,\ldots$$
$$\{c_n\} = 12, 7, 2, -3, -8, -13,\ldots$$

It's not hard to figure out what difference separates any two terms in a sequence. To continue a sequence, you would just continue adding that difference. The larger letter in each case is the name of the sequence (these are sequences *a*, *b*, and *c*). The subscript, *n*, represents the number of the term in the sequence. The expression a_4, for example, represents the fourth term in the *a* sequence, which is 19. The expression b_7 means the seventh term in the *b* sequence, which would be 63.

The typical arithmetic sequence question asks you to figure out the difference between any two successive terms in the sequence, and then calculate the value of a term much farther along. There's just one trick to that—to calculate the value of a_{26}, for example, start by figuring out the difference between any two consecutive terms. You'll find that the terms in the sequence increase at intervals of 6. Now here's the trick: To get to the 26th term in the sequence, you'll start with a_1, which is 1, and increase it by 6 twenty-five times. The term $a_{26} = 1 + (25 \times 6)$, or 151. It's like climbing stairs in a building; to get to the fifth floor, you climb 4 flights. To get to the 12th floor, you climb 11 flights, and so on. In the same way, it takes 11 steps to get to the 12th term in a sequence from the first term. To get to the *n*th term in a sequence, take $(n - 1)$ steps from the first term.

Here's another example—to figure out the value of c_{17}, start with 12 and add –5 sixteen times. The value of $c_{17} = 12 + (16 \times -5)$, or –68. That's all there is to calculating values in arithmetic sequences.

Here's the algebraic definition of the *n*th term of an arithmetic sequence, if the starting value is a_1 and the difference between any two successive terms is *d*.

The *n*th Term of an Arithmetic Sequence

$$a_n = a_1 + (n - 1)d$$

Finding the Sum of an Arithmetic Sequence

You might be asked to figure out the sum of the first 37 terms of an arithmetic sequence, or the first 48 terms, and so on. To figure out the sum of a chunk of an arithmetic sequence, take the average of the first and last terms in that chunk, and multiply by the number of terms you're adding up. For example,

$$\{a_n\} = 5, 11, 17, 23, 29, 35,\ldots$$

What is the sum of the first 40 terms of a_n?

The first term of a_n is 5. The fortieth term is 239. The sum of these terms will be the average of these two terms, 122, multiplied by the number of terms, 40. The product of 122 and 40 is 4,880. That's the sum of the first 40 terms of the sequence. Here's the algebraic definition of the sum of the first n terms of an arithmetic sequence, where the difference between any two successive terms is d.

Sum of the First n Terms of an Arithmetic Sequence

$$\text{sum} = n\left(\frac{a_1 + a_n}{2}\right)$$

Summation

A *summation* (or *series*) is a list of numbers to be added together. First, plug the number below the sigma (Σ) into the formula and get a result. Then do this for every integer up to the number above the sigma. Finally, add up all of your results to get your final answer.

43. $\displaystyle\sum_{k=1}^{8} 2k + 1 =$

(A) 20
(B) 36
(C) 40
(D) 72
(E) 80

Here's How to Crack It

Here, plug $k = 1$ into the formula to get $2(1) + 1 = 3$. Now, repeat for $k = 2$, $k = 3$, etc., up to and including $k = 8$. You end up with $3 + 5 + \ldots + 17$. You could also use the formula for the sum of the first n terms of an arithmetic sequence, and you'd get $8\left(\frac{3+17}{2}\right)$, which is 80. The answer is (E).

Geometric Sequences

A geometric sequence is formed by taking a starting value and multiplying it by the same factor again and again. The College Board often describes this as a "series with a constant ratio between adjacent terms." By "constant ratio," the College Board means the factor you multiply each term by to get the next term. While any two successive terms in an arithmetic sequence are separated by a constant difference, any two successive terms in a geometric sequence are separated by a constant factor. Here are some sample geometric sequences.

$$\{a_n\} = 2, 6, 18, 54, 162, 486,\ldots$$
$$\{b_n\} = 8, 4, 2, 1, 0.5, 0.25,\ldots$$
$$\{c_n\} = 3, 15, 75, 375, 1,875,\ldots$$

Just like arithmetic sequence questions, geometric sequence questions most often test your ability to calculate the value of a term farther along in the sequence. As with arithmetic sequences, the trick to geometric sequences is that it takes 19 steps to get to the 20th term, 36 steps to get to the 37th term, and so on.

To find the value of a_{10}, for example, start with the basic information about the sequence. Its starting value is 2, and each term increases by a factor of 3. To get to the tenth term, start with 2 and multiply it by 3 nine times—that is, multiply 2 by 3^9. You get 39,366, which is the value of a_{10}. As you can see, geometric sequences tend to grow much faster than arithmetic sequences do.

Here's the algebraic definition of the nth term in a geometric sequence, where the first term is a_1 and the factor separating any two successive terms is r.

> **The nth Term of a Geometric Sequence**
>
> $$a_n = a_1 r^{n-1}$$

The Sum of a Geometric Sequence

You may also be asked to find the sum of part of a geometric sequence. This is a bit tougher than calculating the sum of an arithmetic sequence. To add the first n terms of a geometric sequence, use this formula. Once again, the first term in the sequence is a_1, and the factor separating any two successive terms is r.

> **Sum of the First n Terms of a Geometric Sequence**
>
> $$\text{sum} = \frac{a_1\left(1 - r^n\right)}{1 - r}$$

This is not a formula that is called upon very often, but it's good to know it if you're taking the SAT Subject Test Math 2.

The Sum of an Infinite Geometric Sequence

Every now and then, a question will ask you to figure out the sum of an infinite geometric sequence—that's right, add up an infinite number of terms. There's a trick to this as well. Whenever the factor between any two terms is greater than 1, the sequence keeps growing and growing. The sum of such a sequence is infinitely large—it never stops increasing, and its sum cannot be calculated.

> The sum of an infinite geometric series can be calculated only when the constant factor is between –1 and 1.

When the constant factor of a geometric sequence is less than 1, the terms in the sequence continually decrease, and there exists some value that the sum of the sequence will never exceed. For example,

$$\{a_n\} = 1, 0.5, 0.25, 0.125, 0.0625,\ldots$$

The sequence a_n above will never be greater than 2. The more of its terms you add together, the closer the sum gets to 2. If you add all of its terms, all the way out to infinity, you get exactly 2. Here's the formula you use to figure that out. Once again, a_1 is the first term in the sequence, and r the factor between each two terms. Remember that r must be between –1 and 1.

> **Sum of an Infinite Geometric Sequence**
>
> $$\text{sum} = \frac{a_1}{1-r} \qquad \text{for } -1 < r < 1$$

In most cases, though, you can simply use approximation to eliminate ridiculously large or small answer choices. The five formulas in the boxes are all you'll ever need to work with arithmetic and geometric sequences.

Using Your Calculator to Find Sequences and Summations

You can use your calculator to work a sequence or summation by using the algebraic expression of the sequence or summation. Here's an example.

Take the geometric sequence that starts at 2 and has a constant ratio 3. The expression of this sequence would be $2(3^{n-1})$, where n is the place in the sequence. To find this sequence on the TI-84, press 2ND->STAT to enter the LIST menu. The fifth option under OPS is seq. Select that option and you will come to this screen.

```
                    ◆◆◆
  Expr:2(3^(X-1))
  Variable:X
  start:1
  end:5
  step:1
  Paste
```

The first line, Expr, is where you put the algebraic expression of the sequence (be careful with your parentheses!). The second line, Variable, is where you put the variable you are using in the expression. The start and end lines are the values for the variable at the start and the end. Step is the difference between each value of the variable; for the purposes of the SAT Subject Test Math 2, just leave this at 1. When you are complete, select Paste and press ENTER. The calculator will bring the needed information to the main screen; press ENTER again and the calculator will find the sequence.

```
  seq(2(3^(X-1)),X
  ,1,5,1)
      {2 6 18 54 162}
```

Now, let's say that instead of the first five members of the sequence $2(3^{n-1})$, you wanted to find the value of $\sum_{n=1}^{5} 2\left(3^{n-1}\right)$. You start with the seq function above, putting the number below the sigma as the start and the number above the sigma as the end. Next, go back to the LIST menu and go to MATH. The fifth option is sum. To find the summation, select sum. You will be sent to the main screen with the sum function waiting for something to summate. Go back to your sequence through the LIST menu and paste it in after the sum. Hit ENTER and your calculator will work its magic.

```
  sum(seq(2(3^(X-1
  )),X,1,5,1)
                   242
  ▮
```

Knowing these calculator tricks can save you time (and let you score more points) on the SAT Subject Test Math 2.

Recursive Sequences

$$C_{n+1} = C_n + C_{n-1} - 2$$

So this happened. Each year, scores of test-takers see an equation like this one and flee in terror, and it's hard to blame them. Just look at all those subscripts!

However, fear not, because like many things in math, it looks far worse than it actually is. This equation describes what's known as a recursive sequence, which means that there's a sequence of numbers, and you use the numbers in the sequence to figure out the others.

As an example, consider the following sequence.

$$2, 4, 6, 8, 10, 12, 14, \ldots$$

Not so scary right? It's just the even integers starting from 2. But watch this...

$$E_n = E_{n-1} + 2, E_1 = 2$$

Run away! Not really though, because this horrifying equation creates a sequence that is identical to the list above. It's still the sequence of even integers starting from 2 but expressed recursively. The part at the end, $E_1 = 2$, is a fancy way of saying that the first number in the sequence will be 2; the subscript always tells you which element you're at in the sequence.

E_n just means "some number in the list, but we're not telling you which one." E_{n-1} means "the number in the list before that one." For instance, suppose $n = 2$. The equation then becomes

$$E_2 = E_1 + 2$$

All this means is that the second term in the list is going to be the first number in the list plus 2, and since you already know that the first number in the list is 2, then the second number will be 4. Now suppose that $n = 3$.... The equation then becomes

$$E_3 = E_2 + 2$$

and the same thing happens again. The second number 4 increases by 2 and becomes the third number 6. Thus, this formula tells you that any number in the list will be 2 higher than the one before it, and starting from 2, it will yield the positive even integers.

In general, think of recursive sequence equations as being a set of instructions to follow, and remember that the subscripts, which are the scariest parts, do nothing more than tell you where you're at in the sequence.

Let's try an example problem.

In the recursive sequence defined by the equation
$C_{n+1} = (C_n)^3 - 5$, the fourth term in the sequence is 10,643.
Which of the following is equal to $C_3 - C_1$?

(A)   2
(B)   20
(C)   22
(D) 10,621
(E) 10,641

Here's How to Crack It

The question is asking for the difference between C_3 and C_1, which as you'll recall from earlier are the third and first terms in the sequence, respectively. The question also provides the value of the fourth term in the sequence, 10,643, which can be labeled C_4.

Starting with the fourth term, you can now use the equation defining the sequence to work down to the third term C_3, then to the second term C_2, and finally to the first term C_1.

By setting $n = 3$ in the equation, you get

$$C_4 = (C_3)^3 - 5$$

Substitute 10,643 in for C_4.

$$10,643 = (C_3)^3 - 5$$

Solve for C_3 by first adding 5 to, and then taking the cube root of, both sides.

$$10,648 = (C_3)^3$$

$$22 = C_3$$

Therefore, the third term in the sequence is 22. You now could follow the same procedure to get C_2 from C_3 by setting $n = 2$, and then C_1 from C_2 by setting $n = 1$. Or, by recalling that the equation is simply a set of instructions for navigating to each new term, you could alternatively just do the same operations again to move down the list.

Adding 5 to the third term 22 gives 27, and cube rooting then yields 3, so value of the second term is 3. Adding 5 again gives 8, and cube rooting then yields 2, so the value of the first term is 2. Since the problem asked you for the difference between the third term and the first term, you then subtract those terms $C_3 - C_1 = 22 - 2 = 20$. The correct answer is (B).

DRILL 6: SEQUENCES

Try the following practice questions about arithmetic and geometric sequences. The answers can be found in Part IV.

14. In an arithmetic sequence, the second term is 4 and the sixth term is 32. What is the fifth term in the sequence?

    (A)   8
    (B) 15
    (C) 16
    (D) 24
    (E) 25

19. In the arithmetic sequence a_n, $a_1 = 2$ and $a_7 = 16$. What is the value of a_{33}?

    (A) 72.00
    (B) 74.33
    (C) 74.67
    (D) 75.14
    (E) 76.67

26. If the second term of a geometric sequence is 4, and the fourth term of the sequence is 25, then what is the ninth term in the sequence?

    (A)   804.43
    (B)   976.56
    (C) 1864.35
    (D) 2441.41
    (E) 6103.52

34. $3 + 1 + \dfrac{1}{3} + \dfrac{1}{9} + \dfrac{1}{27} + \dfrac{1}{81} \ldots =$

    (A) 4.17
    (B) 4.33
    (C) 4.50
    (D) 5.00
    (E) ∞

38. If the second term of a geometric sequence is 1.5 and the third term of the geometric sequence is 4.5, then what is the sum of the first 10 terms of the geometric sequence?

    (A)   3
    (B)   120
    (C)   9,841.5
    (D)   14,762
    (E)   44,286.5

40. A recursive sequence is defined by the equation
$B_{n+1} = 3B_n - 6$. If $B_3 = 2B_2$ then all of the following are terms
in the sequence EXCEPT

(A) 12
(B) 30
(C) 84
(D) 137
(E) 246

LIMITS

A limit is the value a function approaches as its independent variable approaches a given constant. That may be confusing to read, but the idea is really fairly simple. A limit can be written in different ways, as the following examples show:

$$\lim_{x \to 2} \frac{2x^2 + x - 10}{x - 2} =$$

What is the limit of $\dfrac{2x^2 + x - 10}{x - 2}$ as x approaches 2 ?

If $f(x) = \dfrac{2x^2 + x - 10}{x - 2}$, then what value does $f(x)$ approach as x

approaches 2 ?

These three questions are equivalent. The first of the three is in limit notation and is read exactly like the question, "What is the limit of $\dfrac{2x^2 + x - 10}{x - 2}$ as x approaches 2 ?"

Finding a limit is very simple. Just take the value that x approaches and plug it into the expression. The value you get is the limit. It's so simple that you just know there's got to be a hitch—and there is. The limits that appear on the SAT Subject Test Math 2 share a common problem—tricky denominators. The question introduced above is no exception. Let's take a look at it again.

$$\lim_{x \to 2} \frac{2x^2 + x - 10}{x - 2} =$$

You can find the value of this limit just by plugging 2 into the expression as x. But there's a hitch. When $x = 2$, the fraction's denominator is undefined, and it seems that the limit does not exist. The same solution always applies to such questions. You need to factor the top and bottom of the fraction and see whether there's anything that will make the denominator cancel out and stop being such a nuisance. Let's see how this expression factors out.

$$\lim_{x \to 2} \frac{2x^2 + x - 10}{x - 2} = \lim_{x \to 2} \frac{(x - 2)(2x + 5)}{x - 2} =$$

Now, you can cancel out that pesky $(x - 2)$.

$$\lim_{x \to 2}(2x + 5) =$$

Now the expression is no longer undefined when you plug in 2. It simply comes out to 2(2) + 5, or 9. The limit of $\dfrac{2x^2 + x - 10}{x - 2}$ as x approaches 2 is 9.

That's all there is to limit questions. Just factor the top and bottom of the expression as much as possible, and try to get the problematic terms to cancel out so that the limit is no longer undefined. When it's no longer undefined, just plug in the constant value to find the limit.

One more dirty trick—you might run into a limit problem in which it's impossible to cancel out the term that makes the expression undefined. Take a look at this example.

$$\lim_{x \to -3} \frac{3x^2 + 3x - 36}{x^2 - 9}$$

Because the constant that x approaches, –3, makes the limit undefined, you've got to factor the expression and try to cancel out the problematic part of the denominator.

$$\lim_{x \to -3} \frac{3x^2 + 3x - 36}{x^2 - 9}$$

$$\lim_{x \to -3} \frac{3(x - 3)(x + 4)}{(x - 3)(x + 3)}$$

$$\lim_{x \to -3} \frac{3(x + 4)}{(x + 3)}$$

The expression can be factored, and you can even cancel out a term in the denominator. When the dust clears, however, you find that the denominator of the fraction still approaches zero, and that the limit remains undefined. When this happens, it's said that the limit does not exist, and that would be the correct answer.

You can also graph the function in a limit question on your graphing calculator and see what the value of the function is as the function approaches the requested value. The graphs of functions with defined limits will look like a standard function (line, parabola, or other), but will have a "hole" at the requested value. Use the TRACE function to find the values just before and after the hole to find the limit. If the graph heads off to positive or negative infinity as you approach the requested value, then the limit is undefined at that point.

DRILL 7: LIMITS

Try the following practice questions involving limits. The answers can be found in Part IV.

30. What value does the expression $\dfrac{4x^2 - x - 5}{16x^2 - 25}$ approach as x approaches 1.25 ?

    (A) 0
    (B) 0.225
    (C) 0.625
    (D) 1.275
    (E) 2.250

38. $\displaystyle\lim_{x \to 3} \dfrac{x^2 + x - 12}{2x^2 - 6x} =$

    (A) 1.17
    (B) 2.25
    (C) 3.33
    (D) 6.67
    (E) The limit does not exist.

40. $\displaystyle\lim_{x \to -3} \dfrac{x^3 + 4x^2 - 21x}{x^2 + 10x + 21} =$

    (A) −3.00
    (B) 2.46
    (C) 7.50
    (D) 10.33
    (E) The limit does not exist.

VECTORS

A vector is a visual representation of something that has both direction and magnitude. A vector can represent a force, a velocity, a distance traveled, or any of a variety of physical quantities. On the SAT Subject Test Math 2, vectors usually represent travel.

A vector arrow's orientation indicates the direction of travel. Its length represents the distance traveled (this is the magnitude of the vector). Sometimes, test questions will deal with vectors without telling you what they represent.

Basically, there are only two things you have to do with vectors on the SAT Subject Test Math 2—compute their lengths, and add or subtract them. Computing their lengths is generally done on the coordinate plane, where it's just a matter of using the Pythagorean Theorem. Adding and subtracting vectors is also pretty simple. Here's how it's done.

Adding Vectors

Suppose you wanted to add these two vectors together.

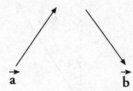

To add them, redraw the second vector so that its tail stands on the tip of the first vector. Then draw the resulting vector, closing the triangle (make sure that the resulting vector's direction is in agreement with the vectors you added). This is what the addition of vectors **a** and **b** looks like.

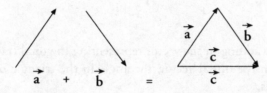

Vector **c** is the sum of vectors **a** and **b**.

If the College Board gives you a figure and asks you to add two vectors, they need to be connected tip-to-tail. If necessary, move one of the vectors, and then try using the Law of Cosines.

Let's look at an example.

---

48. Earl walks 100 m due north. He then walks 75 m at 30 degrees east of due north. Which of the following describes the vector of Earl's trip?

    (A) 175 m at 30 degrees east of due north
    (B) 125 m at 15 degrees east of due north
    (C) 169.161 m at 12.808 degrees east of due north
    (D) 169.161 m at 17.192 degrees east of due north
    (E) 151.329 m at 46.936 degrees east of due north

Here's How to Crack It

First, draw the two initial vectors tip-to-tail.

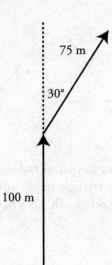

Next, create a triangle by adding in the vector representing the total travel. Because the second vector is 30 degrees from the initial vector, the angle in the triangle opposite the total travel vector will be 150 degrees.

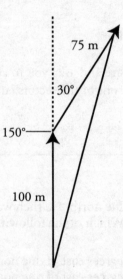

Because you have two sides and an angle, you can use Law of Cosines to find the length of the unknown side. Remember that c in the equation is the side opposite angle C; use the unknown total vector and 150° as c and C, respectively.

$$c^2 = a^2 + b^2 - 2ab \cos C$$

$$c^2 = 100^2 + 75^2 - 2(100)(75) \cos 150°$$

$$c^2 = 28{,}615.381$$

$$c = 169.161$$

This is the length of the vector, so you can eliminate (A), (B), and (E). To find the angle of the vector, use the Law of Sines. You want the angle opposite the 75 m side, as that angle would represent the angle from due north. Once again, remember that in the Law of Sines, side lengths are opposite the angle with the same letter.

$$\frac{\sin A}{a} = \frac{\sin B}{b}$$

$$\frac{\sin 150°}{169.161} = \frac{\sin B}{75}$$

$$75\left(\frac{\sin 150°}{169.161}\right) = \sin B$$

$$0.222 = \sin B$$

$$\sin^{-1} 0.222 = B$$

$$12.808° = B$$

The answer is (C).

―――――――――――――――○―――――――――――――――

Subtracting Vectors

To subtract vectors, you'll use the same technique you used to add them, with one extra step. First, reverse the sign of the vector that's being subtracted. You do this by simply moving the arrowhead to the other end of the vector. Then add the two vectors as you usually would. Here's an example of subtraction using the two vectors you just added. First, reverse the sign of the subtracted vector.

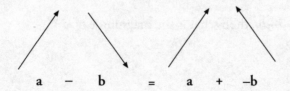

$$\mathbf{a} \quad - \quad \mathbf{b} \quad = \quad \mathbf{a} \quad + \quad -\mathbf{b}$$

And then, add them up.

Tip to Tail
Remember, you're always going to connect vectors tip to tail.

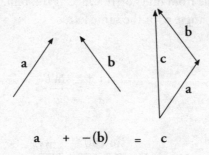

$$a \quad + \quad -(b) \quad = \quad c$$

Vector **c** is the vector produced by subtracting vector **b** from vector **a**.

You can add or subtract two vectors by adding or subtracting their x and y components. For example, if vector **u** has components (1, 3) and vector **v** has components (–1, 5), then the resulting vector **u** + **v** would have components (1 + (–1), 3 + 5) = (0, 8).

DRILL 8: VECTORS

The answers can be found in Part IV.

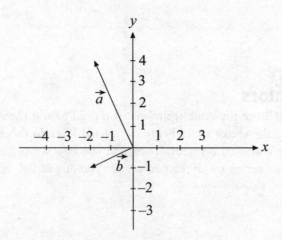

36. If $\vec{c} = \vec{a} + \vec{b}$, then what is the magnitude of $\vec{c}$?

    (A) 2
    (B) 3
    (C) 4
    (D) 5
    (E) 6

41. Vector **a** has components (8, 15), and vector **b** has components (3, 3). If $c = a - b$, what is the magnitude of vector **c** ?

    (A) 10.5
    (B) 13.0
    (C) 15.6
    (D) 16.5
    (E) 21.1

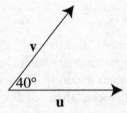

44. If, in the figure above, the magnitude of vector **u** is 9 and the magnitude of vector **v** is 7, what is the magnitude of vector **(u + v)** ?

    (A)   5.79
    (B)   7.00
    (C) 11.40
    (D) 12.26
    (E) 15.05

LOGIC

Every now and then, as you proceed innocently through the SAT Subject Test Math 2, you will come upon a question asked in simple English that seems to have nothing at all to do with math. This is a logic question. Here's a typical example.

24. If every precious stone is harder than glass, which of the following statements must also be true?

    (A) Glass can be a precious stone.
    (B) Every stone harder than glass is a precious stone.
    (C) No stone is exactly as hard as glass.
    (D) Some stones softer than glass are precious stones.
    (E) Every stone softer than glass is not a precious stone.

Here's How to Crack It

This is madness. There's no math here at all. However, there is a rule here for you to work with. The rule states that given one statement, there's only one other statement that is logically necessary, the contrapositive. This is what the contrapositive states:

> **The Contrapositive**
>
> Given the statement $A \rightarrow B$, you also know $\sim B \rightarrow \sim A$.

In English, that means that the statement "If A, then B" also tells you that "If not B, then not A." To find the contrapositive of any statement, switch the order of the first and second parts of the original statement, and negate their meaning. But you can't be sure of anything else. For example, "If not A" doesn't necessarily mean "then not B." And "if B" doesn't necessarily mean "then A." This is how you'd find the contrapositive of the statement, "Every precious stone is harder than glass." Start by making sure that you clearly see what the two parts of the original statement are.

$$\text{stone is precious} \rightarrow \text{stone harder than glass}$$

Then switch the order of the statement's parts, and negate their meanings.

$$\text{stone not harder than glass} \rightarrow \text{stone is not precious}$$

This is the contrapositive. Once you've found it, just check the answer choices for a statement with an equivalent meaning. In this case, (E) is equivalent to the contrapositive. Trap answers will typically say things like "Every stone that is harder than glass is precious" or "Every stone that is not precious is softer than glass."

———○———

Almost all logic questions test your understanding of the contrapositive. There are just a couple of other points that might come up in logic questions.

- If you see the statement "Some A are B," then you also know that "Some B are A." For example, "Some teachers are pretty cool people" also means that "Some pretty cool people are teachers."
- To disprove the claim, "X might be true," or "X is possible," you must show that X is never, ever true, in any case, anywhere.
- To disprove the claim, "X is true," you only need to show that there's one exception, somewhere, sometime.

In other words, a statement that something *may* be true is very hard to disprove; you've got to demonstrate conclusively that there's no way it could be true. On the other hand, a statement that something is *definitely* true is easy to disprove; all you have to do is find one exception. If you remember the three bullet points above and the contrapositive, you'll be prepared for any logic question on the SAT Subject Test Math 2.

DRILL 9: LOGIC

Exercise your powers of logic on these practice questions. The answers can be found in Part IV.

28. At Legion High School in a certain year, no sophomore received failing grades. Which of the following statements must be true?

    (A) There were failures in classes other than the sophomore class.
    (B) Sophomores had better study skills than other students that year.
    (C) No student at Legion High School received failing grades that year.
    (D) Any student who received failing grades was not a sophomore.
    (E) There were more passing grades in the sophomore class than in other classes.

33. "If one commits arson, a building burns." Which of the following is a contradiction to this statement?

    (A) Many people would refuse to commit arson.
    (B) A building did not burn, and yet arson was committed.
    (C) Some buildings are more difficult to burn than others.
    (D) A building burned, although no arson was committed.
    (E) Arson is a serious crime.

35. In a necklace of diamonds and rubies, some stones are not genuine. If every stone that is not genuine is a ruby, which of the following statements must be true?

    (A) There are more diamonds than rubies in the necklace.
    (B) The necklace contains no genuine rubies.
    (C) No diamonds in the necklace are not genuine.
    (D) Diamonds are of greater value than rubies.
    (E) The necklace contains no genuine diamonds.

40. If some pets are dogs, and all dogs are smelly, then which of the following CANNOT be true?

    (A) There is a dog which is not a pet and is not smelly.
    (B) Some pets are smelly.
    (C) Some pets are not smelly.
    (D) If Ralph owns 5 pets, some of which are dogs, then all of Ralph's pets are smelly.
    (E) If Suzy's pet is smelly, then it is a dog.

IMAGINARY NUMBERS

Almost all math on the SAT Subject Test Math 2 is confined to real numbers. Only a few questions deal with the square roots of negative numbers—imaginary numbers. For the sake of simplicity, imaginary numbers are expressed in terms of i. The quantity i is equal to the square root of -1. It's used to simplify the square roots of negative numbers.

Here's an example.

$$\sqrt{-25} = \sqrt{25}\sqrt{-1} = 5\sqrt{-1} = 5i$$
$$\sqrt{-48} = \sqrt{48}\sqrt{-1} = \sqrt{16}\sqrt{3}\sqrt{-1} = 4i\sqrt{3}$$
$$\sqrt{-7} = \sqrt{7}\sqrt{-1} = i\sqrt{7}$$

There are three basic kinds of questions on the SAT Subject Test Math 2 that require you to work with imaginary numbers.

Computing Powers of i

You may run into a question that asks you to find the value of i^{34}, or something equally outrageous. This may seem difficult or impossible at first, but, as usual, there's a trick to it. The powers of i repeat in a cycle of 4 values, over and over.

$$i^1 = i \qquad i^5 = i$$
$$i^2 = -1 \qquad i^6 = -1$$
$$i^3 = -i \qquad i^7 = -i$$
$$i^4 = 1 \qquad i^8 = 1$$

And so on. These are the only four values that can be produced by raising i to an integer power. To find the value of i^{34}, either write out the cycle of four values up to the 34th power, which would take less than a minute, or, more simply, divide 34 by 4. You find that 34 contains eight cycles of 4, with a remainder of 2. The eight cycles of 4 just bring you back to where you started. It's the remainder that's important. The remainder of 2 means that the value of i^{34} is equal to the value of i^2, or -1. In order to raise i to any power, just divide the exponent by 4 and use the remainder as your exponent.

Doing Algebra with *i*

Algebra that includes complex numbers is no different from ordinary algebra. You just need to remember that *i* raised to an exponent changes in value, which can have some odd effects in algebra.

Here's an example.

$$(x - 3i)(2x + 6i) =$$
$$2x^2 - 6ix + 6ix - 18i^2 =$$
$$2x^2 - 18i^2 =$$
$$2x^2 - 18(-1) =$$
$$2x^2 + 18$$

You can also plug in on these questions and use your calculator. On the TI-84, 2ND->"." will give you *i*. Make sure your calculator is in complex number mode (MODE menu, 7th line, select "*a* + *bi*"), plug in for the variables and solve as with regular Plugging In. As in the problem above, don't be surprised if all the imaginary numbers vanish!

A College Board Trick

As you can see, *i* sometimes has a way of dropping out of algebraic expressions. The College Board likes this trick, so keep an eye out for it.

The Complex Plane

A complex number is a specific kind of imaginary number—specifically, the sum of a real number and an imaginary number, such as $5 + 3i$. A complex number is one that takes the form $a + bi$, where *a* and *b* are real numbers and *i* is the imaginary unit, the square root of –1. On the SAT Subject Test Math 2, the principal importance of complex numbers is that they can be represented on the complex plane. This is what the complex plane looks like.

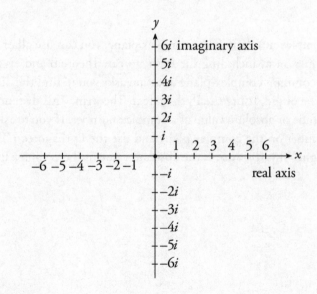

Notice that the complex plane looks just like the ordinary coordinate plane, but the axes have different meanings. On the complex plane, the *x*-axis is referred to as the real axis. The *y*-axis is referred to as the imaginary axis. Each unit on the real axis equals 1—a real unit. Each unit on the imaginary axis equals *i*—the imaginary unit. Any complex number in the form *a* + *bi*, such as 5 + 3*i*, can be plotted on the complex plane almost like a coordinate pair. Just plot *a*, the real component of the complex number, on the *x*-axis; and *bi*, the imaginary component, on the *y*-axis.

Here are several complex numbers plotted on the complex plane.

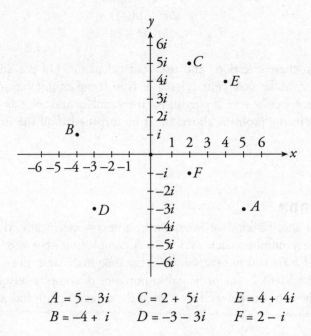

$$A = 5 - 3i \qquad C = 2 + 5i \qquad E = 4 + 4i$$
$$B = -4 + i \qquad D = -3 - 3i \qquad F = 2 - i$$

Once you've plotted a complex number on the complex plane, you can use all of the usual coordinate-geometry techniques on it, including the Pythagorean Theorem and even right-triangle trigonometry. The most common complex-plane question asks you to find the distance between a complex number and the origin, using the Pythagorean Theorem. This distance is most often referred to as the magnitude or absolute value of a complex number. If you're asked to compute $|4 + 3i|$, just plot the number on the complex plane and use the Pythagorean Theorem to find its distance from the origin. This distance is the absolute value of the complex number.

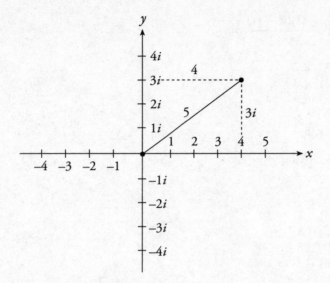

The Pythagorean Theorem will quickly show you that $|4 + 3i| = 5$.

You can also use your calculator to determine the absolute value of a complex number. On the TI-84, press MATH and go to NUM->abs. Input the complex number within the absolute value brackets (i is 2ND->"." on the TI-84) and press ENTER.

DRILL 10: IMAGINARY NUMBERS

Test your understanding of imaginary numbers with the following practice questions. The answers can be found in Part IV.

11. What is the value of i^{51} ?

(A) 0
(B) −1
(C) −i
(D) i
(E) 1

23. Which of the following expressions is NOT equal to zero?

(A) $i^0 - i^{12}$
(B) $i + i^3$
(C) $i^4 + i^{10}$
(D) $i^{11} - i^9$
(E) $i^8 - i^{12}$

40. $\dfrac{(2+4i)(2-4i)}{5} =$

   (A) 2.2
   (B) 4.0
   (C) 4.6
   (D) 5.0
   (E) 8.4

43. $|5-12i| =$

   (A) $7i$
   (B) 7
   (C) 8
   (D) 13
   (E) $13i$

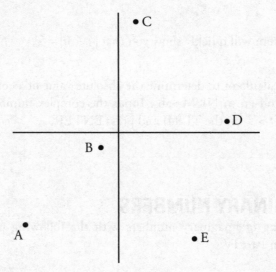

48. On the complex plane shown above, for which of the following points is $|a+bi|$ the least?

   (A) A
   (B) B
   (C) C
   (D) D
   (E) E

POLYNOMIAL DIVISION

Most of the factoring questions on the SAT Subject Test Math 2 will involve nothing more complex than the techniques you saw earlier in the section on quadratics. However, occasionally you may run into a question that requires you to factor a polynomial of a higher degree than a quadratic. You could use polynomial division, a messy algebraic process. But since there are variables in the answer choices of these questions, it's much easier to plug in. See the following for typical questions of this type.

21. If $x^3 + x^2 - 7x + 20 = (x + 4) \cdot f(x)$, where $f(x)$ is a polynomial in x, then $f(x) =$

    (A) $x + 20$
    (B) $x^2 + 5$
    (C) $x^2 - 2x$
    (D) $x^2 - 3x + 5$
    (E) $x^2 - 7x + 20$

Here's How to Crack It

To figure out $f(x)$, you must divide $x^3 + x^2 - 7x + 20$ by $x + 4$. That's polynomial division. Polynomial division is actually just like ordinary division. You set it up like this.

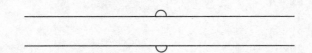

Now, just plug in a number for x. Let's pick $x = 2$. Now, we're just dividing 18 by 6, which gives us 3, with no remainder. So our target answer is 3. Plug in 2 for x in the answers to see which one equals 3. It's (D).

30. What is the remainder when $x^4 - 5x^2 + 12x + 18$ is divided by $(x + 1)$?

    (A) $x^2 - 1$
    (B) $x - 6$
    (C) 6
    (D) 3
    (E) 2

Here's How to Crack It

Once again, just plug in $x = 2$. Now the question is asking for the remainder when 38 is divided by 3. The remainder is 2, our target answer. So the answer is (E). That's all there is to polynomial division. As we mentioned in Chapter 5, don't plug in 0 or 1. When you plug in on polynomial division questions that ask for a remainder, you'll find that bigger numbers, such as 10, are better. If you plug in and something weird happens, plug in a different number.

DRILL 11: POLYNOMIAL DIVISION

Try your talents on these practice questions. The answers can be found in Part IV.

21. If $x^4 - 5x^3 - 2x^2 + 24x = g(x) \cdot (x + 2)$, then which of the following is $g(x)$?

    (A) $x + 12$
    (B) $x^2 + 3x - 18$
    (C) $x^3 - 7x^2 + 12x$
    (D) $x^3 + 10x^2 + 6x$
    (E) $x^4 - 3x^3 + 2x^2 - 6$

27. What is the remainder when $x^3 + 2x^2 - 27x + 40$ is divided by $(x - 3)$?

    (A) 4
    (B) 16
    (C) $2x + 2$
    (D) $x^2 - 5$
    (E) $x^2 + 5x - 12$

41. What is the remainder when $x^5 + 2x^4 - 3x^2 + 2x - 4$ is divided by $(x^2 + 2x)$?

    (A) $x^3 - 3$
    (B) $8x - 4$
    (C) 4
    (D) $2x - 4$
    (E) $20x$

MATRICES

Matrices are a way of presenting information. Matrix questions are rare on the SAT Subject Test Math 2, but there are a few different things which the College Board may ask you to do.

Determinants of Matrices

The determinant of the 2×2 matrix $\begin{bmatrix} a & b \\ c & d \end{bmatrix}$ is $\textbf{\textit{ad}} - \textbf{\textit{bc}}$.

The determinant of a matrix is sometimes indicated by plain vertical bars around the elements, like a big absolute value symbol. The folks at the College Board may simply write $\begin{vmatrix} a & b \\ c & d \end{vmatrix}$ if they want you to find the determinant of the matrix above.

The determinant of the 3×3 matrix

$$\begin{bmatrix} a & b & c \\ d & e & f \\ g & h & i \end{bmatrix}$$ is $\textbf{\textit{aei}} + \textbf{\textit{bfg}} + \textbf{\textit{cdh}} - \textbf{\textit{bdi}} - \textbf{\textit{afh}} - \textbf{\textit{ceg}}.$

If you take the first two columns of the matrix and recopy them to the right of the original matrix, the parts of the formula form diagonal lines of three elements, with the positive parts going from the upper left to the bottom right, and the negative parts going from the upper right down to the bottom left, like this.

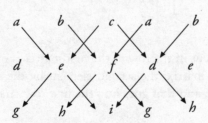

Matrix Multiplication

The simplest sort of multiplication you may be asked to do with a matrix is to multiply a matrix by a single term. In these cases, the product is a matrix the same size as the original matrix, and each position is multiplied by the single term.

A Clue
A good way to remember the determinant of a 2×2 matrix is that you multiply the diagonals and subtract.

A What by What?
When you're looking at a particular matrix, for example, a 3×2 matrix, remember that this describes the matrix as row by column. So there are 3 rows and 2 columns.

For example.

$$3\begin{bmatrix} 2 & 1 \\ 4 & 2 \\ 0 & 5 \end{bmatrix} = \begin{bmatrix} 3\times 2 & 3\times 1 \\ 3\times 4 & 3\times 2 \\ 3\times 0 & 3\times 5 \end{bmatrix} = \begin{bmatrix} 6 & 3 \\ 12 & 6 \\ 0 & 15 \end{bmatrix}$$

WHAT?!?

If these questions seem like a lot of work, well, they are! Understanding matrix multiplication will be helpful in some of your math classes in college, but for the purposes of the SAT Subject Test Math 2, it may be more helpful to skim through this and instead learn how to use your calculator to multiply matrices. Or, considering how rare these questions are, it may be a better use of your time to master the rest of this book!

The more complicated type of matrix multiplication involves multiplying two matrices together. Unlike other types of multiplication in math, order matters when you multiply matrices; i.e., matrix A × matrix B won't typically equal matrix B × matrix A. You can only multiply matrices when the first matrix has the same number of columns as the second matrix has rows. The product matrix will have the same number of rows as the first matrix and the same number of columns as the second matrix.

To illustrate,

$$\begin{bmatrix} - & - \\ - & - \\ - & - \end{bmatrix} \times \begin{bmatrix} - & - & - \\ - & - & - \end{bmatrix} = \begin{bmatrix} - & - & - \\ - & - & - \\ - & - & - \end{bmatrix}, \text{ but } \begin{bmatrix} - & - & - \\ - & - & - \end{bmatrix} \times \begin{bmatrix} - & - \\ - & - \\ - & - \end{bmatrix} = \begin{bmatrix} - & - \\ - & - \end{bmatrix}$$

Now, to determine what goes into the product matrix, you will need to follow some rules. The first row, first column position of the product matrix is the *dot product* of the first row of the first matrix and the first column of the second matrix. The dot product is the sum of the products of the row and column matched by position.

$$\begin{bmatrix} a & b & c \\ - & - & - \end{bmatrix} \times \begin{bmatrix} u & - \\ w & - \\ y & - \end{bmatrix} = \begin{bmatrix} (au + bw + cy) & - \\ - & - \end{bmatrix}$$

In other words, the first element in the row of the first matrix is multiplied by the first element in the column of the second matrix, the second element by the second, and the third by the third. Then you add them up, and that goes into the first row, first column of the product matrix.

The easy way to remember where each dot product ends up in your product matrix is that the **first row, first column** of your product is the **first row** of the first matrix multiplied by the **first column** of your second matrix. The **first row, second column** of the product will be the **first row** of the first times the **second column** of the second, and so on.

$$\begin{bmatrix} a & b & c \\ d & e & f \end{bmatrix} \times \begin{bmatrix} u & v \\ w & x \\ y & z \end{bmatrix} = \begin{bmatrix} (au + bw + cy) & (av + bx + cz) \\ (du + ew + fy) & (dv + ex + fz) \end{bmatrix}$$

Coefficient Matrices

Coefficient matrices are a way of expressing the information given in a system of linear equations. A system of linear equations is a group of equations where none of the variables have exponents (thus, all linear), and you have as many equations as variables.

Let's take an example.

$$3x - y + 2z = 21$$
$$y + 3 = z$$
$$2z + y = 12$$

First, rearrange the equations so each has all the terms with variables on the left side of the equals sign in alphabetical order, and the constants on the right side of the equation.

$$3x - y + 2z = 21$$
$$y - z = -3$$
$$y + 2z = 12$$

Now, you have 3 equations and 3 variables, so your coefficient matrix will be 3×3. Each row will represent one equation. The first column will be the x-value of each equation, the second the y-value, and the third the z-value.

$3x - y + 2z = 21$
$y - z = -3$
$y + 2z = 12$

$$\begin{bmatrix} 3 & -1 & 2 \\ 0 & 1 & -1 \\ 0 & 1 & 2 \end{bmatrix}$$

Note that if an equation does not have a particular variable, that value is a 0 in the matrix. Terms without coefficients are understood to have a coefficient of 1.

You may on rare occasions be asked to express the system of equations using matrices. To do so, you only need add two simple things to your coefficient matrix: the variable matrix and the constant matrix.

The variable matrix is simply your variables listed in order in a column. You multiply the variable matrix by the coefficient matrix.

$$\begin{bmatrix} 3 & -1 & 2 \\ 0 & 1 & -1 \\ 0 & 1 & 2 \end{bmatrix} \begin{bmatrix} x \\ y \\ z \end{bmatrix}$$

The result of this multiplication would return you back to the left side of the equations. The product of these two matrices will be equal to your constants from the original system of equations.

$$\begin{bmatrix} 3 & -1 & 2 \\ 0 & 1 & -1 \\ 0 & 1 & 2 \end{bmatrix} \begin{bmatrix} x \\ y \\ z \end{bmatrix} = \begin{bmatrix} 21 \\ -3 \\ 12 \end{bmatrix}$$

For the purposes of the SAT Subject Test Math 2, this is all you need to know about matrices!

Matrices and Your Calculator

Many calculators can do operations on matrices. The first step for any matrix question will be to input the matrices in your calculator. On the TI-84, press 2ND-> x^{-1} to access the MATRIX menu. The first submenu is titled NAMES; however, you need to start under the EDIT submenu.

The EDIT submenu looks identical to the NAMES submenu, but here you can, well, edit the matrices. To edit a matrix, first input the size of the matrix (rows by columns). Press ENTER after you finish inputting the size of the matrix. Use ENTER to move on to the next position after inputting the value. Use the QUIT function to leave this menu after you are finished.

To find the determinant of a matrix, go back to the MATRIX menu and go to the MATH submenu. The first option, det, is to find the determinant. Select that option. Next, go back to the MATRIX menu and under NAMES select the matrix you wish to find the determinant of. Close the parentheses, press ENTER, and voila!

To multiply matrices, simply enter both matrices in the EDIT submenu, select the first matrix under NAMES, use the normal multiplication key, select the second matrix, and press ENTER. Your calculator will do all the hard work of determining dot products for you.

DRILL 12: MATRICES

If you feel ready for the matrix, try these examples. The answers can be found in Part IV.

30. If matrix X has dimension 3×2, matrix Y has dimension 2×5, and $XY = Z$, then matrix Z must have dimension

    (A) 2×2
    (B) 2×5
    (C) 3×2
    (D) 3×5
    (E) 6×10

40. If $A = \begin{bmatrix} 1 & 2 \\ -1 & 0 \end{bmatrix}$, then what is the determinant of A ?

(A) −2
(B) −1
(C) 0
(D) 1
(E) 2

45. If $\begin{vmatrix} 0 & 1 & 3 \\ -1 & 1 & 2 \\ -2 & 1 & 2 \end{vmatrix} = X$, then $|X| =$

(A) −2
(B) 0
(C) 1
(D) 2
(E) 3

$$2x + 3y - z = 12$$
$$x - 3y + 2z = -5$$
$$x + z = 3$$

46. What is the determinant of the coefficient matrix of the system of equations shown above?

(A) −6
(B) 0
(C) 2
(D) 3
(E) 10

PARAMETRIC EQUATIONS

Another topic that you'll come across on the Math 2 SAT Subject Test is parametric equations, which can often seem scarier than they actually are.

First, consider the following totally ordinary linear equation.

$$y = -2x + 17$$

This linear equation, when graphed in the xy-plane, will produce a line with a slope of −2 and a y-intercept of 17.

A set of parametric equations, by contrast, will look something like this.

$$x = -2t + 6$$

$$y = 4t + 5$$

The way to know that you're dealing with parametric equations is to be on the lookout for a parameter, which will typically be represented by the variable t. While at first glance this set of equations looks quite different to the linear equation above, they're more related than they seem.

In this set of parametric equations, each coordinate pair (x,y) on the graph is defined by what you get when you put in a value for the parameter t. For example, if you make $t = -1$ in each equation, you get

$$x = -2(-1) + 6 = 8$$

and

$$y = 4(-1) + 5 = 1$$

Thus, when you graph this set of parametric equations, the point $(8,1)$ will be on the graph. Something particularly interesting happens when you eliminate the parameter through cancelation. First, multiply the x equation by 2.

$$2 (x = -2t + 6)$$

$$2x = -4t + 12$$

Now add the new x equation and the y equation together.

$$2x = -4t + 12$$

$$+ \quad y = \quad 4t + 5$$

$$2x + y = \qquad 17$$

The $-4t$ and $4t$ terms cancel each other out, and when you solve the resulting equation for y, you get

$$y = -2x + 17$$

which should look familiar, as it is identical to the original, non-parametric equation from earlier. Neat, right? This linear equation will have the same graph as the above set of parametric equations, only now it is missing the parameter. Notice that the example point from earlier (8, 1) still satisfies this new equation, which will also hold true for any other point on the graphs.

$$1 = -2(8) + 17$$

At this point you may be wondering, if the parametric equations and the ordinary linear equation are the same, why bother with the parametrics in the first place? Couldn't you just use linear equations and be done with it? Not exactly. The parameter is useful for communicating additional information that would be missing in the single linear equation. The typical variable you'll see in a set of parametric equations, t, often represents time, and so the t value that produces each x and y tells you when the coordinate pair occurred. This makes parametric equations quite useful for representing physical situations that happen over time. You won't have to worry about this for the SAT Subject Test Math 2, but math concepts are often friendlier when you have some idea of where they come from or what they might be used for.

Let's take a look at an example.

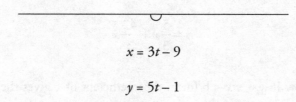

$$x = 3t - 9$$

$$y = 5t - 1$$

If the set of parametric equations shown above were graphed in the xy-plane, what would be the slope of the resulting line?

(A) $\dfrac{3}{5}$

(B) $\dfrac{1}{9}$

(C) $\dfrac{5}{9}$

(D) $\dfrac{5}{3}$

(E) 3

Here's How to Crack It

The problem asks for the slope of the line that results from graphing a set of parametric equations. To get this, you'll first want to convert the parametric equations into $y = mx + b$ form by eliminating the parameter. To do this, multiply each equation by a chosen value that will allow you to cancel the t terms using addition. In this case, multiply the x equation by -5 and the y equation by 3, which yields

$$-5x = -15t + 45$$

$$3y = 15t - 3$$

Add the two equations together to eliminate the parameter.

$$-5x = -15t + 45$$

$$+ \quad 3y = 15t - 3$$

$$-5x + 3y = \qquad 42$$

In the final equation, add $5x$ to both sides.

$$3y = 5x + 42$$

Divide both sides by 3.

$$y = \frac{5}{3}x + \frac{42}{3}x$$

With the equation now in $y = mx + b$ form, the coefficient of x gives the slope, which in this case is $\frac{5}{3}$. The answer is (D).

Comprehensive Miscellaneous Drill

The answers can be found in Part IV.

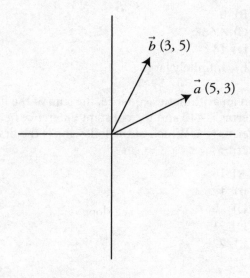

7. If $\vec{c} = \vec{a} - \vec{b}$, then what are the components of $\vec{c}$?

   (A) (8, 8)
   (B) (–2, –2)
   (C) (2, 2)
   (D) (–8, 8)
   (E) (2, –2)

10. $\left| 10 - 24i \right| =$

   (A) –14
   (B) 13
   (C) 24
   (D) 26
   (E) 676

17. Which of the following describes the line equidistant from $f(x) = (x - 2)^2 + 3$ and $g(x) = - (x - 2)^2 - 4$?

   (A) $x = 3.5$
   (B) $y = 0.5$
   (C) $y = -0.5$
   (D) $x = -1$
   (E) $y = (x - 2)^2 - 0.5$

22. $\lim\limits_{x \to 2} \dfrac{x^3 + x^2 - 6x}{x^2 - 5x + 6} =$

   (A) –10
   (B) –3
   (C)   0
   (D) 10
   (E) The limit does not exist.

23. If $7^{\log_5 a} = b$, which of the following is equal to a ?

   (A) $\log_5 7^b$
   (B) $\log_7 b - \log_7 5$
   (C) $5^{\log_7 b}$
   (D) $5b^7$
   (E) $7^5 b$

26. $\log \dfrac{x^3 y}{z} =$

   (A) $3(\log x + \log y - \log z)$

   (B) $\dfrac{\log x + \log y - \log z}{3}$

   (C) $3\log (x + y - z)$

   (D) $\log 3x + \log y - \log z$

   (E) $3\log x + \log y - \log z$

29. If $\log_7 x = 14$, then $\log_{14} x =$

   (A) 1.356
   (B) 1.991
   (C) 2.000
   (D) 8.023
   (E) 10.323

31. What is the quotient when $2x^5 - 3x^4 - 6x^3 + 23x^2 - 25x + 6$ is divided by $2x - 3$?

   (A) $x^4 - 3x^2 + 7x - 2$

   (B) $x^4 + x^3 - 3x^2 + 7x - 2$

   (C) $x^3 - 3x^2 + 7x - 2$

   (D) $x^4 + 6$

   (E) $x^4 + 3x^2 + 7x$

Albert: Double-breasted suits always cost at least $500.

Bethany: But if the customer ordered a double-breasted suit, then the suit won't be ready until after Monday.

Carl: Also, all double-breasted suits are navy blue.

Diana: Don't worry, the customer's suit will be ready on Monday.

32. If all of Albert, Bethany, Carl, and Diana's statements are true, then which of the following must be true?

(A) The customer's suit will not be navy blue.
(B) Diana is a better tailor than Albert, Bethany, or Carl.
(C) The customer's suit will cost less than $500.
(D) The customer did not order a double-breasted suit.
(E) If the suit costs at least $500, then the customer ordered a double-breasted suit.

39. If $\begin{bmatrix} 0 & 0 \\ 2 & 2 \end{bmatrix} \times \begin{bmatrix} x & y \\ z & 0 \end{bmatrix} = \begin{bmatrix} 0 & 0 \\ 0 & 0 \end{bmatrix}$, then which of the following must be true?

I. $x = 0$
II. $y = 0$
III. $x = -z$

(A) I only
(B) II only
(C) I and II only
(D) II and III only
(E) I, II, and III

41. When the parametric equations above are graphed in the xy-plane, which of the following gives the best description of the resulting graph?

(A) Line
(B) Parabola
(C) Circle
(D) Ellipse
(E) The equations cannot be graphed in the xy-plane.

44. $\sum_{n=1}^{\infty} 7\left((-0.5)^{n-1}\right) =$

(A) -14
(B) 0
(C) 4.667
(D) 14
(E) Infinitely large

45. In an arithmetic sequence, the sum of the first 11 terms is 440 and the constant difference between terms is 4. Which of the following is the first term?

(A) 18
(B) 19
(C) 20
(D) 21
(E) 22

Summary

○ A logarithm is another way to write an exponential expression. The rules are all derived from exponent rules, so make sure you're comfortable with those rules!

○ For Visual Perception questions, try to draw out what the question is giving you, and don't forget to use POE!

○ Sequences are series of numbers that follow a certain rule. There are a few ways in which the College Board may test you on sequences.

- An arithmetic sequence is created by adding the same number to the previous member in the sequence.

- The nth term of an arithmetic sequence can be found with the formula $a_n = a_1 + (n-1)d$.

- The sum of the first n terms of an arithmetic sequence can be found with the formula $n\left(\dfrac{a_1 + a_n}{2}\right)$.

- A summation is a list of numbers to be added together. You'll recognize it because of the sigma (Σ). Put the number below the sigma into the equation given. Find the result of that and every following integer up to the number above the sigma. Then add your results.

- A geometric sequence is created by taking an initial value and multiplying it by the same number again and again.

- The nth term of a geometric sequence can be found with this formula: $a_n = a_1 r^{n-1}$.

- The sum of the first n terms of a geometric sequence can be found with this formula: $\dfrac{a_1\left(1 - r^n\right)}{1 - r}$.

- The sum of an infinite geometric sequence is $\dfrac{a_1}{1-r}$. This can be found only if $-1 < r < 1$. If r is bigger than 1, there is no sum, because the sequence never converges.

○ A limit is the value a function approaches as its independent variable approaches a given constant.

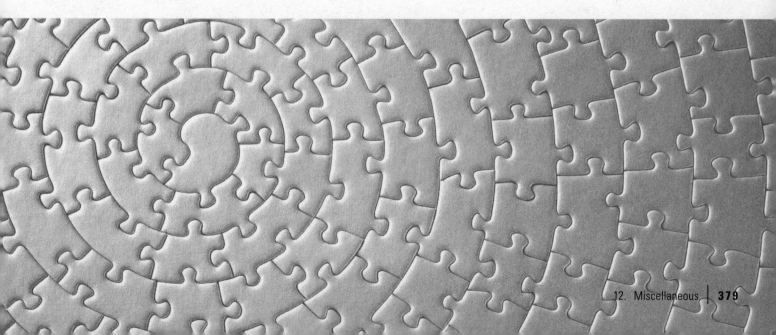

o   A vector contains direction and magnitude and is represented by a line with an arrow. When adding or subtracting vectors, make sure you're connecting tip to tail. When subtracting vectors, add the opposite vector instead.

o   The most important thing to remember for logic questions is the contrapositive. When the problem tells you "If A, then B," you also know that "If not B, then not A" is true. Be suspicious of any other "if...then" statement that doesn't follow the logic of the contrapositive.

o   There are a few things to remember about imaginary numbers:

   •   The definition of i is $\sqrt{-1}$.
   •   The powers of i follow a repeating pattern: i, -1, $-i$, 1. Every exponent of i that is a multiple of 4 is equal to 1; find the nearest multiple of 4 and work the pattern step-wise until you find the answer.
   •   You may need to multiply complex numbers or algebraic expressions with i. Remember to FOIL and simplify i in the last step, or plug in if necessary and use your calculator.
   •   The complex plane represents numbers with real and imaginary components. Real numbers are shown on the equivalent of the x-axis, and imaginary numbers are shown on the equivalent of the y-axis. The absolute value of an imaginary number is the distance from the origin to that point on the complex plane; draw a right triangle and use the Pythagorean Theorem.

o   The best and fastest way to approach polynomial division questions is to plug in. If you're asked to find a remainder, plug in a bigger number (like 10 instead of 2) so you're left with a remainder!

o   Matrix questions may ask you to find the determinant, multiply matrices together, or find the coefficient matrix of a system of linear equations. If you want to tackle these questions, learn the rules or learn how to make your calculator do these questions for you.

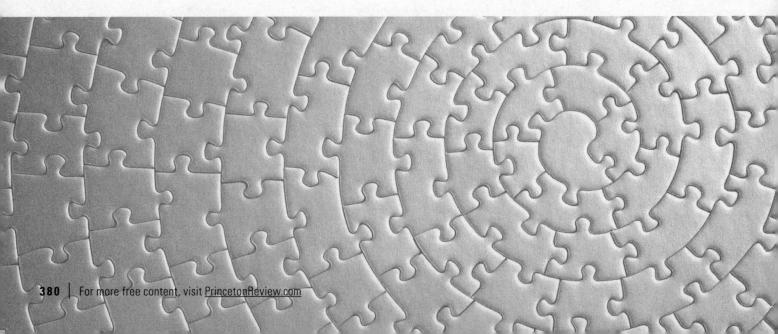

Part IV
Drills:
Answers and
Explanations

CHAPTER 5: ALGEBRA DRILL EXPLANATIONS

Drill 1: Solving Equations, p. 71

1. $x = \{5, -5\}$

   If you're having trouble, think of peeling away the layers of the left side until you get to just x. So you're going to multiply by 17, then add 7, then divide by 3, then take the square root of both sides. Remember that when you take the square root of both sides, you'll end up with two answers: positive and negative.

2. $n = \{0, 5\}$

   This is tricky. You most likely found that the answer is 5. Remember that you can divide both sides by n only if n isn't 0. So you also have to consider whether n could be 0. In this case, it can.

3. $a = 0.75$

   Peel away those layers.

4. $s = 12$

   Keep peeling.

5. $x = 0.875$

   Make sure you didn't cancel the 5's. You can cancel only when numbers are being multiplied or divided, not added or subtracted. Did you get $\dfrac{7}{8}$? Same thing!

6. $m = 9$ or $m = -14$

   Because the left side of the equation is inside absolute value signs, you know it can be either positive or negative. So set up two equations! In the first equation, set $2m + 5$ equal to 23. In the second equation, set $2m + 5$ equal to -23. Then solve each equation for m. These are your two possible values for m.

7. $r = 27$ or $r = -13$

   Set this problem up just like question 6, above. The value inside the absolute value signs can be either positive or negative, so write an equation for each scenario. Solve each equation to come up with the two possible values for r.

8. $\dfrac{9}{8}$

Begin by multiplying both sides by x: $3\sqrt{2x} = 4x$. Then divide both sides by 3: $\sqrt{2x} = \dfrac{4x}{3}$.

Next, square both sides: $2x = \dfrac{16x^2}{9}$. Divide both sides by x: $2 = \dfrac{16x}{9}$. Multiply both sides by 9:

$18 = 16x$. Finally, divide both sides by 16, and simplify: $x = \dfrac{18}{16} = \dfrac{9}{8}$.

9. $\pm\sqrt{\dfrac{1}{27}}$ or ± 0.192

Divide both sides by 2: $\sqrt[3]{y} = 3y$. Next, cube both sides: $y = 27y^3$. Next, divide both sides by y:

$1 = 27y^2$. Divide both sides by 27: $\dfrac{1}{27} = y^2$. Finally, take the square root of both sides, remembering both the positive and negative roots: $y = \pm\sqrt{\dfrac{1}{27}}$ or ± 0.192.

Drill 2: Factoring and Distributing, p. 73

3. **D** This equation can be rearranged to look like: $50x(11 + 29) = 4{,}000$. This is done simply by factoring out 50 and x. Once you've done that, you can add 11 and 29 to produce $50x(40) = 2{,}000x = 4{,}000$. Therefore, $x = 2$.

5. **E** Here, distributing makes your math easier. Distributing $-3b$ into the expression $(a + 2)$ on top of the fraction gives you $\dfrac{-3ab - 6b + 6b}{-ab}$, which simplifies to $\dfrac{-3ab}{-ab}$, which equals 3.

22. **B** The trap in this question is to try to cancel similar terms on the top and bottom—but that's not possible, because these terms are being added together, and you can cancel only in multiplication. Instead, factor out x^2 on top of the fraction. That gives you $\dfrac{x^2\left(x^3 + x^2 + x + 1\right)}{x^3 + x^2 + x + 1}$. The whole mess in parentheses cancels out (now that it's being multiplied), and the answer is x^2.

30. **E** First, work inside the parentheses and factor out x^3 from each term: $(x^3(x^2 + 2x + 1))^{-1}$. Next, the innermost parentheses is a common quadratic in the form $(a + b)^2 = a^2 + 2ab + b^2$, so you can factor: $(x^3 (x + 1)^2)^{-1}$. Finally, a negative exponent means to place the expression in the denominator of a fraction, which leads you to $\dfrac{1}{x^3(x+1)^2}$, (E).

Drill 3: Plugging In, p. 78

1. **E** Plug in $p = 20$, $t = 10$, and $n = 3$. That's 3 items for $20.00 each with 10% tax. Each item would then cost $22.00, and three could cost $66.00. Only (E) equals $66.00.

2. **C** Plug in $x = 5$, $a = 2$, $b = 3$. That means Vehicle A travels at 5 mph for 5 hours, or 25 miles. Vehicle B travels at 7 mph for 8 hours, or 56 miles. That's a difference of 31 miles. Only (C) equals 31.

4. **C** Plug in $n = 3$, then $5 - 3 = 2$ and $3 - 5 = -2$. These numbers have the same absolute value, so the difference between them is zero.

8. **B** Plug in $a = 10$, $b = 1$, $m = 4$. That means that Company A builds 10 skateboards a week and 40 skateboards in 4 weeks. Company B builds 7 skateboards in a week (1 per day), or 28 in 4 weeks. That's a difference of 12 between the two companies. Only (B) equals 12 when you plug in $a = 10$, $b = 1$, $m = 4$.

12. **E** Plug in $a = 4$ and $b = 2$. Okay, all three fail. Let's try some different-sized numbers like $a = 10$ and $b = 2$. Now (I) works; eliminate (B) and (D). Try to make $a + b$ small; Plug in $a = 4$ and $b = -4$. Now (II) and (III) work; eliminate (A) and (C).

18. **A** Plug in $x = 2$ and $y = 3$. Oh well—they all work! Try $x = -3$ and $y = -2$. Now (II) fails; eliminate (C), (D), and (E). Statement (III) also fails; eliminate (B).

35. **B** Plug in $a = 6$. After 3 more passengers get on, there are 9 passengers total. Make $b = 3$ and $c = 2$. If an average of 3 passengers get on over 2 stops, then 6 passengers total get on between those stops, so there are a total of 15 passengers aboard at this point. If $\frac{1}{3}$ get off, then 5 get off, leaving 10 on board. Over the last two stops, an average of 5 passengers will get off at each stop, so 5 is your target. The only answer that equals 5 is (B).

48. **D** Plug in for y. If $y = 4$, then $x^2 = -4$. If you put your TI-80 series into $a + bi$ mode (MODE menu, 7th row, second option), you find that $x = \sqrt{-4} = 2i$. Eliminate (A), (B), and (E). If $y = 2$, then $x = i\sqrt{2}$ or $1.414i$. Eliminate (C) and choose (D).

Drill 4: Plugging In the Answers (PITA), p. 83

1. **D** The answer choices represent Michael's hats. Start with answer (C): if Michael has 12 hats, then Matt has 6 hats and Aaron has 2. That adds up to 20, not 24—you need more hats, so move on to the next bigger answer, (D). Michael now has 14 hats, meaning Matt has 7 and Aaron has 3. That adds up to 24, so you're done.

2. **D** There's a little shortcut you can take if you remember the Average Pie. Since the total is 3,200 and you have two parts, you know that the average will be 1,600. This means that the difference will be 800. Work through the answer choices, starting with (C). A ratio of 2:5 has 7 parts. Divide 3,200 by 7. Each part would be 457.14—it doesn't work out with whole numbers, so it can't be right. Then move on to (D); a ratio of 3:5 has 8 parts, each of which would be 400. That means the shipment is divided into shares of 1,200 and 2,000. Their difference is 800, and their average is 1,600, which is what you're looking for!

12. **D** Start with (C); if the largest of the three integers is 5, then the total of the other two integers would have to be 15 − 5 or 10. No two numbers less than 5 have a sum of 10, so eliminate (A), (B), and (C). If you plug in (D), 9 is the largest number. For the product of all three integers to be 45, the product of the other two integers must be 5. So these two integers can only be 5 and 1. Now find the sum of all three numbers. 9 + 5 + 1 = 15, so (D) is the correct answer.

40. **E** Begin with (C) by making $x = 2$. The formula for the volume of a cylinder is $\pi r^2 h$. If the diameter is 2, then $r = 1$, so the volume of the cylinder would be $\pi(1)^2 2 = 2\pi$. The surface area of a sphere is $4\pi^2$, so if the radius is 2, then the surface area is $4\pi(2^2) = 16\pi$. You want the surface area to equal to the volume of the cylinder, so eliminate (C). It may be difficult to decide which way to go in this problem, but (A) and (B) will be harder to deal with than (D) or (E), so try (D). If $x = 4$, then for the cylinder $r = 2$, and the volume of the cylinder is $\pi(2^2)4 = 16\pi$. The surface area of the sphere would be $4\pi(4^2) = 64\pi$. Not quite equal, but the sphere is only 4 times bigger, whereas it was 8 times bigger in (C), so you're moving in the right direction. Eliminate (A), (B), and (D), and choose (E).

Drill 5: Inequalities, p. 85

1. $n \geq 3$

2. $r < 7$

3. $x \geq -\dfrac{1}{2}$

4. $x < \dfrac{1}{8}$

5. $t \leq 3$

6. $n \leq 4$

7. $p > \dfrac{1}{5}$

8. $s \geq 1$

9. $x \geq -7$

10. $s \geq \dfrac{2}{5}$

11. $-8 \leq x \leq 4$

12. $z < -2$ or $z > 2$

Drill 6: Working with Ranges, p. 86

1. $-8 < -x < 5$

2. $-20 < 4x < 32$

3. $1 < (x + 6) < 14$

4. $7 > (2 - x) > -6$

5. $-2.5 < \dfrac{x}{2} < 4$

Drill 7: More Working with Ranges, p. 89

1. $-4 \leq b - a \leq 11$

2. $-2 \leq x + y \leq 17$

3. $0 \leq n^2 \leq 64$

4. $3 < x - y < 14$

5. $-13 \leq r + s \leq 13$

6. $-126 < cd < 0$

7. $-1 \leq x \leq 7$

Because the absolute value is less than 4, whatever's inside the absolute value must be between -4 and 4. Therefore, $-4 \leq 3 - x \leq 4$. Start solving this by subtracting 3 from all three sides: $-7 \leq -x \leq 1$. Then divide through by -1 (remember to flip the direction of the inequality signs because you're dividing by a negative number): $7 \geq x \geq -1$.

8. $a \leq -10$ or $a \geq 3$

Because the absolute value is greater than 13, the stuff inside the absolute value must be either less than -13 or greater than 13. Therefore, you have two inequalities: $2a + 7 \leq -13$ or $2a + 7 \geq 13$. Solve each inequality separately.

Drill 8: Direct and Inverse Variation, p. 91

2. **C** There are variables in the answers, so plug in! Quantities in inverse variation always have the same product. That means that $ab = 3 \cdot 5$, or 15, always. Plug in a number for x, such as 10. Now set up your proportion: $3 \cdot 5 = a \cdot 10$. So $10a = 15$, and $a = 2.5$. Plug $x = 10$ into the answers and find the answer choice that gives you 2.5. Only (C) does.

3. **D** Remember your formulas. Direct means divide. Quantities in direct variation always have the same proportion. In this case, that means that $\frac{n}{m} = \frac{5}{4}$. When $m = 5$, solve the equation $\frac{5}{4} = \frac{n}{5}$. Multiply both sides by 5 and you'll find that $n = 6.25$.

9. **A** Direct variation means the proportion is constant, so that $\frac{p}{q} = \frac{3}{10}$. To find the value of p when $q = 1$, solve the equation $\frac{3}{10} = \frac{p}{1}$; p must be 0.3.

11. **B** Remember that direct means divide. Set up your proportion: $\frac{24}{3.7^2} = \frac{y}{8.3^2}$. If you simplify this, you get 120.77, which is (B). Be careful. If you answered (E), you forgot that the direct variation was between y and x^2, not y and x.

26. **D** Begin by translating English to math. If "the square of x varies inversely with the cube root of the square of y," then $(x_1)^2 \sqrt[3]{(y_1)^2} = (x_2)^2 \sqrt[3]{(y_2)^2}$. Make $x_1 = \frac{1}{2}$, $y_1 = 8$, and $y_2 = \frac{1}{2}$:

$\left(\frac{1}{2}\right)^2 \sqrt[3]{8^2} = (x_2)^2 \sqrt[3]{\left(\frac{1}{2}\right)^2}$. Solve for x_2:

$$\left(\frac{1}{4}\right)\sqrt[3]{64} = (x_2)^2 \sqrt[3]{\frac{1}{4}}$$

$$\left(\frac{1}{4}\right)(4) = (x_2)^2 (0.630)$$

$$1 = (x_2)^2 (0.630)$$

$$1.587 = (x_2)^2$$

$$1.260 = x_2$$

Choose (D).

39. **A** Begin by translating English to math. "The cube root of the sum of x and 2" is $\sqrt[3]{x+2}$. If that is inversely proportional to "the square of y," then $(\sqrt[3]{x_1+2})((y_1)^2)=(\sqrt[3]{x_2+2})((y_2)^2)$. Make $x_1=6, y_1=3$ and $y_2=6$: $(\sqrt[3]{6+2})(3^2)=(\sqrt[3]{x_2+2})(6^2)$, so $18=(\sqrt[3]{x+2})(36)$ or $\sqrt[3]{x+2}=0.5$. Cube both sides: $x+2=0.125$. Finally, subtract 2 from both sides: $x=-1.875$, (A).

Drill 9: Work and Travel Questions, p. 93

1. **C** The important thing to remember here is that when two things or people work together, their work rates are added up. Pump 1 can fill 12 tanks in 12 hours, and Pump 2 can fill 11 tanks in 12 hours. That means that together, they could fill 23 tanks in 12 hours. To find the work they would do in 1 hour, just divide 23 by 12. You get 1.9166, which rounds up to 1.92.

2. **A** To translate feet per second to miles per hour, take it one step at a time. First, find the feet per hour by multiplying 227 feet per second by the number of seconds in an hour (3,600). You find that the projectile travels at a speed of 817,200 feet per hour. Then divide by 5,280 to find out how many miles that is. You get 154.772, which rounds up to 155.

5. **B** The train travels a total of 400 miles (round-trip) in 5.5 hours. Now that you know distance and time, plug them into the formula and solve to find the rate. $400 = r \times 5.5$, so $r = 72.73$.

10. **D** Plug in! Say Jules can make 3 muffins in 5 minutes ($m=3, s=5$). Say Alice can make 4 muffins in 6 minutes ($n=4, t=6$). That means that Jules can make 18 muffins in 30 minutes, and Alice can make 20 muffins in 30 minutes. Together, they make 38 muffins in 30 minutes. That's your target number. Take the numbers you plugged in to the answers and find the one that gives you 38. Choice (D) does the trick.

28. **A** Plug in $x=100, y=2$ and $z=3$. If the race is 100 meters, then Samantha runs the first 40 meters at 2 m/s, so it takes her $\frac{40}{2}=20$ seconds for that leg of the race. If she runs the remaining 60 meters at 3 m/s, then it takes her $\frac{60}{3}=20$ seconds. Therefore, she takes 40 total seconds to run the race. Plug your values for x, y, and z into each answer choice; only (A) equals 40.

Drill 10: Average Speed, p. 95

7. **D** Find the total distance and total time. The round-trip distance is 12 miles. It takes $\frac{1}{2}$ hour to jog 6 miles at 12 mph, and $\frac{2}{3}$ hour to jog back at 9 mph, for a total of $1\frac{1}{6}$ hours. Do the division, and you get 10.2857 mph, which rounds up to 10.3.

11. **D** This one is easier than it looks. Fifty miles in 50 minutes is a mile a minute, or 60 mph. Forty miles in 40 minutes is also 60 mph. The whole trip is made at one speed, 60 mph.

25. **B** Plug in an easy number for the unknown distance, like 50 miles. It takes 2 hours to travel 50 miles at 25 mph, and 1 hour to return across 50 miles at 50 mph. That's a total distance of 100 miles in 3 hours, for an average speed of $33\frac{1}{3}$ mph. Choices (A) and (E) are traps.

49. **C** If Amy and Bob walk 5 m/s and 2 m/s, respectively, toward one another, that means they are approaching each other at 7 m/s. Because they start 250 m apart, it will take $\frac{250}{7} = 35.71$ seconds until they meet. During those 35.71 seconds, Charlie is running at 13 m/s, so Charlie will run $35.71 \cdot 13 = 464.29$ m, (C).

Drill 11: Simultaneous Equations, p. 99

17. **C** Here, you want to make all of the b terms cancel out. Add the two equations, and you get $5a = 20$, so $a = 4$.

27. **E** Here, you need to get rid of the z term and cancel out a y. The way to do it is to divide the first equation by the second one, $\frac{xyz}{y^2z} = \frac{4}{5}$. The z and a y cancel out, and you're left with $\frac{x}{y} = \frac{4}{5}$, or 0.8. Even though there are more variables than equations, the College Board questions almost always have a trick to let you solve them the easy way.

28. **D** Here, you need to get x and y terms with the same coefficient. If you subtract the second equation from the first, you get $10x - 10y = 10$, so $x - y = 1$.

33. **D** The question is solvable by multiplication. Multiplying all three equations together gives you $a^2b^2c^2 = 2.25$. Don't pick (B)! Take the positive square root of both sides, and you get $abc = 1.5$.

35. **A** First, simplify the given terms. If $\sqrt{abc} = 7$ and $\sqrt[3]{ab^2c} = 8$, then $abc = 49$ and $ab^2c = 512$. You can then isolate b: $\frac{ab^2c}{abc} = b$, so $b = \frac{512}{49} = 10.449$. To find b^{-4}, use the exponent function on your calculator: $10.449^{-4} = 0.00008398$, which equals (A).

Drill 12: FOIL, p. 101

1. $x^2 + 9x - 22$

2. $b^2 + 12b + 35$

3. $x^2 - 12x + 27$

4. $2x^2 - 3x - 5$

5. $n^3 - 3n^2 + 5n - 15$

6. $6a^2 - 11a - 35$

7. $x^2 - 9x + 18$

8. $c^2 + 7c - 18$

9. $d^2 + 4d - 5$

10. $z^4 - 5z^3 + 24z^2 - 10z + 44$

11. $18x^4 + 16x^2 + 24x - 10$

Drill 13: Factoring Quadratics, p. 103

1. $a = \{1, 2\}$ Factor to $(a - 1)(a - 2) = 0$.

2. $d = \{-7, -1\}$ Factor to $(d + 7)(d + 1) = 0$.

3. $x = \{-7, 3\}$ Factor to $(x + 7)(x - 3) = 0$.

4. $x = \{-5, 2\}$ Factor to $3(x^2 + 3x - 10) = 3(x + 5)(x - 2) = 0$.

5. $x = \{-11, -9\}$ Factor to $2(x^2 + 20x + 99) = 2(x + 11)(x + 9) = 0$.

6. $p = \{-13, 3\}$ Factor to $(p + 13)(p - 3) = 0$. Subtract 39 from both sides first.

7. $c = \{-5, -4\}$ Factor to $(c + 5)(c + 4) = 0$.

8. $s = \{-6, 2\}$ Factor to $(s + 6)(s - 2) = 0$.

9. $x = \{-1, 4\}$ Factor to $(x + 1)(x - 4) = 0$.

10. Factor the expression $(n^2 - 5)(n^2 + 2) = 0$. So $n^2 = 5$ or -2. But n^2 is never negative, so $n = \pm\sqrt{5}$.

Drill 14: Special Quadratic Identities, p. 105

3. **A**   Remember that $n^2 - m^2 = (n - m)(n + m)$. So fill in what you know and solve for what you don't: $24 = (-3)(n + m)$. You don't need to find each variable individually.

5. **B**   Remember that $(x + y)^2 = x^2 + 2xy + y^2$. Again you have all the parts except for what the question is asking for: $3^2 = 8 + 2xy$. So $2xy = 1$ and $xy = 0.5$.

10. **D**   Translate into math. You know that $x + y = 9$ and $x^2 + y^2 = 36$. It's asking for xy. The pieces that the question gives you relate to $(x + y)^2 = x^2 + 2xy + y^2$. So, $9^2 = 36 + 2xy$; $2xy = 45$; and $xy = 22.5$. Notice that (E) is a partial answer.

39. **D**   To eliminate the radical in the denominator, multiply the fraction by $\dfrac{2x + 4\sqrt{2x}}{2x + 4\sqrt{2x}}$. This will eliminate the radical by using the $x^2 - y^2 = (x + y)(x - y)$ quadratic identity while keeping the value constant. This results in $\left(\dfrac{4x}{2x - 4\sqrt{2x}}\right)\left(\dfrac{2x + 4\sqrt{2x}}{2x + 4\sqrt{2x}}\right) = \dfrac{4x(2x + 4\sqrt{2x})}{(2x)^2 - (4\sqrt{2x})^2} = \dfrac{4x(2x + 4\sqrt{2x})}{4x^2 - 32x}$. Factor $4x$ out of the denominator and simplify: $\dfrac{4x(2x + 4\sqrt{2x})}{4x(x - 8)} = \dfrac{2x + 4\sqrt{2x}}{x - 8}$, (D).

Drill 15: The Quadratic Formula, p. 107

1.   2 distinct real roots; $x = \{0.81, 6.19\}$

2.   2 distinct imaginary roots: $0.5 \pm 1.44i$

3.   2 distinct real roots; $s = \{0.76, 5.24\}$

4.   2 distinct real roots; $x = \{-1.41, 1.41\}$

5.   1 real root; $n = -2.5$ (2 identical real roots, that is, a "double root")

6.   Two imaginary solutions, $\pm 3i$

7.   Two real solutions, 0.752 and -16.244

8.   Two imaginary solutions, $-0.316 \pm 3.578i$

Comprehensive Algebra Drill, p. 110

4. **D** First, solve each equation for a^2. For the first equation, start by multiplying both sides by 3: $a^2 + 2x = 15$. Then, subtract $2x$ from both sides: $a^2 = -2x + 15$. For the second equation, simply subtract 2 from both sides: $a^2 = \dfrac{7x}{5} - 2$. Because each right-hand side is equal to a^2, you can set them equal to one another: $-2x + 15 = \dfrac{7x}{5} - 2$. Solve for x or plug in the answers and find that $x = 5$, which is (D).

8. **C** There are two ways to solve this problem. You can plug in the answers for k and use the quadratic formula to see if there is only one distinct solution. You can also use the discriminant; if there is only one distinct real solution, then $b^2 - 4ac = 0$. You can use this to solve for k, which represents the c value: $3.5^2 - 4(1)(k) = 0$; $k = 3.0625$.

10. **D** Plug in the answers! Start with the middle answer and make $x = 25$; $25 + \sqrt[3]{25} = 27.924$. This is too small; eliminate (A), (B), and (C). Try $x = 27$; $27 + \sqrt[3]{27} = 30$, so choose (D).

14. **D** Begin by translating English to math. "y subtracted from $4x$ is the cube root of 2" means $4x - y = \sqrt[3]{2}$ in math. "$3x$ subtracted from $2y$ is the square of 3" is $2y - 3x = 3^2$. To solve for "the sum of x and y," stack the equations and add:

$$4x - y = \sqrt[3]{2}$$
$$+(-3x + 2y = 3^2)$$
$$x + y = \sqrt[3]{2} + 3^2$$

Therefore, $x + y \approx 10.26$. Choose (D).

16. **A** If the maximum value of a function is -2, then the function can never equal 0, as $0 > -2$. In order to have real roots, there must be a value of x at which the function equals 0, which is impossible if the greatest value of the function is negative. Therefore, the function cannot have any real roots; only I is true, so choose (A).

24. **E** If there are no real solutions, then the discriminant ($b^2 - 4ac$) must be less than 0. You know $a = 2$, so $b^2 - 4(2)c < 0$, or $b^2 < 8c$. Try each answer choice; the only choice that makes $b^2 < 8c$ is (E).

26. **A** When you have an absolute value with inequalities, you need to flip the inequality sign when finding the negative of the absolute value. Therefore, if $\left| \dfrac{x^3 + 5}{2} \right| < 6$, then $\dfrac{x^3 + 5}{2} < 6$ and $\dfrac{x^3 + 5}{2} > -6$. To solve the first inequality, begin by multiplying both sides by 2: $x^3 + 5 < 12$. Next, subtract 5 from both sides: $x^3 < 7$. Finally, take the cube root of both sides with your calculator. You find that $x < 1.91$. For the second inequality, start similarly by multiplying both sides by 2: $x^3 + 5 > -12$.

Next, subtract 5 from both sides: $x^3 > -17$. Finally, take the cube root of both sides, and you find that $x > -2.57$ (remember you can take the odd root of a negative number). Because x can satisfy both inequalities at once, it is an inclusive range; choose (A).

36. **D** Graph the function on your calculator and count the number of times it crosses the x-axis.

40. **A** First, if a and b are real, then $(a + b)^2$ cannot be negative; eliminate (C) and (D). Next, you can plug in. Make $a = 0$ and $b = 0$, so $(a + b)^2 = 0$; eliminate (B) and (E) and choose (A).

46. **A** Plug in! Make $x = 3$, so $\dfrac{3^3 - 2(3)^2 + 4(3) - 8}{3^4 - 16} = 0.2$. Plug in $x = 3$ into each answer choice; (A) and (D) work, but you can eliminate (B), (C), and (E). Plug in again, making $x = 4$, so $\dfrac{4^3 - 2(4)^2 + 4(4) - 8}{4^4 - 16} = 0.167$. Between (A) and (D), only (A) equals 0.167 when $x = 4$; choose (A).

49. **E** Graph the two functions on your calculator. The graphs intersect twice; eliminate (A) and (B). $f(x)$ crosses the x-axis four times [eliminate (D)], and $g(x)$ crosses the x-axis once [eliminate (C)]. To confirm (E), use CALC-> intersect to find the points of intersection ((2.043, 7.087) and (–2.654, –2.307)); neither point is located between $-2 < x < 2$.

CHAPTER 6: FUNDAMENTALS DRILL EXPLANATIONS

Drill 1: PEMDAS and Your Calculator, p. 119

1.   5

2.   35

3.   12

4.   35

5.   0

6.   2.5 or $\dfrac{5}{2}$

7.   0.333... or $\dfrac{1}{3}$

Drill 2: Word Problem Translation, p. 122

1. $6.5 = \dfrac{x}{100} \cdot 260$; $x = 2.5$

2. $20 = \dfrac{n}{100} \cdot 180$; $n = 11.11$

3. $\dfrac{30}{100} \cdot \dfrac{40}{100} \cdot 25 = x$; $x = 3$

4. $x = \sqrt{\dfrac{1}{3} \cdot 48}$; $x = 4$

5. $\sqrt{y} = \dfrac{1}{8} \cdot y$; $y = \dfrac{1}{64} y^2$; $\dfrac{1}{y} = \dfrac{1}{64}$; $y = 64$

6. $\sqrt[3]{\dfrac{y}{2} + z} - x^3$

7. $x = \sqrt[n]{2 + 3^2}$

Drill 3: Percent Change, p. 123

2. **B** You already know that the difference is going to be 25. Set up your formula: $\dfrac{25}{150} \cdot 100 = 16.67$. So, adding 25 gallons to 150 gallons is a 16.67% increase.

3. **B** The decrease from 5 to 4 is a 20% decrease, and the increase from 4 to 5 is a 25% increase. So the difference is 5%.

4. **C** Using the formula $12 = (150 \div x)100$, you get $x = 1,250$, so 1,250 must have been the original amount. $1,250 + 150 = 1,400$. Be careful to read "after the deposit" in the question.

18. **B** Plug in! Make $n = 3$. $f(3) = \dfrac{1}{3}(3) + 2 = 3$ and $f(6) = \dfrac{1}{3}(6) + 2 = 4$. Then use the formula:

    $\dfrac{4-3}{3} \cdot 100 = 33.333... = 33\dfrac{1}{3}$ %.

Drill 4: Repeated Percent Change, p. 127

20. **D** Using the formula, you get $1,000(1.05^{12}) = 1,795.856$.

25. **E** For this question, you need to compute 100 annual increases of 8%, so you must multiply the starting amount, 120,000, by 1.08^{100}, which gives you 263,971,350.8—which can also be written as 2.6×10^8. If you weren't sure, multiply the answers in your calculator to check your work.

28. **C** This question is a little trickier. For each annual decrease of 4%, you must multiply by 0.96. The easiest way to solve the question is to start with 2,000 and keep multiplying until the result is less than 1,000—just count the number of decreases it takes. The seventeenth annual decrease makes it less than 1,000, so the sixteenth is the last one that is not less than 1,000—and 1995 + 16 = 2011. You can also use logs, which we'll get to in a little while.

40. **D** Plug in and use PITA! Make the starting value of the account 100. To find the resulting price you would use $100(1+0.025)^n$, where n is the number of years. Plug in each answer for n to determine which one equals 200. The answer which is closest to 200 is (D).

Drill 5: Averages, p. 129

1.   There were 9 people at dinner.

2.   All told, 4,500 apples were picked.

3.   The average height of a chess club member is 5.5 feet.

Drill 6: Multiple Average Questions, p. 131

18. **D** Nineteen donations averaging $485 total $9,215. Twenty donations averaging $500 total $10,000. The difference is $785.

20. **A** The *Tribune* received 80 letters in the first 20 days and 70 for the last 10 days. That's a total of 150 in 30 days, or $150 \div 30 = 5$ letters per day on average.

21. **A** One day in five out of a year is 73 days. At 12 a day, that's 876 umbrellas sold on rainy days. The rest of the year (292 days) is clear. At 3 umbrellas a day, that's another 876 umbrellas. A total of 1,752 umbrellas in 365 days makes a daily average of 4.8 umbrellas.

42. **E** Plug in $x = 100$ and $n = 5$. If her average score on the first 5 tests is 100, then her total score to this point is $100 \cdot 5 = 500$. On the last 3 tests, she scores an average of 120, making $120 \cdot 3 = 360$ points for the last three tests. She therefore has a total of 860 points over 8 tests for an average of $\frac{860}{8} = 107.5$ for all tests. Use the chosen variables to check all five answers and only (E) works.

Drill 7: Irrational Numbers, p. 133

33. **A** Type each answer into your calculator, then use MATH->FRAC to see if the result is equal to any simple fraction. To test (C) and (D), use the change of base formula: $\log_B A = \dfrac{\log A}{\log B}$. (See the section on logarithms in Chapter 12.) The only answer that does NOT result in an integer or simple fraction is (A), so (A) is irrational.

35. **C** Plug in! Make $x = 3$. Plug $x = 3$ into each answer choice and use MATH->FRAC to see if it is equivalent to a fraction. The only answer which becomes a fraction is (C).

Drill 8: Exponents, p. 140

1. $b = 3$ (1 root)

2. $x = 11, -11$ (2 roots)

3. $n = 2$ (1 root)

4. $c = \sqrt{10}, -\sqrt{10}$ (2 roots)

5. $x = 3, -3$ (2 roots)

6. $x = -2$ (1 root)

7. $d = 3, -3$ (2 roots)

8. $n =$ any real number except for 0; everything to the 0 power is 1 (infinitely many roots).

9. **C** Remember that the top is the exponent and the bottom is the root. So in your calculator, put in 4^(3/2). This is the same as cubing 4 and then taking the square root of your result (or taking the square root of 4 and then cubing that result). Any way you slice it, the answer is 8.

10. **D** Remember your rules. A negative exponent means flip it. And a fractional exponent means the top is the exponent and the bottom is the root. You may have ended up with $\dfrac{1}{\left(\sqrt[4]{x}\right)^3}$, which isn't wrong. It just happens to not be in the answers. The only correct answer is $\dfrac{1}{\left(\sqrt[4]{x^3}\right)}$.

11. **A** Flip and square it: $\left(\dfrac{3}{2}\right)^2 = 2.25$. Don't forget your parentheses in your calculator.

12. **E** Flip and take the third root.

13. **A** In your calculator it goes, either as is (with parentheses) or if you need to take more steps, just remember that the numerator is the exponent and the denominator is the root. Or notice that $\sqrt[3]{25}$ must be less than $\sqrt{25}$ and use POE.

14. **D** What's anything raised to the zero power? That's right, 1.

Comprehensive Fundamentals Drill, p. 142

1. **A** Be careful to follow PEMDAS! Start with the innermost parentheses in the numerator: $2 + \sqrt[3]{5} = 3.71$. Multiply by 4 and you get 14.84. $14.84 + \sqrt{3} = 16.57$; $\sqrt[3]{16.57} = 2.55$. The denominator is thankfully easier, but start with the parentheses: $2 + 9 = 11$; multiplying by 3 gives you 33; adding 49 gives you 82. $\sqrt{82} = 9.06$. Finally, $2.55 \div 9.06 = 0.281$.

2. **E** Plug in $x = 3$ and $y = 7$. The only choice that is even is (E).

10. **B** Because "is" means "equals," you can break this problem into two pieces: what comes before the "is" and what comes after. "The cube root of the sum of one-third m and n" means you multiply m by $\frac{1}{3}$, add that product to n, then take the cube root of the entire operation: $\sqrt[3]{\frac{1}{3}m + n}$. You can eliminate (C), (D), and (E), because they do not include the equivalent of this expression. This expression must be equal to "the cube of one-third of the sum of m and n." You must add m and n, multiply that sum by $\frac{1}{3}$, then take that result to the power of 3: $\left(\frac{1}{3}(m+n)\right)^3$. The only answer that has accurate equivalents to both of these expressions is (B).

15. **B** Use fractional exponents in order to combine these two radicals. Square roots are equivalent to the $\frac{1}{2}$ power, and cube roots are the $\frac{1}{3}$ power, so $\sqrt{x^3 y^5} \cdot \sqrt[3]{x^2 y} = (x^3 y^5)^{\frac{1}{2}} \cdot (x^2 y)^{\frac{1}{3}}$. Next, distribute the fraction within the parentheses: $(x^3 y^5)^{\frac{1}{2}} \cdot (x^2 y)^{\frac{1}{3}} = (x^{\frac{3}{2}} y^{\frac{5}{2}})(x^{\frac{2}{3}} y^{\frac{1}{3}})$. When you multiply with the same base, add the exponents, but to add fractions you need a common denominator. Make the denominators equal to 6 and add the exponents: $(x^{\frac{3}{2}} y^{\frac{5}{2}})(x^{\frac{2}{3}} y^{\frac{1}{3}}) = (x^{\frac{9}{6}} y^{\frac{15}{6}})(x^{\frac{4}{6}} y^{\frac{2}{6}}) = x^{\frac{13}{6}} y^{\frac{17}{6}}$. Because the exponents are improper fractions, you can "pull out" from the radical by rewriting the exponent as an integer plus a fraction: $x^{\frac{13}{6}} y^{\frac{17}{6}} = x^{2+\frac{1}{6}} y^{2+\frac{5}{6}} = x^2 x^{\frac{1}{6}} y^2 y^{\frac{5}{6}}$. Finally, you can rewrite the fractional exponents as under the radical $\sqrt[6]{\ }$: $x^2 y^2 \sqrt[6]{xy^5}$, (B).

18. **A** If the average of a, b, c, d, and e is 86, then the sum of of a, b, c, d, and e is $86 \cdot 5 = 430$. The sum of a, b, and c is $84 \cdot 3 = 252$, and the sum of c, d, and e is $82 \cdot 3 = 246$. If you add the sum of a, b, and c to the sum of c, d, and e, you get $(a + b + c) + (c + d + e) = 498$. Because c occurs twice in this equation, if you subtract $a + b + c + d + e = 430$ from $(a + b + c) + (c + d + e) = 498$, you are left with $c = 68$.

20. **D** Plug in! Make the edge length 2, which makes the area of each face 4 and the total surface area $x = 24$. Therefore, the volume of cube A will be $2^3 = 8$. For cube B, the total surface area will be $24 \cdot 4 = 96$; if you divide by 6 you find the area of each face is 16. $\sqrt{16} = 4$ gives you the edge of cube B. The volume of cube B will be $4^3 = 64$. To find percent change, you take the difference divided by the original and multiply by 100: $\frac{64 - 8}{8} \cdot 100 = 700$, which is (D).

23. **C** When you are adding (or subtracting) with exponents, you can factor out the largest common factor of the two terms. If you do this to the numerators and denominators of both fractions, you get $\frac{x^3(x+3)}{2x^4(x+3)} + \frac{x^2y(x+2)}{2x^3y(x+2)}$. You can cancel the binomials in both equations, leaving $\frac{x^3}{2x^4} + \frac{x^2y}{2x^3y}$. Simplify both fractions and add to get $\frac{1}{2x} + \frac{1}{2x} = \frac{2}{2x} = \frac{1}{x}$, (C).

35. **D** PITA! The formula for repeated percent change is original$(1 - \text{rate})^{\text{number of changes}}$. The answers represent the number of changes, so if you start with (C), you find that $4395(1 - 0.10)^7 = 2102.11$. Close, but not small enough; eliminate (A), (B), and (C). Try (D) $4395(1 - 0.10)^8 = 1891.90$. There are no lesser answers which work, so choose (D).

37. **C** Plug in $x = -3$, $y = -2$, and $z = -1$. All of the answers are true except (C).

43. **C** PITA! If you need a 400 mL solution which is at 45% concentration, you need $\frac{45}{100} \cdot 400 = 180$ mL of solution in your final product. Try (C). If you use 120 mL of the 80% concentration, you will have $\frac{80}{100} \cdot 120 = 96$ mL of solution. This leaves 280 mL of the 30% solution, which contributes $\frac{30}{100} \cdot 280 = 84$ mL of solution. $96 + 84 = 180$ mL of solution in your final product, so your answer is (C).

45. **E** Plug in $x = 5$, $y = 4$, and $z = 2$. If 5 elements have an average of 4, then the sum of those elements is 20. If 3 of those elements have an average of 2, then their total is 6, which means the other 2 elements add up to 14. The average of the remaining 2 elements therefore must be 7. The only answer choice which equals 7 is (E).

CHAPTER 7: PLANE AND SOLID GEOMETRY DRILL EXPLANATIONS

Drill 1: Triangles in Rectangular Solids, p. 160

17. **D** Use the formula for the long diagonal of a cube. Given that the cube's edge is the cube root of 27, or 3, the formula will be $3^2 + 3^2 + 3^2 = d^2$. If you simplify this, you'll see that the cube's long diagonal must be 5.2.

22. **E** Be careful here; you won't be using the Super Pythagorean Theorem. The sides of this triangle are the diagonals of three of the solid's faces. *BD* is the hypotenuse of a 3:4:5 triangle, and *BE* is $\sqrt{4^2 + 12^2}$ = 12.65. For *DE*, use the Pythagorean Theorem with a = 3 and b = 12: $DE = \sqrt{153}$ = 12.37. The sum of the three sides is 5 + 12.37 + 12.65 = 30.02.

25. **A** This is a long-diagonal question, with a twist. Each edge of the cube is 1, but you're actually finding the long diagonal of a quarter of the cube. Think of it as finding the long diagonal of a rectangular solid with dimensions $1 \cdot \dfrac{1}{2} \cdot \dfrac{1}{2}$. Plug those three numbers into the Super Pythagorean Theorem. You could also solve this by finding the length of *CN* and then using the Pythagorean Theorem on triangle *MCN*.

41. **B** Plug in s = 2. Each side of $\triangle DEG$ is a diagonal of a square with side length 2; therefore, *DE*, *EG*, and *DG* are all equal to $2\sqrt{2}$. This makes $\triangle DEG$ an equilateral triangle. Use the equation $A = \dfrac{s^2\sqrt{3}}{4}$, where s is the side of triangle (and NOT the side of the cube, which is what the s in the question stands for), to find the area: $\dfrac{\left(2\sqrt{2}\right)^2 \sqrt{3}}{4} = \dfrac{8\sqrt{3}}{4} = 2\sqrt{3}$. $2\sqrt{3}$ is the target. The question originally defined s as the side length of the cube, so plug s = 2 into each answer choice, and you find that only (B) equals $2\sqrt{3}$.

Drill 2: Volume, p. 162

1. **D** PITA! Quickly move through the answer choices (starting in this case with the smallest, easiest numbers), calculating the volumes and surface areas of each. The only answer choice that makes these quantities equal is (D).

2. **B** If the cube's surface area is $6x$, then x is the area of one face. Pick an easy number to plug in! Suppose x is 4. That means that the length of any edge of the cube is 2, and that the cube's volume is 8. Just plug x = 4 into all of the answer choices, and find the one that gives you 8. Choice (B) does the trick. Choice (E) is the formula for the volume of a cube with edge x.

10. **E** This one's a pain. The only way to do it is to try out the various possibilities. The edges of the solid must be three factors which multiply to 30, such as 2, 3, and 5. That solid would have a surface area of 62. The solid could also have dimensions of 1, 5, and 6, which would give it a surface area of 82. Keep experimenting, and you find that the solid with the greatest surface area has the dimensions 1, 1, and 30, giving it a surface area of 122.

15. **C** So you don't know the formula for the area of a pentagon? You don't need to. Just use the formula for the volume of a prism, $V = Bh$.

26. **C** Plug in! Suppose the sphere's original radius is $r = 2$, which would give it a surface area of 50.3. If that radius is then increased by $b = 1$, the new radius is 3. The sphere would then have a surface area of 113.1. That's an increase of 62.8. Plug $r = 2$ and $b = 1$ into the answer choices; the one that gives you 62.8 is correct. That's (C).

35. **B** Just plug in any values for b and h that obey the proportion $b = 2h$. Then plug those values into the formula for the volume of a pyramid.

42. **B** The sphere has a volume of 4.19. When submerged, it will push up a layer of water having equal volume. The volume of this layer of water is the product of the area of the circular surface (50.27) and the height to which it's lifted—it's like calculating the volume of a very flat cylinder. You get the equation $50.27h = 4.19$. Solve, and you find that $h = 0.083$.

Drill 3: Inscribed Solids, p. 166

17. **B** The long diagonal of the rectangular solid is the diameter of the sphere. Just find the length of the long diagonal and divide it in half.

19. **C** Calculate the volume of each shape separately. The cube's volume is 8; the cylinder, with a radius of 1 and a height of 2, has a volume of 6.28. The difference between them is 1.72.

25. **B** The cube must have the dimensions 1 by 1 by 1. That means that the cone's base has a radius of 0.5 and that the cone's height is 1. Plug these numbers into the formula for the volume of a cone, and you should get 0.26.

37. **D** If the volume of Cube A is 1,000, then the edge length is $\sqrt[3]{1000} = 10$. That makes the diameter of Sphere S also 10. Cube B's diagonal will be equal to 10; to find the edge of Cube B, use the Super Pythagorean Theorem: $a^2 + b^2 + c^2 = d^2$. Because all the edges are equal, this becomes $3a^2 = d^2$, or $3a^2 = 10^2$, so $a = 5.774$. To find the surface area, use the formula $SA = 6s^2 : 6(5.774^2) = 200$, which is (D).

Drill 4: Rotation Solids, p. 169

19. **C** This rotation will generate a cylinder with a radius of 2 and a height of 5. Its volume is 62.8.

29. **D** This rotation will generate a cone lying on its side, with a height of 5 and a radius of 3. Its volume is 47.12.

40. **D** Here's an odd one. The best way to think about this one is as two triangles, base to base, being rotated. The rotation will generate two cones placed base to base, one right-side-up and one upside-down. Each cone has a radius of 3 and a height of 3. The volume of each cone is 28.27. The volume of the two together is 56.55.

Drill 5: Changing Dimensions, p. 171

3. **E** Just plug in a value for the radius of sphere A, say 2. So the radius of sphere B is 6. Use the volume formula: A has volume $\frac{4}{3}\pi(2)^3 = \frac{4}{3}\pi(8)$, and B has volume $\frac{4}{3}\pi(6)^3 = \frac{4}{3}\pi(216)$. If you make a ratio, the $\frac{4}{3}\pi$ cancels, and you have $\frac{8}{216} = \frac{1}{27}$.

5. **D** Plug in for the dimensions of the rectangular solid so that the volume is 24. So pick $l = 3$, $w = 4$, and $h = 2$. The volume of the solid which the question asks for will then be $\left(\frac{3}{2}\right)\left(\frac{4}{2}\right)\left(\frac{2}{2}\right) = 3$.

10. **B** Plug in for the length of the edge of the cube—try 2. So the surface area formula gives you $6(2)^2 = 24$, and the volume of the cube is 8. Increasing this by a factor of 2.25 gives you a new surface area of 54. Setting the surface area formula equal to this gives you a length of 3 for the new, increased edge. So the new volume is 27. $27 \div 8$ gives you 3.375 for the increase between the old and new volumes, which approximates to (B).

33. **C** Plug in for the dimensions of the original cylinder. Make the radius 3 and the height 4. This makes the original volume $= \pi(3^2)(4) = 36\pi = x$. Doubling the radius and halving the height makes $r = 6$ and $h = 2$. Find the new area: $= \pi(6^2)(2) = 72\pi$. Plug $x = 36\pi$ into each answer choice; the only choice which equals 72π is (C).

46. **C** The volume of a prism is Bh, where B is the area of the base and h is the height perpendicular to that base. Plug in for the hexagonal base and the height; make $B = 3$ and $h = 2$, so the initial volume is 6. Doubling the dimensions of each rectangular face will double the length of each side of the hexagonal bases. If you double the dimensions of a 2-dimensional figure, you increase its area by a factor of four, so the new base area is 12. The lengths of the rectangular faces are also the height of the prism, so once the length is doubled, the new height is 4. Using the new base and height, you find that the new volume is $(12)(4) = 48$, which is 8 times bigger than the original volume of 6, so choose (C).

Comprehensive Plane and Solid Geometry Drill, p. 173

3.   **A**   First, you need the height of the cone to find the volume. To find the height, use the radius and the given distance from the base to the apex to form a right triangle with a leg of 4 and a hypotenuse of 5. Using the Pythagorean Theorem, $a^2 + 4^2 = 5^2$; the height is 3. (Note this is a Pythagorean Triplet: $3^2 + 4^2 = 5^2$. Recognizing these can save you time!) Next, use the formula for volume of a cone: $\frac{1}{3}\pi r^2 h$, so $\frac{1}{3}\pi(4^2)(3) = 50.265$, which is (A).

14.   **D**   You could use the distance formula to find the sides of the original rectangle, solve for area, triple the coordinates, find the distance, solve for area, and compare. Or, remember your dimension change rules: change in area is the square of the change in length. Therefore, if the lengths triple, the area increases by a factor of 9, which is (D).

19.   **E**   Draw it.

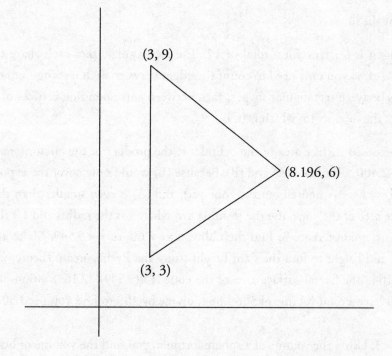

(8.196, 12) is 6 units above the rightmost vertex. This creates a line segment parallel to and the same length as the two leftmost points; this would create a parallelogram. Eliminate (C) and (D). (8.196, 0) is similar, just 6 units below the rightmost vertex. This point would also create a parallelogram; eliminate (A). Finally, (−2.196, 6) is 5.196 units to the left of the line created by (3, 3) and (3, 9), whereas (8.196, 6) is 5.196 units to the right. Because this new point would create another equilateral triangle with (3, 3) and (3, 9), the resulting shape would be a parallelogram. Choose (E).

25. **C** The best way to approach this problem is to draw it. Draw two hexagons and connect each vertex to its corresponding vertex in the other hexagon.

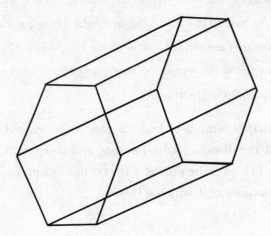

Then count the lines.

Each hexagon is 6 edges, for a total of 12. The rectangular faces each share two edges with the hexagon bases, so you only need to count the edges between each rectangular face. There are 6 distinct edges between rectangular shapes, each between corresponding vertices of the hexagon bases. This brings the total to 18, which is (C).

26. **C** First, the exposed surface area of the cylinder is the product of the circumference and the height: $60 \times 40 = 2{,}400$. Eliminate (A) and (B), because (B) would only cover the exposed part of the cylinder (and we haven't figured out the cone yet), and (A) is even smaller than that. To find the lateral surface area of the cone, use the formula $\pi r l$, where r is the radius and l is the slant height. Use $2\pi r$ with the circumference to find the radius: $2\pi r = 60$, so $r = 9.549$. Make a right triangle with the radius and height to find the slant height using the Pythagorean Theorem: $20^2 + 9.549^2 = c^2$, so $c = 22.164$. The lateral surface area of the cone is $\pi(9.549)(22.163) = 664.884$. Add this to the cylinder to have a total volume of 3064.884; divide by 100 to find you need 30.649 gallons, (C).

32. **A** Plug in $x = 3$. Using the volume of a sphere formula, you find the volume of both shapes is $\frac{4}{3}\pi(3)^3$ $= 36\pi$. Next, use the volume of a cone formula, using y for the radius and $x = 3$ for the height: $\frac{1}{3}$ $\pi(y)^2(3) = 36\pi$. Solve for y and you find $y = 6$. Plug in $y = 6$ into each answer and look for the choice which equals 3. Only (A) works; choose (A).

38. **D** To find the area of the equilateral triangle, all you need is a side and the formula $A = \dfrac{s^2\sqrt{3}}{4}$. The distance between the first two points can be determined by using the distance formula:

$$\sqrt{\left(x_1 - x_2\right)^2 + \left(y_2 - y_1\right)^2} =$$

$$\sqrt{\left((a+3)-(a-3)\right)^2 + \left(b-(b+8)\right)^2} =$$

$$\sqrt{(a+3-a+3)^2 + (b-b-8)^2} =$$

$$\sqrt{6^2 + (-8)^2} = 10$$

If the side is 10, then the area is $\dfrac{(10)^2\sqrt{3}}{4} = 25\sqrt{3}$, which is (D).

41. **D** If the diameter is equal to the height and the radius is r, then $2r = h$. The surface area is of a cylinder is $2(\pi r)^2 + 2\pi rh$. This is equal to the volume, so $2(\pi r)^2 + 2\pi rh = \pi r^2 h$. Plug in $2r$ for h, then solve for r.

$$2(\pi r)^2 + 2\pi r(2r) = \pi r^2(2r)$$

$$2\pi r^2 + 4\pi r^2 = 2\pi r^3$$

$$6\pi r^2 = 2\pi r^3$$

$$3 = r$$

To find the longest distance within the cylinder, make a right triangle with one leg the height and the other the diameter. Because height equals diameter, they are both equal to 6. The hypotenuse of an isosceles right triangle is $\sqrt{2}$ times the length of the legs, so the longest distance is $6\sqrt{2}$.

If you were stuck on this question, you could ballpark away a few answers. If the diameter equals the height, and you want the longest distance within the cylinder, you know you're looking for the hypotenuse of an isosceles right triangle. From there, you can eliminate (A), (C), and (E), because the hypotenuse of the isosceles right triangle will be $\sqrt{2}$ times the leg length. At this point, you can use PITA to see which answer fits the criteria of the question.

45. **A** If the shape is rotated around AB, then the height of the resulting cylinder will be the length of AB. Only (A) has a length of 7 for AB. Alternatively, the segments perpendicular to AB will be the resulting cylinder's radius; if the cylinder has a diameter of 9, you need a radius of 4.5. Once again, only (A) fits.

48. **B** In polar coordinates, the first number is the distance from the origin. Because one point is the origin and the other two known points are $(2, \frac{\pi}{6})$ and $(4, 0)$, you know the two sides of the parallelogram are 2 and 4. $\frac{\pi}{6}$ gives you one angle in the parallelogram because one side of the parallelogram is the x-axis (the θ value is 0) and the other side is at $\frac{\pi}{6}$ radians from the x-axis. Use the formula for finding the area of a parallelogram using trigonometry: $ab \sin \theta$. Therefore, the area is $(2)(4)\sin\frac{\pi}{6} = 4$, which is (B). If you chose (A), your calculator is in degrees, not radians!

50.   **A**   Plug in $s = 2$. To find the height of the pyramid, create a right triangle. One leg will be the height of the pyramid, the other leg will extend from a vertex of the base of the pyramid to the center of the base, and the hypotenuse will be the edge of the pyramid from the vertex of the base to the top. You already know the hypotenuse is $s = 2$. The base is a square; the leg on the base is half the diagonal of the square. If the side of the square is 2, then the diagonal is $2\sqrt{2}$ and the leg is $\dfrac{2\sqrt{2}}{2} = \sqrt{2}$. You now have the hypotenuse and one leg of the triangle; use the Pythagorean Theorem to find the remaining leg, which is the height of the pyramid.

$$a^2 + b^2 = c^2$$

$$\left(\sqrt{2}\right)^2 + b^2 = 2^2$$

$$2 + b^2 = 4$$

$$b^2 = 2$$

$$b = \sqrt{2}$$

Plug $s = 2$ into your answers and you find that only (A) equals $\sqrt{2}$.

CHAPTER 8: COORDINATE GEOMETRY DRILL EXPLANATIONS

Drill 1: The Coordinate Plane, p. 183

1.   Point E, Quadrant II

2.   Point A, Quadrant I

3.   Point C, Quadrant IV

4.   Point D, Quadrant III

5.   Point B, Quadrant I

Drill 2: The Equation of a Line, p. 185

1. **A** You can plug the line's slope m and the given point (x, y) into the slope-intercept equation to get $1 = 0.6(3) + b$. So $b = -0.8$. So the equation is $y = 0.6x - 0.8$.

    To find the point that is also on this line, go to each answer choice and plug the x-coordinate into the formula. You'll have the right answer when the formula produces a y-coordinate that matches the given one.

2. **E** Once again, get the line into slope-intercept form, $y = 5x - 4$. Then plug in zero. You get a y-value of -4. Notice that this is the y-intercept (the value of y when $x = 0$).

4. **B** Put the line into the slope-intercept formula by isolating y. So $y = -3x + 4$ and the slope is -3.

6. **D** You can figure out the line formula ($y = mx + b$) from the graph. The line has a y-intercept (b) of -2, and it rises 6 as it runs 2, giving it a slope (m) of 3. Use those values of m and b to test the statements in the answer choices.

Drill 3: Slope, p. 188

1. **C** Use the slope formula on the point $(0, 0)$ and $(-3, 2)$: $\dfrac{2-0}{-3-0} = -\dfrac{2}{3}$.

5. **D** Draw it. Remember that perpendicular lines have slopes that are negative reciprocals of each other. A line containing the origin and the point $(2, -1)$ has a slope of $-\dfrac{1}{2}$. The perpendicular line must then have a slope of 2. Quickly move through the answer choices, determining the slope of a line passing through the given point and the origin. The one that gives a slope of 2 is correct.

13. **A** Once again, the slope-intercept formula is your most powerful tool. Isolate y, and you get $y = -3x + 5$. The line must then have a slope of -3 and a y-intercept of 5. Only (A) and (D) show lines with negative slope, and the line in (D) has a slope which is between -1 and 0, because it forms an angle with the x-axis that is less than 45°.

37. **D** Remember that perpendicular lines have slopes that are negative reciprocals of each other. The slopes of x and y are therefore negative reciprocals—you can think of them as x and $-\dfrac{1}{x}$. The difference between them will therefore be the sum of a number and its reciprocal: $x - \left(-\dfrac{1}{x}\right) = x + \dfrac{1}{x}$.

    If $x = 1$, then the sum of x and its reciprocal is 2; if $x = 5$, then the sum of x and its reciprocal is 5.2; but no sum of a number and its reciprocal can be less than 2. A sum of 0.8 is impossible.

Drill 4: Line Segments, p. 192

2. **D** Use the distance formula on the points (−5, 9) and (0, 0).

6. **E** Drawing a rough sketch and approximating allows you to eliminate (A) and (B). Then, plug the points you know into the midpoint formula and PITA for the coordinates of B. The average of −4 and the x-coordinate of B is 1. The average of 3 and the y-coordinate of B is −1. That makes B the point (6, −5).

12. **D** You'll essentially be using the distance formula on (2, 2) and the points in the answer choices. (−5, −3) is the point at the greatest distance from (2, 2).

28. **E** To find the area of the circle, you need the radius. Since the given line segment goes through the center, that segment is a diameter. Find the length of the diameter using the distance formula:

$$d = \sqrt{(18-5)^2 + (22-4)^2} = 22.204$$. Divide by 2 to find the radius, which is 11.102. Finally, use the formula for area of a circle: $\pi(11.102)^2 = 387.201$, which is (E).

Drill 5: General Equations (Parabolas), p. 196

21. **C** This is a quadratic function, which always produces a parabola. If a parabola has a maximum or minimum, then that extreme value is the parabola's vertex. Just find the vertex. The x-coordinate is $-\dfrac{b}{2a}$, which is 3 in this case. The y-coordinate will be $f(3)$, or −1.

22. **B** Use that vertex formula again. The x-coordinate is $-\dfrac{b}{2a}$, which is −1 in this case. That's enough to get you the right answer. (If you needed the y-coordinate as well, you'd just plug in $x = -1$ and solve for y.)

25. **D** At every point on the x-axis, $y = 0$. Plug each of the answer choices in for x, and see which one gives you $y = 0$. You could also put in 0 for y and solve for x; the solutions are 1 and 5.

36. **B** The parabola opens downward, so you know in the standard form of the equation $y = a(x-h)^2 + k$ that a must be negative; eliminate (E). The axis of symmetry is negative, so h must be negative. This means in the standard form of the equation the parentheses must be $(x + h)$; eliminate (A) and (C). Finally, the vertex of the parabola is positive, so k must be positive; eliminate (D) and choose (B).

Drill 6: General Equations (Circles), p. 198

18. **B** Just plug each point into the equation. The one that does *not* make the equation true is not on the circle.

20. **E** If S and T are the endpoints of a diameter, then the distance between them is 8. If they are very close to each other on the circle, then the distance between them approaches zero. The distance between S and T cannot be determined.

45. **C** Notice that because the y's equal 0, you can cancel out the y's in all the answer choices. Plug in the points: (2, 0) works in (C), (D), and (E), but (10, 0) works in (A), (B), and (C). It must be (C).

50. **A** First, rewrite the equation into the Standard Form. Begin by rearranging the equation so your x-terms and y-terms are together and the constants are on the other side of the equation.

$$x^2 + 4x + y^2 + 8y = -4$$

Next, complete the square for both the x-terms and the y-terms. To do so, take the b coefficient, divide by 2, square the result, and add that to each term and to the other side of the equation.

$$\left(x^2 + 4x + 4\right) + \left(y^2 + 8y + 16\right) = -4 + 4 + 16$$

You have just created two perfect squares. Factor as follows:

$$\left(x + 2\right)^2 + \left(y + 4\right)^2 = 16$$

Now the equation is in the standard form. The center of the circle is at (–2, –4) and the circle has a radius of 4. You are looking for a circle with the center in the third quadrant and tangent to the x-axis: (A) meets these criteria.

Drill 7: General Equations (Ellipses), p. 202

15. **E** Because $a = 4$ and $b = 5$, the minor axis is 2(4) = 8 and the major axis is 2(5) = 10.

40. **C** For an ellipse in its general form, the center is (h, k), which in this case is (–5, 3).

45. **E** There is no denominator under the y^2, so it is understood to be 1. Therefore, the form of this ellipse centered at the origin is $\dfrac{x^2}{16} + \dfrac{y^2}{1} = 1$. Because the a^2 value (denominator of the x-term) is greater than the b^2 value (denominator of the y-term), the ellipse's major axis is horizontal. Eliminate (A), (B), and (D). You can now plug the points given into the original equation. Alternatively, if you can remember that if $a^2 = 16$ then $a = 4$, then you know the distance along the horizontal axis is $2a = 8$. Therefore, the distance from the origin is 4. Either way, the answer is (E).

Drill 8: General Equations (Hyperbolas), p. 205

38. **B** Like circles and ellipses, hyperbolas in general form have their centers at (h, k). This one is centered at $(-4, -5)$.

45. **A** If the hyperbola is opening to the left and right, the form of the equation is $\dfrac{(x-h)^2}{a^2} - \dfrac{(y-k)^2}{b^2} = 1$, where the center is (h, k). Eliminate (B) and (D), since those hyperbolae open up and down. Eliminate (E) because it isn't the equation of a hyperbola: rather, it is the equation of an ellipse. The center of the hyperbola shown is in the fourth quadrant; h should be positive and k should be negative, which means the sign in the x-term should be negative and the sign in the y-term should be positive. Choice (A) fits these criteria.

Drill 9: Triaxial Coordinates, p. 207

14. **C** This is once again a job for the Super Pythagorean Theorem, which is simply another version of the 3-D distance formula. It's just like finding the long diagonal of a box which is 5 by 6 by 7. Set up this equation: $d^2 = 5^2 + 6^2 + 7^2$, and solve.

19. **B** A point will be outside the sphere if the distance between it and the origin is greater than 6. Use the Super Pythagorean Theorem to measure the distance of each point from the origin.

37. **D** First, Point D is not on the y-axis, so its x-coordinate cannot be 0; eliminate (A) and (B). Point B shares x- and y-coordinates with point D directly below it. Make the origin point O. Triangle OCD will have a right angle at D. $\overline{OD}$ and $\overline{CD}$ are each edges of the cube with length 5. This is an isosceles (45-45-90) right triangle; therefore, $\overline{OC}$ will have length $5\sqrt{2} = 7.071$. Point D will have a y-coordinate of half the length of $\overline{OC}$, or 3.536; eliminate (C) and (E) and choose (D).

Comprehensive Coordinate Geometry Drill, p. 209

1. **A** The x-intercept must have a y-value of 0; eliminate (E). Next, use the slope formula to find the slope of the line: $\dfrac{18-7}{-4-19} = -\dfrac{11}{23}$. Next, use this slope, one of the given points, and the x-intercept coordinates $(x, 0)$ in the slope formula to solve for the x-intercept: $-\dfrac{11}{23} = \dfrac{18-0}{-4-x}$. Cross-multiply: $44 + 11x = 414$, so $x = 33.636$. The x-intercept is therefore $(33.636, 0)$, which is (A).

2. **C** First, find the slope of the given line by solving for y.

$$4x + 7y = 23$$

$$7y = 4x + 23$$

$$y = -\frac{4}{7}x + \frac{23}{7}$$

The slope of this line is the x coefficient: $-\frac{4}{7}$. A perpendicular line will have a slope which is the negative reciprocal of this line, $\frac{7}{4}$, which is (C).

5. **D** You need an equation that results in a hyperbola that opens vertically. Choices (A) and (B) describe parabolas and would give you only half of what you need ((A) could be the part of the graph above the x-axis, but not below; (B) could be the part of the graph below the x-axis, but not above); eliminate (A) and (B). Choice (E) describes an ellipse, because you are adding the two terms; eliminate it. If the x-term is positive, the hyperbola opens horizontally; eliminate (C) and choose (D).

12. **B** The x-value of the vertex of a parabola given in the general form of the equation, $y = ax^2 + bx + c$, is found by using $-\frac{b}{2a}$. This is $-\frac{5}{2(-3)} = 0.833$. Eliminate (A), (D), and (E). To find the y-value, plug this x-value into the original equation: $-3(0.833)^2 + 5(0.833) - 11 = -8.917$. These x- and y-values match (B).

18. **A** Start by finding the center of the circle by finding the midpoint of the diameter shown:

$\left(\frac{4+16}{2}, \frac{-9+(-4)}{2} \right) = (10, -6.5)$. Because the standard form of the equation of a circle is

$(x-h)^2 + (y-k)^2 = r^2$, the answer must have $(x-10)^2 + (y+6.5)^2$; eliminate (B), (D), and (E).

Next, find the radius by finding the distance between the center and one of the points on the

circle: $\sqrt{(10-4)^2 + (-6.5-(-9))^2} = 6.5$. The right side of the equation must be radius squared, or

42.25; choose (A).

22. **D** First, find the midpoint of $\overline{AB}$: $x = \frac{-2+0.5}{2} = -0.75$, and $y = \frac{4+12}{2} = 8$. Next, use the distance formula to find the distance between $(-0.75, 8)$ and $(7, -5)$: $d = \sqrt{(-0.75-7)^2 + (8-(-5))^2} = 15.134$, (D).

25. **A** The equation for an ellipse centered on the origin is $\dfrac{x^2}{a^2} + \dfrac{y^2}{b^2} = 1$ where $2a$ is the width and $2b$ is the height of the ellipse. If the ellipse contains the point $(4, 0)$ as its widest point on the x-axis, then its width must be 8, which means $a = 4$. The equation needs to include $\dfrac{x^2}{16}$; only (A) fits this criteria. Alternatively, you can plug the x- and y-values of the points given into each equation and eliminate the equations that are not true with the given values.

28. **E** First, because there is no negative sign before the $(x-2)^2$, the parabola should open up; eliminate (A) and (B). Next, $(x-2)^2$ would move the vertex to the right of the y-axis; eliminate (C) because the vertex is to the left. Finally, $\leq$ means that the shaded region should be below the parabola; eliminate (D) and choose (E).

36. **B** If the point is on the y-axis, the x value must be 0; eliminate (A). Next, you have a few options. First, you can draw and ballpark; the only answer which is not obviously closer to $(0, 2)$ than $(6, 0)$ is (B). Or, you can use PITA; start with (C) or (D) and find the distance from $(0, 2)$ and $(6, 0)$ for each answer.

Finally, mathematically, the distance from $(0, 2)$ will be the difference in y-coordinates, or $y - 2$.

The distance from $(6, 0)$ can be found using the distance formula: $\sqrt{(x_2 - x_1)^2 + (y_2 - y_1)^2} = \sqrt{(6-0)^2 + (0-y)^2} = \sqrt{36 + y^2}$.

Set these two equations equal to each other and solve.

$$y - 2 = \sqrt{36 + y^2}$$

$$y^2 - 4y + 4 = 36 + y^2$$

$$-4y = 32$$

$$y = -8$$

Therefore, the answer is (B).

42. **E** If point E is at $(0, 3.5)$, then the y-coordinates of both point B and point C must also be 3.5. Use the function given to find the x-coordinate of points B and C by making $f(x) = 3.5$.

$$3.5 = -2x^2 + 10$$

$$-6.5 = -2x^2$$

$$3.25 = x^2$$

$$\pm 1.803 = x$$

The distance from point B to point C will be the difference in their x-values, which is 3.606. The distance from point A to point B will be the y-value of 3.5. To find the area of the rectangle, multiply length times width: $3.606 \times 3.5 = 12.619$, (E).

49.   **E**   Every point on a sphere with radius 5 will be 5 units away from the center of the sphere. You could use the 3D distance formula $d = \sqrt{\left(x_2 - x_1\right)^2 + \left(y_2 - y_1\right)^2 + \left(z_2 - z_1\right)^2}$, but there's something else going on here. Each point in the answers shares at least one coordinate with the center of the sphere, so you can look at the other two points and use the simpler 2D distance formula. For (A) you don't even need to go that far: the y- and z-coordinates are the same as the center, and the x-coordinate differs by 5. Similarly, (B) shares the x- and z-coordinates and differs from the center by 5 along the y-axis: eliminate (A) and (B). Choices (C) and (D) both share an x-coordinate with the center, so you can find the difference between the y- and z-coordinates of each point and the center of the circle. In both cases, you create a 3:4:5 Pythagorean triple; these points are a distance of 5 from the center of the circle, so eliminate (C) and (D) and choose (E).

CHAPTER 9: TRIGONOMETRY DRILL EXPLANATIONS

Drill 1: Trig Functions in Right Triangles, p. 216

1. $\sin \theta = \dfrac{3}{5} = 0.6$; $\cos \theta = \dfrac{4}{5} = 0.8$; $\tan \theta = \dfrac{3}{4} = 0.75$

2. $\sin \theta = \dfrac{5}{13} = 0.385$; $\cos \theta = \dfrac{12}{13} = 0.923$; $\tan \theta = \dfrac{5}{12} = 0.417$

3. $\sin \theta = \dfrac{24}{25} = 0.96$; $\cos \theta = \dfrac{7}{25} = 0.28$; $\tan \theta = \dfrac{24}{7} = 3.429$

4. $\sin \theta = \dfrac{6}{10} = 0.6$; $\cos \theta = \dfrac{8}{10} = 0.8$; $\tan \theta = \dfrac{6}{8} = 0.75$

Drill 2: Completing Triangles, p. 219

1. $AB = 3.38$; $CA = 7.25$; $\angle B = 65°$

2. $EF = 2.52$; $FD = 3.92$; $\angle D = 40°$

3. $HJ = 41.41$; $JK = 10.72$; $\angle J = 75°$

4. $LM = 5.74$; $MN = 8.19$; $\angle N = 35°$

5. $TR = 4.0$; $\angle S = 53.13°$; $\angle T = 36.87°$

6. $YW = 13$; $\angle W = 22.62°$; $\angle Y = 67.38°$

Drill 3: Trigonometric Identities, p. 225

10. **D** Use FOIL on these binomials, and you get $1 - \sin^2 x$. Because $\sin^2 x + \cos^2 x = 1$, you know that $1 - \sin^2 x = \cos^2 x$.

16. **C** Express $\tan x$ as $\dfrac{\sin x}{\cos x}$. The cosine then cancels out on the top of the fraction, and you're left with $\dfrac{\sin x}{\sin x}$, or 1.

24. **A** The term $(\sin x)(\tan x)$ can be expressed as $(\sin x)\left(\dfrac{\sin x}{\cos x}\right)$ or $\dfrac{\sin^2 x}{\cos x}$. The first and second terms can then be combined: $\dfrac{1}{\cos x} - \dfrac{\sin^2 x}{\cos x} = \dfrac{1 - \sin^2 x}{\cos x}$. Because $1 - \sin^2 x = \cos^2 x$, this expression simplifies to $\cos x$.

38. **E** Break the fraction into two terms, as follows: $\dfrac{\tan x}{\tan x} - \dfrac{\sin x \cos x}{\tan x}$. The first term simplifies to 1, and the second term becomes easier to work with when you express the tangent in terms of the sine and cosine: $\dfrac{\sin x \cos x}{\tan x} = \dfrac{\sin x \cos x}{\dfrac{\sin x}{\cos x}} = \cos^2 x$. The whole expression then equals $1 - \cos^2 x$, or $\sin^2 x$.

45. **D** First, FOIL the numerator (or note the common quadratic $(a + b)(a - b) = (a^2 - b^2)$ to get $1 - \sin^2 \theta$, which is equal to $\cos^2 \theta$ when you rearrange $\sin^2 \theta + \cos^2 \theta = 1$. Next, factor the denominator. The denominator is the common quadratic $a^2 + 2ab + b^2 = (a + b)^2$. Don't be fooled by the exponent to the power of 4; in this case $a = \sin^2 \theta$ and $b = \cos^2 \theta$. So far, the fraction looks like the following:

$$\frac{\cos^2 \theta}{\left(\sin^2 \theta + \cos^2 \theta\right)^2}$$

Because $\sin^2 \theta + \cos^2 \theta = 1$, the denominator is 1 and the expression is equal to $\cos^2 \theta$, which is (D).

Drill 4: Other Trig Functions, p. 227

19. **E** Express the function as a fraction: $\dfrac{1}{\cos^2 x} - 1$. You can then combine the terms by changing the form of the second term: $\dfrac{1}{\cos^2 x} - \dfrac{\cos^2 x}{\cos^2 x}$. This allows you to combine the terms, like this: $\dfrac{1 - \cos^2 x}{\cos^2 x} = \dfrac{\sin^2 x}{\cos^2 x} = \tan^2 x$.

23. **D** Express the cotangent as a fraction, as follows: $\dfrac{1}{\sin x \cot x} = \dfrac{1}{\sin x \dfrac{\cos x}{\sin x}}$. The sin x then cancels out,

leaving you with $\dfrac{1}{\cos x}$, or sec x.

24. **A** Express the cotangent as a fraction, and the second term can be simplified:

$(\cos x)(\cot x) = \cos x \dfrac{\cos x}{\sin x} = \dfrac{\cos^2 x}{\sin x}$. Express both terms as fractions, and the terms can be com-

bined: $\dfrac{\sin^2 x}{\sin x} + \dfrac{\cos^2 x}{\sin x} = \dfrac{\sin^2 x + \cos^2 x}{\sin x} = \dfrac{1}{\sin x}$, or csc x.

38. **E** Start by putting everything into either sin or cos. You'll notice that almost everything is over cos x, so rewrite the 1s in the denominator as $\dfrac{\cos x}{\cos x}$.

$$\dfrac{\left(\dfrac{1}{\cos x} + \dfrac{\sin x}{\cos x}\right)\left(\dfrac{1}{\cos x} - \dfrac{\sin x}{\cos x}\right)}{\left(\dfrac{1}{\cos x} + \dfrac{\cos x}{\cos x}\right)\left(\dfrac{1}{\cos x} - \dfrac{\cos x}{\cos x}\right)}$$

Now that all the terms in each set of parentheses are over the same denominator, you can combine the numerators within each set of parentheses.

$$\dfrac{\left(\dfrac{1 + \sin x}{\cos x}\right)\left(\dfrac{1 - \sin x}{\cos x}\right)}{\left(\dfrac{1 + \cos x}{\cos x}\right)\left(\dfrac{1 - \cos x}{\cos x}\right)}$$

Multiply the fractions in the numerator and denominator.

$$\dfrac{\left(\dfrac{1 + \sin x}{\cos x}\right)\left(\dfrac{1 - \sin x}{\cos x}\right)}{\left(\dfrac{1 + \cos x}{\cos x}\right)\left(\dfrac{1 - \cos x}{\cos x}\right)} = \dfrac{\dfrac{1 - \sin^2 x}{\cos^2 x}}{\dfrac{1 - \cos^2 x}{\cos^2 x}}$$

Divide by multiplying the numerator by the reciprocal of the denominator. The $\cos^2 x$ will cancel, making the multiplication straightforward.

$$\left(\dfrac{1 - \sin^2 x}{\cos^2 x}\right)\left(\dfrac{\cos^2 x}{1 - \cos^2 x}\right) = \dfrac{1 - \sin^2 x}{1 - \cos^2 x}$$

Next, use the trig identity to simplify the numerator and denominator: $\dfrac{\cos^2 x}{\sin^2 x}$.

You know that $\dfrac{\sin\theta}{\cos\theta} = \tan\theta$; because cotangent is the inverse function of tangent, $\dfrac{\cos\theta}{\sin\theta} = \cot\theta$.

Therefore, $\dfrac{\cos^2 x}{\sin^2 x} = \cot^2 x$, which is (E).

Another way to approach this question is to plug in. Make $x = 20°$. Now the problem reads

$\dfrac{\left(\sec 20° + \tan 20°\right)\left(\sec 20° - \tan 20°\right)}{\left(\sec 20° + 1\right)\left(\sec 20° - 1\right)}$. Secant is $\dfrac{1}{\cos}$, so $\sec x = \dfrac{1}{\cos 20°} = 1.064$ and $\tan 20° =$

0.364. You can then rewrite the problem: $\dfrac{(1.064+0.364)(1.064-0.364)}{(1.064+1)(1.064-1)} = \dfrac{1.000}{0.132} = 7.576$. This

is your target answer. You can immediately eliminate (A) and (B) (because sin and cos are always

between −1 and 1, inclusive, their product must also be in between these values). Plug 20° into

each answer choice (remember that $\csc^2 20° = \dfrac{1}{\left(\sin 20°\right)^2}$). Only (E) comes close.

Drill 5: The Unit Circle, p. 233

18. **A** Draw the unit circle. −225° and 135° are equivalent angle measures, because they are separated by 360°. Or just PITA, to see which value of x works in the equation.

21. **D** Draw the unit circle. 300° and 60° are not equivalent angles, but they have the same cosine. It's a simple matter to check with your calculator. Or you could just PITA.

26. **B** PITA and use your calculator!

30. **C** PITA and use your calculator!

36. **D** Plug in a value for θ from the ranges in the answer choices. If $\theta = 60°$, then (sin 60°)(cos 60°) = 0.433, which is not less than zero. So cross off any answer choices that contain 60°—(A), (B), (C), and (E).

40. **E** Use your calculator and plug in the numbers in each statement. Remember that $\cot x = \dfrac{1}{\tan x}$, so

$\cot 40° = \dfrac{1}{\tan 40°} = 1.192$. Statements (I) and (III) are both equal to 1.192; choose (E).

Drill 6: Degrees and Radians, p. 236

Degrees	Radians
30°	$\dfrac{\pi}{6}$
45°	$\dfrac{\pi}{4}$
60°	$\dfrac{\pi}{3}$
90°	$\dfrac{\pi}{2}$
120°	$\dfrac{2\pi}{3}$
135°	$\dfrac{3\pi}{4}$
150°	$\dfrac{5\pi}{6}$
180°	π
225°	$\dfrac{5\pi}{4}$
240°	$\dfrac{4\pi}{3}$
270°	$\dfrac{3\pi}{2}$
300°	$\dfrac{5\pi}{3}$
315°	$\dfrac{7\pi}{4}$
330°	$\dfrac{11\pi}{6}$
360°	2π

Drill 7: Non-Right Triangles, p. 241

1. $a = 8.26$, $\angle B = 103.4°$, $\angle C = 34.6°$ Your calculator will give you $\angle B = 76.6°$, but you need $180° - 76.6° = 103.4°$ in order to have an obtuse angle with the same distance from 90° as 76.6°.

2. $\angle A = 21.79°$, $\angle B = 120.0°$, $\angle C = 38.21°$

3. $c = 9.44$, $\angle B = 57.98°$, $\angle C = 90.02°$

4. $b = 13.418$ $\angle B = 125.710°$ $\angle C = 21.290°$. Use Law of Sines to find $\angle C$: $\dfrac{\sin 33°}{9} = \dfrac{\sin C}{6}$. Cross-

multiply to get $6\sin 33° = 9\sin C$, then divide both sides by 9: $\sin C = \dfrac{6\sin 33°}{9}$. Use the inverse

function of sine to find the unknown angle: $\angle C = \sin^{-1}\left(\dfrac{6\sin 33°}{9}\right) = 21.290$. There is another

value for $\angle C$, which is 158.70° (because sin 21.290° = sin 158.70°, as discussed in the section on

the unit circle), but that would result in a triangle with more than 180°, so it can be ignored. If

$\angle C = 21.290°$, then $\angle B$ is $180 - 33 - 21.290 = 125.710°$. To find side b, you can use either Law of

Sines or Law of Cosines; either way, its value is 13.418.

Drill 8: Polar Coordinates, p. 245

39.   **C**

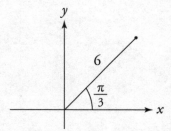

Draw it! The x-coordinate of the point is $6\cos\dfrac{\pi}{3}$, or 3. The y-coordinate is $6\sin\dfrac{\pi}{3}$, which is 5.196.

42.   **B**

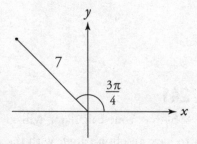

Draw it! The y-value of a point is its distance from the x-axis. The y-coordinate of this point is $7\sin\dfrac{3\pi}{4}$, which equals 4.949.

45.   **B**

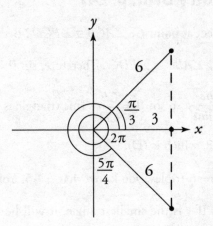

Draw it! In rectangular coordinates, A, B, and C have x-coordinates of 3. This means that they are placed in a straight vertical line. They define a straight line, but not a plane or space.

50.   **C**

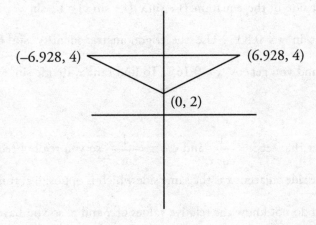

Draw it! Start by converting the polar coordinates using $x = r \cos \theta$ and $y = r \sin \theta$. You find the points of the triangle are (0, 2), (6.928, 4), and (−6.928, 4). Once you draw the triangle, you can see that the base is the distance between (6.928, 4) and (−6.928, 4), or 13.856. The height is the distance from (0, 2) to the perpendicular base on the line $y = 4$, so $h = 2$. The area of the triangle is $\frac{bh}{2}$; therefore, $\frac{13.856(2)}{2} = 13.856$, which is (C).

Comprehensive Trigonometry Drill, p. 247

7. **D** Because $\overline{BD}$ and $\overline{AE}$ intersect at point C, $\angle ACB \cong \angle ECD$. Because both triangle ABC and triangle CDE are right triangles, $\angle ABC \cong \angle EDC$. Therefore, sin θ = sine of $\angle EDC$. SOHCAHTOA

indicates that sin = $\dfrac{opposite}{hypotenuse}$, so sin θ = $\dfrac{CE}{CD}$. This triangle is one of the Pythagorean triples, so

CD = 5, and sin θ = $\dfrac{4}{5}$ = 0.8, which is (D).

10. **A** If you know your Pythagorean triples, you know that b = 5. You can always use the Pythagorean

Theorem to find it as well. If x is the smallest angle, it will be opposite the smallest side; in this

case, opposite the side with length 5. Secant is the inverse operation of cosine, so start by using

SOHCAHTOA to find that cos = $\dfrac{adjacent}{hypotenuse}$. For secant, you want $\dfrac{hypotenuse}{adjacent}$, which is (A).

13. **E** To find $\tan^2 x$ you can use the identity $\tan x = \dfrac{\sin x}{\cos x}$. In this case, $\tan^2 x = \dfrac{\sin^2 x}{\cos^2 x}$. Start by using

FOIL on the left side of the equation: $(1 - \sin x)(1 + \sin x) = 1 - \sin^2 x$. Manipulate the full equa-

tion to find that $\sin^2 x = 0.835$. Use the trigonometric identity $\sin^2 \theta + \cos^2 \theta = 1$ to substitute

$\sin^2 x = 0.835$, and you get $\cos^2 x = 0.165$. To find $\tan^2 x$, divide $\sin^2 x$ by $\cos^2 x$: $\dfrac{0.835}{0.165} = 5.061$,

which is (E).

20. **C** For (I), remember that sec $x = \dfrac{1}{\cos x}$ and csc $z = \dfrac{1}{\sin z}$, so you really need to know whether cos x =

sin z. Because the side adjacent x is the same side which is opposite z, this is true; eliminate (B) and

(D). For (II), you do not know the relative values of x and z, so you have no idea whether they are

equal; eliminate (E). Finally, to compare sin x to tan x, use SOHCAHTOA: sin x is $\dfrac{O}{H}$ and tan x

is $\dfrac{O}{A}$. O is the same in both fractions, and in any given right triangle the hypotenuse will be larger

than either leg. Therefore, because its denominator is greater and the numerators are equal, sin x

will be less than tan x; (III) is true, so choose (C).

25. **C** This is a right triangle question. Create a triangle using Carl's eye level, the tip of the rocket, and a

point on the rocket 1.6 m off the ground. The hypotenuse travels through Carl's eye, and to keep

Carl's body 500 m from the rocket, you need to make sure his eye is also that far from the rocket.

Because Carl's eye is 1.6 m above ground level and the rocket is 150 m above ground level, that leg of the triangle should be $150 - 1.6 = 148.4$ m, NOT 150 m:

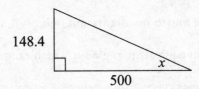

For this triangle, you know the sides opposite and adjacent to the x. To find the value of x, use tan $x = \dfrac{148.4}{500}$, then solve for x using $\tan^{-1}$: $\tan^{-1}\left(\dfrac{148.4}{500}\right) = 16.531$, which is (C).

34. **C** Because you know three sides, you can use the Law of Cosines: $c^2 = a^2 + b^2 - 2ab\cos C$. In this case, because you want to find $\angle A$, make a your "c" value and $\angle A$ your C. (Remember that in the Law of Cosines, c is the side opposite $\angle C$.) Therefore, to find $\cos A$, the equation becomes:

$\left(\sqrt{20}\right)^2 = 7^2 + 9^2 - 2(7)(9)\cos A$, and solving for $\cos A$ you find $0.873 = \cos A$. To find secant, you need $\dfrac{1}{\cos A}$; therefore, $\dfrac{1}{0.873} = 1.145$, which is (C).

35. **B** PITA! Be sure your calculator is in radians, then start trying the answers! If $x = \dfrac{\pi}{4}$, then $\sin\left(\dfrac{\pi}{4} + \dfrac{\pi}{6}\right) = 0.966$, and $\cos\dfrac{\pi}{4} = 0.707$. Eliminate (C). It can be difficult to determine whether you need a greater or lesser value of x, so just pick a direction. If you try (B), then

$\sin\left(\dfrac{\pi}{6} + \dfrac{\pi}{6}\right) = 0.866$, and $\cos\dfrac{\pi}{6} = 0.866$; choose (B).

40. **E**

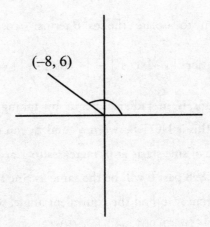

Start by drawing the point, including the angle it makes with the x-axis. Remember that polar coordinates are in the form (r, θ), where r is the distance from the origin, and θ is the angle in radians. Start by using the Pythagorean Theorem to find r: $6^2 + 8^2 = r^2$, $r = 10$. Eliminate (A). Next, to find θ, you can use $\tan^{-1}\left(\dfrac{y}{x}\right) = \theta$. Your calculator will tell you that $\tan^{-1}\left(\dfrac{6}{-8}\right) = -0.644$. However, this angle is in the fourth quadrant, and point $(-8, 6)$ is in the second quadrant. Eliminate (C). You need to find an equivalent angle for which tangent equals $-\dfrac{6}{8}$. Because tangent is a periodic function which repeats every π units, there is an equivalent angle π units away. Therefore, if you add π to -0.644, you get the equivalent angle in the second quadrant, which is 2.498. Eliminate (B). If $r = -10$, then the angle is measured from its equivalent in the fourth quadrant, which you found earlier to be -0.644. Neither (D) nor (E) has a $\theta = -0.644$. However, you can find the angle with the same terminal side by adding 2π. When you add 2π to -0.644, you get 5.639, so choose (E).

45. **D** First, the value of cosine must always be between -1 and 1, inclusive, so eliminate (E). Next, if $-90° \le \theta \le 90°$, then θ is in either the first or fourth quadrants. Cosine is positive in both of those quadrants; eliminate (A) and (B). Cosecant is $\dfrac{1}{\sin}$, so $\dfrac{1}{\sin\theta} = -1.556$. Solving for $\sin \theta$, you find that $\sin \theta = -0.643$. If you take the inverse sine of -0.643 you get $-40°$, and $\cos -40° = 0.766$, which is (D).

47. **C** Use the trigonometric identity $\sin^2 \theta + \cos^2 \theta = 1$ and substitute $1 - \cos^2 \theta$ for each $\sin^2 \theta$ in the equation: $\left(1 - \cos^2\left(\dfrac{\pi}{x}\right)\right) + \left(1 - \cos^2\left(\dfrac{\pi}{y}\right)\right) + \left(1 - \cos^2\left(\dfrac{\pi}{z}\right)\right) = 2.34$. Next, subtract 3 from both sides of the equation to isolate the $\cos^2 \theta$ terms: $-\cos^2\left(\dfrac{\pi}{x}\right) - \cos^2\left(\dfrac{\pi}{y}\right) - \cos^2\left(\dfrac{\pi}{z}\right) = -0.655$. Finally, multiply both sides by -1: $\cos^2\left(\dfrac{\pi}{x}\right) + \cos^2\left(\dfrac{\pi}{y}\right) + \cos^2\left(\dfrac{\pi}{z}\right) = 0.655$, (C).

48. **E** Be sure your calculator is in radians! Begin by taking the inverse sine of 0.782 to find x: $\sin^{-1} 0.782 = 0.898$. This is NOT between $\dfrac{\pi}{2}$ and π; you need to find the equivalent angle in the given range. The value of sine starts at 0, increases to 1 at $\dfrac{\pi}{2}$, and decreases symmetrically to 0 at π. Therefore, sine at 0.898 past 0 will be the same as sine at 0.898 radians before π. To find x you must subtract 0.898 from π to find the equivalent angle, which is 2.244. Finally, find cosine of 3 times 2.244: $\cos(3(2.244)) = 0.901$, which is (E).

CHAPTER 10: FUNCTIONS DRILL EXPLANATIONS

Drill 1: Weird Symbols as Functions, p. 254

19. **B** Just follow instructions on this one, and you get –64 – (–27), or –64 + 27, which is –37. (C) is a trap answer.

20. **A** You've just got to plow through this one. The original expression ¥5 + ¥6 becomes $5(3)^2 + 5(4)^2$, which equals 125. Work through the answer choices from the top to find the one that gives you 125. Choice (E) is a trap answer.

21. **B** The function §a leaves even numbers alone and flips the signs of odd numbers. That means that the series §1 + §2 + §3…§100 + §101 will become (–1) + 2 + (–3) + 4 + (–5) … + 100 + (–101). Rather than adding up all those numbers, find the pattern: –1 and 2 add up to 1; –3 and 4 add up to 1; and so on, all the way up to –99 and 100. That means 50 pairs that add up to 1, plus the –101 left over. 50 + –101 = –51.

Drill 2: Functions Using Standard Notation, p. 256

1.   **E** $f(–1) = (–1)^2 – (–1)^3 = 1 – (–1) = 1 + 1 = 2$

3.   **B** $f(7) = 10.247$. $f(8) = 11.314$. That's a difference of 1.067.

11. **B** $g(3) = 3^3 + 3^2 – 9(3) – 9 = 0$

14. **D** $f(3, –6) = \dfrac{3(–6)}{3 + (–6)} = \dfrac{–18}{–3} = 6$

15. **A** PITA for n, plug each answer choice into $h(x)$, and see which one spits out 10. Alternately, you could solve $10 = n^2 + n – 2$ by setting n equal to 0 and factoring; the solutions are –4 and 3.

19. **E** The greatest factor of 75 not equal to 75 is 25. Therefore, $f(75) = 75 \cdot 25 = 1,875$.

20. **E** If $y = 3$, then $g(–y) = g(–3)$. Because $–3 < 0$, $g(–3) = 2|–3| = 2(3) = 6$.

37. **E** First, determine which part of the split function you need to use in order to find $f(2,3)$ and $f(0.5,4)$. In both cases xy equals an even number, so you only need to deal with the first part of the split function. Then, simply plug in the given values.

$$f(2,3) = \frac{(2)(3)^2}{2} = 9$$
$$f(0.5,4) = \frac{(0.5)(4)^2}{2} = 4$$

$$f(2,3) + f(0.5,4) = 9 + 4 = 13$$

Choose (E).

Drill 3: Compound Functions, p. 262

2. **D** Plug in a number for x. Try 3. $f(g(3)) = f(7) = 21$, and $g(f(3)) = g(9) = 13$, so the difference is 8.

8. **E** To evaluate $f(g(-2))$, first find the value of $g(-2)$, which equals $(-2)^3 - 5$, or -13. Then put that result into $f(x)$: $f(-13) = |-13| - 5 = 13 - 5 = 8$.

9. **B** Use PITA. Plug in 3 for $g(x)$: $f(3) = 5 + 3(3) = 14$. Nope—eliminate (A). Now plug in 4 for $g(x)$: $f(4) = 5 + 3(4) = 17$. Any of the other choices would leave a variable in the compound function, so (B) is the answer.

16. **D** Just plug in a nice little number, perhaps $x = 3$. You get $g(f(3)) = g(64) = 12$. Now just plug 3 into the answers for x, to see which one hits your target number, 12.

20. **C** $f(g(3)) = 5$. $g(f(3)) = 3.196$. The difference between them is 1.804.

22. **E** PITA! You are looking for the choice that makes $f(x) = 2$. Start with (C): $f(10) = \log\left(\frac{20}{2}\right) = 1$. This is too small; eliminate (A), (B), and (C). Next, try (D): $f(100) = \log\left(\frac{100}{2}\right) = 1.699$; also too small, so eliminate (D) and pick (E).

35. **B** Plug in $x = 3$, so $f(g(3)) = \frac{1-3^2}{3^2} = -\frac{8}{9}$. Next, plug $x = 3$ into each answer choice.

(A) $\frac{(3)-1}{(3)} = \frac{2}{3}$

(B) $\frac{1}{3}$

(C) $\frac{1}{(3)^2} = \frac{1}{9}$

(D) $\frac{1}{(3)-1} = \frac{1}{2}$

(E) $2 - (3) = -1$

Finally, plug each answer into $f(x)$ and look for the answer that equals $-\frac{8}{9}$. Only (B) works.

Drill 4: Inverse Functions, p. 265

7. **B** Plug a number into $f(x)$. For example, $f(2) = 1.5$. Since $g(1.5) = 2$, the correct answer is the function that turns 1.5 back into 2. Choice (B) does the trick.

18. **B** PITA, starting with (C). Take each answer choice, plug it in for x in $f(x)$, and see which one spits out 9.

30. **E** The fact that $f(3) = 9$ doesn't tell you what $f(x)$ is. It's possible that $f(x) = x^2$, or that $f(x) = 3x$, or that $f(x) = 2x + 3$, and so on. Each of these functions would have a different inverse function. The definition of the inverse function cannot be determined.

31. **C** Plug in! This question is looking for the inverse of $f(x)$. Make $x = 10$, so $f(10) = \sqrt{\dfrac{10+2}{3}} = \sqrt{4} = 2$.
    Next, plug 2 into each answer choice and look for an answer that equals 10. Only (C) fits.

Drill 5: Domain and Range, p. 273

9. **A** This function factors to $f(x) = \dfrac{1}{x(x-3)(x+2)}$. Three values of x will make this fraction undefined: -2, 0, and 3. The function's domain must exclude these values.

15. **E** This function factors to $g(x) = \sqrt{(x+2)(x-6)}$. The product of these binomials must be nonnegative (that means positive or zero), since a square root of a negative number is not a real number. The product will be nonnegative when both binomials are not positive ($x \leq -2$) or when both are nonnegative ($x \geq 6$). The function's domain is $\{x: x \leq -2 \text{ or } x \geq 6\}$.

16. **D** Take this one step at a time. Because a number raised to an even power can't be negative, the range of a^2 is the set of nonnegative numbers—that is, $\{y: y \geq 0\}$. The range of $a^2 + 5$ is found by simply adding 5 to the range of a^2, $\{y: y \geq 5\}$. Finally, to find the range of $\dfrac{a^2+5}{3}$, divide the range of $a^2 + 5$ by 3, $\left\{y: y \geq \dfrac{5}{3}\right\}$, or $\{y: y \geq 1.67\}$. The correct answer is (D).

19. **D** Because this is a linear function (without exponents), you can find its range over the given interval by plugging in the bounds of the domain. $f(-1) = -1$, and $f(4) = 19$. Therefore, the range of f is $\{y: -1 \leq y \leq 19\}$.

28. **E** Start by finding the smallest value for $f(x)$ within the domain $-3 \leq x \leq 3$. Because x^4 is a variable to an even exponent, the smallest value for that term is 0. If $x^4 = 0$, then the fraction becomes $\dfrac{0-2}{3} = -\dfrac{2}{3} = -0.667$, which is the lowest part of the range of $f(x)$; eliminate (A) and (C). Next,

check the extremes of the domain: $f(3) = \dfrac{(3)^4 - 2}{3} = 26.333$ and $f(-3) = \dfrac{(-3)^4 - 2}{3} = 26.333$.

Checking values between -3 and 3 confirms that 26.333 is the greatest value for $f(x)$; choose (E).

Drill 6: Identifying Graphs of Functions, p. 278

1. **D**   It's possible to intersect the graph shown in (D) twice with a vertical line, where the point duplicates an x-value on the curve.

3. **B**   It's possible to intersect the graph shown in (B) more than once with a vertical line, at each point where the graph becomes vertical.

Drill 7: Range and Domain in Graphs, p. 284

17. **A**   The graph has a vertical asymptote at $x = 0$, so 0 must be excluded from the domain of f.

24. **D**   Only two x-values are absent from the graph, $x = 2$ and $x = -2$. The domain must exclude these values. This can be written as $\{x: x \neq -2, 2\}$ or $\{x: |x| \neq 2\}$.

28. **C**   The graph extends upward forever, but never goes lower than -3. Its range is therefore $\{y: y \geq -3\}$.

37. **C**   Plug in a big number, such as $x = 1{,}000$. It looks like y approaches 5.

48. **E**   Plug the numbers you are given into the equation to see what happens to the graph. In (I), if $x = 2$, then $y = -\dfrac{1}{0}$, which does not exist. Therefore I is definitely an asymptote, and you should eliminate answer choices without (I) in them, that is, (B) and (C). Now, try plugging in a big number for x, like $x = 1{,}000$. The value of y heads toward -1, which means $y = -1$ is also an asymptote, and (III) is correct. Cross off answer choices without (III) in them, in other words, (A) and (D). The correct answer is (E).

Drill 8: Roots of Functions in Graphs, p. 286

16. **D**   PITA! Plug in each choice for x into $f(x)$ to see which one spits out 0.

19. **C**   The function $g(x)$ can be factored as $g(x) = x(x + 3)(x - 2)$. Set this function equal to zero and solve for x. You'll find the function has three distinct roots, -3, 0, and 2.

25. **D**   The roots of a function are the x-values at which $f(x) = 0$. In short, the roots are the x-intercepts—in this case, -4, -1, and 2.

Drill 9: Symmetry in Functions, p. 290

6. **D** "Symmetrical with respect to the x-axis" means reflected as though the x-axis were a mirror. That is, the values of the function above the x-axis should match corresponding values below the x-axis.

17. **E** An even function is one for which $f(x) = f(-x)$. This is true by definition of an absolute value. Confirm by plugging in numbers.

30. **A** For an odd function, all points are reflected across the origin. Therefore, every point in Quadrant I will have a reflection in Quadrant III, and every point in Quadrant II will have a reflection in Quadrant IV. The only graph which satisfies this requirement is (A).

34. **C** If $f(x)$ is a function, it has no more than one y-value for any x-value; therefore, it cannot be symmetrical with respect to the x-axis. Eliminate (D) and (E). For any even function, $f(-x) = f(x)$, so plug some numbers in. Try $x = 2$ and $x = -2$. If $x = 2$, then $f(2) = 0.296$, and if $x = -2$, then $f(-2) = -0.296$. These are not equal; eliminate (B). If a function is odd, then $f(-x) = -f(x)$. In this case, you can see that $f(-2) = -f(2)$. You can plug in other values to confirm, but each choice will satisfy $f(-x) = -f(x)$, so the function is odd. Choose (C).

Drill 10: Degrees of Functions, p. 298

8. **B** Count the number of times the graph crosses the x-axis. Each intersection is a distinct real root.

17. **E** The graph shown has five visible distinct x-intercepts (zeros), so it must be at least fifth-degree. The degree of a function is determined by its greatest exponent. Only the function in (E) is at least a fifth-degree function.

20. **D** Since the degree of a function is determined by its greatest exponent, all you need to do in order to find the fourth-degree function is figure out the greatest exponent in each answer choice when it's multiplied out. Remember, you don't need to do all of the algebra; just see what the greatest exponent will be. Choice (A) is a second-degree function, because its highest-order term is x^2. Choices (B) and (C) are third-degree functions, because the highest-order term in each function is x^3. Choice (E) is a fifth-degree function, since $x \cdot x \cdot x^3 = x^5$. Only (D) is a fourth-degree function.

Comprehensive Functions Drill, p. 300

1. **B** Start by putting 3 and 1.5 into the function for x and y: $(3)^2(1.5) + 2(3)(1.5) - (1.5) = 21$. Next, plug each answer choice into the function, using the first term for x and the second term for y. The only one that equals 21 is (B).

3. **C** Start with the inside function: $g(2.7) = \sqrt[3]{(2.7)} = 1.392$. Then plug this value into $f(x)$:

$$f(1.392) = \frac{(1.392)^2 + 3}{2} = 2.469, \text{(C)}.$$

5. **E** Because the numerator is an odd root, it does not affect the domain of $g(x)$. The restrictions on the domain are entirely due to the denominator. You cannot have a denominator of 0; therefore, x cannot equal 3. Eliminate (B), (C), and (D). You cannot take the square root of a negative number, so x cannot be less than 3 either. Eliminate (A) and choose (E).

11. **E** For a function to be even, it must be reflected across the y-axis. This function does not fit that description; points in the first quadrant do not have their corresponding points in the second. Eliminate (A) and (D). An odd function has symmetry across the origin. The algebraic definition is that $f(-x) = -f(x)$ for all points in the domain. This is the case for this graph, so (II) is true; eliminate (C). Finally, if you draw the line $y = -x$, you find that the function is symmetrical across this line. Statement (III) is also true, so choose (E).

18. **D** The function $g(x)$ is an upward-opening parabola with its vertex on the origin. $f(x)$ opens downward, so you need a function with a $-g(x)$; eliminate (A) and (B). $f(x)$ is shifted to the left of the y-axis, so you need to add within the parentheses; eliminate (E). Finally, $f(x)$ has its vertex above the x-axis, so you need to add outside the parentheses; eliminate (C) and choose (D).

27. **C** To have an asymptote, a function must be a fraction. Eliminate (B) and (E). A function has a vertical asymptote wherever its denominator is equal to 0. Plug $x = 3$ into the denominator of each function. The only denominator that equals 0 when $x = 3$ is (C).

28. **D** To find $f(f(f(-2)))$ start with the innermost term. Because $-2 < -1$, use the uppermost definition for the first term: $f(-2) = (-2)^2 - 3 = 1$. Now, find $f(f(1))$. 1 falls into the middle range, so apply that definition: $f(1) = e^1 = 2.718$. Finally, find $f(2.718)$ by using the last definition: $f(2.718) = \ln 2.718 = 1$, (D).

32. **A** Plug in $x = 4$, so $f(4) = \frac{2}{(4)^2} = 0.125$. Plug 0.125 into each answer choice and look for the answer that equals 4. Only (A) works.

44. **B** Plug in $x = 3$, so $f(g(3)) = 2(3)^2 = 18$ and $g(3) = (3)^2 - 1 = 8$. Plug 8 into each answer choice and look for the answer that equals 18. Only (B) works.

45. **D** In (A), taking the absolute value of a function will reflect any negative portion of the function across the x-axis, and the negative absolute value will reflect the result back across the x-axis. However, the function will remain periodic. Choice (B) moves the whole function left two units and up two units, but the function will remain periodic. Choice (C) stretches the function vertically by a multiple of 3 and shifts the graph to the right 2 units, but it still is periodic. In (D), you find a

different kind of transformation. Multiplying $f(x)$ by x will change the value of the function in a non-repeating manner because x keeps changing (as opposed to the other answer choices in which the transformation is constant). For example, take $f(x) = \cos x$. The period is 2π, so $f(0) = f(2\pi) = 1$. However, if you multiply $f(x)$ by x, the function is now $xf(x) = x\cos x$, so $(0)f(0) = (0)\cos(0) = 0$ but $(2\pi)f(2\pi) = (2\pi)\cos(2\pi) = 2\pi$. Other values of x will also show that $xf(x)$ is no longer periodic.

If $f(x)$ is periodic, (E) will also be periodic, as you are repeatedly dividing 1 by the same values of $f(x)$.

49. **D** If $f(g(x)) = x$, then $g(x)$ is the inverse of $f(x)$. To find the inverse, choose points on the graph of $f(x)$ and eliminate answer choices that do not have a corresponding point. Estimate that the y-intercept of $f(x)$ is $(0, 2)$. If $f(0) = 2$, then $g(2) = 0$, so you need a graph that includes the point $(2, 0)$. Eliminate (A), (B), and (E). Next, estimate that x-intercept of $f(x)$ is $(-2, 0)$. This means $g(x)$ must include the point $(0, -2)$. Eliminate (C) and choose (D).

CHAPTER 11: STATISTICS AND SETS DRILL EXPLANATIONS

Drill 1: Statistics, p. 308

11. **B** If the sum of a list's elements is zero, then the mean must also be zero. It's impossible to know what the median is; the list could be {0, 0, 0, 0, 0, 0, 0, 0, 0, 0} or {−9, 1, 1, 1, 1, 1, 1, 1, 1, 1}. Both lists add up to zero, but have different medians. The mode is not necessarily zero for the same reasons.

35. **C**

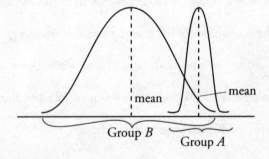

You can either draw a nice pair of bell curves like the ones we've made, or just plug in some numbers. Imagine that Group A has the scores 5, 5, 5 and Group B has the scores 1, 5, 6. The mean of A is greater, and the standard deviation of B is greater (simply because the values are more spread out), but (A), (B), (D), and (E) are all false. Choice (C) may sound vague, but go complain to the College Board. Really, the stuff about the mean is just a smokescreen.

37. **B** A boxplot does not give you information about the sum of the data or the number of data points. Therefore, you cannot find the mean from a boxplot; eliminate (A), (D), and (E). To find the interquartile score, find the difference between the first and third quartiles (the ends of the box): 130 − 85 = 45. The number in the middle of the box is the median, so the range from the highest score to the median score is 160 − 115 = 45; choose (B). The range of all the students is 160 − 60 = 100, which is not twice the interquartile range.

Drill 2: Probability, p. 314

1. **A** There are only two things that can happen, rain or not rain. If 5 out of 12 possible outcomes mean rain, then the other 7 of the 12 possible outcomes must mean no rain.

3. **A** The probability that two events will occur together is the product of the chances that each will happen individually. The probability that these two events will happen together is $\frac{2}{5} \cdot \frac{1}{3}$ or $\frac{2}{15}$.

6. **B** Out of a total of 741 cookies, 114 are burned. The probability of getting a burned cookie is therefore $\frac{114}{741}$. That reduces to $\frac{1}{6.5}$, which is equivalent to $\frac{2}{13}$.

11. **B** For the product of the numbers to be odd, both numbers must be odd themselves. There's a $\frac{3}{6}$ chance of getting an odd number on each die. The odds of getting odd numbers on both dice are $\frac{3}{6} \cdot \frac{3}{6} = \frac{9}{36} = \frac{1}{4}$.

30. **C** This one's pretty tricky. It's difficult to compute the odds of getting "at least one basket" in three tries, since there are so many different ways to do it (basket-basket-basket, miss-miss-basket, basket-basket-miss, and so on). It's a simpler solution to calculate the odds of Heather's missing all three times. If the probability of her making a basket on any given try is $\frac{4}{5}$, then the probability of her missing is $\frac{1}{5}$. The probability of her missing three times in a row is $\frac{1}{5} \cdot \frac{1}{5} \cdot \frac{1}{5}$, or $\frac{1}{125}$. That means that Heather makes no baskets in 1 out of 125 possible outcomes. The other 124 possible outcomes must involve her making at least 1 basket.

45. **D** Plug in $b = 3$, $r = 4$, and $g = 5$. The probability that the first marble is blue is $\frac{3}{12}$. Once you've removed that blue marble, you have 11 marbles left, so the probability that the second marble is red is $\frac{4}{11}$. The probability of both events occurring will be the product: $\left(\frac{3}{12}\right)\left(\frac{4}{11}\right) = \frac{12}{132} = \frac{1}{11}$. Plug in to each answer choice and look for that one that equals $\frac{1}{11}$. Only (D) works.

Drill 3: Permutations, Combinations, and Factorials, p. 323

12. **B** All committee questions are combination questions, because different arrangements of the same people don't count as different committees. The number of permutations of 12 items in 4 spaces is $12 \times 11 \times 10 \times 9$, or 11,880. To find the number of combinations, divide this number by $4 \times 3 \times 2 \times 1$, or 24. You get 495.

18. **D** The number of permutations of 6 items in 6 spaces is $6 \times 5 \times 4 \times 3 \times 2 \times 1$, or 720.

31. **A** Compute the number of combinations of females and males separately. The number of combinations of 17 females in 4 spaces is $\dfrac{17 \cdot 16 \cdot 15 \cdot 14}{4 \cdot 3 \cdot 2 \cdot 1}$, or 2,380. The number of combinations of 12 males in 3 spaces is $\dfrac{12 \cdot 11 \cdot 10}{3 \cdot 2 \cdot 1}$, or 220. The total number of combinations is the product of these two numbers, $220 \times 2,380$, or 523,600.

49. **E** Plug in $n = 5$. This is a combination question, as you are looking for the number of possible groups. Start by finding the number of arrangements of 3 teachers when you have 5 teachers available. You do so by making 3 spots, then putting in the number of available options for each spot: $5 \times 4 \times 3 = 6$. Because order doesn't matter, you then divide by the factorial of the number of spots, or $3 \times 2 \times 1$: $\dfrac{60}{6} = 10$. This is your target; make $n = 5$ in each answer choice. Only (E) works.

Drill 4: Group Questions, p. 325

10. **A** Remember the group problem formula: Total = Group 1 + Group 2 + Neither − Both. Then Plug In the numbers from the question, so $530 = 253 + 112 + N − 23$, and $N = 188$.

13. **C** Remember the group-problem formula: Total = Group 1 + Group 2 + Neither − Both. Then Plug In the numbers from the question, so $T = 14 + 12 + 37 − 9 = 54$.

28. **B** Plug in a number of tourists that you can easily take $\dfrac{1}{3}$, $\dfrac{2}{5}$, and $\dfrac{1}{2}$ of—like 30. If the total number of tourists is 30, then 10 speak Spanish, 12 speak French, and 15 speak neither language. Once again, plug these numbers into the group formula to get $30 = 10 + 12 + 15 − B$. This simplifies to $30 = 37 − B$, so $B = 7$. Seven tourists speak both Spanish and French. That's $\dfrac{7}{30}$ of the whole group.

Comprehensive Statistics and Sets Drill, p. 326

3. **D**   In this boxplot, the "whisker" between 65 and 100 represents 25% of the students. Therefore, 25% of 400, or 100, students scored in that range.

4. **C**   Remember that each number to the right of the line represents an element with the tens digit of what comes to the left of the line and the units digit of what comes to the right. In other words, this set of data contains the elements 30, 30, 30, 31, 31, 32, 32, 32, 38, and 39 in the 30-39 range. To find the median, the easiest thing to do is to cross out the highest and lowest values until you are left with the middle values. In this set, there are an even number of elements, so you take the mean of the two middle values (39 and 40) to find the median, which is 39.5.

14. **A**   Find the mean by adding up the total bacteria count for the week and dividing by 7: $2{,}071{,}768 \div 7 = 295{,}967$. A value within 30,000 of this will be between 265,967 and 325,967. No days are within this range.

15. **A**   Standard deviation is a measure of how closely packed the elements are around the mean. Choice (A) is a set of values all equal to each other, so the standard deviation is lower than all the other choices.

16. **A**   Use the group equation: Total = Group 1 + Group 2 + Neither − Both. In this case, no one is in the neither group, so you have $350 = 179 + \text{Soda} + 0 - 57$. Solving for Soda, you find that 228 people bought soda. You want to find how many more people bought only soda than only popcorn, so subtract: $228 - 179 = 49$, which is (A).

18. **B**   Make slots and fill in the numbers. You only want Monday through Friday, so there are five slots. Don has 14 choices for Monday, 13 left for Tuesday, etc., until he has 10 left for Friday. Then multiply: $14 \times 13 \times 12 \times 11 \times 10 = 240{,}240$, which is (B).

23. **C**   Find the probability of each event happening independently, then multiply the probabilities together. The probability of the first record being crunk is $\frac{6}{28}$. Because records cannot be played more than once, there are only 27 possible records that can be played second, so the probability that the second album is punk is $\frac{10}{27}$. Similarly, there are 26 choices left for the third album, so the probability that the third album is funk is $\frac{12}{26}$. Multiply the probabilities together: $\frac{6}{28} \times \frac{10}{27} \times \frac{12}{26} = \frac{10}{273}$, which is (C).

27. **A**   Make slots and fill in the numbers. Treat the group of men separately from the group of women. For men, you are choosing 2 out of 7. That means there are $\frac{7 \times 6}{2 \times 1} = 21$ different groups of men.

For women, you are choosing 3 out of 5: $\dfrac{5 \times 4 \times 3}{3 \times 2 \times 1} = 10$ different groups of women. Each group of men could be paired up with each group of women, so multiply the two together to find the total number of groups: $21 \times 10 = 210$. Finally, use your calculator to determine the value of the answer choices given. On the TI-80 series, the factorial function is found by MATH->PRB->!. The only answer that equals 210 is (A).

32. **C** One way to approach this question is by ballparking. Probability can never be greater than 1; eliminate (D) and (E). If the probability that Jerry wins his second fencing match is already 0.94, then the probability that he wins that match or his first match must be greater; eliminate (A) and (B), and choose (C).

To solve this problem mathematically, find the probability that Jerry does not win either match, and subtract that from 1. If his chance at winning his first match is 0.57, then his chance of not winning is $1 - 0.57 = 0.43$. Similarly, if his chance of winning his second match is 0.94, then his chance of not winning is 0.06. The chance of Jerry not winning either match is $0.43 \times 0.06 = 0.03$. His chance of winning at least one match is therefore $1 - 0.03 = 0.97$.

38. **D** If Laura Jane has drawn two cards, then there are 38 cards remaining in the deck. If there is a 50% chance that the third card is between the first and second cards drawn, then there must be 19 cards between 8 and Laura Jane's second card. If you add 19 to 8, you get 27, but that's the 19th card. Because you need 19 cards in between 8 and the second card, the second card must be a 28, which is (D).

43. **E** This question, like many challenging probability questions, is easier to approach by determining the probability of the desired event NOT happening and subtracting that from 1. If nickels are worth 5 cents and dimes worth 10 cents, then the only way to get a total value of 6 cents or less is to have all pennies. It is easiest to find the probability of all pennies and subtract that from 1 to find the probability of getting at least one nickel or dime. The probability of choosing only pennies is $\left(\dfrac{32}{75}\right)\left(\dfrac{31}{74}\right)\left(\dfrac{30}{73}\right) = 0.07345$. Therefore, the probability of at least one nickel or dime is $1 - 0.07345 = 0.92655$, which rounds to the value in (E).

CHAPTER 12: MISCELLANEOUS DRILL EXPLANATIONS

Drill 1: Logarithms, p. 331

1. $2^5 = 32$, so $\log_2 32 = 5$

2. $3^4 = 81$, so $x = 81$

3. $10^3 = 1,000$, so $\log 1,000 = 3$

4. $4^3 = 64$, so $b = 4$

5. Exponents and logs undo each other, so $x^{\log_x y} = y$.

6. $7^0 = 1$, so $\log_7 1 = 0$

7. $\log_x x = 1$

8. x to what power is x^{12}? The 12th power, of course! $\log_x x^{12} = 12$

9. 1.5682—use your calculator

10. 0.6990—use your calculator

Drill 2: Logarithmic Rules, p. 333

1. $\log 20$

2. $\log_5 2$

3. $\log 3$

4. $\log_4 16 = 2$

5. $\log 75$

Drill 3: Logarithms in Exponential Equations, p. 335

1. Take the log of both sides and use the power rule. Your new equation will be $4 \log 2 = x \log 3$. Now divide both sides by $\log 3$ and you get $4\dfrac{\log 2}{\log 3} = x$. Using your calculator, you get $x = 2.5237$.

2. Use the Change of Base formula: $\log_5 18 = \dfrac{\log 18}{\log 5} = 1.7959$.

3. Use the definition of a logarithm to convert the equation: $n = \log 137 = 2.1367$.

4. Use the Change of Base formula: $\log_{12} 6 = \dfrac{\log 6}{\log 12} = 0.7211$.

5. $4^{x+2} = (4^x)(4^2) = 80$. Here's a great place to use the rule of multiplying exponents with like bases.

6. Use the Change of Base formula: $\log_2 50 = \dfrac{\log 50}{\log 2} = 5.6439$.

7. $3^{x+1} = (3^x)(3^1) = 21$

8. Use the change of base formula for the left side of the equation. $\dfrac{\log 12}{\log 3} = 2.2619$. So you know that $\log_4 x = 2.261$. Now use the definition of logs to see that $4^{2.2619} = x$, and x is about 23. Make sure not to round too early so that your answer is as close to the College Board's answer as possible.

Drill 4: Natural Logarithms, p. 339

8. **E** The graph of $\ln x$ is negative at just above $x = 0$ and then crosses the x-axis; the given graph never crosses the x-axis. Eliminate (A). The graph of $-\ln x$ therefore starts positive and then cross the x-axis, so eliminate (B) as well. The graphs of e^x and e^{-x} will always be in positive territory; eliminate (C) and (D) and choose (E).

    You can also plug in on this problem. When $x = 0$, the function must be negative. Choices (A) and (B) are undefined when $x = 0$, and (C) and (D) equal 1 when $x = 0$. The only choice that is negative at $x = 0$ is (E).

18. **B** The equation $e^z = 8$ converts into a natural logarithm: $\ln 8 = z$. To find the value of z, just type $\ln 8$ into your calculator and see what happens. You'll get 2.07944.

23. **C** All you need to know to solve this one is that $\pi \approx 3.14$ and $e \approx 2.718$. Then it's easy to put the quantities in order; just remember that you're supposed to put them in descending order.

38. **A** To solve this equation, start by isolating the e term.

$$6e^{\frac{n}{3}} = 5$$

$$e^{\frac{n}{3}} = \frac{5}{6}$$

Then, use the definition of a logarithm to change the form of the equation.

$$\ln \frac{5}{6} = \frac{n}{3}$$

$$n = 3\ln \frac{5}{6}$$

Finally, use your calculator to evaluate the logarithm.

$$n = 3(-0.1823)$$

$$n = -0.5469$$

40. **D** The equation "$\ln 1.5x = 1.5$" is equivalent to $e^{1.5} = 1.5x$, so solve this second equation:

$x = \dfrac{e^{1.5}}{1.5} = 2.988$, which is (D). Another approach is to use PITA. If you start with (C), you find

that $\ln(1.5 \times 0.405) = -0.498$, which is way too small, so eliminate (A), (B), and (C). Plugging in

(D), however, gives you $\ln(1.5 \times 2.988) = 1.5$, which makes (D) the answer.

Drill 5: Visual Perception, p. 343

12. **A**

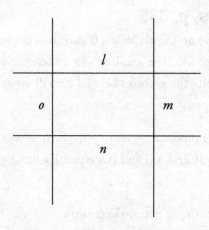

Drawing the described set of lines results in something looking like the above. As you can see, line *l* is parallel to line *n*, but neither of the other two statements is true.

30. **D** Whenever a circle intersects with a face of cube and pokes through (as opposed to touching at just one point), it creates a circle.

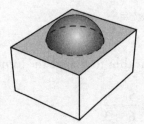

It's probably easiest to get six intersections by having the sphere intersect with all six faces of the cube.

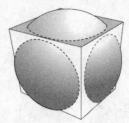

It's also possible to get five by having nearly the same picture but moving the sphere up a little so as not to intersect with the base of the cube. Seven is too complicated, though; there are only six faces of the cube, so how are there going to be seven circles?

47.   **D**   Draw it! Start by drawing circles A and B, with circle B on the inside and the radius of A twice that of B.

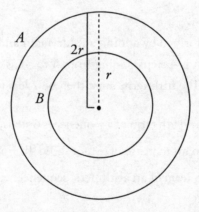

You are looking for the maximum number of regions you can create with your two chords, so draw them one at a time. Chord XY, on its own, can split both circles into two regions.

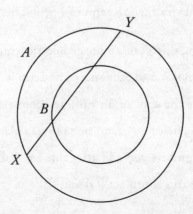

Chord *YZ* can also split both circles into two regions. Because chord *YZ* must share point *Y* with chord *XY*, it cannot split the regions created by *XY*.

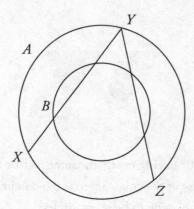

You can count the regions and find there are 7, which is (D).

Drill 6: Sequences, p. 351

14. **E** An arithmetic sequence is formed by adding a value again and again to an original term. From the second term to a sixth term is 4 steps. Going from 4 to 32 is a change of 28 in four steps, making each step an increase of 7. The fifth term must then be 7 less than the sixth term, or 25.

19. **E** Going from the first to the seventh term of a sequence is 6 steps, and going from 2 to 16 is a difference of 14. That makes each step an increase of $\frac{14}{6}$, or 2.33. To find the 33rd term, plug these numbers into the formula for the *n*th term of an arithmetic sequence: $a_{33} = 2 + (33 - 1)\ \frac{7}{3} = 2 + 74\ \frac{2}{3} = 76.67$.

26. **D** From the second term of a sequence to the fourth is two steps—that is, 4 is multiplied by the factor *r* twice to get to 25. That means that $4 \times r^2 = 25$. Solve for *r* and you'll find that $r = 2.5$. Just punch 4 into your calculator as the second term, and keep multiplying by 2.5 until you've counted up to the ninth term. *Or* figure out that the first term in the sequence is $\frac{4}{2.5}$, or 1.6. Then just plug those values into the formula for the *n*th term of a geometric sequence: $a_9 = 1.6 \times 2.5^8 = 2441.41$.

34. **C** Because no end term is given, this is an infinite geometric sequence. It's decreasing, not increasing, so its sum is finite. Its first term is 3, and each successive term is multiplied by a factor of $\frac{1}{3}$. Plug those values into the formula for the sum of an infinite geometric sequence, Of course, you can also approximate. If you add the first four terms on your calculator, you get 4.4444. So you can eliminate (A) and (B). All the numbers you add after this are really tiny, so you'll never reach 5.0 or an infinite size. Therefore, you can eliminate (D) and (E).

38. **D** Use the formula for the sum of a geometric sequence: $\text{sum} = \dfrac{a_1\left(1-r^n\right)}{1-r}$, where a_1 is the first term

in the sequence, r is the factor between terms, and n is the number of terms. 1.5 is the second term

and 4.5 is the third term, so r will be $\dfrac{4.5}{1.5}=3$. If 1.5 is the second term, the first term is $\dfrac{1.5}{3}=0.5$.

You want the first 10 terms, so your equation is $\dfrac{0.5\left(1-3^{10}\right)}{1-3}=14{,}762$, (D).

40. **D** The question asks which answer is <u>NOT</u> in the sequence. Since the equation $B_{3'} = 2B_2$ provides information about the second and third terms in the sequence, set $n = 3$ to get $B_3 = 3B_2 - 6$. Substitute $2B_2$ in for B_3 to get $2B_2 = 3B_2 - 6$. Add 6 to and subtract $2B_2$ from both sides to get $B_2 = 6$. Thus, the second term in the sequence is 6. Plug the second term 6 in for B_2 into the equation $B_3 = 3B_2 - 6$ to get $B_3 = 3(6) - 6 = 12$. Thus, the third term in the sequence is 12. Since this is an EXCEPT question, write "Yes" next to (A). At this point, you can either continue setting n equal to higher values to get further terms using the equation. Alternatively, you can read the equation as a set of instructions telling you that each term in the sequence is 3 times the previous term minus 6. Therefore, since the third term is 12, multiply it by 3 and subtract 6 to get 30, the fourth term in the sequence. Write "Yes" next to (B). Multiply 30 by 3 and subtract 6 to get 84, the fifth term. Write "Yes" next to (C). Multiply 84 by 3 and subtract 6 to get 246, the sixth term. Write "No" next to (D) since the sequence did not yield 137, and "Yes" next to (E). Since you have 4 "Yes" answers and only 1 "No," the answer is (D).

Drill 7: Limits, p. 354

30. **B** This expression factors into $\dfrac{(4x-5)(x+1)}{(4x-5)(4x+5)}$. The binomial $4x - 5$ cancels out, leaving you with

$\dfrac{(x+1)}{(4x+5)}$. This expression is no longer undefined when x equals 1.25, so just plug 1.25 into the

expression—the result is the limit. Alternatively, plug something very close to 1.25 (say, 1.24999)

into the expression and use your calculator to evaluate it. It should be very close to (B).

38. **A** This expression factors into $\dfrac{(x+4)(x-3)}{2x(x-3)}$. The binomial $x - 3$ cancels out, leaving you with $\dfrac{x+4}{2x}$.

This expression is no longer undefined when $x = 3$, so just plug $x = 3$ into the expression to obtain

the limit. Alternatively, plug in a number very close to 3 (say, 2.99) into the expression and use

your calculator to evaluate it. The result should be very close to (A).

40. **E** This expression factors into $\dfrac{x(x+7)(x-3)}{(x+7)(x+3)}$. The binomial $x + 7$ factors out, leaving you with $\dfrac{x(x-3)}{(x+3)}$. Notice, however, that the expression is *still* undefined when $x = -3$. The limit remains undefined and does not exist. Alternatively, plug in a number very close to -3 (say, -2.99) and evaluate the expression. Notice that it doesn't appear to be close to any of the numbers in the answer choices. If you want to verify that it's not going anywhere, try numbers even closer to -3 (say, -2.999 or -2.9999) until you're convinced that the limit does not exist.

Drill 8: Vectors, p. 358

36. **D** You can see from the graph that the components of $\vec{a}$ are $(-2, 4)$, and the components of $\vec{b}$ are $(-2, -1)$. So the components of $\vec{c}$ must be the result of adding the components, $(-4, 3)$. If you draw this, you can see that the magnitude of $\vec{c}$ is the length of the hypotenuse of a 3:4:5 triangle.

41. **B** Subtracting the components of **a** and **b**, you get $(5, 12)$. So the magnitude of **c** is the length of the hypotenuse of a 5:12:13 triangle.

44. **E**

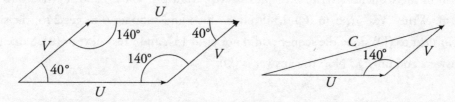

Either move **u** so that its tip points to the tail of **v**, or vice-versa; you'll get the same result either way. In any event, the angle between the vectors is now 140°. Draw in the resulting vector (we've labeled it with a length of c) from tail to head, closing off the triangle. The Law of Cosines then gives $c^2 = 9^2 + 7^2 - 2(9)(7) \cos 140°$. So $c = 15.05$. You could also approximate c, once you draw in the resulting vector.

Drill 9: Logic, pp. 361

28. **D** The basic statement here is: sophomore → not failing. The contrapositive of this statement would be: failing → not sophomore. Choice (D) is the contrapositive.

33. **B** The basic statement here is: arson → building burns. The contrapositive would be: no building burns → no arson. Choice (B) directly contradicts the contrapositive.

35. **C** The basic statement here is: not genuine → ruby. The contrapositive would be: not ruby → genuine. Choice (C) paraphrases the contrapositive.

40. **A** You are looking for the answer choice which is ALWAYS false. Reading carefully is important throughout the SAT Subject Test in Math 2, but especially on logic questions such as this. If all dogs are smelly, it doesn't matter whether or not a certain dog is a pet; it will always be smelly. Therefore, (A) is always false; it is impossible according to the information to have a dog that is not smelly. Choice (B) must be true, because you know some pets are dogs, and all dogs are smelly, so eliminate it. Choice (C) could be true, because you do not know about the smelliness of any non-dog pet. Because it could be true, (C) is not MUST be false, so eliminate it. Similarly, (D) could be true because maybe pets other than dogs are smelly, or maybe all of Ralph's pets are dogs; eliminate (D). Choice (E) is tricky; it is certainly not the case that it is necessarily true. However, it is possible with the given information that all smelly pets are dogs (though not necessary). So (E) could be true with the given information; eliminate (E).

Drill 10: Imaginary Numbers, p. 365

11. **C** Remember that the powers of i repeat in a cycle of four. Divide 51 by 4, and you'll find that the remainder is 3. i^{51} will be equal to i^3, which is $-i$.

23. **D** Only (D) contains two values that do not cancel each other out. $i^{11} = i^3(i^8) = i^3(1) = i^3 = -i$, and $i^9 = i(i^8) = i(1) = i$. So $-i - i = -2i$, not 0.

40. **B** Use FOIL on the top of the fraction, and you get $\dfrac{4 - 16i^2}{5}$, or $\dfrac{4 + 16}{5} = \dfrac{20}{5} = 4$.

43. **D** Plot the point on the complex plane; it will have a real coordinate of 5 and an imaginary coordinate of -12. The Pythagorean Theorem will give you the point's distance from the origin, 13.

48. **B** Remember that $|a + bi|$ is the distance from the origin in the complex plane. Therefore, this question is asking for the point which is closest to the origin.

Drill 11: Polynomial Division, p. 368

21. **C** Divide both sides by $(x + 2)$. Now Plug In $x = 2$. $g(2) = \dfrac{16}{4} = 4$, your target number. Plug in 2 for x in the answer choices, to see which one turns into 4. Only (C) works.

27. **A** Plug in $x = 10$, and use your calculator. When 970 is divided by 7, you get 138.571. Well, $7 \times 138 = 966$, so the remainder is 4, your target number. Choice (B) is wrong. Choices (C), (D), and (E) are nowhere near 4, so only (A) can be correct. Choice (E) is the answer without the remainder.

41. **B** Plug in! Because you want remainders, you want to choose a larger value of x. Make $x = 10$. Putting x into both statements, you find that you want the remainder when 119,716 is divided by 120.

A trick to find the remainder at this point is to do the division in your calculator: you find that 119,716 ÷ 120 = 997.633. Subtract what comes before the decimal, so your calculator reads 0.633. Then multiply by what you divided by: 0.633 × 120 = 76, which is your remainder. Finally, plug $x = 10$ into each answer choice, looking for that one that equals 76. The only choice that works is (B).

Drill 12: Matrices, p. 372

30.　**D**　In matrix multiplication, the two inner dimensions (the number of columns in the first matrix and the number of rows in the second matrix) must be equal; the resulting matrix will have as many rows as the first matrix and as many columns as the second matrix.

40.　**E**　The determinant is $(1)(0) - (2)(-1) = 2$.

45.　**C**　You can write the matrix next to itself; then the six parts of the formula form straight (diagonal) lines. So you get $0 + (-4) + (-3) - (-2) - 0 - (-6) = 1$. Alternatively, if you have a calculator that can do matrices, use your calculator.

46.　**A**　Make a matrix out of the coefficients on the left-hand side of the equations.

$$\begin{bmatrix} 2 & 3 & -1 \\ 1 & -3 & 2 \\ 1 & 0 & 1 \end{bmatrix}$$

The determinant is $-6 + 6 + 0 - 3 - 0 - 3 = -6$.

Alternatively, if you have a calculator that can do matrices, use your calculator.

Comprehensive Miscellaneous Drill, p. 377

7.　**E**　To find $\vec{a} - \vec{b}$, find $\vec{a} + \left(-\vec{b}\right)$. If $\vec{b} = (3, 5)$, then $-\vec{b} = (-3, -5)$, so

$\vec{a} + \left(-\vec{b}\right) = (5, 3) + (-3, -5) = (2, -2)$, (E).

10.　**D**　To find the absolute value of a complex number, use the Pythagorean Theorem: $10^2 + \left(-24^2\right) = c^2$, $676 = c^2$, $c = 26$. Choice (D) is correct.

You can also use your calculator on this question. On the TI-84, press MATH -> NUM -> abs to find absolute value, then input the expression (i is 2ND -> "." on the TI-84), close the parenthesis, and press ENTER.

17. **C**

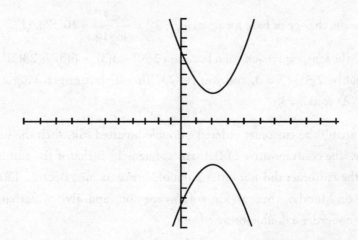

Draw it! The graph of $f(x) = (x-2)^2 + 3$ is a parabola 2 units to the right of the y-axis and 3 units above the x-axis, while $g(x) = -(x-2)^2 - 4$ is a downward-opening parabola 2 units to the right of the y-axis and 4 units below the x-axis. Both parabolas change value at equal rates, so the line equidistant between the two will be a horizontal line; eliminate (A), (D), and (E). The midpoint between the two parabolas will be below the x-axis, so you need a line for which y is negative; choose (C).

22. **A** Factor the expression: $\lim\limits_{x \to 2} \dfrac{x^3 + x^2 - 6x}{x^2 - 5x + 6} = \dfrac{x(x+3)(x-2)}{(x-3)(x-2)}$. Cancel out the $(x-2)$ terms, and you

are left with $\lim\limits_{x \to 2} \dfrac{x(x+3)}{x-3} =$. Plug in $x = 2$ and you find $\lim\limits_{x \to 2} \dfrac{2(2+3)}{2-3} = -10$, (A).

23. **C** The question asks which expression is equal to a. In order to isolate a, use inverse operations to first invert the base of 7 by taking the log base 7 of both sides to get $\log_7 \left(7^{\log_5 a}\right) = \log_7 (b)$. The log base 7 and the base of 7 will cancel, leaving you with $\log_5 a = \log_7 b$. Next, invert the log base 5 by giving a base of 5 to both sides $5^{\log_5 a} = 5^{\log_7 b}$. The base of 5 and the log base 5 will cancel, leaving you with $a = 5^{\log_7 b}$. The answer is (C).

26. **E** Plug in $x = 2$, $y = 3$, and $z = 5$. The expression becomes $\log \left(\dfrac{(2^3)(3)}{5} \right) = 0.681$. The only choice that matches is (E).

Alternatively, use logarithm rules: multiplication of terms after log is the same as adding the logarithms, and division is the same as subtraction, so $\log \left(\dfrac{x^3 y}{z} \right) = \log x^3 + \log y - \log z$. The power rule lets you pull the exponent out in front of the log as multiplication:

$\log x^3 + \log y - \log z = 3\log x + \log y - \log z$.

29. **E**   The equation $\log_7 x = 14$ tells you the same information as $x = 7^{14}$. Therefore, you are looking for $\log_{14} 7^{14}$. Use the change of base formula: $\log_{14} 7^{14} = \dfrac{\log 7^{14}}{\log 14} = 10.323$, (E).

31. **A**   Plug in $x = 3$. The long expression then becomes $2(3)^5 - 3(3)^4 + 6(3)^3 + 23(3)^2 - 25(3) + 6 = 219$. You can divide that by $2(3) - 3 = 3$, and you get 73. That is your target. Plug $x = 3$ in to each answer choice. Only (A) equals 73.

32. **D**   Bethany says that if the customer ordered a double-breasted suit, then the suit won't be ready until after Monday. The contrapositive of Bethany's statement is that if the suit is ready on Monday or earlier, then the customer did not order a double-breasted suit. Because Diana states that the suit will be ready on Monday, then we know from the contrapositive of Bethany's statement that the customer did not order a double-breasted suit.

39. **D**   Because you need to test (III), plug in numbers for x and z that are opposite, like 3 and -3, and set y equal to 0, as in (II). If you now multiply these matrices on your calculator, you will see that this works. Because x wasn't set to zero, (I) doesn't have to be true, and (A), (C), and (E) can be eliminated. Both (B) and (D) say that (II) works, so test (III) again. If you make $x = 3$, $y = 0$, and $z = -4$, the product matrix does not work. Statement (III) must always be true, so choose (D).

You can also approach this question using matrix multiplication. The product of the two matrices (ignoring the given product for the moment) would be $\begin{bmatrix} 0 & 0 \\ 2 & 2 \end{bmatrix} \times \begin{bmatrix} x & y \\ z & 0 \end{bmatrix} = \begin{bmatrix} 0x + 0z & 0y + 0 \\ 2x + 2z & 2y + 0 \end{bmatrix}$.

The first row will obviously equal the given zeroes, so you only have to make sure that $2x + 2z = 0$ and that $2y = 0$. Solving each equation, you find that $x = -z$ and $y = 0$, so Statements (II) and (III) are true.

41. **B**   The question asks for the best description of the graph produced by the parametric equations. To determine this, first eliminate the parameter. In this case, the parameter cannot be eliminated by adding or subtracting the equations, so use substitution. First, isolate t in the x-equation by subtracting 3 from both sides.

$$t = x - 3$$

Next, substitute in $x - 3$ for t in the y-equation.

$$y = 9 - (x - 3)^2$$

At this point, you may recognize that by changing the order of the terms to $y = -(x - 3)^2 + 9$, the equation will be in the vertex form of a quadratic, and thus will yield a parabola when graphed. If you're less familiar with the vertex form, however, you can continue by foiling the $(x - 3)^2$ to produce

$$y = 9 - (x^2 - 6x + 9)$$

$$= 9 - x^2 + 6x - 9$$

$$= -x^2 + 6x$$

which is the $ax^2 + bx + c$ general form. In either form, the answer is (B).

44. **C** All the weird symbols break down into asking for the sum of an infinite geometric sequence: $\sum\limits_{n=1}^{\infty}$ is telling you to add all the values of the function for each n from one to infinity, and $7\left((-0.5)^{n-1}\right)$ is the algebraic form of a geometric sequence starting at 7 and with a constant ratio of -0.5. Because the constant ratio is between -1 and 1, you know that there will be a value for the infinite series, so eliminate (E). Next, use the formula $\dfrac{a_1}{1-r}$ to find the sum of the infinite series, where a_1 is the starting term and r is the common ratio: $\dfrac{7}{1-(-0.5)} = 4.667$, (C).

45. **C** Plug In the Answers! Start with (C). If the first term is 20, then you need to find the 11th term using the formula $a_n = a_1 + (n-1)d : a_{11} = 20 + (11-1)4 = 60$. To find the sum of the first n terms, use the formula $\text{sum} = n\left(\dfrac{a_1 + a_n}{2}\right) : 11\left(\dfrac{20+60}{2}\right) = 440$. This is what you want, so choose (C).

Part V
Final Practice Test

Chapter 13
Practice Test 2

MATHEMATICS LEVEL 2

For each of the following problems, decide which is the BEST of the choices given. If the exact numerical value is not one of the choices, select the choice that best approximates this value. Then fill in the corresponding oval on the answer sheet.

Notes: (1) A scientific or graphing calculator will be necessary for answering some (but not all) of the questions on this test. For each question, you will have to decide whether or not you should use a calculator.

(2) For some questions in this test you may have to decide whether your calculator should be in the radian mode or the degree mode.

(3) Figures that accompany problems on this test are intended to provide information useful in solving the problems. They are drawn as accurately as possible EXCEPT when it is stated in a specific problem that its figure is not drawn to scale. All figures lie in a plane unless otherwise indicated.

(4) Unless otherwise specified, the domain of any function f is assumed to be the set of all real numbers x for which $f(x)$ is a real number. The range of f is assumed to be the set of all real numbers $f(x)$, where x is in the domain of f.

(5) Reference information that may be useful in answering the questions on this test can be found below.

THE FOLLOWING INFORMATION IS FOR YOUR REFERENCE IN ANSWERING SOME OF THE QUESTIONS ON THIS TEST.

Volume of a right circular cone with radius r and height h:

$$V = \frac{1}{3}\pi r^2 h$$

Lateral area of a right circular cone with circumference of the base c and slant height ℓ: $S = \frac{1}{2}c\ell$

Volume of a sphere with radius r: $V = \frac{4}{3}\pi r^3$

Surface area of a sphere with radius r: $S = 4\pi r^2$

Volume of a pyramid with base area B and height h:

$$V = \frac{1}{3}Bh$$

USE THIS SPACE FOR SCRATCHWORK.

1. If $xy \neq 0$ and $3x = 0.3y$, then $\dfrac{y}{x} =$

 (A) 0.1
 (B) 1.0
 (C) 3.0
 (D) 9.0
 (E) 10.0

2. If $f(x) = \left(3\sqrt{x} - 4\right)^2$, then how much does $f(x)$ increase as x goes from 2 to 3 ?

 (A) 1.43
 (B) 1.37
 (C) 1.00
 (D) 0.74
 (E) 0.06

GO ON TO THE NEXT PAGE

3. What is the equation of a line with a *y*-intercept of 3 and an *x*-intercept of –5 ?

    (A) $y = 0.6x + 3$
    (B) $y = 1.7x - 3$
    (C) $y = 3x + 5$
    (D) $y = 3x - 5$
    (E) $y = -5x + 3$

USE THIS SPACE FOR SCRATCHWORK.

4. For what positive value of *a* does $a - \sqrt{5a + 18}$ equal –4 ?

    (A) 0.56
    (B) 1.00
    (C) 1.12
    (D) 2.06
    (E) 4.12

5. If the second term in an arithmetic sequence is 4, and the tenth term is 15, what is the first term in the sequence?

    (A) 1.18
    (B) 1.27
    (C) 1.38
    (D) 2.63
    (E) 2.75

6. If $g(x) = \left| 5x^2 - x^3 \right|$, then $g(6) =$

    (A) –54
    (B) –36
    (C) 36
    (D) 216
    (E) 396

GO ON TO THE NEXT PAGE

7. Which of the following graphs of functions is symmetrical with respect to the line $y = x$?

(A)

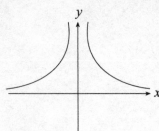

(D)

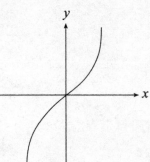

(B)

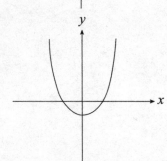

(E)

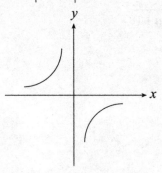

(C)

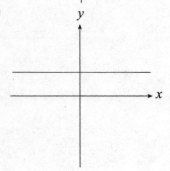

8. If $0° \le A \le 90°$ and $\sin A = \dfrac{1}{3} \sin 75°$, then $A =$

(A) 12.9°

(B) 18.8°

(C) 25.0°

(D) 32.2°

(E) 45.0°

GO ON TO THE NEXT PAGE

MATHEMATICS LEVEL 2—*Continued*

9. If $f(x) = \frac{1}{2}x^2 - 6x + 11$, then what is the minimum value of $f(x)$?

(A) −8.0
(B) −7.0
(C)   3.2
(D)   6.0
(E) 11.0

USE THIS SPACE FOR SCRATCHWORK.

10. $|x - y| + |y - x| =$

(A) 0

(B) $x - y$

(C) $y - x$

(D) $2|x - y|$

(E) $2|x + y|$

$$0° \leq A \leq 90°$$
$$0° \leq B \leq 90°$$

11. If $\sin A = \cos B$, then which of the following must be true?

(A) $A = B$
(B) $A = 2B$
(C) $A = B + 45$
(D) $A = 90 - B$
(E) $A = B + 180$

GO ON TO THE NEXT PAGE

USE THIS SPACE FOR SCRATCHWORK.

	Total Units Production	Flawed Units
April	569	15
May	508	18
June	547	16

12. Each month, some of the automobiles produced at the Carco plant have flawed catalytic converters. According to the table above, what is the probability that a car produced in one of the three months shown will be flawed?

(A) 0.01
(B) 0.02
(C) 0.03
(D) 0.04
(E) 0.05

13. Adamsville building codes require that a wheel-chair ramp must rise at an angle (θ) of no less than 5° and no more than 7° from the horizontal. If a wheelchair ramp rises exactly 3 feet, as shown in Figure 2, which of the following could be the length of the ramp?

(A) 19.0 feet
(B) 24.0 feet
(C) 28.0 feet
(D) 35.0 feet
(E) 42.0 feet

GO ON TO THE NEXT PAGE

USE THIS SPACE FOR SCRATCHWORK.

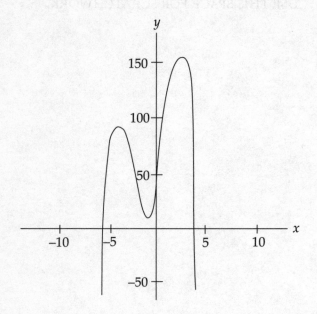

14. The figure above represents the graph of the function $y = -x^4 - 4x^3 + 14x^2 + 45x - n$. Which of the following could be the value of n?

   (A) −50
   (B) −18
   (C)   50
   (D) 100
   (E) 150

15. What value does $\dfrac{x^2 - x - 6}{3x + 6}$ approach as x approaches −2?

   (A) −1.67
   (B) −0.60
   (C)   0
   (D)   1.00
   (E)   2.33

GO ON TO THE NEXT PAGE

16. In Titheland, the first 1,000 florins of any inheritance are untaxed. After the first 1,000 florins, inheritances are taxed at a rate of 65%. How large must an inheritance be, to the nearest florin, in order to amount to 2,500 florins after the inheritance tax?

    (A) 7,143
    (B) 5,286
    (C) 4,475
    (D) 3,475
    (E) 3,308

17. In an engineering test, a rocket sled is propelled into a target. If the sled's distance d in meters from the target is given by the formula $d = -1.5t^2 + 120$, where t is the number of seconds after rocket ignition, then how many seconds have passed since rocket ignition when the sled is 10 meters from the target?

    (A) 2.58
    (B) 8.56
    (C) 8.94
    (D) 9.31
    (E) 11.26

18. $\displaystyle\sum_{k=1}^{10}(3k-2) =$

    (A) 25
    (B) 28
    (C) 145
    (D) 280
    (E) 290

19. If $e^x = 5$, then $x =$

    (A) 0.23
    (B) 1.61
    (C) 1.84
    (D) 7.76
    (E) 13.59

USE THIS SPACE FOR SCRATCHWORK.

GO ON TO THE NEXT PAGE

MATHEMATICS LEVEL 2—*Continued*

20. If the greatest possible distance between two points within a certain rectangular solid is 12, then which of the following could be the dimensions of this solid?

    (A) $3 \times 3 \times 9$
    (B) $3 \times 6 \times 7$
    (C) $3 \times 8 \times 12$
    (D) $4 \times 7 \times 9$
    (E) $4 \times 8 \times 8$

USE THIS SPACE FOR SCRATCHWORK.

21. Runner A travels *a* feet every minute. Runner B travels *b* feet every second. In one hour, runner A travels how much farther than runner B, in feet?

    (A) $a - 60b$
    (B) $a^2 - 60b^2$
    (C) $360a - b$
    (D) $60(a - b)$
    (E) $60(a - 60b)$

22. A right triangle has sides in the ratio of 5:12:13. What is the measure of the smallest angle in the triangle, in degrees?

    (A) 13.34
    (B) 22.62
    (C) 34.14
    (D) 42.71
    (E) 67.38

GO ON TO THE NEXT PAGE

23. If $f(x) = \dfrac{1}{x+1}$, and $g(x) = \dfrac{1}{x}+1$, then $g(f(x)) =$

USE THIS SPACE FOR SCRATCHWORK.

(A) 2

(B) $x + 2$

(C) $2x + 2$

(D) $\dfrac{x+2}{x+1}$

(E) $\dfrac{2x+1}{x+1}$

24. If $f(x) = (x - \pi)(x - 3)(x - e)$, then what is the greatest possible distance between points at which the graph of $y = f(x)$ intersects the x-axis?

(A) 0.14
(B) 0.28
(C) 0.36
(D) 0.42
(E) 0.72

25. $\dfrac{x!}{(x-2)!} =$

(A) 0.5
(B) 2.0
(C) x
(D) $x^2 - x$
(E) $x^2 - 2x + 1$

GO ON TO THE NEXT PAGE

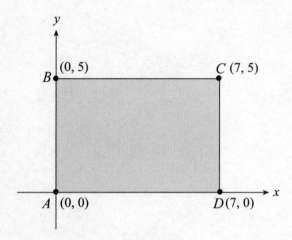

26. What is the volume of the solid created by rotating rectangle *ABCD* in the figure above around the *y*-axis?

   (A) 219.91
   (B) 245.00
   (C) 549.78
   (D) 769.69
   (E) 816.24

27. If $f(x, y) = \dfrac{x^2 - 2xy + y^2}{x^2 - y^2}$, then $f(-x, -y) =$

   (A) 1

   (B) $\dfrac{1}{x+y}$

   (C) $\dfrac{-x+y}{x+y}$

   (D) $\dfrac{-x+y}{x-y}$

   (E) $\dfrac{x-y}{x+y}$

GO ON TO THE NEXT PAGE

28. In order to disprove the hypothesis, "No number divisible by 5 is less than 5," it would be necessary to

   (A) prove the statement false for all numbers divisible by 5
   (B) demonstrate that numbers greater than 5 are often divisible by 5
   (C) indicate that infinitely many numbers greater than 5 are divisible by 5
   (D) supply one case in which a number divisible by 5 is less than 5
   (E) show that a statement true of numbers greater than 5 is also true of numbers less than 5

USE THIS SPACE FOR SCRATCHWORK.

29. A parallelogram has vertices at $(0, 0)$, $(5, 0)$, and $(2, 3)$. What are the coordinates of the fourth vertex?

   (A) $(3, -2)$
   (B) $(5, 3)$
   (C) $(7, 3)$
   (D) $(10, 5)$
   (E) It cannot be determined from the information given.

30. The expression $\dfrac{x^2 + 3x - 4}{2x^2 + 10x + 8}$ is undefined for what values of x?

   (A) $x = \{-1, -4\}$
   (B) $x = \{-1\}$
   (C) $x = \{0\}$
   (D) $x = \{1, -4\}$
   (E) $x = \{0, 1, 4\}$

GO ON TO THE NEXT PAGE ⟩

31. For which of the following functions is $f(x) > 0$ for all real values of x ?

   I. $f(x) = x^2 + 1$
   II. $f(x) = 1 - \sin x$
   III. $f(x) = \pi(\pi^{x-1})$

(A) I only
(B) II only
(C) I and III only
(D) II and III only
(E) I, II, and III

USE THIS SPACE FOR SCRATCHWORK.

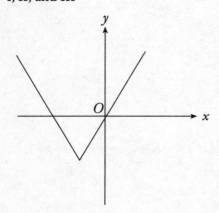

32. The graph of $y = f(x)$ is shown in the figure above. Which of the following could be the graph of $y = -f(-x)$?

(A)
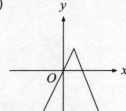

(B)
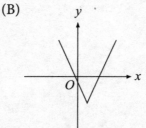

(C)
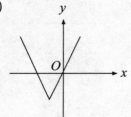

(D)
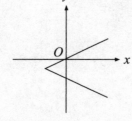

(E)
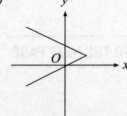

GO ON TO THE NEXT PAGE

33. A wire is stretched from the top of a two-foot-tall anchor to the top of a 50-foot-tall antenna. If the wire is straight and has a slope of $\dfrac{2}{5}$, then what is the length of the wire in feet?

    (A)   89.18
    (B)   120.00
    (C)   123.26
    (D)   129.24
    (E)   134.63

USE THIS SPACE FOR SCRATCHWORK.

34. If $\dfrac{3\pi}{2} < \theta < 2\pi$ and $\sec \theta = 4$, then $\tan \theta =$

    (A)   −3.93
    (B)   −3.87
    (C)   0.26
    (D)   3.87
    (E)   3.93

35. Circle O is centered at $(-3, 1)$ and has a radius of 4. Circle P is centered at $(4, -4)$ and has a radius of n. If circle O is externally tangent to circle P, then what is the value of n ?

    (A)   4.00
    (B)   4.37
    (C)   4.60
    (D)   5.28
    (E)   6.25

GO ON TO THE NEXT PAGE →

36. In triangle ABC, $\dfrac{\sin A}{\sin B} = \dfrac{7}{10}$ and $\dfrac{\sin B}{\sin C} = \dfrac{5}{2}$. If angles A, B, and C are opposite sides a, b, and c, respectively, and the triangle has a perimeter of 16, then what is the length of a ?

(A) 2.7
(B) 4.7
(C) 5.3
(D) 8.0
(E) 14.0

USE THIS SPACE FOR SCRATCHWORK.

x	$h(x)$
−1	0
0	3
1	0
2	3

37. The table of values above shows selected coordinate pairs on the graph of $h(x)$. Which of the following could be $h(x)$?

(A) $x(x + 1)(x - 1)$
(B) $(x + 1)^2(x - 1)$
(C) $(x - 1)(x + 2)^2$
(D) $(x - 1)^2(x + 3)$
(E) $(x - 1)(x + 1)(2x - 3)$

$$a + b + 2c = 7$$
$$a - 2b = 8$$
$$3b + 2c = n$$

38. For what values of n does the system of equations above have no real solutions?

(A) $n \neq -1$
(B) $n \leq 0$
(C) $n \geq 1$
(D) $n > 7$
(E) $n = -15$

GO ON TO THE NEXT PAGE

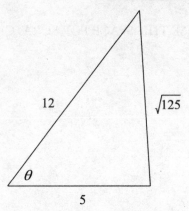

Note: Figure not drawn to scale.

USE THIS SPACE FOR SCRATCHWORK.

39. In the figure above, what is the value of θ in degrees?

(A) 62.00
(B) 65.38
(C) 65.91
(D) 68.49
(E) 68.70

40. If $\begin{vmatrix} l & m & n \\ p & q & r \\ s & t & u \end{vmatrix} = A$, then $\begin{vmatrix} 2l & 2m & 2n \\ 2p & 2q & 2r \\ 2s & 2t & 2u \end{vmatrix} =$

(A) $2A$
(B) $4A$
(C) $6A$
(D) $8A$
(E) $18A$

41. In the function $g(x) = A[\sin(Bx + C)] + D$, constants are represented by A, B, C, and D. If $g(x)$ is to be altered in such a way that both its period and amplitude are increased, which of the following constants must be <u>increased</u>?

(A) A only
(B) B only
(C) C only
(D) A and B only
(E) C and D only

GO ON TO THE NEXT PAGE

42. All of the elements of list M and list N are arranged in exactly 20 pairs, such that every element from list M is paired with a distinct element from list N. If in each such pair, the element from list M is larger than the element from list N, then which of the following statements must be true?

(A) The median of the elements in M is greater than the median of the elements in N.
(B) Any element of M is greater than any element of N.
(C) The mode of the elements in M is greater than the mode of the elements in N.
(D) The range of the elements in M is greater than the range of the elements in N.
(E) The standard deviation of the elements in M is greater than the standard deviation of the elements in N.

USE THIS SPACE FOR SCRATCHWORK.

43. If 3, 5, 8.333, and 13.889 are the first four terms of a sequence, then which of the following could define that sequence?

(A) $a_0 = 3;\ a_{n+1} = a_n + 2$

(B) $a_0 = 3;\ a_{n+1} = 2a_n - 1$

(C) $a_0 = 3;\ a_n = a_{n-1} + \dfrac{40}{9}$

(D) $a_0 = 3;\ a_n = \dfrac{5}{3}a_{n-1}$

(E) $a_0 = 3;\ a_n = \dfrac{7}{3}a_{n-1} - \dfrac{40}{9}a_{n-1}$

44. If $0 \le n \le \dfrac{\pi}{2}$ and $\cos(\cos n) = 0.8$, then $\tan n =$

(A) 0.65
(B) 0.75
(C) 0.83
(D) 1.19
(E) 1.22

GO ON TO THE NEXT PAGE

45. The height of a cylinder is equal to one-half of *n*, where *n* is equal to one-half of the cylinder's diameter. What is the surface area of this cylinder in terms of *n* ?

(A) $\dfrac{3\pi n^2}{2}$

(B) $2\pi n^2$

(C) $3\pi n^2$

(D) $2\pi n^2 + \dfrac{\pi n}{2}$

(E) $2\pi n^2 + \pi n$

46. If $(\tan\theta - 1)^2 = 4$, then which of the following could be the value of θ in radian measure?

(A) −0.785
(B)   1.373
(C)   1.504
(D)   1.512
(E)   3

47. Which of the following expresses the range of values of $y = g(x)$, if $g(x) = \dfrac{5}{x+4}$?

(A) $\{y:\ y \neq 0\}$
(B) $\{y:\ y \neq 1.25\}$
(C) $\{y:\ y \neq -4.00\}$
(D) $\{y:\ y > 0\}$
(E) $\{y:\ y \leq -1 \text{ or } y \geq 1\}$

GO ON TO THE NEXT PAGE ⇒

MATHEMATICS LEVEL 2—*Continued*

48. If $\csc\theta = \dfrac{1}{3t}$, then where defined, $\cos\theta =$

USE THIS SPACE FOR SCRATCHWORK.

(A) $3t$

(B) $\sqrt{1-3t^2}$

(C) $\sqrt{1-9t^2}$

(D) $\dfrac{3t}{\sqrt{1-3t^2}}$

(E) $\dfrac{3t}{\sqrt{1-9t^2}}$

49. If $f(x, y) = \dfrac{xy+y}{x+y}$, then which of the following

statements must be true?

   I.   If $x = 0$ and $y \neq 0$, then $f(x, y) = 1$.
   II. If $x = 1$, then $f(x, x) = 1$.
   III. $f(x, y) = f(y, x)$

(A) I only
(B) II only
(C) I and II only
(D) I and III only
(E) I, II, and III

50. A triangle is formed by the x-axis, the y-axis, and the line $y = mx + b$. If $m = -b^3$, then what is the volume of the cone generated by rotating this triangle around the x-axis?

(A) $\dfrac{\pi}{9}$

(B) $\dfrac{\pi}{3}$

(C) π

(D) 3π

(E) 9π

STOP

IF YOU FINISH BEFORE TIME IS CALLED, YOU MAY CHECK YOUR WORK ON THIS TEST ONLY.
DO NOT WORK ON ANY OTHER TEST IN THIS BOOK.

Chapter 14
Practice Test 2:
Answers and
Explanations

PRACTICE TEST 2 ANSWER KEY

Question Number	Correct Answer	Right	Wrong	Question Number	Correct Answer	Right	Wrong
1	E	___	___	26	D	___	___
2	B	___	___	27	E	___	___
3	A	___	___	28	D	___	___
4	A	___	___	29	E	___	___
5	D	___	___	30	A	___	___
6	C	___	___	31	C	___	___
7	E	___	___	32	A	___	___
8	B	___	___	33	D	___	___
9	B	___	___	34	B	___	___
10	D	___	___	35	C	___	___
11	D	___	___	36	C	___	___
12	C	___	___	37	E	___	___
13	C	___	___	38	A	___	___
14	A	___	___	39	D	___	___
15	A	___	___	40	D	___	___
16	B	___	___	41	A	___	___
17	B	___	___	42	A	___	___
18	C	___	___	43	D	___	___
19	B	___	___	44	D	___	___
20	E	___	___	45	C	___	___
21	E	___	___	46	A	___	___
22	B	___	___	47	A	___	___
23	B	___	___	48	C	___	___
24	D	___	___	49	C	___	___
25	D	___	___	50	B	___	___

PRACTICE TEST 2 EXPLANATIONS

1. **E**   The statement $xy \neq 0$ means that neither x nor y is zero. To find the value of $\frac{y}{x}$, rearrange the equation so that $\frac{y}{x}$ is isolated on one side of the equals sign; whatever's on the other side will be the answer. In this case, the easiest way to isolate $\frac{y}{x}$ is to divide each side of the equation by x, getting $3 = \frac{0.3y}{x}$, and then divide both sides by 0.3, getting $\frac{3}{0.3} = \frac{y}{x}$. Your calculator will tell you that $\frac{3}{0.3}$ is equal to 10, so the answer is (E).

2. **B**   To find the increase in $f(x)$ as x goes from 2 to 3, calculate $f(2)$ and $f(3)$ by plugging those numbers into the definition of the function. You'll find that $f(2) = 0.0589$ and $f(3) = 1.4308$. The increase in $f(x)$ is the difference between these two numbers, 1.3719. The answer is (B).

3. **A**

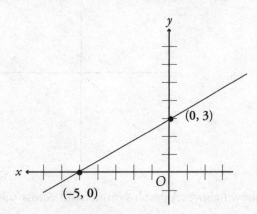

Since you are given the two intercepts, draw a rough sketch like the one above and approximate. The slope is positive, but less than 1, since the line runs more than it rises. Only (A) matches this description. You could also notice that since the y-intercept is 3, the equation of the line (in slope-intercept form) must look like $y = mx + 3$, which narrows it down to (A) or (E). But (E) has a negative slope, which doesn't fit your sketch, so the answer is (A).

4. **A**   PITA. Starting with (C), plug in the values from the answer choices for a in the original expression. Plugging in (C) will give you $1.12 - \sqrt{5(1.12) + 18} = .56 - 4.8580 = -4.2980$. Eliminate (C). It will be difficult here to tell which direction you should go next, so just pick one and keep moving. When you reach (A), you'll find that $.56 - \sqrt{5(.56) + 18} = .56 - 4.56 = -4$. The answer is (A).

5. **D**   An arithmetic series is one in which each term increases by a constant added amount. From 4 to 15 is a total increase of 11, which happens from the second term in the arithmetic series to the tenth, taking 8 steps. This means that each step is equal to one-eighth of 11, $\frac{11}{8}$, or 1.375. That's the constant amount added to each term in the series to get the next term. To find the first term in the series, just take one step backward from the second term, that is, subtract 1.375 from 4. You get 2.625.

You can also solve this problem by using the formula for the nth term of an arithmetic sequence: $a_n = a_1 + (n-1)d$. You'd start by figuring out d (the difference between any two consecutive terms) just as you did above, finding that $d = 1.375$. Then, take one of the terms you're given (for example, $a_2 = 4$, in which case $n = 2$) and use these values to fill in the formula, $4 = a_1 + (2-1)(1.375)$. Then solve for a_1. Once again you'll find that $a_1 = 2.625$. Either way, the answer is (D).

6. **C** This function question just requires you to plug 6 into $g(x)$. You can start with some POE. Eliminate (A) and (B), because the entire function is contained within an absolute value sign, so it can't produce negative values. To find the exact value of $g(6)$, plug in the number. You get $\left|5(6)^2 - (6)^3\right|$, or $|-36|$, which equals 36, so the answer is (C).

7. **E**

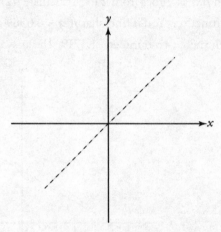

The line $y = x$ is shown above. A graph symmetrical across this line will look like it is reflected in this line as though it were a mirror. Another way to think about it is that the two halves of a curve symmetrical across the line $y = x$ would meet perfectly if you folded the paper along that line. Of the five choices, only (E) has this kind of symmetry.

8. **B** Just use your calculator. Make sure that your calculator is in degree mode.

$$\sin A = \frac{1}{3}\sin 75°$$

$$\sin A = \frac{1}{3}(0.9659)$$

$$\sin A = 0.3220$$

$$\sin^{-1}(\sin A) = \sin^{-1}(0.3220)$$

$A = 18.8°$

The answer is (B).

9. **B** This is the equation of a parabola which opens upward. The minimum value will be the y-value of the vertex, which you can find using the vertex formula. The x-coordinate of the vertex is given by $x = \dfrac{-b}{2a}$, which gives you $x = \dfrac{-(-6)}{2\left(\dfrac{1}{2}\right)} = 6$ in this case. Plug this value back into the equation to get

the y-coordinate of the vertex, $\frac{1}{2}(6)^2 - 6(6) + 11 = -7$. The function's minimum value is -7. The answer is (B).

10. **D** This is a great question for Plugging In. Plug in a couple of simple values, like $x = 3$ and $y = 5$, and solve. $|3 - 5| + |5 - 3| = |-2| + |2| = 2 + 2 = 4$. The correct answer must also equal 4. This is the target number. Plug in $x = 3$ and $y = 5$ into each answer choice. You'll find that only (D) gives you the correct value.

11. **D** Plugging In works very well here. Find simple values that make the original equation true, like $A = 90°$ and $B = 0°$, so $\sin 90° = 1$ and $\cos 0° = 1$. Then go through the answer choices to find the one that is also true when $A = 90°$ and $B = 0°$. In this case, only (D) works. Alternatively, you can also recall from trigonometry that when two angles are between 0° and 90°, the sine of one angle equals the cosine of another angle when the two angles are complements, or have a sum of 90 degrees. This is expressed in (D). This can also be written out using the trigonometric identity $\sin A = \cos (90° - A)$. The answer is (D).

12. **C** To figure out a probability, divide the number of things that satisfy the condition (in this case, flawed automobiles) by the total (all automobiles produced).

	Total Units Production	Flawed Units
April	569	15
May	508	18
June	547	16

Since you're calculating the odds for the entire three-month period, you have to add up the two columns of the chart. You find that 49 flawed automobiles were produced out of a total of 1,624. Divide 49 by 1,624 to find the probability, 0.03. The answer is (C).

13. **C**

The easiest way to find the possible ramp lengths is to find the shortest and longest legal lengths.

The length of the ramp is the hypotenuse of a right triangle. Using the SOHCAHTOA definition of sine $\left(\sin = \frac{O}{H} \right)$, you can set up equations to find the lengths of a 5°-ramp and a 7°-ramp. $\sin 5° = \frac{3}{H}$ and $\sin 7° = \frac{3}{H}$. Solve for H in each by multiplying both sides of both equations by H and then use your calculator to divide both sides of the first equation by sin 5° and both sides of second equation by sin 7°. Make sure your calculator is in degree mode! You'll find that the shortest possible hypotenuse has a length of 24.62, while the longest has a length of 34.42. Only (C) is between these limits.

14.   **A**   This question is simpler than it looks. The constant term $-n$ represents the y-intercept (where $x = 0$) of the whole complicated function. Just look to see where the function crosses the y-axis. It does so at $y = 50$. That means that $-n$, the y-intercept, equals 50. Just plain n, however, equals -50. Watch out for (C), a trap answer! The answer is (A).

15.   **A**   Here's a classic limit question. You can't just plug the x-value in the question into the function, because it makes the denominator equal zero, which means the function is undefined at that point. To find the limit of the function approaching that point (assuming the limit exists), try to cancel out the denominator by factoring. First, factor the top and bottom of the function, $\dfrac{(x+2)(x-3)}{3(x+2)}$. As you can see, the term $(x + 2)$ occurs in the numerator and the denominator, so you can cancel it out. You're left with $\dfrac{(x-3)}{3}$. Now you can plug $x = -2$ into the function without producing an undefined quantity. The result, $\dfrac{-2-3}{3} \approx -1.67$, is the limit of the function as x approaches -2. The answer is (A).

16.   **B**   This is a great PITA question. When you receive an inheritance in Titheland, you get the first 1,000 florins free and clear. After that, you get only 35% of the remaining amount; the government keeps the other 65%. To find the right answer, take the numbers from the answer choices and see which one would give you 2,500 florins after taxes.

Choice (C) is 4,475 florins. Starting with that amount, you'd get 1,000 florins free and clear, and 3,475 would be taxed. The government would take 65% of 3,475, or 2,258.75. That would leave you with 1,216.25 plus the first 1,000, for a total of 2,216.25 florins after taxes—not enough. Your next step is to select the next larger answer choice and try again. Choice (B) is 5,286 florins, which will give you 1,000 untaxed and 4,286 taxed. That means the government takes 65% of 4,286, or 2,785.9 florins, leaving you with 1,500.1. Add the untaxed 1,000, and you've got a total of 2,500.1 florins after taxes—right on the money. The answer is (B).

17.   **B**   Since the question provides a value for d, plug in! Setting $d = 10$ in the equation yields $10 = -1.5t^2 + 120$. Solve for t. Subtract 120 from both sides to get $-110 = -1.5t^2$. Divide both sides by -1.5 to get $t^2 \approx 73.3333$. Take the square root of both sides to get $t \approx 8.5635$. The answer is (B).

18. C Plug in 1 for k in the expression $3k - 2$; then repeat for 2, 3, 4, etc., all the way up to 10, and add up all the results. This gives $1 + 4 + 7 + ... + 28$. This is an arithmetic sequence where you keep adding 3. The formula for the sum of the first n terms of an arithmetic sequence is $\text{sum} = n\left(\dfrac{a_1 + a_n}{2}\right)$, which, in this case, gives $\text{sum} = 10\left(\dfrac{1 + 28}{2}\right) = 145$. The answer is (C). You can also use your calculator to solve this problem. On the TI-84, press 2ND->STAT to access the LIST menu. Under MATH, choose the fifth option: sum. Next, go back to the LIST menu and under OPS select the fifth option: seq. Input the expression under Expr (use x instead of k), the variable is x, start 1, end 10, and step 1. Paste and close the bracket and then hit ENTER. Either way, the answer is (C).

19. B Since the equation $e^x = 5$ has the variable x as an exponent, you can use inverse operations to cancel the base e by taking the natural logarithm, ln, of both sides. This yields $\ln e^x = \ln 5$. The ln and the base e cancel, leaving you with $x = \ln 5$. And that's something you can just punch into your calculator. The natural logarithm of 5 is 1.60944, which rounds to 1.61. The correct answer is (B). As an alternative, you can PITA, starting with (C), to see which value, when plugged in for x, makes the equation true.

20. E The greatest distance within a rectangular solid is the length of the long diagonal—the line between diagonally opposite corners, through the center of the solid. The length of this line can be determined using the Super Pythagorean Theorem, $a^2 + b^2 + c^2 = d^2$, where a, b, and c are the dimensions of the solid, and d is the length of the diagonal. To find the possible coordinates of the box, use the Super Pythagorean Theorem on each of the answer choices, and find the one that gives a diagonal of 12. Only (E) produces the right number, $4^2 + 8^2 + 8^2 = d^2$, and so $d = \sqrt{144}$, or 12.

21. E The variables in the answer choices tell you that this is a perfect Plugging In question. Pick a rate for each runner. Say runner A travels 100 feet every minute ($a = 200$) and runner B travels 2 feet for every second ($b = 2$). Since one hour contains 60 minutes or 3,600 seconds, A travels 60 × 200 feet, or 12,000 feet, while B travels 3,600 × 2 feet, or 7,200 feet. In this case, A travels 4,800 feet farther than B. This makes 4,800 your target number—the number the correct answer will equal. Only (E) equal 4,800 using these values. The answer is (E).

22. B Draw it!

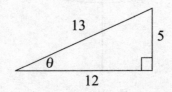

The hypotenuse of a right triangle is always its largest side, so the 13 must be opposite the right angle. The smallest angle will be opposite the side length 5, which you can call θ. Knowing this, you can use SOHCAHTOA to find the degree measurement of θ. Here, the sine will equal the opposite side over the hypotenuse. This yields $\sin \theta = \dfrac{5}{13}$, so $\theta = \sin^{-1} \dfrac{5}{13} = 22.62°$, which is (B).

23. **B** Since the question and answer choices contain variables, plug in for x. Suppose, for example, that $x = 2$. To evaluate the expression $g(f(2))$, start on the inside, $f(2) = \dfrac{1}{2+1}$, or $\dfrac{1}{3}$. Then, work with the outside function, $g\left(\dfrac{1}{3}\right) = \dfrac{1}{\frac{1}{3}} + 1$, or $3 + 1$, which equals 4. That's the value of $g(f(2))$. The correct answer choice will be the one that gives the same value (4) when you plug in $x = 2$. Choice (B) is the only one that does.

24. **D** The values at which a function intercepts the x-axis, also called the roots of the function, are those values that make the expression equal to zero. In this case, there are three roots—π, 3, and e. The greatest distance between any two roots will be the distance between the greatest and least roots. To figure out which are the greatest and least roots, use your calculator to find the values of π (3.14159…) and e (2.71828…). These are the greatest and least roots, so subtract them to find their difference, 0.42331.

25. **D** Plug in $x = 4$. Then $\dfrac{x!}{(x-2)!} = \dfrac{4!}{2!} = \dfrac{4 \times 3 \times 2 \times 1}{2 \times 1} = 12$. The correct answer will be the one that equals 12 when $x = 4$, which is (D).

26. **D** A rectangle rotated around one edge generates a cylinder. This rectangle is being rotated around the vertical axis, so the cylinder will have a radius of 7 and a height of 5, as in the figure below.

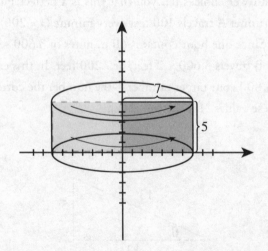

Just plug these values into the formula for the volume of a cylinder, $V = \pi r^2 h$ to get $V = \pi (7)^2 (5) =$ $245\pi \approx 769.69$. The answer is (D).

27. **E** Since there are variables in both the question and the answer choices, Plug in for x and y, for example $x = 2$ and $y = 3$. The question asks for $f(-x, -y)$, so plug these in as negatives.

$$f(-2,-3) = \frac{(-2)^2 - 2(-2)(-3) + (-3)^2}{(-2)^2 - (-3)^2}$$
$$= \frac{4 - 12 + 9}{4 - 9}$$
$$= -\frac{1}{5}$$

This is the target number. Since the answer choices are expressed in terms of x and y, not $-x$ and $-y$, make sure to test the answer choices using $x = 2$ and $y = 3$, looking for the one that gives you $-\frac{1}{5}$. The only one that works is (E).

28. **D** The question asks you to disprove the hypothesis "No number divisible by 5 is less than 5." When trying to disprove a hypothesis, the only thing necessary is to find a single counterexample. Many of the answer choices use phrasing like " all numbers," "often," or "numbers"(plural), which would indicate that many counterexamples are necessary. Since you only need to find one number less than 5 which is divisible by 5 to disprove the statement, the correct answer is (D), which says that you need "one case."

29. **E** Draw it!

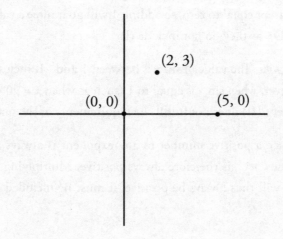

With these 3 points, there are multiple options to create a parallelogram: $(-3, 3)$, $(3, -3)$, or $(7, 3)$ would all give you different parallelograms. Because this is the case, you cannot answer the question given the information provided, so the answer is (E).

30. **A** An expression is undefined when its denominator equals zero, so first factor the expression. You'll find it equals $\dfrac{(x+4)(x-1)}{2(x+4)(x+1)}$. Two values will make this expression undefined: $x = -1$ and $x = 4$, both of which make the denominator equal to zero. Choice (A) is correct. (Note: It's true that the term $(x + 4)$ cancels out of the factored expression. That doesn't mean that the original expression is defined at $x = -4$, however. It just means that you can calculate the limit of the expression as x approaches -4. Don't confuse the existence of a limit with the defined/undefined status of an expression.) You can also PITA to see which values from the answer choices cause problems for the expression. In this case, pick an easy value that shows up in 2 or 3 answer choices, so you can eliminate the greatest number of them. Try $x = 0$. Plugging this in gives you $-\dfrac{1}{2}$, which does not have a denominator of 0. So eliminate answer choices that contain 0: eliminate (C) and (E). Next, try $x = -1$. This causes the denominator to become 0, so you know that -1 is in the correct answer. Therefore, eliminate answer choices that don't contain -1: eliminate (D). The only difference between (A) and (B) is -4. When you test $x = -4$, the denominator again becomes 0, so -4 must be in the correct answer, which is (A).

31. **C** In a Roman numeral question, tackle each statement one at a time, remembering to use Process of Elimination on the five answer choices. The expression in (I) must always be positive, as x^2 must always be greater than or equal to zero, so adding 1 will guarantee a value that is always 1 or greater. Eliminate (B) and (D), as they do not include (I).

Statement (II) is trickier. The value of $\sin x$ is between 1 and -1, inclusive, so most values of $1 - \sin x$ are positive. However, when $\sin x$ is equal to 1 (such as when $x = 90°$), then $1 - \sin x = 0$, which is not positive. Statement (II) does not fulfill the requirements of the question; eliminate (E).

Finally, for (III), since a positive number to any exponent is always a positive number, the value within the parentheses, π^{x-1}, is therefore always positive. Multiplying this by π will keep the value positive. Since (III) will thus always be positive, it must be included in the answer. The answer is (C).

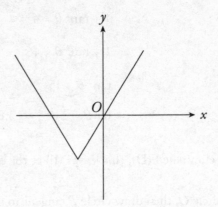

32. **A**

Changing the sign of x in the expression $f(x)$ will reflect the function's graph over the x-axis. Change the sign of the whole function to produce $-f(-x)$ will reflect the function's graph over the y-axis as well. Choice (A) is correct, because its graph represents the original graph reflected both horizontally and vertically.

33. **D** Draw it!

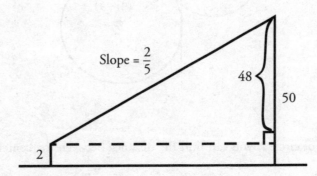

The wire rises 48 feet from the anchor to the antenna. If the slope of the wire is $\dfrac{2}{5}$, then the wire rises 2 feet for every 5 vertical feet it covers. You can use a proportion to find the horizontal distance between the anchor and the antenna: $\dfrac{2}{5} = \dfrac{48}{x}$, so $x = 120$. However, don't pick (B); that's a trap, since the question asks for the length of the wire, not the horizontal distance. The wire is the hypotenuse of a right triangle with legs 120 and 48. Therefore, you can use the Pythagorean Theorem to find the hypotenuse: $48^2 + 120^2 = c^2$, $c = 129.24$, (D).

34. **B** To start, you can do some useful elimination. The statement $\dfrac{3\pi}{2} < \theta < 2\pi$ tells you that you're working in the fourth quadrant of the unit circle, where the tangent is negative. You can immediately eliminate (C), (D), and (E). Next, since the question provides the secant and asks for the tangent, the simplest way forward is to use the Pythagorean identity $1 + \tan^2 \theta = \sec^2 \theta$. Plugging in the secant of 4 yields

$$1 + \tan^2 \theta = 4^2$$

$$1 + \tan^2 \theta = 16$$

$$\tan^2 \theta = 15$$

$$\tan \theta = \pm\sqrt{15} \approx \pm 3.8730$$

Since you've already eliminated (D), this leaves (B) as the correct answer.

35.   **C**   Draw it! Start with circle O, then draw circle P tangent to circle O:

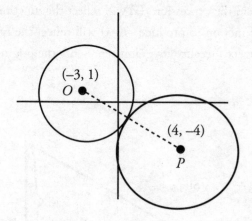

To find the radius of circle P, you can find the distance between the centers of the two circles and subtract the radius of circle O. To find the distance, use the distance formula $d = \sqrt{(x_2 - x_1)^2 + (y_2 - y_1)^2}$: $d = \sqrt{(-3 - 4)^2 + (1 - (-4))^2} = 8.6023$. Because circle O has a radius of 4, circle P must therefore have a radius of $8.6023 - 4 = 4.6023$, which is (C).

36.   **C**   The equations in the beginning of this question can be rearranged into the Law of Sines. A little algebraic manipulation gets you $\dfrac{\sin A}{7} = \dfrac{\sin B}{10}$ and $\dfrac{\sin B}{5} = \dfrac{\sin C}{2}$. Since both equations contain $\sin B$, make the $\sin B$ portion of each equation look the same by dividing the second equation by 2 on both sides to produce $\dfrac{Sin B}{10} = \dfrac{Sin C}{4}$. Now you're able to combine the two equations together to yield $\dfrac{\sin A}{7} = \dfrac{\sin B}{10} = \dfrac{\sin C}{4}$, which is the Law of Sines. This tells you that the lengths of the triangle's sides are in a ratio of 7:10:4. So, you can call the sides $7x$, $10x$, and $4x$. The perimeter is 16, so $7x + 10x + 4x = 21x = 16$, and $x = 0.7619$; side a has length $7x$, which equals approximately 5.3333. The answer is (C).

37.   E

x	$h(x)$
−1	0
0	3
1	0
2	3

Test each expression with the values from the table. The easiest one to use is 0; when you make $x = 0$, the function should equal 3. Only (D) and (E) equal 3 when $x = 0$. Then, notice that the function is equal to zero when $x = 1$ or −1. Therefore, these values must be roots of the function. Only (E) contains both 1 and −1 as roots. It's the right answer.

38.   A   This is a tricky simultaneous-equations problem. After some experimentation, you might notice that the second and third equations can be added together, yielding $a + b + 2c = n + 8$, which is very similar to the first equation, $a + b + 2c = 7$. From this, you can determine that $n + 8 = 7$, and therefore that $n = -1$. If n is any value other than −1, then no values of a, b, and c can make this system of equations true. Therefore, there is no solution for this system if $n \neq -1$. The answer is (A).

39.   D

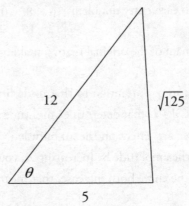

Note: Figure not drawn to scale.

When you know all three sides of a triangle, and you need to determine the measures of the angles, it's time to use the Law of Cosines, $c^2 = a^2 + b^2 - 2ab \cos C$. Just plug in the lengths of the sides, making sure that you make c the side opposite θ. $\sqrt{125}^2 = (12)^2 + (5)^2 - 2(12)(5) \cos \theta$. Simplifying this gives you the equation $\cos \theta = 0.3667$. Taking the inverse cosine of both sides (after making sure your calculator is in degree mode) shows that $\theta = 68.4898°$.

40.   D   The formula for the determinant of a 3 × 3 matrix tells you that $A = lqu + mrs + npt - mpu - lrt - nqs$. You can visualize this if you take the first two columns of the matrix and recopy them to the right of the original matrix, and make diagonal lines connecting the elements.

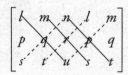

Now do the same thing with the second matrix. Since each element in the matrix now has a coefficient of 2, you'll find that each term in the determinant will now have a coefficient of 8. For example, the *mrs* term will now be $(2m)(2r)(2s)$, or $8mrs$. Thus, the determinant is now $8lqu + 8mrs + 8npt - 8mpu - 8lrt - 8nqs$. Factor out 8, and it's clear that this determinant is $8A$. The answer is (D).

Want an easier way to solve this? Go to the MATRIX menu on your graphing calculator and enter a random 3×3 matrix, like $\begin{bmatrix} 9 & 2 & 5 \\ 3 & 4 & 0 \\ 6 & 8 & 1 \end{bmatrix}$. Your calculator will tell you that the determinant of this matrix is 30. Now enter the matrix with each entry doubled: $\begin{bmatrix} 18 & 4 & 10 \\ 6 & 8 & 0 \\ 12 & 16 & 2 \end{bmatrix}$. The determinant of this matrix is 240. This is 8 times the determinant of the original matrix, making (D) the answer once again.

41. **A** This is a little tricky; you've got to pay attention to that underlined word, "increased." The values in the equation $g(x) = A[\sin (Bx + C)] + D$ that determine amplitude and period are A and B, respectively. Quantities C and D do not have any effect on the amplitude or period, so (C) and (E) are out. The trick is that while you increase the amplitude by increasing A, you increase the period by *decreasing B*. If the amplitude and period of the curve both increase, that means that A increases and B decreases.

42. **A** All the fancy language in this question basically boils down to this: List M and list N each contains 20 elements; each element in list M is larger than the corresponding element in list N.

Once you have a clear idea of what that means, tackle the answer choices one at a time. Since the middle two values of M are bigger than the middle two values of N, the median of M must be greater, and (A) is correct. If you don't see this right away, you can always eliminate the other answer choices. You can eliminate (B) because it's quite possible that the largest value in list N is larger than the smallest value in list M. You don't know anything about the modes of the two lists, so cross off (C). For (D), suppose that each element in M is exactly 1 greater than the corresponding element in N. The ranges would be identical, so you can cross off (D). In that same situation, the standard deviations of the two lists would be identical, so you can cross off (E).

43. **D** This problem looks scary, but it's really just a matter of plugging in. Each answer choice says that the first term is 3, and then each one gives a different definition of the sequence. In the

given sequence, $a_0 = 3$, $a_1 = 5$, $a_2 = 8.333$, and $a_3 = 13.889$. Plug in values of n to see if the terms you are given fit the equations in each answer choice. If you plug $n = 0$ into (A), you get $a_{0+1} = a_0 + 2$. Well, $5 = 3 + 2$, so this seems to work. Now plug $n = 1$ into (A). This gives $a_{1+1} = a_1 + 2$. But $8.333 \neq 5 + 2$, so (A) doesn't define the sequence. In (B), plug in $n = 0$ again, which gives $a_{0+1} = 2a_0 - 1$. This works, because $5 = 2(3) - 1$. But when you try $n = 1$, you get $a_{1+1} = 2a_1 - 1$, which is wrong, because $8.333 \neq 2(5) - 1$. Cross off (B). Repeating this process for (C), plug in $n = 1$, which fails. Choice (D) works for all the terms given. It turns out that this is a geometric sequence with a constant factor of $\frac{5}{3}$. Finally, check (E) by plugging in $n = 1$, which fails as well. The answer is (D).

44. **D** The statement $0 \leq n \leq \frac{\pi}{2}$ tells you that you're working in the first quadrant of the unit circle where both sine and cosine are never negative. The unit $\frac{\pi}{2}$ tells you that you'll be working with angles in radians, not degrees. Make sure your calculator is in the correct mode. The question tells you that the cosine of the cosine of n is 0.8. To find n, just take the inverse cosine of 0.8, and then take the inverse cosine of the result. You should get 0.8717—that's n. If you get an error, your calculator is probably in degree mode. Finally, take the tangent of 0.8717. You should get 1.1895.

45. **C** This cylinder has a radius of n (because n is half the diameter) and a height of $\frac{n}{2}$. Just plug these values into the formula for the surface area of a cylinder, $SA = 2\pi r^2 + 2\pi rh$. You get $2\pi n^2 + \pi n^2$, or $3\pi n^2$.

46. **A** PITA. Plug in each answer choice for θ to see which one makes the equation true. Make sure your calculator is in radian mode. Only (A) works: $(\tan(-0.785) - 1)^2 \approx (-2)^2 = 4$.

47. **A** A good way to tackle this one is by trying to disprove each of the answer choices. If you start with (A), you're lucky. The only way for a fraction to equal 0 is for the numerator to be 0, but in this case, the numerator is 5. Thus, the fraction cannot equal 0 and (A) is the right answer. Even if you weren't sure, the other answer choices can be disproven. Just set $\frac{5}{x+4}$ equal to a quantity prohibited by each answer choice, and solve for x. If there's a real value of x that satisfies the equation, then the value *is* in the range after all, and the answer choice is incorrect. Another method is to graph the function on your calculator and see what y-values seem impossible.

48. **C** $\csc\theta = \dfrac{1}{\sin\theta}$, so rewrite the given equation as $\dfrac{1}{\sin\theta} = \dfrac{1}{3t}$. That means $\sin\theta = 3t$. Now, plug in an easy number for θ, such as 30°. So you have $\sin 30° = 3t$. Therefore, $t = 0.167$. The question asks for $\cos 30°$, which is 0.866, the target number. Now, plug in 0.167 for t in the answer choices to see which one becomes 0.866. Choice (C) is the only one that comes close. As an alternative, once you know that $\sin\theta = 3t$, you could use SOHCAHTOA to construct a right triangle with opposite side $3t$ and hypotenuse 1, and then use the Pythagorean Theorem to solve for the adjacent side. Then, use SOHCAHTOA again to get the cosine. Either way, the answer is (C).

49. **C** There's no sophisticated math here. It's just an annoying function question with a lot of steps. As usual with Roman numeral questions, tackle the statements one at a time and remember to use POE. Statement (I) must be true—if $x = 0$, then the function comes out to $\dfrac{y}{y}$, which equals 1 no matter what y is (since y can't be zero). Choice (B) can be eliminated since it doesn't contain (I). Statement (II) must be true. When the statement says $f(x, x)$, it can be tempting to think that the statement is doing something very complicated, but all that has happened is that y has been replaced by x. Thus, anywhere that you see a y in the function, just put x there instead. In the case of this statement, the value of x is 1. Since the value 1 is being plugged into the function in the x and y positions, the function will always equal $\dfrac{2}{2}$, or 1. Choices (A) and (D) can be eliminated because they don't include (II). Finally, (III) is not necessarily true; $f(x, y) = \dfrac{xy + y}{x + y}$, and $f(y, x) = \dfrac{xy + x}{x + y}$. If x and y have different values, then these expressions will not be equal, due to the differing second term in the numerator. Choice (E) can be eliminated because (III) is not always true. That leaves only (C).

50. **B** Start by plugging in. Because there are no numerical values given for m and b, you can plug in numbers as long as they satisfy the equation $m = -b^3$. Make $m = -8$ and $b = 2$. The line's equation is therefore $y = -8x + 2$. At this point, it helps to draw the triangle.

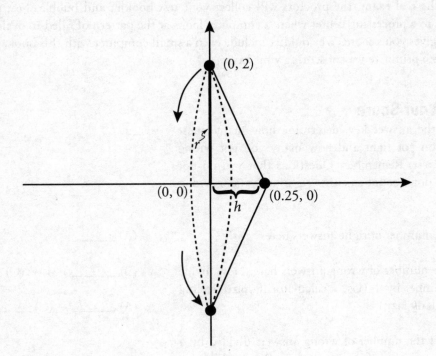

As shown, the equation gives you an x-intercept of 0.25 and a y-intercept of 2. If you rotate this triangle around the x-axis, you will create a cone with a radius of 2 and a height of 0.25. Using the formula for volume of a cone ($V = \frac{1}{3}\pi r^2 h$), you find that $V = \frac{1}{3}\pi(2)^2(.25) = \frac{\pi}{3}$. Therefore, the answer is (B).

HOW TO SCORE
PRACTICE TEST 2

When you take the real exam, the proctors will collect your test booklet and bubble sheet and send your bubble sheet to a processing center where a computer looks at the pattern of filled-in ovals on your bubble sheet and gives you a score. We couldn't include even a small computer with this book, so we are providing this more primitive way of scoring your exam.

Determining Your Score

STEP 1 Using the answer key, determine how many questions you got right and how many you got wrong on the test. Remember: Questions that you do not answer don't count as either right answers or wrong answers.

STEP 2 List the number of right answers here.

(A) _____

STEP 3 List the number of wrong answers here. Now divide that number by 4. (Use a calculator if you're feeling particularly lazy.)

(B) _____ ÷ 4 = (C) _____

(A) _____ − (C) _____ = _____

STEP 4 Subtract the number of wrong answers divided by 4 from the number of correct answers. Round this score to the nearest whole number. This is your raw score.

STEP 5 To determine your real score, take the number from Step 4 and look it up in the left column of the Score Conversion Table on the next page; the corresponding score on the right is your score on the exam.

PRACTICE TEST 2
SCORE CONVERSION TABLE

Raw Score	Scaled Score	Raw Score	Scaled Score	Raw Score	Scaled Score
50	800	25	630	0	350
49	800	24	630	−1	330
48	800	23	620	−2	320
47	800	22	610	−3	300
46	800	21	600	−4	280
45	800	20	590	−5	270
44	800	19	590	−6	250
43	800	18	580	−7	230
42	790	17	570	−8	220
41	780	16	560	−9	200
40	770	15	560	−10	200
39	760	14	540	−11	200
38	750	13	530	−12	200
37	740	12	520		
36	730	11	500		
35	720	10	490		
34	710	9	470		
33	700	8	460		
32	690	7	440		
31	690	6	430		
30	680	5	400		
29	670	4	400		
28	660	3	380		
27	650	2	370		
26	640	1	360		

Completely darken bubbles with a No. 2 pencil. If you make a mistake, be sure to erase mark completely. Erase all stray marks.

1.

YOUR NAME: _____
(Print)   Last   First   M.I.

SIGNATURE: _____   DATE: __/__/__

HOME ADDRESS: _____
(Print)   Number and Street

_____
City   State   Zip Code

PHONE NO.: _____
(Print)

IMPORTANT: Please fill in these boxes exactly as shown on the back cover of your test book.

2. TEST FORM

3. TEST CODE

4. REGISTRATION NUMBER

5. YOUR NAME

First 4 letters of last name				FIRST INIT	MID INIT

A A A A   A A
B B B B   B B
C C C C   C C
D D D D   D D
E E E E   E E
F F F F   F F
G G G G   G G
H H H H   H H
I I I I   I I
J J J J   J J
K K K K   K K
L L L L   L L
M M M M   M M
N N N N   N N
O O O O   O O
P P P P   P P
Q Q Q Q   Q Q
R R R R   R R
S S S S   S S
T T T T   T T
U U U U   U U
V V V V   V V
W W W W   W W
X X X X   X X
Y Y Y Y   Y Y
Z Z Z Z   Z Z

6. DATE OF BIRTH

Month	Day		Year	
○ JAN				
○ FEB	0	0	0	0
○ MAR	1	1	1	1
○ APR	2	2	2	2
○ MAY	3	3	3	3
○ JUN		4	4	4
○ JUL		5	5	5
○ AUG		6	6	6
○ SEP		7	7	7
○ OCT		8	8	8
○ NOV		9	9	9
○ DEC				

Test Code columns:
0 A J 0 0
1 B K 1 1
2 C L 2 2
3 D M 3 3
4 E N 4 4
5 F O 5 5
6 G P 6 6
7 H Q 7 7
8 I R 8 8
9

Registration Number: 0-9 columns

7. SEX
○ MALE
○ FEMALE

The Princeton Review®

Start with number 1 for each new section.
If a section has fewer questions than answer spaces, leave the extra answer spaces blank.

1. A B C D E
2. A B C D E
3. A B C D E
4. A B C D E
5. A B C D E
6. A B C D E
7. A B C D E
8. A B C D E
9. A B C D E
10. A B C D E
11. A B C D E
12. A B C D E
13. A B C D E
14. A B C D E
15. A B C D E
16. A B C D E
17. A B C D E
18. A B C D E
19. A B C D E
20. A B C D E
21. A B C D E
22. A B C D E
23. A B C D E
24. A B C D E
25. A B C D E
26. A B C D E
27. A B C D E
28. A B C D E
29. A B C D E
30. A B C D E

31. A B C D E
32. A B C D E
33. A B C D E
34. A B C D E
35. A B C D E
36. A B C D E
37. A B C D E
38. A B C D E
39. A B C D E
40. A B C D E
41. A B C D E
42. A B C D E
43. A B C D E
44. A B C D E
45. A B C D E
46. A B C D E
47. A B C D E
48. A B C D E
49. A B C D E
50. A B C D E

The **Princeton Review**®

Completely darken bubbles with a No. 2 pencil. If you make a mistake, be sure to erase mark completely. Erase all stray marks.

1.

YOUR NAME: _____
(Print)
     Last   First   M.I.

SIGNATURE: _____ DATE: ___ / ___ / ___

HOME ADDRESS: _____
(Print)
         Number and Street

_____
  City   State   Zip Code

PHONE NO.: _____
(Print)

IMPORTANT: Please fill in these boxes exactly as shown on the back cover of your test book.

2. TEST FORM

3. TEST CODE

4. REGISTRATION NUMBER

5. YOUR NAME

First 4 letters of last name				FIRST INIT	MID INIT

6. DATE OF BIRTH

Month	Day		Year	
JAN				
FEB	0	0	0	0
MAR	1	1	1	1
APR	2	2	2	2
MAY	3	3	3	3
JUN		4	4	4
JUL		5	5	5
AUG		6	6	6
SEP		7	7	7
OCT		8	8	8
NOV		9	9	9
DEC				

7. SEX
- MALE
- FEMALE

The **Princeton Review**®

Start with number 1 for each new section.
If a section has fewer questions than answer spaces, leave the extra answer spaces blank.

1. A B C D E
2. A B C D E
3. A B C D E
4. A B C D E
5. A B C D E
6. A B C D E
7. A B C D E
8. A B C D E
9. A B C D E
10. A B C D E
11. A B C D E
12. A B C D E
13. A B C D E
14. A B C D E
15. A B C D E
16. A B C D E
17. A B C D E
18. A B C D E
19. A B C D E
20. A B C D E
21. A B C D E
22. A B C D E
23. A B C D E
24. A B C D E
25. A B C D E
26. A B C D E
27. A B C D E
28. A B C D E
29. A B C D E
30. A B C D E

31. A B C D E
32. A B C D E
33. A B C D E
34. A B C D E
35. A B C D E
36. A B C D E
37. A B C D E
38. A B C D E
39. A B C D E
40. A B C D E
41. A B C D E
42. A B C D E
43. A B C D E
44. A B C D E
45. A B C D E
46. A B C D E
47. A B C D E
48. A B C D E
49. A B C D E
50. A B C D E

STUDY GUIDE FOR THE SAT SUBJECT TEST IN MATH 2

Bad news first: there's no one right way to study for a test. If you're looking for a surefire shortcut, there simply isn't one. The good news, however, is that if you're reading this, you're already on the right track—you're putting in the three key resources for successful study habits: time, energy, and focus. The following study guide features a few suggested ways to tackle the SAT Subject Test in Math 1, depending on whether the test is just around the corner (**1 Week Cram**) or if you've got more time to practice (**7 Week Stretch**).

Remember that these plans are simply suggestions; everybody learns in their own way and at their own pace. When choosing where to begin, use what you know about your own study habits. If cramming for a test hasn't been effective for you in the past, perhaps it's time to try spreading out your practice over a longer period of time. On the other hand, if you find yourself forgetting key material just before the test, you might want to try an intense refresher in the week leading up to the exam.

If you're not sure how best to prepare, we recommend using Practice Test 1 (pages 24–43) as a diagnostic, which means giving yourself enough time to mirror what will be allotted to you on test day, and then working in a quiet and uninterrupted environment. When you're done, check answers against the key on page 46. If you're happy with your results, you might just spend a week focusing on the specific section for which you had wrong answers. On the other hand, if you're struggling across the board, you may be best served by building up those content gaps over the course of a few months. Here are our recommendations.

1 Week Cram

The following schedule is an extremely abbreviated way of gaining maximum exposure to the course. It involves reinforcement over a limited amount of time, so you'll be touching on each bit of content three times—once when you skim the chapter to get a general sense of the ideas within, again when you read the summary to remind yourself of what you're expected to have learned, and finally when you test your knowledge against the drill questions.

When we suggest "skimming," that means glancing at the topics and reviewing any that you're not sure about. Use the drills within each chapter to help you prioritize; if you can't solve the drill questions, you likely haven't yet reinforced your knowledge of that subject enough.

We don't recommend spending more than four hours studying on any given day, especially since you probably have other things to take care of! (Your mind needs time to absorb everything.) That said, if you have extra time on any given day, we recommend fully reading the portions of each content chapter that you feel least comfortable with.

Day 0, Sunday [1 hour]
Take Practice Test 1. Keep the results of the test in mind as you go through the next week, and slow down your skimming when you hit a section where you struggled.

Day 1, Monday [1.5 hours]
- Review the format of the SAT Subject Test in Math 1 in Chapter 1, "Introduction."

- Familiarize yourself with some pacing and test-taking strategies in Chapter 2, "Strategy."

- Skim Chapter 5, "Algebra," and the drills on pages 71, 73–74, 78–80, 83, 85, 86, 89, 91–92, 93–94, 95–96, 99, 101, 103, 105, and 107.

Day 2, Tuesday [2 hours]

- Review the Summary (pages 112–113) for Chapter 5. Circle any concepts you forgot.

- Skim Chapter 6, "Fundamentals," and the drills on pages 119, 122, 123, 127–128, 129, 131–132, 133, and 140–141.

- Skim Chapter 7, "Plane and Solid Geometry," and the drills on pages 160–161, 162–164, 166–167, 169–170, and 171–172.

Day 3, Wednesday [2.5 hours]

- Review the Summary (pages 144–145) for Chapter 6. Circle any concepts you forgot.

- Skim Chapter 8, "Coordinate Geometry," and the drills on pages 183, 185–186, 188–189, 192–193, 196–197, 198–200, 202–203, 205–206, and 207–208.

- Review the Summary (pages 176–179) for Chapter 7. Circle any concepts you forgot.

- Complete the Comprehensive Drill for Chapter 5 (pages 110–111).

- Skim Chapter 9, "Trigonometry," and the drills on pages 216–217, 219–220, 225, 227, 233–234, 236, 241–242, and 245–246.

Day 4, Thursday [2.5 hours]

- Review the Summary (page 212) for Chapter 8. Circle any concepts you forgot.

- Complete the Comprehensive Drill for Chapter 6 (pages 142–143).

- Review the Summary (page 249–250) for Chapter 9. Circle any concepts you forgot.

- Complete the Comprehensive Drill for Chapter 7 (pages 173–175).

- Skim Chapter 10, "Functions," and the drills on pages 254, 256–257, 262–263, 265–266, 273–274, 278–279, 284–285, 286–287, 290–292, and 298–299.

Day 5, Friday [2.5 hours]

- Review the Summary (page 303–304) for Chapter 10. Circle any concepts you forgot.

- Complete the Comprehensive Drill for Chapter 8 (pages 209–211).

- Complete the Comprehensive Drill for Chapter 9 (pages 247–248).

- Skim Chapter 11, "Statistics and Sets," and the drills on pages 308–309, 314–316, 323, and 325.

Day 6, Saturday [3 hours]

- Review the Summary (page 328) for Chapter 11. Circle any concepts you forgot.

- Complete the Comprehensive Drill for Chapter 10 (pages 300–302).

- Skim Chapter 12, "Miscellaneous," and the drills on pages 331, 333, 335, 339, 343, 351–352, 354, 358–359, 361, 365–366, 368, and 372–373.

- Take Practice Test 2 (pages 450–467).

Day 7, Sunday [2.5 hours]

- Review the Summary (pages 379–380) for Chapter 12. Circle any concepts you forgot.

- Complete the Comprehensive Drill for Chapter 11 (pages 326–327).

- Complete the Comprehensive Drill for Chapter 12 (pages 377–378).

- Take Practice Test 3 (optional; download from your online student tools).

This is it, your final chance to review. Look at all the circled concepts and the questions you got wrong on Practice Tests 2 (and 3). If there's any overlap, that's a clear sign that you need more practice in that section, so spend any remaining time reviewing that content. That said, you've been working hard, so don't burn yourself out by pushing for more than two hours. Rest is an important part of studying, too: it's when the mind processes everything.

7 Week Stretch

This schedule doesn't break things into a day-to-day calendar but helps to establish what you should aim to accomplish within a given week. For some, that may be a matter of evenly distributing the reading material across the week. For others, it may be to spend one day studying, one day reviewing, and one day testing. We have arranged the material by EARLY, MID, and LATE week.

Week 1

- EARLY: Take Practice Test 1 (pp. 24–43).

- MID: Review results of Practice Test 1.

- LATE: Read Chapter 5. Review the summary, rephrase its concepts in your own words (to internalize the ideas), and complete all drills, especially the comprehensive one on pages 110–111.

Week 2

- EARLY: Read Chapters 6 and 7.

- MID: Review the summaries of Chapters 6 and 7. Try rephrasing these concepts in your own words so that you internalize the ideas.

- LATE: Complete all drills in Chapters 6 and 7, especially the comprehensive ones on pages 142–143 and 173–175.

Week 3

- EARLY: Read Chapters 8 and 9.

- MID: Review the summaries of Chapters 8 and 9. Try rephrasing these concepts in your own words so that you internalize the ideas.

- LATE: Complete all drills in Chapters 8 and 9, especially the comprehensive ones on pages 209–211 and 247–248.

Week 4

- EARLY: Read Chapter 10.

- MID: Review the summary of Chapter 10. Try rephrasing these concepts in your own words so that you internalize the ideas.

- LATE: Complete all drills in Chapter 10, especially the comprehensive one on pages 300–302.

Week 5

- EARLY: Read Chapter 11.

- MID: Review the summary of Chapter 11. Try rephrasing these concepts in your own words so that you internalize the ideas.

- LATE: Complete all drills in Chapter 11, especially the comprehensive one on pages 326–327.

Week 6

- EARLY: Read Chapter 12.

- MID: Review the summary of Chapter 12. Try rephrasing these concepts in your own words so that you internalize the ideas.

- LATE: Complete all drills in Chapter 12, especially the comprehensive one on pages 377–378. Take Practice Test 2 (pages 450–467).

Week 7

- EARLY: Review Answers and Explanations for Practice Test 2.

- MID: Take Practice Test 3 (download from your online student tools).

- LATE: Go over any topics you still feel uncomfortable, especially those for which you got questions wrong in Practice Tests 2 and 3.

FINAL NOTES

Don't feel as if you have to limit yourself to one of these templates. This is your test and your book; the most effective practice is likely to be that which you feel most comfortable with and able to commit to. That said, here are a few final pointers for adapting the book:

- Spread out the practice tests so that you can track progress and learn from mistakes.

- Don't gloss over reviewing answers, even to problems that you got right, especially if you guessed.

- If possible, don't cram. Your goal isn't to remember material for a single day—unless you're taking the test tomorrow—so the more that you can check back in on how much you remember from a section over the course of your review, the more you'll be able to retain for test day.

Feel free to use other resources! We've given you the best content review and practice tests at our disposal, but if you're still struggling over a difficult concept, and your teacher can't help, another perspective can only help. (Just make sure you fact-check the source!) The College Board's website features an overview of each Subject Test as well as practice questions:

https://collegereadiness.collegeboard.org/sat-subject-tests/subjects/mathematics/mathematics-2

NOTES

NOTES

NOTES

NOTES

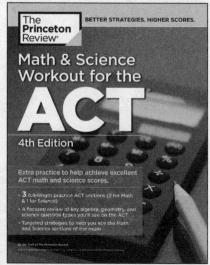